PHENOMENOLOGY
Background, Foreground, & Influences

Edited by
Professor Maurice Natanson
Yale University

A Garland series

PHENOMENOLOGY
Background, Foreground, & Influences

36.00

Phenomenological Psychology

ERWIN W. STRAUS

Garland Publishing, Inc. • New York & London
1980

This facsimile edition is published by permission of
Basic Books, Inc.

This facsimile has been made from a copy in
the Yale University Library (BF204.5.S78)

*The volumes in this series have been printed on acid-free,
250-year-life paper.*

Library of Congress Cataloging in Publication Data

Straus, Erwin Walter Maximilian, 1891–
Phenomenological psychology.

(Phenomenology, background, foreground & influences ; 15)
Reprint of the 1966 ed. published by
Basic Books, New York.
Includes bibliographies and index.
1. Phenomenological psychology.   I. Title.
II. Series.
[BF204.5.S7   1980]   155.19′2   78-66759
ISBN 0-8240-9555-3

Printed in the United States of America

Phenomenological Psychology

THE SELECTED PAPERS OF ERWIN W. STRAUS

Phenomenological Psychology

TRANSLATED, IN PART, BY ERLING ENG

BASIC BOOKS, INC., PUBLISHERS
NEW YORK

Preface

In a preface to the French edition of the *Principles of Philosophy*, Descartes compared "philosophy as a whole" to a tree "whose roots are metaphysics, whose trunk is physics, and whose branches that issue from this trunk are all the other sciences." No direct reference was made to the tree that once had been planted in the Garden of Eden. Yet, ending the allegory with a concealed reference to the biblical word, "By their fruits you shall know them," Descartes examined and praised the fruits of his tree of knowledge. These were no forbidden fruits. On the contrary. With no false modesty, Descartes predicted—three hundred years before Hiroshima—that many centuries would pass "before all the truths that may be deduced from these principles are so deduced." After all, science does not grow on trees. It is an exquisitely human creation, and we may well marvel how this wondrous artifact enables man to reach so far beyond the boundaries of his physical existence.

Whoever sees the Golden Gate Bridge realizes that it must be manmade, that it is not fashioned by nature. The bridge outdistances nature. Even so, it is exposed to wear and tear, threatened by tidal waves and earthquakes; it demands constant repair. There the Latin adage *tempus edax rerum* proves true. The Archimedean principle, however, formulated more than two thousand years ago, has not been corroded by time Lobachevski and Riemann did not force Euclid into retirement. Science is not consumed by usage. At a party, the arrival of unexpected guests may well embarrass a host, for a meal prepared for ten will not serve twenty; but a speaker addressing an audience much larger than expected will enjoy the situation. Science obviously is not a thing among other things. Scientific propositions are statements about. . . . The so-called laws of nature are no forces in nature. Chemistry does not consist of any chemical elements; it contains no compounds, known or unknown. A scientist may leave all his property to his heirs; he cannot bequeath his knowledge to them.

There is a striking ontological difference between things known and the human knowledge of things. The physicist who determines the velocity of light as a ratio of distance to time, com-prehends spatial and temporal distances; he brings beginning and end of the travel together. A measurement of speed is not a descriptive copy of natural events. It reaches beyond the concrete situation. Although living in time with every breath and heartbeat, man is able to conceive time as time and ascribe numerical values to it. Science surpasses nature. It opens for man the door of his capsule, and he, without leaving his homestead, reaches out through the open door, far beyond himself, into space and time— traveling on the wings of words, meaning, and mathematics.

Since science is a human creation, the question arises whether or how far the methods of physics could be turned back and applied to the artificer, to man himself. In more technical terms, the question is whether psychology is, can, or must be a branch of natural science. No doubt the great majority of contemporary psychologists would answer the question with an unrestricted "Yes." Captivated by the metaphysical tradition and impressed by the tremendous success of scientific research in physics, chemistry, and biology, they have widely accepted the thesis that there is but one Science, that the methods of objective observation, experiment, and measurement have a claim to universal validity, that, with their application to the *animal rationale*, no antitrust suit was to be feared.

"To understand man the doer," Boring told innocent freshmen and sophomores, "we must understand his nervous system, for upon it his actions depend."[1] This statement leads to a historical impasse, for, if we accept it at its face value, we would have to exclude Socrates and Plato, Augustine and Luther, Sophocles and Shakespeare, Caesar and Napoleon from the ranks of those who could understand man "the doer." Only those born after Broca, Hitzig, Cajal, and Sherrington could ever hope to be admitted into the circle of experts.

Yet a Gallup Poll today would find but few who could claim first-hand knowledge in the field of neurobiology, probably not more than one among 15,000. Nevertheless, all the 15,000 go more or less successfully about their business, completely unaware that "the nervous system connects stimulus with response" and that "action . . . always occurs as a response to excitation."[2] It is more than doubtful that anybody would advise newlyweds to put a psychological text into their luggage to enhance their mutual understanding, love, and pleasure. Of course, one

[1] E. Boring, H. Langfeld, and H. Weld. *Introduction to Psychology* (New York: John Wiley & Sons, Inc., 1939), p. 3.
[2] *Loc. cit.*

may argue that such everyday-life understanding is on a prescientific level, that it could not stand comparison with the results of scientific methods relating output to input.

Yet, if understanding of the nervous system requires first-hand information, who would be able to take and stand the test? Even the wisest and most learned among the neurophysiologists owe a great deal of their knowledge to others, to the teachers with whom they were in direct contact, to the books and journals that they studied. Their own understanding of the nervous system is therefore necessarily preceded by the direct understanding of other men and their oral and written communications. Those who study "verbal behavior" have good reason to wonder how statements bound to the actual functioning of a particular nervous system could be detached from the moment of "verbalization," preserved, and even multiplied, with no limit to number.

The widespread search for the "neurophysiological basis of mind" is, despite experiment and clinical observation, a kind of metaphysical exercise. A distinction has been made between two ontological levels— a genuine and a spurious one. Full reality is granted to the nervous system and its function, while experience is interpreted as a kind of phantasma, at best an assemblage of purely secondary qualities somehow related to the true events within the nervous system. In theory, the structure and function of the nervous system is the primary agent; but, through a nasty trick, nature limited our direct experience to a deceptive surface. Théodule Ribot, the French psychologist who attached to a centuries-old metaphysics the new label of epiphenomenology, degraded consciousness (before Freud) to a shadow existence, to a mere accompaniment of nervous processes. "Consciousness could interfere with those processes as little as a wanderer's shadow could modify his steps." Cartesian dualism has been replaced by the one-and-a-half-ism of the real thing and its shadow. Unfortunately, those shadows are all that we immediately possess.

Let us consider the sufficiently trivial situation of one entering a travel agency with the intention of buying an airplane ticket. The prospective traveler who may well qualify as a doer and the agent (who also qualifies) understand each other pretty well. How could an understanding, the most perfect understanding, of the nervous system improve this situation? Should the traveler understand the agent's nervous system, and vice versa, or should his nervous system understand the nervous system of the agent? And would this not imply that his nervous system (each nervous system) must understand itself? Must we substitute for the customer the nervous system of the buyer and, for the salesman, the nervous system of the seller and try to record their action and interaction in biochemical and biophysical terms on the molecular, molar, or nuclear level? How is it possible to compare man the doer with the functions of his nervous system? What is the common ground on which these two such divergent chains of events can be brought together? And who should perform the comparison?

Following this torrent of perplexing questions, the last one is—or at least seems—easy to answer. Who else could it be if not the scientist who conceived the problem, arranged the experiments, registered the results, and finally reported—refreshed by a liberal dose of introspection —his findings in words and writ? In everyday life, one may be satisfied with this answer. In science, however, such reference to the obvious could not be accepted. Have we not learned that, in order to understand man the doer, we must understand his nervous system? The behavioral scientist cannot claim a privileged status for himself. We must lift the observer's mask and turn our attention to his cerebral apparatus—the real actor in this, as in any other, drama of experience. Since, in every psychological experiment, two nervous systems are involved, our interest must be switched from the nervous system observed to the observing nervous system.

At this moment, a transformation of catastrophic dimension occurs. The laboratory, as a well-illuminated environment furnished with visible and tangible instruments disappears; gone are the experimental animals and subjects; gone is the observer himself—at least as we know him in everyday life. Nothing is left but the invisible machinery of the observer's nervous system, equipped with receptors and afferent pathways, with the synaptic apparatus, and all the efferent pathways activating muscles and glands. Whatever happens occurs as a particular event within the confines of this machine. The nervous-system-observer receives stimuli, but has no relations to another nervous system, organism, or fellow man as objects of observation or communication. The afferent impulses release the efferent, but do not anticipate them. The efferent impulses do not know the synaptic connections that activated them. In everyday life, we once believed that we listened to the observer's talk, but now we realize that the observer cannot even hear himself. Efferent impulses acting on organs of articulation produce certain sounds; these phonemes are nothing but a set of stimuli that may release another set of responses far remote from the so-called object of observation, its output and input.

A legion of eminent scholars is busy these days demonstrating that and how "information" is coded and decoded by the machinery of the nervous system. Fascinated by the job to be done, spellbound by the magic of a venerated metaphysics, they completely forget to investigate their own situation. The result is an amazing and unpardonable confusion of stimuli and objects. Stimulus is a central concept of behaviorism; but, whenever it is used, there is a good chance that it will be badly misused, signifying things rather than stimuli. Yet the relation of stimuli to receptors differs radically from that of experiencing creatures to objects. Stimuli are pure physical agents, unstained by any secondary qualities. Stimuli are not visible, audible, tangible. The wall over there, the writing pad, the pen and the ink—none of these are stimuli. The light reflected from the wall, from the paper, might be called a stimulus, provided it has already reached and acted on receptors; for stimuli have no existence independent of the receiving nervous system. Because stimulation precedes response, nobody can handle, nobody can manipulate, stimuli; they are out of reach. I as an experiencing being may stretch my hand toward the pen on my desk; a motor response cannot be directed to optical stimuli already received in the past.

Since stimuli act exclusively on a particular nervous system they are strictly private events. A light beam that hits the retina of a rat, a monkey, or a man will never stimulate the observer's eye. Acting with and after incorporation, stimuli can never be shared by an observer and his subjects. Stimuli are not for sale; they are not listed in Sears Roebuck's catalogue. Lacking all substance, stimuli cannot be exchanged in trade; one cannot buy a pound of them. The hyphenated term "stimulus-object" is a sham.

To be consistent, the psychologist must either accept his subjects as experiencing persons, like himself, sharing with him a world of visible and audible things, or he must interpret his own behavior also in terms of stimuli and response. Should he decide on the second alternative, he will have to admit that in psychological experiments two sets of stimuli and responses occur—one belonging to the subjects, the other to the experimenter himself. The observation reported must be understood as his—or, better, as his brain's—response to all those stimuli that had acted on its receptors. The observer's response, is, therefore, by no means identical with the subject's own response, which actually functions as a stimulus in relation to the observer. Obviously, this cause of the observer's response cannot be at the same time an object of his observation. Since this route is blocked, we shall try the other one.

The observer makes an observation; rather, he makes it an observation, through his silent questions and anticipation of possible answers. An observation is not a simple procedure of recording that could just as well be left to a registering scale; the observer is an indispensable participant in any experiment, active even when watching the scene through a one-way mirror. His situation has much in common with that of a spectator in a theater, who is expected not to interfere with the events on the stage, displayed before his eyes in a plane at a right angle to the direction of his sight. The spectator is not involved in the drama, but his presence is required to make the play a show. In an experiment, the scientist acts as his own playwright; he sets the scene, calls in the actors, raises the curtain, but then, when everything is arranged, he withdraws to the parterre to watch the outcome. He is not involved, yet he is affected. Were he not affected by light and sound, he could not observe and at the end report his observations. He sees, though he is less interested in his own act of seeing than in the events visible to him. Although he establishes a causal connection between them, they are *objects* for him.

This relation of the observer to the objects of his observation we call "intentional"—using, though with some bias, Husserl's terminology. In science, no less than in everyday life, we take our capacity to see, to observe, to describe, for granted. In psychology, however, it becomes our task to make this naïve prethematic attitude thematic, to withdraw our interest from things observed and to reflect on our own situation as observers. There we discover that we deal with persons and things, with plants and animals—in short, with objects and not with stimuli. Actually, this is not a discovery to be reached by cumbersome experiments; it is an insight familiar to every one of us in everyday life or, to use once more one of Husserl's terms, in the *Lebenswelt*. It is a rediscovery made necessary because philosophy and science have passed over and distorted in disdain the basic "axioms of everyday life."[8]

That we see things in their own right, over there at a distance, that they present themselves to us without being incorporated like air and food, that they are, so to speak, here and there at the same time is the paradox of sensory experience. Accepted without the slightest shadow of a doubt in everyday life, the paradox is thrown out of the high court of theory.

Senses and sensory experience belong to the greatest gift nature has bestowed on man and animals. Through the senses, the gates to the world are opened to us. Sensory experience is an ontological enrichment. Yet for ages sensory experience has been disparaged, condemned as deceptive, belittled as a hodgepodge of confused ideas, discredited as a mirage, listed as a liability rather than as an asset. Those who accept

---

[8] Cf. my paper on "Aesthesiology and the Hallucinations" in *Existence*, Ed. May, Ellenberger, and Angel (New York: Basic Books, Inc., 1958).

the verdict and try to work their way out of the enchanted region are not inclined to stop and to inspect carefully their own position. Despite all their efforts to escape, to blot out the secondary qualities, and to base everyday experience on a solid scientific ground, it is just the *Lebenswelt* that makes all these acts of observing, describing, counting, and measuring possible.

The result is a bewildering inconsistency. The *Lebenswelt* is despised; at the same time, too much is taken for granted. The search for the "neurophysiological basis of mind" requires and actually presupposes the validity of that which it denies. Boring's precept is a good example. "To understand man the doer," he said, "we must understand his nervous system." Well, then *we* must understand! To whom is this advice given? Who are "we"? No doubt you and I—all of us who move around on the premises of the *Lebenswelt*. There, as a rule, our curiosity is startled by the unusual, by the abnormal—the Siamese twins, the highest tower in the world, or the smallest camera. Perhaps someone would like to know how this camera is built or how it works. The psychological possibility of making and recognizing pictures is taken for granted.

Schematic representations of the nervous system are not unusual in psychological tests. Nobody seems to wonder that those few black lines in a printed diagram could represent pathways in a—no, in *the*—nervous system. Obviously, stimuli could not do that. The question how something could represent something else is not even asked.

The psychologist's first task is, therefore, to turn back to the origins, to discover the problems hidden in the familiar. To decipher the unwritten constitution of everyday life was and is the leitmotif of the papers brought together in this volume. The title was chosen to express an affiliation with the phenomenological movement in its early, still more in its recent, phases. Since the writer does not follow Husserl on his path to transcendental reduction, the agreement is in the spirit rather than in the letter. Even so, the attempt to explore human experience, revealing its depth and wealth, instead of reducing it, complies well with Husserl's appeal: "Back to the things themselves!"

•

My thanks and appreciation go to Erling Eng, Ph.D., who accepted the demanding task of translating chapters One, Two, Six, Nine, Twelve, and Seventeen and fully lived up to my expectations.

Lexington, Kentucky
December 1965   ERWIN W. STRAUS

Contents

Plates containing figures 14–1 to 14–2, 14–7 to 14–8, 18–1 to 18–22 follow page 274.

PART I

Phenomenological Studies

CHAPTER ONE

The Forms of Spatiality

Goal-Directed Movement and Presentifying Movement

In earlier writings I have tried to show that, since the experience of time is a basic medium for experience in general, there are modifications of temporal experience which determine other kinds of experience, thoughts, actions, and effects through their dependency, both in form and content, on such modifications. Considering the role of space as well as time in the constitution of the phenomenal world, it would not have been amiss to have approached the field of spatial structures with corresponding questions. But the observations and reflections I am going to present did not originate in such a shift of inquiry from one area to another. The initial impetus stemmed, rather, from a more remote and, I might say, accidental event.

In the years just following World War I, many attempts were made to create new forms in the art of the dance. It was then the fashion to talk about "absolute dance." Dance was no longer to pine away in the bonds of musical invention but was to be freed of the tyranny of music. But, after actually observing such muffled dances without accompaniment, it became evident that the tie between music and the dance was by no means accidental. In its absolute form, dance had not lost the ground from under its feet, to be sure, but it had lost the space that is idiomatic for dance. Evidently, there is an essential connection that ties the movement of the dancer to the music and to the spatial structure produced by the music—a tie that cannot be set aside arbitrarily.

This observation forced me to take note of a problem whose solution required that the whole field of inquiry be broadened. What I wish to discuss is the question of the correlation between spatial qualities, forms of movement, and modes of perception. Despite the circumstances of its birth, the following treatment of spatial structures is in essential agreement with my studies of lived time. In the present context, I hope the justification for this approach can be even more readily demonstrated than was possible in my earlier discussions of time.

If we wish to represent the primary lived experience *(Erleben)* of space, then we must emancipate ourselves from the concepts of space prevailing in physics and mathematics. We must guard against judgments and decisions borrowed from other sciences, even when they are based upon well-established findings. Logically and systematically, these concepts of space are posterior, even though they are historically prior to analyses of the primary forms of lived experience. Therefore, we need not enter into discussion of the physical bases and physiological conditions of space perception; nor need we be concerned with the psychological genesis and dominance of particular sensory fields, like the optical or tactile, over others.

We may now state our inquiry more precisely: Does the spatial present itself in different modes in the various spheres of sensory experience—for example, the optical and acoustical—and are there different forms of motor activity and perception that correspond to them?

The Phenomenal Modes of Color and Tone

This approach violates a widely accepted view in psychology—that a spatial order is connate only for the optical, tactile, and kinesthetic spheres, while, for the other senses, mere complexes of feelings with spatial features are admitted. When we inquire into the rationale of this doctrine, we find that they fall into two groups that, although at variance with each other, have in common that they ignore the phenomenally given. The first is a group of completely untested assumptions about the structure of space as lived that are accepted without question; the second is a set of deductions from observation of the anatomical structure and functions of the auditory organ, used to deny the possibility of an original spatial character.

Concerning the latter, there is no reason to doubt the validity of experiments that have, for example, demonstrated the significance of differences in time and intensity for the binaural localization of sound. But do these experiments demonstrate anything about the validity of the empiricist theory of spatial perception? We certainly do not perceive acoustical stimuli; rather, we hear tones and noises on the basis of such stimuli. In this process, both ears are active, along with the central projection area, as a unitary system. I find, in considering spatial organization, no principal difference between it and the optical system: retina, calcarina, and variations of their topical values. Moreover, child psychology has shown that it is just the auditory stimuli that occasion voluntary focusing of the infant's gaze in the third month of life. It is certainly doubtful whether we can, in such a case, assume involvements with other sensory presentations, unconscious conclusions, or judgments, for temporal differences do not endow tones and noises with a spatial character they originally did not have. Such temporal differences have nothing to do with the spatiality of sound but only with the *particular direction* of sound in space. Now, if a sound can be said to be shifted in a particular direction, it must originally have presented itself as spatial.

The empiricist theory would scarcely have been so widely adopted and so long defended against arguments from experience had it not been supported by the first group of reasons mentioned above. Both nativists and empiricists presuppose that the space whose mode of perceptual givenness we are discussing must be Euclidean—i.e., in the last analysis, the constructive schema of empty, homogeneous, three-dimensional space. Of course, if one's research follows these lines, vision and touch must take precedence over the other senses.

It goes without saying that Euclidean space is important for our practical activity and theoretical scientific knowledge. Yet our lived experience is not confined to these functions. Significant phenomena of psychic life must remain inaccessible to psychological understanding when psychologists define their sphere of investigation too narrowly—with regard to purposive, calculated activity and scientific knowledge only. In consequence, they fail to note the various modes in which spatiality occurs for us; they take instead the optical space of detached observation or even empty space for space itself. But, if we proceed from the phenomena themselves, without any such prejudices, we are indeed justified in raising the question "Whence?" of every sound that meets our ears. Such a question does not originate in reflection about the sound, its source, and the existence of things in space; it coincides with hearing itself.

Here, it is important to proceed with circumspection so as not to lose sight of the necessary distinctions. First, we must distinguish between the localization of the sound and the localization of the source of the sound. When we perform the Weber test, we do not ask the subjects for the actual location of the source; it is already known to them from the tuning fork placed against their forehead. We inquire instead *where* they hear the sound. Whether or not the sound is lateralized in the Weber test depends on the condition of the physiological apparatus that conducts and registers the sound. But we are not interested here in the physiological conditions of lateralization. Instead, we are concerned with the phenomenal mode in which the sound is given, which shows up with particular clarity in this examination. In this instance, as in all instances, we attempt to determine the direction or location of the sound source from the sound alone; the sound itself must be endowed with an original spatial character.

The distinctive features of the spatiality of sound can most readily be demonstrated by a comparison of the optical and acoustical spheres. We can accomplish this in two ways: by comparing the modes of spatiality for sound and color, on the one hand, and, on the other, by comparing the determination of the actual location of the sound source with the determination of the actual location of the illuminated colored object. It would be incorrect to make a comparison directly between sound source and light source; the comparison ought to be limited, as we have pointed out, to the differences and similarities in the appearances of the sounding object and the colored object. Many obscurities have arisen from the failure to stringently carry through the strict separation of aims required at this point with the result that the sound source and the colored object, sound and color, have been incorrectly matched, for what is valid with regard to the spatial character of the sound source is not at all valid for the sound itself.

The direction in which the source of a sound is to be sought, and therewith its actual direction in space, is often difficult to determine. With a colored object, however, the direction is readily determined by the direction of seeing, although its actual location, distance, and position are often no less ambiguous. We see the stars at a distance that in no way agrees with their actual remoteness. Estimations of land distances, as well as the position of an object in relation to other points of the terrain, are often extremely difficult and uncertain. But, although determinations of the actual location of the sound source and of the colored object are not appreciably different, there is a radical difference in quality between the phenomenally given modes of spatiality for color and pure tone.

To represent the phenomenal difference with maximum clarity, we will limit ourselves, for the moment, to a comparison of the appearance modes of surface colors and tones. Further, even as physics achieves a representation of elementary events by experimentally reducing an abundance of effective factors by abstraction and purification of phenomena whose lawfulness can then be mathematically stated, we may not just take any experience here as our point of departure. In phenomenal analysis, too, we must look for the "pure case," whether it presents itself naturally or is obtainable only through special experimental arrangements. In our natural environment, optical and acoustical data mingle and unite with data from other sensory spheres, forming connections with nonvisual givens. Only after we have apprehended the essence of the phenomenon in the pure case can we consider the more complex and obscure cases usually encountered under natural conditions.

It is in the tones of music that the spatiality of sound is most fully actualized. Hence, in making our comparison, we must start from the tone and then show how, in noises that indicate the presence or closeness of an object, the purely spatial character of tone is changed through the tone's function of "pointing to something."

Even though the actual location of a colored object may remain indefinite, the direction in which we see the colors themselves is precisely determinable. The principles of physical and physiological optics—our knowledge that light rays travel from the object and impinge on our retina—do not affect the phenomenon of color in the least. We always see colors over *there*, i.e., in a direction and at a distance, somewhere vis-à-vis ourselves. The colors are both bounded and, in turn, boundary setting; they confine space, differentiating it into partial spaces ordered sideways and in depth.

A resonating tone is altogether different. Often, we can say of a sound source that it is impossible to determine reliably the direction where it is localized. But this directional quality does not hold true for the sound itself. Even though we may describe the direction of the sound source as indeterminate, we still maintain that it is determinable—i.e., we state that it must be in this direction, that direction, or a third direction. But the tone itself does not extend in a single direction; rather, it approaches us, penetrating, filling, and homogenizing space.[1] Thus, the tone is not confined to a single spatial position. This lack of *topical* determination accounts for the denial of any original *spatiality* in the acoustical sphere.

We may now summarize our initial group of comparisons: Colors appear opposite to us, over there, confined to one position; they demarcate and differentiate space into partial spaces, appearing side by side and behind one another. Tones, on the contrary, approach us, come to us, and, surrounding us, drift on; they fill space, shaping themselves in temporal sequences.

[1] How this homogenization differs from the homogeneity of empty Euclidean space will be discussed later.

To fully understand the remarkable relationship of tone to time, we must return once more to the question of color in relation to the colored object and tone in relation to the sound source. The very phrase "sound source" shows that the tone emanates from the resonating body much like ripples of water from their source. Color clings (phenomenally) to the object while the tone produced by an object separates itself from it. Color is the mark of a thing, whereas tone is the effect of an activity. We say, for example, that a cock *is* white or multicolored; on the other hand, we do not mention crowing as one of his attributes, but as his activity. We say that he crows, that he *does* crow. But we do not mean that his color is one of his characteristics because the cock always appears white or multicolored whereas his crowing is observed to be discontinuous. A brook murmurs continuously day and night and can even be heard when both banks and water have disappeared in darkness and become invisible. Although a brook's murmuring—the "audible" of it —is more continuous than any of its visible features, we nevertheless persist in considering the rustling its activity. It is just here that the significance of the phenomenally given modes of color and sound becomes evident, for the interpretation in terms of characteristic versus activity is in full agreement with the phenomena. It does not derive from certain experiences about things and their characteristics, which would call rather for correction.

Thus the sound is experienced as the effect of an action because it is of the essence of sound to separate itself from the sound source. While color and form—optical givens in the broadest sense of the term—constitute the object, sound, both as tone and noise, merely points to the object and only indicates it. The sound that detaches itself from the sound source can take on a pure and autonomous existence; but this possibility is fulfilled solely in the tones of music, while noise retains the character of indicating and pointing to.[2]

Here, we must consider the distinction between tone and noise. If we find ourselves in surroundings whose spatial organization and population of things is thoroughly familiar to us and if we hear a specific noise, such as the sound of a motor, then what was said earlier about tone is not fully applicable. We then hear a noise outside in the definite spot where we localize the source of the sound. Nevertheless, in this experience, the optical blends with the acoustical and with what is known although unfigured. If, on the other hand, we are not in familiar surroundings but in the hubbub of a foreign city with a strange language, customs, and

[2] The significance of the twofold nature of sound for the development of speech in its double function of expression and communication cannot be pursued here.

ways, then noises already begin to lose their particular effects and approach the phenomenal mode of the existence of tone, of which music is the perfect realization. Under these conditions, noise, too, penetrates and fills space; by homogenizing space, it makes orientation difficult and increases confusion and strangeness. A jumble of voices differs in its mode of spatial appearance from that of words and sentences overheard on the crowded street, words and sentences that we could understand. As noises grow increasingly confused and lose their ostensive function, they tend to approach the phenomenal mode of givenness of musical tones.

There is no visual art that is analogous to music, and there can be none because color does not separate itself from the object as tone does. In music alone tone reaches a purely autonomous existence. Music is the complete realization of the essential possibilities of the acoustical. We may invent specific sounds as signals, but we no longer wish to hear such reference in the purely musical sphere. Consequently, we prefer the string quartet to the piano quartet because we can still hear the piano as a sound source in the latter case while the former furnishes us with the ideal possibility of pure harmony.

The forms and structures of art mentioned here and later are not merely for illustration; it is not our intention to explain them. Rather, we contemplate them as *facta* and ask what conditions make them possible. When we do this, we are at once directed to the distinctions in the modes of being between color and sound that we encountered earlier.

The cadenza of the violin concerto is an aesthetic structure that owes its existence to a compromise between two conflicting tendencies—the need of the virtuoso to display his technical bravura and the requirement of the work of art that the solo voice be subordinated to the work as a whole. In the concerto, the composer gives the virtuoso a chance to shine with his own ideas, taste, and ability. After a great upsweep, the orchestra hushes. Then the cadenza begins, with arpeggios, runs, and double chords racing with great bounds through the instrument's entire gamut of tones; increasing in tempo, the notes come thicker and thicker upon the hearer until finally, with an ascending trill, the turbulent floods of tone stream together, grow peaceful, and flow over into the theme of the movement that the orchestra resolves in a rapid close. While all this is happening, it is impossible to listen meditatively to the music; it is necessary to see, hear, and look at the player himself. It is no longer a matter of simply taking in the tones, for they themselves compel us to observe the process of their origination and to admire their originator.

But the folk singer also wants to hear *himself* and to be heard *himself*. Song is a means of erotic wooing for him or just a means of self-representation. Consequently, the folk singer does everything in his power to emphasize the bodily character of the song while the art song strives for just the opposite. The scoring by many of the great masters for the human voice as if it were an instrument is in accord with this. In the late Baroque period, the forms of style favored the development of absolute music and, at a time of gradual decline in the plastic arts, raised musical creation to new heights. By contrast, musical composition during the nineteenth century gave increasing importance to the song text. At the same time, with the invention of program music, the leitmotif and Wagner's concept of the "total art work," music gradually ceased sounding and began to talk, say, or mean something. These two trends can be pursued throughout the entire history of music. Both derive from the phenomenal nature of tone; tone can simply point to or indicate something objective or it can attain a purely autonomous existence. Only when this latter has been reached can we fully comprehend the spatial mode of the tone's existence—the filling and homogenizing of space, on which we have already commented, and the temporal form of existence, of which we intend to speak.

As the tone is achieving its purely autonomous existence, we hear it originate and disappear; we are aware of its emergence, its becoming, and its dying away. In the instance of color, there is nothing to compare with this. When a color crosses our field of vision, we see the *movement* of an object. When we observe a succession of colors in a single place, we see an object *changing*. We see the glowing light die away, i.e., the shining object passes through a succession of hues. Even at sunset, it is the sky, the ocean, or the mountains on which the change of colors takes place. The succession of colors actually requires the permanence of the object. But all of this is different for music; here, the succession of tones brings the temporal character of its existence to the fore; its temporal differentiation differentiates time in turn. It is the autonomous existence of tone and its relatedness to time that endow its sounding rhythms with such rich significances (*Prägnanz*). This cannot be realized with optical materials. It is impossible to produce with lights and colors appearing and disappearing in a well-defined sequence the same clear experience of rhythm in the beholder as when he hears a rhythmically articulated succession of tones. This difference in the appearance of rhythm between optical and acoustical presentations is not based on any difference between acoustical and optical stimuli; it cannot be explained physiologically at all but can only be derived from the phenomena. To focus on physiological explanations here would be to ignore other highly significant differences.

The difference between experiences of optically and acoustically produced rhythm is not limited to the reception. Not only are we able to hear a rhythm better than we can see one, but, as everyone knows, a rhythmic series of tones compels us to move in a way that is characteristically different from everyday walking, running, and jumping. Is this induced movement merely an indirect effect of the charged meaning (*Prägnanz*) of the auditory rhythm, or is there a direct link between hearing and movement? This is the decisive choice of alternatives. Whoever takes the first alternative must assume two distinct psychic processes: hearing the rhythm and spontaneous production of movements independent of the first but referring to it. We could, perhaps, conceive of the tie between them as having been produced by a concealed delight in imitation. Then we would be inclined to imitate a rhythmic series of sounds more than a rhythmic series of images simply because the former provided us with a better model for imitation.[3] But experience shows us that there is no such preference and that, without any additional activity on our part, we are captivated and carried away by the musical rhythm. The "link" between the "stimulus," the rhythm heard, and its response, the rhythmic movement, is a completely direct one.

The Gnostic and the Pathic Moment in Perception

To gain a better understanding of these relationships, we must be ready to fundamentally broaden and develop our usual way of regarding and representing sensation. Up to now, psychologists have talked almost exclusively about sensation but never about sensing. Of experience as a whole, it has been always the *gnostic* and never the *pathic* moment that has been remarked and considered. If the unmediated bond between the hearing of a rhythm and rhythmic movement itself is a fact—and ample evidence will be given for this below—then we can no longer refuse to give special attention to the pathic moment in sensation. Vision, hearing, and the other senses do not just provide sensory impressions, do not just enable color and sound to appear before us; at the same time that we perceive objects, we also sense the colors and tones, i.e., they take hold of us and influence us in a lawfully determinate way.

[3] This is like the situation in group gymnastic exercises where the individual participant tries to imitate the movement or position of the leading gymnast as closely as possible. In this instance, the two events—reception of the model and its imitation—are separated in time. The complete antithesis between the modeling of a visual schema and the lived "rapture" of dance or march music is particularly clear here.

Here I would like to anticipate several unfortunate misinterpretations. Firstly, by the pathic moment, we mean the immediate communication we have with things on the basis of their changing mode of sensory givenness. Thus, we do not relate the pathic dimension—and this should be made explicit—to the fixed or changing properties of the objects, and this means not to objects capable of attracting, frightening, or oppressing us by their properties. If we were to attach the pathic moment to objects, we would have included it in the conceptual sphere, and the distinction between gnostic and pathic would have been obliterated. The pathic is a characteristic feature of primordial experience; it is for this reason that it is so difficult to understand conceptually, being the immediately present, sensually vivid, still preconceptual communication we have with appearances.

The expressions used earlier—"sensation" and "sensing"—could easily give rise to another misunderstanding, for this separation of sensing from sensation recalls the distinctions we are familiar with in phenomenology, especially the thesis, so often repeated with emphasis by Husserl, that every perception is perception *of something*. It could be thought that the distinction between sensation and sensing is only a repetition of the phenomenological division between act and intentional object. But this is incorrect. The distinction between sensation and sensing remains completely within the sphere of the experience content. The gnostic moment merely develops the *what* of the given in its object character, the pathic the *how* of its being as given. For this reason, I think it objectively and terminologically more accurate to use my earlier expressions of gnostic and pathic moments.

There are a series of additional reasons which can be most meaningfully presented by a discussion of a few recent studies in which a similar line of thought has been followed. A recent paper of Heinz Werner is entitled "The Experimental Study of Sensing" (1929). In his comments on this paper, Metzger (1929) referred to points of agreement with his own work as well as with that of von Hornbostel (1926). Werner's principal finding was that four stages could be experimentally discriminated in the experiencing of an objectively presented tone:

(1) The stage of highly charged [hochprägnant] object tone (analogous to surface color); (2) the stage of spatial tone (analogous to plane color); (3) the stage of tone entering the body which becomes a resonant container; (4) in the fourth stage subject and object approach even more closely, so that eventually an experienced bodily condition is dominant. The first and second stages can be termed stages of perception, the third and fourth as stages of sensation, demonstrably present for tones as well as for colors. As one shifts from objectally certain, well defined perception in the direction of subjectivized experiencing,

phenomena of sensing appear which have the quality of specific bodily conditions (1929).

In contrast to our view, Werner comprehends the pathic not as a moment fundamental in perceptual experience but as limited to particular temporal stages of the perceptual process, where it is taken as the experiencing of a bodily condition.

Here Werner has apparently succumbed to an illusion. He has, of course, not obtained his findings from a phenomenological analysis of experience but through experimental studies. He has succumbed to the error of taking particulars arising solely from the structure and design of the experiment for features belonging to the essence of the phenomenon itself. The complexity of the What and How of the given must somehow be elucidated and made temporarily distinct in every experiment if it is to be grasped by the experimental subject. Even the brief abstract of this experiment shows that Werner interpreted his findings incorrectly, for it is not true that perception ceases and sensation begins with the third or even the fourth stage. The tone is still definitely and continuously present as a perceptual object or as the What of experience, and it is only the How as a way of being apprehended that emerges more distinctly as a bodily condition. Consequently, it is entirely unjustifiable to limit the pathic moment to particular stages of experience, construing it merely as a bodily state.

The same error of limiting the universality of the pathic to particular instances is also committed by von Hornbostel and Metzger. Von Hornbostel (1926, p. 701) calls "the existence and factual being of things 'outside us' the objective objectal form of being given," perception and "that we are so and so disposed," the subjective nonobjectal form of being given he calls "sensation." Metzger (1929) has correctly objected that what is given in a sensation is no mere being disposed, i.e., is not only a condition of myself but that there is a something still persistent and that a relationship between me and it is still present. Yet, curiously enough, Metzger limits such relationships to special instances. He says, "An object which I face, an object before me, can also be said to be outside me, to 'exclude' me; it is simply there and doesn't affect me" (1929, p. 20). He then proposes to speak of sensation in the new specific sense "whenever an external appearance is no longer simply there, but enters into relation with me, affects me without intellectual detours, making me disposed in such and such a way" (1929, p. 20).

The error of limiting phenomena to those special instances where they show clearly appears an inveterate one in psychology. In so doing, the neutral point is taken as nullity, with the consequence that the full significance of observations in the single case is lost. It escapes Metzger that simply being there, being over against, and being excluded are all forms of the relationship between me and the appearance. He is unable to see that these relationships do not arise at the particular moment in time when the object begins to affect me noticeably. It escapes him that they are only variations in generic relationships, a change in communication with the object, actually a change of the pathic moment. It is just as if a physicist were to regard rest and movement as two fundamentally different kinds of phenomenon. But the pathic moment does not only belong to individual cases or particular stages in perception; it belongs to perception generally and in each case. Finally, it does not have the same significance as a specific bodily disposition.[4]

A few more words on the last point. The notion that sensing is only a matter of a bodily state appears to find support in the psychology of disgust. There are objects enough whose sight, to be sure, we can bear but whose contact and bodily ingestion we vigorously resist. Here, it actually seems as if a completely new experience arises with the encroachment on and penetration of the boundary of the body. But doesn't it merely seem so? Aren't we familiar with exactly the opposite behavior? Isn't it normal that when a men is passionately moved to touch and fondle the body of a woman in its most intimate parts, he avoids looking at them? Nevertheless, it remains the self-same object whose contact is so vigorously sought and whose sight is so modestly avoided. This discrepancy in behavior is not based on the objective difference between optical and tactile data but on a difference in communication, i.e., on a difference of the pathic moments. In experiencing disgust, the pathic moment begins as little with bodily contact as in the second case it comes to an end with bodily contact. The change takes place entirely within the sphere of communication. In the shift from touching to looking, there is a change in the relative dominance of pathic and gnostic moments in experience. In touching, the pathic is dominant; in looking, the gnostic dominates. "Looking at" brings every object into the domain of the objective and general. The veiling gesture of modesty tries to fend off this process of depersonalization and deanimation.

With the foregoing discussion, we have entered the threshold of the psychology of shame and disgust, for which the distinction between pathic and gnostic moments is of such basic importance. Yet, we do not

[4] Herder was the first, as far as I know, to elaborate this distinction on a broad scale. Nevertheless, his paper, "On Understanding and Sensing," which was not awarded a prize by the Prussian Academy, has remained without influence on the development of modern psychology.

wish to cross over this threshold here but only to represent the characteristic features of the pathic moment as far as our special interest requires.

At this moment, we will confine ourselves to demonstrate that the union and mutual interpenetration of the pathic and gnostic in music first endows the acoustically presented rhythms with the power to elicit corresponding forms of movement. We can accomplish this most easily by returning to the comparison of optical and acoustical appearances.

The colored object, we said, appears there, over against us, in a particular direction and at a particular limited and delimiting distance. Unlike a tone that approaches us, the color retains its place. To experience the color, we must turn toward it, look at it, actively master it. The Greco-Roman theory of vision, which assumed that rays passed from the eye to the object, was based on the phenomenal character of the optical appearance. This theory is untenable when used outside the phenomenal sphere to account for physiological phenomena in terms of cause and effect. Such an error is exactly the reverse of that most commonly met with today: the tendency to extend causal relationships to immediate experience and its laws or even to replace the latter by the former. The theory of the rays emanating from the eye continues to make good sense in the phenomenal sphere in spite of all the physical and physiological knowledge developed since antiquity which makes it unacceptable today as a physiological theory.

Whether an object attracts us, i.e., invites our approach, or whether it is dreadful, i.e., threatens us with its import, the tension of confrontation always remains. In seeing, we are behaving actively, whether approaching or avoiding, attacking or taking flight.

Jossmann (1928) has explored the relationships between the structure of perceptual experience and the terms referring to it. He has pointed out that numerous expressions used for optical perceptual experiences—like "seeing," "looking," "peering," "gazing," "being aware of," and "observing"—are etymologically related to or identical with words for certain movements. The German word *sehen* (to see) has the same root as the Latin *sequi* (to follow); the verb *blicken* (to glance) is synonymous with *strahlen* (to beam), which is related to the Old High German *Strahla* (arrow). To this it should be added that, in these words and in metaphors like "casting a look or eye at someone," the activity of seeing is emphasized along with the sense of movement. Thus language not only discloses how vision articulates space by its movements, as Jossmann brings out, but these terms also point to the spontaneity of visual perception.

Stimulated by such observations, it is not at all difficult to discover that the phenomenal character of musical experience has also left its mark on language. This is manifest in the semantic relatedness of words like *hören* (to hear), *horchen* (to hearken), and *gehorchen* (to obey). Tone has an activity all its own; it presses in on us, surrounds, seizes, and embraces us. Only in a later phase are we able to defend ourselves against sound, only after sound has already taken possession of us, while in the visual sphere we begin to take flight before we have been prehended. The acoustical pursues us; we are at its mercy, unable to get away. Once uttered, a word is there, entering and owning us. Nor can it be rendered unspoken through any pretense or apology.

All hearing is presentic. For this reason, repetition is possible in the acoustical sphere, while the optical sphere is limited to reduplication. In sound, we apprehend the happening presentically, while in color we lay hold of Being at a distance. That this interval puts the things we see also at a temporal distance is not quite so apparent when they form part of our immediate surroundings, as in the case of a far-off point in space like, say, the goal of a day's hike. Even though we take in that mountain top or that village with this glance, it appears to us as something that is not yet or any longer present. What we see lies at a distance before or behind us. The space that expands before us is, thus, a metaphor of the approaching future; the space that lies behind is a metaphor of the past that has receded from us.[5] When we hear something, we have already heard it. Language joins hearing (*hören*) and belonging (*Gehören*) and hearing and servile (*hörig*) closely together. Obviously, these concepts are linked, as in the case of seeing, by the common character of pathicity or, more accurately, by an original correspondence between the pathic character of sensory experience and the structure of possession. We are, today, all too inclined to bestow our attention solely on that which has a gnostic character. So it is important to observe that words may be linguistically related not only on the basis of their conceptual and object contents but also, occasionally, on the basis of a common pathic quality.

The distinctive quality of the pathic moment in its different ways of appearing in optical and acoustical space is far from adequately rendered by the antithesis of "taking" and "being taken." Color not only presents itself from over there, opposite to us, but also is demarcated at the same time that it demarcates, articulating space as regions, laterally and in depth. In optical space, things stand out from one another with sharply defined boundaries; the articulation of optical space is governed by contour. The optical image appears as a representative of the concept, just as

---

[5] That this is no mere metaphor we learn from the oculogyric crises of encephalitics.

the melody serves as a natural representative of the unity of the *Gestalt*. The contour, the sharp definition, and the juxtaposition of visible things has been the most significant factor in the frequent attempts in the history of philosophy and psychology to replace the concept by the representation, i.e., the visually given image. On the other hand, there have been ages in which the graphic and plastic arts aimed at surmounting the differentiation and separation of things as articulated in optical space. Artistic activity is dependent on the pathic moment of the optical phenomenon—reactively dependent down to the tiniest details of technique. Baroque painters did everything to keep things from appearing as simply juxtaposed; to reduce the contours through representation in the plane, they manipulated such devices as the density of paint on the canvas, the distribution of light, the picture's dimensions, its frame, chiaroscuro modelling as in etching, and indirect representation of contour. One need only call to mind the works of Rembrandt, especially his famous landscapes.[6]

Not only art is able to overcome apartness and distance and to create a second world by proclaiming the harmony of appearances. Twilight is intimate because here nature veils the boundaries separating things from one another as well as the distances that divide us from them. Still more, twilight, like night, fills space with effects like those of music, filling and homogenizing space, unifying and binding together everything that strives apart.

Here I would like to introduce some lines from a poem of Goethe ("*Wiederfinden*" [Reunion] in the West-East Divan) in which the antithesis of light and sound has been superbly rendered.

> When the world in primal depths
> Lay on God's eternal breast,
> He evoked the earliest hour,
> Rejoiced in his creation's flower,
> Said the word, So let there be!
> Then a painful ah! resounded
> As the All of might unbounded
> Fragmented to realities.

[6] Wölfflin (1923) conceives of the contrast between Renaissance and Baroque styles as a change from tangible plastic form to purely visual graphic form. He sees this transition as a rational psychological process—a transformation of the visual schema on which the artistic representation is founded—and as demonstrating a fundamentally different kind of interest in the world. "There [in the Renaissance] it is the defined shaped, here [in the Baroque] it is the changing appearance; there it is the continuing form, measurable and confined, here it is movement, form in function; there the things in themselves, here the things in their relationships" (p. 31). "There the accent falls on the outlines of things, here appearance merges with infinity. Plastic vision that places the emphasis on contours isolates things, while pictorial vision

The light arose, and shyly
The darkness drew away from it,
While all at once the elements
Flew all apart, and bit to bit.
Wildly, wanton dreaming, each one races
To gain the distance opened wide,
Frozen in unmeasured spaces,
No longing in, no sound outside.

Muted all, deserted, still,
Lonely for the first time God!
Then he made the morning light
Who took pity on his plight,
And unfolded to his sadness
A play of colors, sounding gladness,
And now all could love again
That only fell apart just then.[7]

The thoughts expressed in the last few lines are closely related to Goethe's theory of color. The phrase "a play of colors, sounding" is particularly important in the present connection. While the dispersion of elements and loss of tone represent the disintegration of unity, it was Goethe's original intention for the reunion to occur through color alone. Burdach (1900) has shown that the third from the last line in the original version reads, "a play of colors ever renewed" and that this was only later changed by Goethe to, "a play of colors, sounding . . . ." As in the opening words of the Prologue in Heaven (Faust, Part I), it is once more tone and sound, and not light and color, that fill, suffuse, and unify space.

Many, perhaps, may raise their eyebrows at quoting from poetry to support a scientific presentation. But these verses are not chance products of poetic inspiration nor of unrestrained fantasy. Their impact derives, as their connection with Goethe's color theory published several years earlier also shows, from what Goethe personally referred to as exact sensuous fantasy. Additional discussion here would probably show that those who frown on our turning to poets themselves take the reports of subjects in psychological experiments as primary data. But it would be sheer self-deception to believe that the reports of experimental subjects are able to transmit to us the subjects' immediate experiences intact. Subjects trained and untrained, gifted and ungifted, are able to conceptually formulate and express only so much of their immediate experiences as have already been structured by language in general or by

---

brings them together" (p. 15). I have used these quotations, which could be multiplied many times, because it seemed desirable to have the support of Wölfflin's authority in this field.

[7] Translated by E. E.

the scientific knowledge they have acquired. Invariably, their reports refer only to special instances or combinations of the already known. As we call out to our experimental subjects, so the answer comes echoing back. It is the experimenter, of necessity, who establishes the general frame of reference according to his hypothesis, his experimental design, and his discussion of theoretical background. It is just here—where we do not want to descend to the details but to reveal the basic forms of perception—that we cannot hope to secure critical evidence from protocols or statements made by experimental subjects.

Actually, all perceptual experience is controlled by modes of the spatial as basic forms. We respond to distinctions in the pathic sphere in a lawful way, although we are rarely able to account to ourselves for our own responses. Any effort on our part to do so meets with considerable resistance because, practically, we are more disposed to analyze particular sensations than to analyze sensing in general. It is easier for us to become aware of differences in immediate experiences than of the fundamental structures underlying all immediate experiences. It is more in keeping with the natural attitude to compare individual rhythms with one another and to observe their differences than to submit rhythm itself to intellectual reflection. Microscopic examination, preoccupation with details, can be carried out in a more systematic manner than the macroscopic view of elementary forms. Science, accustomed to the pursuit of knowledge through the concept, prefers to use materials already conceptually preformed in everyday life and tends to be suspicious of what is not. Of course, there is a systematic study of works of art and a psychology of artistic creativity; but they use psychological knowledge developed elsewhere and in a different way to explain the creative process. To do the reverse—to use artistic products as legitimate and fully valid evidence for psychological views—is unusual and, to many, will seem methodologically dubious. Despite the rationale I have earlier given for this approach, I can hardly expect that my references to Goethe or to the graphic and plastic arts will be considered adequate support for my theses.

Luckily, however, everyone is in a position to observe for himself, in everyday life, the significance of spatial qualities, the pathic moment in particular, in the formation of immediate experience. Whenever you visit the cinema, you can make the test. When a film is shown without music, the pictures appear at a different remove—unusually remote; they are marionette-like and lifeless.[8] We lack contact with what is being

---

[8] Reference here is to the silent films, usually accompanied by a piano in front of and below the screen. This now obsolete test, unhappily enough, has been replaced by the possibility of using television for the same test. (E. E.)

represented, which glides by in front of our eyes in a spiritless, barren manner. We are spectators at, and not participants in, what is occurring. As soon as the music starts, contact is re-established. It is not even necessary for the music to be somehow appropriate to the images. Space filled with sound is enough to establish a connection between viewer and picture. The difference is even more appreciable between rhythms presented optically and acoustically. A troop of soldiers marching across the screen without musical accompaniment fails to elicit any sympathetic movements from us, whereas we are immediately physically stirred by march music. March music does not elicit just any movement but a particular sort of movement. Forms of movement such as marching and dancing are possible only with music, the music founding the structure of space within which the dancing movement can occur. Optical space is the space of directed, measured, and purposive movement; acoustical space is the space of dance. Purposive movement and dance cannot be understood as different combinations of the same elements. They are two entirely different basic forms of movement, related to two different modes of the spatial.

Although study of these relationships is far from complete, we have now arrived at the point where we can make some use of the foregoing analysis and, at the same time, put it to the test. We are also fortunate in being able to call on everyday observations as evidence. We can do without novel experiments since we need only cite experiences familiar to everyone from everyday life; although these experiences are generally ignored by science, they bring together what belongs together. Our task is limited to elucidating a factual connection so that it reveals its inherent meaningfulness.

Physiology has paid little attention to the dance. The most recent comprehensive treatise in physiology, by Bethe (Steinhausen, 1930), discusses movement and equilibrium; stance and posture; positions of rest; and walking, running, and jumping, but it does not discuss the dance. Physiology, satisfied with an account of the mechanics of the body in motion, can do no more than to represent dance movement as a combination of motor elements. Dance is an expressly psychological problem. Yet, in spite of its empirical and grand theoretical significance, especially for psychopathology, psychology has scarcely given it serious consideration.

Closer examination discloses a real gap. We have, to be sure, a psychology of action and a physiology of movement. A psychology of motion, however, is lacking. This situation is easily demonstrated by attempts to classify movements, e.g., by von Monakow (1910) and others.

It is made crystal clear in Hugo Liepmann's studies of apraxia (1905), in his well-known "movement formula." The progressive transformation of the small g (partial goal representations) into the I (innervations) corresponding to them—i.e., where the motor apraxia is located, according to his formula—simultaneously signifies the transition from the psychology of action, the action project, to the physiology of movement. The goal representations and partial goal representations, both optical and kinesthetic, do not pertain to the movement themselves; they are a project of the movement's path. In relation to objects, they have come to denote particular directions and places in space, with particular positionings of limbs anticipated in imagination and perceived in action. In this manner, Liepmann emphasizes, it is possible to subdivide every partial act of an action into any number of finer acts. There is actually no limit to segmentation if we analyze not the movement but the path.

The unique character of dance movement, however, cannot be derived from Liepmann's movement formula if we seriously consider the form of its appearance, its mode of being experienced, and its correspondence to acoustical space. The psychology of movement remains as a special task that does not coincide with that of the psychology of action—i.e., analyzing its path—nor with that of the physiology of movement—analyzing its innervations. The immediate experience of movement does not merely consist in the projection and perception of the path. Liepmann's movement formula, however, segments the path into a series of stations traversed, one succeeding the other in objective time. The formula projects a purely spatial order in which the sequence of movement acts is replaced by a row of spatial positions. Thus, the formula gives a constructive schema of an already objectivized movement, while the immediate experience of moving oneself is not considered. My critique does not deny the correctness of the Liepmann formula as such, but I have tried to show that, besides such an analysis of action, it is also possible and necessary to develop a psychology of movement concerned not with partial goal representations and innervations but with the forms of appearance, the various types of immediately experienced movement, and their connection with modes of the spatial. So let us begin.

On a Psychology of Movement[9]

If we ask a group of persons to walk to march music or, even better, if we try to enliven a column of trudging soldiers with a march, we observe that their heavy steps become lighter, their gaits firmer and more buoyant, their bodies more energetic and erect, and that they raise their eyes from the ground and their immediate surroundings and look toward the distant.

Their measured, directed movement from A to distant B has been transformed into animated movement no longer restricted to a prescribed destination. Walking is no longer just a means for getting from A to B, for overcoming spatial distance. While marching to music we experience ourselves, the action of our live body as it reaches out in space. What we immediately experience is not the action but our vital doing. While the pedestrian had to advance by leaving step after step behind him, the marching person enters the space ahead. Spatial direction and distance are replaced by symbolic space qualities; the stretch extending into the distance is replaced by the wide, open space ahead. From the changed mode in which the live body is immediately "given," from the distance now having become unimportant, from the widely opening space, the marcher receives the propulsion manifested in his "lively" step. But even though we can show how markedly marching and ordinary walking differ, dancing will conclusively reveal the fundamental differences between the forms of movement corresponding to optical and acoustical space. I will first describe the form of its appearance, then analyze it as a mode of immediate experience, and, finally, examine its relationship to the acoustical style of the spatial.

If we begin by asking someone to walk as he usually does, then ask him to tread to march music, and, finally, to move to the music of a minuet, it takes no expert to notice the radical changes in performance. Walking is converted into stepping, i.e., the foot is no longer set down heel first, as in walking and even in marching, but is set down from its point. In emphasizing this difference, I select from the entire altered pattern of movement just one easily observable detail. It indicates that the roles played by the trunk and the limbs in the movement as a whole have changed in favor of the movements of the trunk. This enhancement of the *motor activity of the trunk* is a critical feature; we find it in all dances, modern as well as earlier and ancient forms, dances sacred and profane, and the dances of nonliterate as well as literate peoples. To use an image, we might say that in walking we move our trunk like the king in chess, i.e., with a minimum of self-deployment and maximum avoidance of danger. The sense organs and limbs protect the trunk just as the pawns and other pieces protect the king. The existence of the whole is involved with the presence and integrity of the trunk, just as with the king in chess despite his limited radius of action.

The eyes and ears protect against what is distant, while the hands shield against what is close up. The blind person uses his arms and cane to feel his way, while persons who can see extend their hands in the dark for orientation and protection. In the dance, to the contrary, we find a completely different movement schema. Here, the trunk is no longer a passively compliant part of the live body; rather, the moving trunk itself dominates the moving figure. Stepping, in the minuet, requires compensatory trunk movements different from those of ordinary walking. Without them, the flow of movement slackens and the rhythmic step is replaced by the clog-step. In promenading, trunk movements are still limited to departures from and returns to the sagittal plane. In other styles of dancing, the movements are further embellished with bowings, turnings, displacements of the trunk as a whole, or by an enhanced lordotic or kyphotic stance, viz. by more variegated attitudes of the trunk as differentiated in its parts. Dancers who are not truly talented, who "don't know what to do with their arms and hands," betray how much the attitude and movement of the trunk determine the movement of the limbs. Through all these turning movements, the trunk abandons the rigid vertical while venturing into space.

From a purely physiological standpoint, one could, perhaps, object that these movements mainly require the activity of the muscles of the legs and abdomen rather than a small number of trunk muscles. The answer to this objection is that we do not experience our muscle innervations, but rather we experience the motion of our body and limbs in the same way that we see others moving. If, on the other hand, we consider the movement from a merely technical viewpoint—which is entirely legitimate—and if we ask about its effect and utility in locomotion, then we must begin with the negative statement that all these trunk movements—the turning and bowing, lowering and raising, inclining and rocking—are not particularly functional for advancing in a straight line. They do not help to keep the body in one direction, but, rather, they force it out of a straight line. Not only is this true for the movements of the trunk, but it also applies to all other dance steps, just as it applies, in the last analysis, to the movement of the dance as a whole.

The dance is not related to any particular direction; we do not dance to get from one point to another in space. Among primitive peoples, there are many dances in which no change of place occurs. Since the dance is not goal directed, it must also lack reference to distance. Walking, we move *through* space from one point to another; dancing, we move *within* space. In walking, we leave a certain distance behind; we traverse space. The dance, on the contrary, is nondirected and nonlimited movement. It has no reference to spatial measure nor to spatial and temporal limit. The dance floor can be of any shape. It confines the dancer, not the dance. The mere fact that dance floors vary widely in form and size shows that dance movement, though bounded, is not hampered by its perimeter.

Walking, however, is, from the very beginning, limited both by its point of departure and its goal. Wherever dance has not been shaped by social conventions or aesthetic intentions, it is free of temporal limits and terminates in exhaustion or ecstasy. Moreover, even in its contemporary forms, dance knows of no intrinsic limitations. Just as the perimeter of the dance floor does not mark the extension of a dance spatially, so the formal ending of the musical score does not set the limits of the dance temporally. The dance can be continued for as long as one wishes beyond the closing chord simply by reviving the music. Walking, however, is measured, directed, numbered. Measure and number are originally alien to dance movement, which is free of reference to direction or limit. Measure and number invade the dance when it is naïvely or artistically stylized or when the dance movement is subordinated to pantomimic representation.

If the dance is not oriented in terms of direction and distance or, pragmatically speaking, in terms of path and distance, what remains as a frame of reference for dance movement? For dance, like any movement, needs a frame of reference. Here, where we do not yet consider the dance in its experiential meaning but simply and utterly in its formal appearance, the characterization of its movement as nondirected and nonlimited has only negative significance. Yet, earlier, when speaking of trunk movements, we emphasized that these movements release the trunk from its vertical position and bring it into its spatial surroundings. This motif, of the expansion of the experienced body space into the space of the environment, as initially observed in the movements of the trunk, now repeats itself in forward-and-backward steps, in sideways trotting, and in turning. Ultimately, we discover the identical motif in the over-all movement of the dancer. The dance movement fills space in all directions. The frame of reference of dance movement is formed by the *symbolic spatial qualities.*

Here, we must confine ourselves to merely introducing this concept in a very general way that does not do justice to its significance. Only subsequent exposition can give it more substantial content. The various moments we have pointed out in succession—viz. the enhanced motor activity of the trunk, the abolition of direction and distance, the filling of space, the reference to symbolic spatial qualities, the dependency on tone and rhythm—do not accidentally occur together; they are all necessarily and reciprocally related and in agreement with the modes and forms of the spatial. Consequently, it is impossible to strictly separate the forms of appearance from the modes of experiencing and the spatial forms of movement in our discussion. The different modes of experience and the forms of spatiality, in particular, do not allow of description one after the other but only through and with one another. Thus, many details will first become comprehensible when the whole is viewed in retrospect. Even though we have just referred to a filling of space, we want this term to be understood in a more specific sense than is usual in psychology, for we are here anticipating that mode of the spatial which will be precisely characterized later.

Dance, it appears, has originated "on the spot" among all peoples and at all times. Dance is one of the primary human creations like language, clothing, ornamentation, and using tools. Consequently, it must stem from a basic and pervasive need. Despite the variety of origins and developmental periods, we encounter the same structure of movement everywhere, so long as we confine ourselves to pure dance movement and do not include pantomimic representations. What is it that brings man to perform movements which, from the standpoint of locomotive technique, would be completely unnatural? If we search for an answer to this question through analysis of the modes of experience, we meet with a formal difficulty virtually insurmountable.

How can we describe such experiences without using an idiom full of images and therefore inappropriate for the conceptual rigor and sober restraint of scientific writing? This must be one of the reasons why science has shown so little interest in a phenomenon like the dance, whose primordial character and universal appearance ought to provoke scientific curiosity. Every so often, we see how an investigator hesitates in bringing such phenomena into the scope of his inquiry, phenomena which, as experiences, are remote from or even in opposition to the experience of scientific thinking.

On the other hand, should we undertake an analysis of experience as called for here and, at the same time, try to avoid metaphorical expression, then we are accused of having forced the irrational into a rational frame. Nevertheless, if we now try to show how the dance originates in a kind of immediate experience poles apart from theoretical knowledge —from purposive, planned, and calculating action and the technical control of things—we do not mean to imply that the change as conceived is the sought-for end of that immediate experience. When we say that the tension between subject and object, between I and world, is dissolved in the immediate experience of dancing, we do not claim that this achievement is linked with any reflection which would yet have to per-mit—even if it were theoretically capable of resolving it—this antith-esis to factually continue to exist. So it would be completely incorrect to charge us with having rationalized the irrational. Even though we seek to make the immediate experience of dancing accessible to reason, we never for a moment forget that the experience itself is not conceptual, that the dance does not overcome the subject–object dichotomy con-ceptually, but that it actualizes a union of the separated in a far more elementary manner—by em-bodying its meaning.

The crescendo of motor activity in the trunk accentuates the functions expressive of our vital being at the expense of those which serve knowl-edge and practical action. This centering of motor activity in the trunk is also accompanied by a characteristic transformation in one's immedi-ate experience of his own body. Corresponding to the dominant posi-tion of the trunk in motor activity, there is a transposition of the ego relative to the body schema. The "I" of the awake, active person is cen-tered in the region at the base of the nose, between the eyes; in the dance it descends into the trunk.[10]

The expression "localization of the ego relative to the body schema" must not be misinterpreted. What we mean to say is that the live body in immediate experience is organized as a totality. The principle of this unifying articulation is the relative closeness of the various parts of the organism to the "I." For example, our feet, as a rule, are farther from the "I" than the eyes; they are more of a part, more of a possession, an or-gan or tool. When we tell someone to look at us, we expect him to look us in the eye. We would not be satisfied if he were to look at our feet or at our neck. The shyness of many persons' gaze is indicated by their tendency to avoid that direct communication between the alien "I" and their own which occurs when one looks into another's eyes. The "I" of the man of action is assumed, in terms of the live body, by the eyes. When the "I" is shifted from the region of the eyes to the trunk, the emphasis on the gnostic attitude is reduced and the pathic moment in experience comes to the fore. Now we are no longer directed to particu-lar objects of the external world in comprehending, observing, willing, and acting, but we experience our existence, our being alive, our sensi-bility, in an immediate manner.

A group of important feeling terms, such as "weighed down," "elat-ed," "hemmed in," "constricted," "liberated," "inclination," "aver-sion," "upright," and "bowed down" all refer to the posture or mode of

[10] See Balzac's *La Théorie de la démarche*.

sensation of the live body and its organs. Amplifying the suggestion made by Klages (1923) it must be added that all of these terms refer solely to the trunk and not to the head or limbs. This narrowing down of the concept of live body to one part of the total agrees perfectly with the character of the body (*Leib*) as it is present in experience, viz. as differentiated into predominantly pathic and predominantly gnostic, pragmatic portions.

When we say that accentuation of motor movements in the trunk shifts the emphasis from the gnostic to the pathic moment, we do not mean that the movements of the trunk enable us to receive different, more numerous, or more intense organ sensations. When we speak of proprioceptive sensation, we are considering the body (*Körper*); however, where we speak of the gnostic and pathic moments, we are definitely comprehending the experience of the live body (*Leib*) in relation to its surroundings or to the world. This and only this is our topic here and below.

The opening wide of live body space into its surroundings is an expression used to characterize the form in which the movement of the dance appears; but it may also serve us as a description of experience. In regular walking, live body space is expanded into the surroundings through the swinging of arms; in simply standing, live body space is expanded merely by the way the arms are held. (Naturally, "the live body" is meant here in the pregnant sense of the phrase as discussed earlier.) Of course, we are all aware that the swinging movement of the arms is physiologically conditioned. But the way it occurs—back and forth, its amplitude, the relation between swings, the distance of the plane of swinging from the trunk, the outward swinging and use of hand movements to brake the arm movements, reversing the forward swing into the swing backward and the other way around—gives to the pendulum-like movements of the arms a distinctive stamp. Consequently, it is a distinguishing feature of a person's walk, and we are able to infer ways of behavior, character traits, and moods from it. The swinging becomes expressive, revealing the active relation of the individual to space, i.e., to the world.

The position of the arms in standing, interpreted by Goldstein (1934) as "optimum biological behavior," is, no doubt, codetermined by the expressive moment. This position varies; it changes continually with mood and situation. The anxious person draws his arms toward his trunk, while they sink to the body of the depressed, who is beset, encumbered, and overpowered by the surrounding space. Someone who needs to defend, assert, or seclude himself from his surroundings folds his arms across his chest; yet he does not do so in order to draw his arms to his trunk. On the contrary, the arms function, as it were, like a bulwark for his body, repelling what is alien to the personal sphere. Very slightly modified, however, this position can be interpreted in an entirely different way. By slightly lifting the forearms crossed over the chest, the gesture changes from one of unambiguous defense into one of humble obedience. In both instances, the hands and forearms cross the midline and are thus removed from their spheres of effective action. Nevertheless, it is not their interference with action or the ability to do anything that endows these gestures with expressive meaning, but, simply, it is the symbolism of space. On what other basis could folding the arms and crossing them over the chest have such different meanings? In the attitude of humility, we see how the live body space is contracted and how surrounding space, following the arms' movement, presses in on the body, enclosing it; here, again, we sense the letting happen, the not resisting, the submission. Lastly, a comparison of the bodily attitudes of an ancient Greek and of a Christian at prayer must remove all doubts about the expressive meaning of these gestures and the spatial symbolism underlying them.

We do not need to multiply our examples. Those given ought to be sufficient to show that, in analyzing the movements that express the tendency of live body space to expand against surrounding space and to actualize itself symbolically, we remain throughout within the confines of the observable and empirical method. Without theoretical reflection, we respond in an appropriate manner to the expressive meaning of such movements perceived in others, while we are unable to alter voluntarily the course of our own movements controlled by these expressive characters.

The opening wide of live body space is fullest when the trunk itself is inserted into the movement, as in dancing.

Since every opening wide of body space can be experienced as enrichment or as jeopardy, the very same movements are passionately sought by some and shyly avoided by others. The sports field and the gymnasium furnish an abundance of examples. To be obliged to launch one's trunk into space, as in the pole vault, limits many a person's performance. Some persons who can dive into the water from great heights do not venture a jump in which the body must be moved from the vertical out into space. Objectively considered, the risk is not appreciably different in the two cases or, if different, is not more dangerous in the first case than in the second. Not the objective measure of danger, but the peril experienced in abandoning the customary position is responsible for the limited performance.

For this reason, many persons are unable to surrender to the dance movement and attempt—vainly, of course—to compose one from steps and jumps derived from purposive movement. Expressive movement cannot be produced apart from the immediate experience of which it forms an integral part. The immediate experience and the movement in which it actualizes its meaning are indivisible; the movement is not the cause of the immediate experience; neither is the immediate experience the purpose of the movement. The harmony of trunk movements with those of the legs and the total encompassing movement prevents us from assuming that particular movements are invested with particular tones of pleasure, so that, while performing them for pleasure, we would incidentally slip into the characteristic movement of the dance. No, the affinity with the symbolic qualities of space—the nondirected and the nonbounded—determines the specific character of the immediate experience in dancing. The individual motion in itself is not pleasurable, but, rather, it becomes so within the total encompassing movement of the dance. The observation that dances reach a climax and occasionally conclude in ecstasy might suggest, albeit incorrectly, that the dance in its entirety, all the movements that terminated in ecstasy, were performed for the sole purpose of bringing about such a state.

There are many forms of movement that can drive one to the point of dizziness, loss of consciousness, and ecstasy. Of them all, turning around is one of the most widely distributed forms. It appears early in children's "ring-around-the-rosy," and we find it everywhere as an element of dance movement. We are so familiar with it that we no longer wonder at it. Nevertheless, it is quite surprising and noteworthy that, in dancing, we find a movement to be pleasurable that is extremely unpleasant and disturbing in other circumstances. The simplest solution would be to say that turning around is acceptable in dancing only because it may eventually lead to ecstasy. However convenient this explanation may be, experience shows that it cannot be correct. There are many dances which do not end in ecstasy, even though they include the turning movement. As we may realize in ourselves and easily observe in others, each particular phase of moving has its own intrinsic value. The single phase of moving is enjoyable in itself; it is not endowed with a flavor of pleasure through its relation to a goal, a condition still momentarily lacking, only to be eventually attained by the movement itself. In sport, however, the situation is altogether different. For the mountain climber, it is his movement that *results in* his experiencing victory, of elevation, of the conquest of space. But his exertion remains exactly that. Although we call on the runner to give his all, admiring his victory which is also a victory over his own body, we do not want to see any exertion in the dancer. Compare the facial expression of a dancer with that of a runner crossing the finish line and you will realize how differently the movements are integrated into the total immediate experience.

Thus, in the optically structured space of purposive action, the individual turning movement is, by itself, experienced quite differently than in the space of the dance. In the first instance, the turning is disagreeable because it may end in dizziness and loss of orientation. The loss of orientation is the crucial feature. Optical space has an established system of directions by which we direct ourselves. When we are turning around or being turned around, this is no longer possible, and the movement becomes disagreeable. The feeling of dizziness increases our discomfort. However, it is possible to bear the dizziness in many different ways. When we ride the merry-go-round, whirling to the rhythms of music, vertigo adds an element of thrill as long as we do not resist the rotating movement but go along with it, giving ourselves entirely up to it.

In both cases, the proprioceptive sensations remain unchanged, but they are embodied in different structures of immediate experience. The space in which we move on the merry-go-round or in dance—which we are discussing here—has lost its directional stability. Of course, it is still a space with extension and direction, but direction is no longer disposed in a certain way around a fixed axis; rather, direction moves and turns with us as it were. The dissolution of defined direction, and, correspondingly, of topical valences, homogenizes space. In a space of such modality, it is no longer possible to act; one can only enter into it as a participant. Actually, we don't live in space but in spaces, spaces somehow demarcated and stabilized by a system of fixed axes. One need only imagine a room perfectly quadratic, without windows and indirectly illuminated; in the middle of each wall is a door, while furniture and pictures are arranged in a strictly symmetrical manner so that each wall appears as a mirror image of the opposite wall. If one were to spend some time in this room and then walk back and forth several times, one would become confused about the entrance, having lost his orientation to neighboring, surrounding areas; one would be bewildered and bewitched like a person in a magic maze. To enter such a space in fantasy is sufficient to show why we make our rooms rectangular rather than

square, why we prefer asymmetry—a clearly and distinctly apprehended difference between length and width, as proportions in the ratio of
the Golden Mean. Action demands a system of definite, distinct directions and determining loci with valences varying in accord with their
relationship to the directional system. When the spatial structure
changes, as happens in dance, the immediate experience of confrontation also changes that tension between subject and object which, in ecstasy, completely dissolves. When we turn around while dancing, we
are, from the very start, moving in a space completely at odds with oriented space. But this change of spatial structure occurs only in pathic
participation, not in a gnostic act of thinking, contemplating, or imagin-
ing. That is to say, presentic experience actualizes itself *in* the movement; it does not produce itself *by means of* the movement. Even though
a dance occupies a considerable interval in objective time, the entire
movement is still integrally presentic. In itself, it does not produce any
changes in immediate experience nor any changes in the external situation, as does action which must abandon its starting point to reach its
goal. Every action demands that a particular condition or position be left
behind in order to reach another condition, another position. This defines both direction and limits for action. When the new condition is
reached, the old one belongs to the past; action is a historical process.
Presentic movement, on the other hand, is free of direction or limits;
it knows only waxing and waning, ebbing and flooding.[11] It does not
bring about change; it is not a historical process. It is for just this reason that we term it "presentic," despite its duration in objective time.[12]
The dissolution of the subject–object tension, culminating in ecstasy,
is not the aim of the dance; rather, the very experience of dancing originally arises within it.

We are speaking of the dance here in a very general way. But one
need only compare a minuet and a waltz to see how much dances can
differ. The dancer of the minuet performs his steps over the basic
rhythm. The "filling" of space is only figuratively represented by the
formation of couples, the "visits," etc. The dancer of the minuet senses
the harmonizing influence of the music without yielding to it entirely;

[11] Such movement is especially well developed in gypsy music. The singular quality
of presentness prevails in the music of "nonliterate" peoples or wherever music is not
produced as independent works of art, i.e., where music still belongs to the landscape
rather than to architecture, church, chamber, or concert hall. One need only listen to
the endlessly reiterated rhythms and brief melodic phrases of primitive music. The
significance of meter, particularly the preference for asymmetrical rhythms to interrupt the symmetry of walking movements, cannot be taken up here.

[12] Action and presentic movement are only distinguishable within a historiological
perspective and not within one that is biological-functional.

he remains an individual. Rulers do not join in dancing. The different ways of life of social classes and the changes of sentiment dominating different historical periods are directly reflected in their forms of dancing. The sequence: minuet, waltz, jazz strikingly demonstrates the extent to which individual existence has been abandoned and swallowed up by mass movements.

The reduction of subject–object tension as it develops throughout the dance, perhaps even to ecstasy, is not experienced as the subject's dissolution but as his "merging with." Hence, the dancer requires a partner, either an individual or a group; that is also why he needs music, which bestows its own movement on space so that the dancer can participate in it. The dancer is drawn into the movement, becoming part of a harmonious movement that embraces space, his partner, and himself.

In the myth of Orpheus, men and animals, trees, forests, and even rocks, mountains, and streams followed his sounding lyre. Here we have a simple, telling expression of the compelling power of music to which all nature, both living and nonliving, bends. Should we happen to conjure up the schema of Euclidean space in this context, we are likely to smilingly dismiss the myth as merely anthropomorphic. Then an expression like the one used earlier, that the dancer is drawn into the movement of space, seems an unpardonable lapse. But those words were no slip of the pen; they were used deliberately with full awareness. The space in which we live is as different from the schema of empty Euclidean space as the familiar world of colors differs from the concepts of physical optics. Anybody who takes the systematic concepts of physics and physiology as a guide in describing experience and its laws must necessarily fail in his purpose. Consequently, we ought not to attach ourselves to these systems if we wish to reveal space and its structure in immediate experience. And then it will make sense to speak of the "movement of space." As immediately experienced, space is always a filled and articulated space; it is nature or world.

We have now returned to the point from which we started. It is unnecessary to add anything to what we have said earlier about pregnant rhythm and the compelling power of music. But we do need to once more take up the theme of the homogenization of space; for this phenomenon alone enables us to show convincingly that spatiality presents itself in a variety of modes and that we are not merely dealing with different modes of spatial appearance peculiar to color and sound.

Previously, when discussing the turning movement, we showed that turning around in the dance requires a particular spatial structure. We wish to elaborate on this point now, using another example, to see what we can further discover about modes of spatiality, the optical space of directed movement, and the acoustical space of dance movement. Again, we will use a simple fact for our starting point.

Moving backward and turning around have much in common as types of movement. Going backward in optical space is disagreeable to us just as is turning around, and we try to avoid it. In dancing, however, the seemingly similar kind of motor activity is taken for granted; in dancing, we notice none of the trouble and resistance experienced whenever we have to walk backward. We experience walking backward as an unwelcome imposition, but we experience dancing backward as a spontaneous activity. We could of course try to relate—and, thereby, to explain—this difference in experience to the different circumstances: In dancing, we need not be afraid that we will stumble over anything on the open dance floor, which is quite unlike the usual situation in which we have to walk backward. Still, we can reverse each one of these external conditions of movement without producing any change in our mode of experiencing. No matter how empty a room may be, it is still disagreeable to walk backward in it. Even when assured there are no obstacles so that we do not have to turn our heads to check, we will still note tendencies toward such orienting movements. When dancing on a floor with several other couples, it may well happen that while moving backward we neglect the necessary precautions and have a collision. Every attempt to explain the difference in experience by the hypothesis that the need for orientation and certainty is better satisfied in one situation than in the other is vain, for the simple reason that the need for orientation and certainty does not accompany the backward movement in dancing as it does in walking. Such need is not felt because the dancing movement occurs in a space with a different structure from that of the space of purposive movement.

In this connection, it must become even clearer than in the analysis of the turning movement that experienced movement is never related to empty Euclidean space but always to a space with its own characteristic structure and articulation. This articulation is not determined by a system of directions—right–left, over–under, before–behind—anchored in the live body; it is independent of such a system. Of course, the synergy of backward movement as such is the same in dancing as in walking. However, if it is experienced so differently in the two instances, the cardinal directions alone cannot be decisive. The cardinal directions are changeable. With every change in the position of the body, they, too, change. After an "about face" that which was behind is now before, and what was on the left lies on the right and vice versa. In walking *forward*, however, we *re-turn*. The way thither and the way hither are not determined by the cardinal directions. When we ride in an automobile from home to our place of work the way thither remains just that, even if we sit with our back toward the direction in which we are going. What is to our rear preserves the character of "forward." In the corresponding case, with conditions reversed, what lies before us preserves its character of re-turn.

In other words, the space in which we live is a historical space. Just as we experience time from a particular now, from our age, our years, our present, so space is ordered for us with regard to a central point, a firm and immovable Here.

Wherever we are, we direct ourselves with regard to this definite Here. For example, we "go away" or are "on the way," we "de-part" or "turn back." Thus, we have a Here that is steadfast, and a Here that is mobile or, in more concrete terms, a "home" and a "camping place." The bounded spaces in which we live are constantly being joined together, articulated as partial spaces for themselves, and as a whole through the relationship of "camping place" to "home." Thus it is that the region of sunrise has such an elementary significance for nomadic peoples. It is as though it were their home. The word "orient-ation" indicates, of course, that "camping place" is originally determined in relation to the region of sunrise. While limited areas of space, like a room or street, already have a system of fixed axes, various spaces, through their relation to the steadfast Here, are joined together into historical space, and their directions acquire a dynamic momentum.[13]

In the typical situation, the articulation of space into the cardinal directions "ahead" and "behind" coincides with the historical differentiation into regions of "fight" and "flight." So movement backward is actually against the dynamic tendency of historical space. While dancing, we seem not to register the dynamics of historical space. This falls into line with our earlier discussion. Dancing, we no longer move in a bounded region of space related to a steadfast Here, we move in homogeneous space, freed from differences in direction and topical valences. While dancing, the movement backward does not take place in opposition to the dynamic impulses conditioned by space; consequently, there is nothing disagreeable about it, as there is in walking backward in optical space.

Analysis of backward movement has obliged and aided us to uncover one last feature essential for a psychology of movement—the distinction between historical and presentic space. It is just the presentic

[13] See E. Minkowski's discussion (1933) of my and F. Fischer's paper.

that characterizes the acoustical mode of the spatial as well as its corresponding experience. Historical action is suspended while dancing; the dancer is lifted from the stream of historical becoming. The dancer's experience is a mode of being present that does not point to any future end and is, thus, spatially and temporally unlimited. The dancer's movement is a nondirectional motility that resonates to the autonomous movement of the space by which it is pathically induced. Space filled with tone and homogenized by a single pervading movement—and in this the homogeneity of the acoustical mode of the spatial differs from that of empty metrical space—has itself a presentic character. Dance space is not a part of directed, historical space but is a symbolic region of the world. It is determined not by distance, direction, and magnitude but through the "wide openness," loftiness, profundity, and autokinesis of space. While a distance extends from here to there and, thus, has a definite position and spot in space, a spot and a position have a different relation to "wide openness." "Wide openness" is neither here nor on the horizon, nor is it on a line connecting the here with any other points of space or such points with each other; it is not quantifiable but is rather a quality of space. Thus, we can legitimately say that dance movement is ordered according to the symbolic qualities of space.

Thus we see how a remarkable mode of spatiality establishes itself on the nature of sound; its autonomous existence; its temporal unfolding; and its moments of homogenization, of induction, and of the presentic. We have further seen how this mode of the spatial promotes and facilitates the experience of unification, actualized in nondirected and nonbounded movement, which, guided by the fullness (*Prägnanz*) of rhythm, opens and extends the live body into space. This demonstration of the full correspondence between the nature of sound, mode of spatiality, kind of immediate experiencing, and the phenomenal form of movement may be taken as a signal confirmation of our theses.

Now whatever one's position may be with regard to these views as a whole, one must acknowledge that any analysis and theory of movement which does not account for the structure of the space in which the movement occurs remains incomplete. But, if one reviews the literature on motion and willed actions, one will discover that the problem of space has been neglected both in the contributions of clinicians as well as those of psychologists. Pragmatically, such an omission is of least consequence in the treatment of purposive movement; but, in the analysis of the more primitive forms of movement, viz. psychomotor disturbances of presentic movements and of expressive movements, it cannot be passed over. It is characteristic of the status of this problem that even Klages terms the expressive movement a metaphor of action. In his definition that "every expressive body movement actualizes the experienced impulsion of the feeling expressed in it" (1923), he also seems to be relating the expressive movement to an abstract space of unspecified modality. He fails to even consider any other possible derivation. The interpretation of expressive movement as action, however, is appropriate only for a certain group of expressive movements. This interpretation is invalid for all those expressive movements which do not actualize *an* impulse but which are presentic behavior—which are related not to historical space and its directions but to presentic space and the symbolic qualities of space.

I do not wish to discuss this antithesis in greater detail here. Some may feel that we have by now strayed far enough from clinical problems. Yet, our treatment of dance in such detail, with regard to its phenomenal form and mode of experience, has served to explicate the modes of the spatial and the general features of presentic movements. Once we have grasped the general features, we are able to accommodate the individual case, especially the pathological case. In fact, we are not very far removed from the clinic here. The relation of phobias to the symbolic qualities of space, of perversions and psychopathic states to the distinction of gnostic and pathic, and of catatonia to presentic movement are readily apparent. Finally, if we recall those occasional encephalitic patients who can only move forward with the greatest difficulty while they are able to move backward with the greatest ease or can even dance, then we can see how close the connection actually is.

In this context, the further question also arises of the articulation of the sensorimotor sphere and the correspondence between spatial structure and movement. If we find that, as a rule, the sounds of a minuet convert walking into stepping, we are certainly not going to assume that a "stimulus" has acted directly on the triceps surae, or on the central representation of the extension of the foot in the cerebrum. Here we encounter problems like those taken up by Kleist (1922), Isserlin (1910), Steiner (1922), Bostroem (1924), and others in discussing the relation of catatonic disturbances of movement to those based on a lesion in the striatum. But neither the physiological theory of Kleist nor the will psychology of Isserlin and Bostroem are entirely satisfactory.

The distinction between purposive movement and presentic movement has, by and large, extended the scope of our problems. At the same time, it has definitely provided us with a point of departure for a fresh solution—one that could prove fruitful over and beyond the psychomotor sphere. But, before we are in a position to assume these tasks, we must still attempt to extend the basis of our thinking through an analysis of the relationships between the forms of space and perception.

References

Bostroem, A. Encephalitische und Katatone Motilitätsstörungen. *Klinische Wochenschrift* 3 (1924).

Burdach, K. (Ed.) Notes to Goethe, *Gesammelte Werke*. Stuttgart and Berlin: Cotta, 1900. V, 398.

Goldstein, K. *Der Organismus*. Eng. trans., *The Organism*. New York: American Book Co., 1939. P. 340.

Herder, G. *Vom Erkennen und Empfinden der menschlichen Seele* [1778], *Gesammelte Werke* (Berlin: 1876), 17, 163–219.

Isserlin A. Über die Beurteilung von Bewegungsstörungen bei Geisteskranken, *Zeitschrift für die gesamte Neurologie und Psychiatrie*, 3 (1910).

Jossmann, P. Über Beziehungen zwischen Struktur and Benennung von Wahrnehmungserlebnissen, *Zentralblatt für die gesamte Neurologie und Psychiatrie*, 50 (1928), 307.

Klages, L. *Ausdrucksbewegung und Gestaltungskraft*. Leipzig: Barth, 1923.

Kleist, K. Die psychomotorischen Erscheinungen und ihr Verhältnis zu den Motilitätsstörungen bei Erkrankungen der Stammganglien, *Monatsschrift für Psychiatrie*, 52 (1922).

Liepmann, H. *Über Störungen des Handelns bei Gehirnkranken*. Berlin: Karger, 1905.

Metzger, W. Optische Untersuchungen am Ganzfeld, *Psychologische Forschung*, 13 (1929), 17–34.

Minkowski, E. *Le Temps vécu*. Paris: Collection de l'Évolution Psychiatrique, 1933. Book II, chaps. 3, 7,

Steiner, G. Encephalitische und katatonische Motilitätsstörungen, *Zeitschrift für die gesamte Neurologie und Psychiatrie*, 78 (1922).

Steinhausen, W. Mechanik des menschlichen Körpers in Correlation der Bewegungen, *Handbuch der normalen und pathologischen Physiologie*. Berlin: Springer Verlag, 1930. Vol. 15, Pt. I.

Straus, E. Die Aesthesiologie und ihre Bedeutung für das Verständnis der Halluzinationen, *Zeitschrift für Psychiatrie und Neurologie* (1949), 182. Trans. in R. May, E. Angel, & H. F. Ellenberger (Eds.), *Existence*. New York: Basic Books, 1958.

von Hornbostel, E. Psychologie der Gehörserscheinungen, *Handbuch der normalen und pathologischen Physiologie*. Berlin: Springer Verlag, 1926. Vol. 11.

von Monakow, C. Aufbau und Lokalisation der Bewegungen beim Menschen, *Monakow's Arbeiten*, 4 (1910).

Werner, H. Das Empfinden und seine experimentelle Prüfung, *Bericht über den XI. Kongress der Deutschen Gesellschaft für Psychologie, Wien, 1929*. Jena: G. Fischer Verlag, 1930.

Wölfflin, H. *Kunstgeschichtliche Grundbegriffe*. 6th ed.; München: Hugo Bruckmann Verlag, 1923.

CHAPTER TWO

Lived Movement

The title of this paper refers to ideas which, in recent years, have steadily become more succinct for me. This presentation, from the very beginning and without intention on my part but from inner necessity, took the shape of an offering to the *genius loci* or, to be more exact, to the geniuses of your city. True, this praise occasionally takes on, as you will see, the character of a polemic; it assumes the stance of tournament rather than paying tribute. But this is necessary, since struggle, discussion, and the drawing of distinctions are essential for scientific thought. Even our soliloquies and lectures are dialogues we hold with our comrades in letters living and dead.

The title "Lived Movement" will evoke an analogous phrase for you. I am thinking of the notions of "lived time" and "lived space" introduced into psychology by Minkowski (1933). This convergence of my work and that of Minkowski does not simply occur, I must admit, out of inner necessity; it is intentional. It is my way of saying that my conception of the problems of psychology and psychopathology agrees, in many respects, with that of Minkowski, who received decisive impulses from Bergson's philosophy. Hence, the title of this lecture should allow me a place among your previous acquaintances, even though I come before you as a stranger.

But "lived movement" is not only an expression of amity. It is also a cry to battle. The adjective "lived" (*vécu*) denotes a kind of movement contrary to what is usually meant when one speaks of movement alone without any further qualification. Movement in general is taken as the motion whose laws have been formulated by classical physics in direct descent from the philosophy of Descartes.

Cartesian philosophy and with it the Cartesian notion of movement has never ceased to be influential. Now it is just this Cartesian theory of movement that we are challenging—that we must challenge—if we are to understand human and animal movements.

Descartes himself likened philosophy as a whole to a tree, with metaphysics for its roots and medicine, mechanics, and morals for its three main branches. Just as the trunk grows out of the roots and the branches from the trunk, so a reliable knowledge of truth in the special sciences depends on a prior knowledge of material things based, in turn, on a knowledge of metaphysical truths. Descartes always insisted on the necessity of respecting the solidarity of the parts belonging to a single whole. Yet, the rich development of the special sciences has gradually drawn our attention away from general principles and directed it instead to single questions, with a consequent narrowing of our view. The physicists' notions of movement are taken for granted even in those special sciences which have little in common with physics. They are applied without hesitation to nonphysical movements, as if no problems were involved in such transfer. The natural philosophical bases of the notion of movement have been virtually forgotten, as have all the accompanying assumptions, difficulties, contradictions, and paradoxes; all such matters have apparently lost their actuality today. And so it happens that a doctrine founded on the powerful abstraction of a genius, replete with deep and hazardous riddles, is almost accepted as nature itself today.

Contemporary physicists, however, remain generally cautious. One of the most outstanding among them, Heisenberg, has recently written:

within a system of laws which are based on certain fundamental ideas only certain quite definite ways of asking questions make sense, and thus a system is separated from others which allow different questions to be put. Thus, the transition in science from previously investigated fields of experience to new ones will never consist simply of the application of already known laws to these new fields. On the contrary, a really new field of experience will always lead to the crystallization of a new system of scientific concepts and laws. They will be no less capable of rational analysis than the old ones but their nature will be fundamentally different. . . . Thus the hope of understanding all aspects of intellectual life on the principles of classical physics is no more justified than the hope of a traveller who believes he will have obtained the answer to all problems once he has journeyed to the end of the world (1952, pp. 23–24).

Thus, the physicist himself not only gives the physiologist and psychologist the right to develop his own principles—the system appropriate for his science—he also makes it his duty.

It is necessary to understand the natural philosophical hypotheses implicit in the notion of movement in classical physics to see why Descartes and, after him, a good many psychologists believed there could be only one kind of movement and why they thought there is no room for the concept of lived movement in the structure of science. This knowledge is also indispensable if we are to develop a theory of lived movement in opposition to that viewpoint. We ought to know where the divergence occurs.

Of course, I cannot go into too many details here, but the conceptions of Descartes are so broad, and his basic ideas have had such far-reaching consequences, that it is possible to clarify the historical situation with a few references.

In his "Sixth Meditation" we find this short paragraph on movement.

I am also acquainted with several other abilities, like those of changing location, of assuming different attitudes, etc., which could not be conceived any more than the previous ones without some substance to which they would be attached, nor without which they could not exist. But it is very apparent that these abilities, if it is true that they exist, must belong to some material or extended substance, and not to a thinking substance, since their clear and distinct concept certainly contains some kind of extension, but nothing at all of intelligence.

These few words, a consequence and necessary interpretation of the Cartesian doctrine of substances, have determined the fate of the psychology of movement for centuries. Sensation and movement are fundamentally separated; they belong to different worlds—sensation to the thinking thing (*res cogitans*) and movement to the realm of extension (*res extensa*). Descartes separated them, and this separation continues right up to the present. So powerful has been the influence of his thought that the problem concerning us here has, at times, been lost from view.

If now, for a moment, we turn our attention toward the phenomenon of lived movement, making an effort to rid ourselves of all preconceptions, it will be evident that there is an intrinsic connection between sensation and movement, whether or not we are Cartesians. I move myself, I leave here to go there, I launch myself into space; my movement occurs in a certain direction, at a certain speed, and with a certain output of energy. But the direction, the speed, and the length of my steps are all imposed by my surroundings. I set my foot down variously on the pavement or muddy ground, in a field or on a mountain, in light or in the dark; there at an obstacle I draw back. Or, yet another example: I don't hold a pen as I grip an umbrella when it is storming. How firmly I grasp something depends on its resistance—its tendency to get away from me. We always sense an intrinsic connection between sensation and movement. As a sensing and moving being, I am one and the same person, and it is as such a person that I look into my world, which is *one* world. Our question is, then: Should we not conceive the relation between sensation and movement as an intrinsic one, i.e., as a unity and not as a juncture? In addition, we must ask how we are able to realize such a range of sensations and movements within the form of this unity.

Yet, according to Descartes, the only possible relation is an extrinsic one—a linkage and influence that is both reciprocal and *external,* corresponding to the connections between sensory and motor centers. The postulate of the organism's unity did not derive from physiological observations. It is given to physiology, having originated simply and solely from our awareness of the object of physiology as a *living* organism. In its position vis-à-vis the world, the animated human or animal body is an organic unity, but it is not an isolated organism affected by just any events and responding in just any way. The more psychology assimilates itself to physiology, the more it interprets sensations as the content of awareness accompanying afferent impulses; and the more it conceives of moving itself as a mere muscular function, the less it is able to realize the internal relation between sensation and movement.

But, Descartes explicitly teaches that the psychology of movement is completely dependent on physiology. He does not recognize lived movement; instead, he interprets it entirely as a process and execution of muscular motion *within* a body. The body, my body as well as the bodies of all other men and animals, must be comprehended in a purely mechanical fashion. Since every movement is a mode of extension for Descartes and since every bodily event is real or true only to the extent that it can be mathematically formulated, there is no longer any place for an autonomous psychology of movement since there can be no such thing as lived movement.

It is unnecessary for me to show in detail how faithful psychology has remained to this idea of Descartes right down to the present day. Open any psychology textbook to the discussion of movement, and a single glance will show you how nearly everything has been fitted into the Cartesian schema.

In introducing the idea lived movement, we must, therefore, first examine whether there are sufficient reasons for subordinating the psychology of movement to physiology. Has the psychology of movement no other task than to book the results of physiological investigations as its own? We should not forget that Descartes saw the difference between the living and the dead body as exactly like that between a wound-up watch and one with a broken spring. This is the metaphor he uses in his treatise on *The Passions of the Soul.* But, if life is not a particular mode of being, then lived movement cannot be a particular form of movement. It is necessary for us to inquire about the characteristics of the subject of lived movement and about the mode of its being.

Generally, we agree that every movement is the movement of some entity. Whenever we mention movement, we involuntarily refer, with or without awareness, to something in motion. Every statement of movement is, at the same time, a statement about the nature of what is in motion. Thus, the question of the subject of lived movement and its mode of being is an ontological question. Yet, there are still many scholars in various disciplines who believe it possible to get along without metaphysics. They do not seem to recognize that the basic concepts of the specialized sciences and even of the exact sciences derive from a metaphysics worked out in detail. Of course, one is free to disclaim such an ancestry, just as one can deny his forebears, but that does not factually dispose of it. Another metaphor may be even more illuminating. If we want a new variety of rose, we don't get it by coloring petals or cutting off leaves; we must change the seed itself. This is our situation at the moment. If we want to distinguish lived movement from mechanical motion, we must go to the germ of the doctrine, i.e., to metaphysics.

In the time-honored view, lived movement, or the impression we have of moving ourselves, is an illusion. It is a secondary quality like our impressions of colors, sounds, and so forth. The only exceptions to this are movements elicited by the will. Discussion of these will be postponed until later for the sake of clarity in presentation. What is real, then, in lived movement is the *performance* of the movement. This performance occurs within the organism, but it effects a change of the body's location in space. We note this change of place from sensations of sight and touch. But these sensations, even though attached to the performance of movement, could never produce our intuition of active movement. The inside and outside are still separated. Psychophysiology remains incapable of accounting for our illusory impression that we move ourselves by ourselves. This confusion—of internal sensations that represent external processes, of external sensations that govern internal processes, of representations oriented toward the future and yet being realized in the present—cannot be brought to order with a few additions and corrections. The basic approach needs to be corrected.

Earlier, I used a brief passage from the *Meditations* as a starting point for our analysis of the Cartesian doctrine of movement. However, my presentation up to this point does not rest on an interpretation of this passage alone; I have tried to relate it to Descartes' work as a whole. At the same time, I am going to return to this quotation since its content is far from exhausted. What it says is that sensation is not only separate from movement but that the experiencing subject is simultaneously separate from his world. As a thinking entity, I occupy, so to speak, a place outside the world of bodies. The ego perceives the world from outside it, and the soul's link with the body remains a mysterious one. Apparently the soul is able to recognize its own body by means of certain signs that distinguish it from other bodies, while, at the same time, the soul remains separate from its own body.

In later centuries, science abandoned the Cartesian doctrine of substance. No one today accepts the pineal gland as the locus of an intimate cohesion between the soul and body. Yet, the subject has retained its extramundane character. The subject of sensation and movement—of necessity, a limited subject in a state of constant becoming—continues to make its appearance in clothes borrowed from the Cartesian ego.

This is apparent in many places, most of all, perhaps, in the psychology of space. Actually, the entire debate between nativism and empiricism (particularly, the controversies about depth perception) has been conducted as if space were perceived by extramundane spirits. The real problem is not how vision enables us to perceive space but the *actuality* of our being in space, for it is only as I am a being who exists in the world that I am able to feel and move myself.

The space that presents itself to the soul is, according to Descartes, homogeneous, three-dimensional space. This makes the world, and not the surroundings of a self-moving being, the frame of reference for human and animal movement. But is it possible, even approximately, to describe lived movement in terms of a space uniformly extended in height, breadth, and depth? It doesn't seem so to me; in any event, it is not possible without greatly minimizing or even ruling out everything of importance for the phenomenon of lived movement. Hence, if it is impossible to understand or derive lived movement from homogeneous space in any exact manner, we must ask what is the structure of the space in which lived movement occurs? what is its relation to the space of physics? what is its ontological significance?

The notion of visual space is an old and familiar one in the psychology of sensation. Yet, in the psychology of movement, the Cartesian notion of space has remained unchallenged. Because Descartes regarded movement as a process of motion in the body taken as a machine, he could not recognize any other system of reference for lived movement outside of Euclidean space. Our situation, however, is no longer the same as his was.

Knowledge of the laws of mechanical movement does not lead to an understanding of lived movements. To illustrate: Can we, with the same principles, describe and understand the movement of a falling body, the peristaltic movements of intestinal muscles, contraction of the pupil to light, automatic movements that maintain our equilibrium, a gesture of greeting, a grasping movement, and jumping over a ditch? I emphasize *with the same principles*, in the sense of Descartes. It is obvious that these movements differ in certain ways. Even so, there is the possibility they could all be reduced to a common denominator. Let us take a closer look. The time we use to measure peristaltic movement is the objective time of the pendulum, while the space in which we observe them is the inner space of the body taken partly as objective space. Still, if I wish to comprehend a phenomenon like jumping, I must radically change my way of seeing things. I can, of course, measure its duration exactly from start to finish. I can also measure, by means of an objective spatial rule, the height or length of a jump. This is an everyday affair in sports. But what is it that I have measured? I already said it is the jump. De facto it is not the jump we are concerned with here—however unclearly I may have expressed myself—but the *action* of jumping itself. What interests us is not the spatial and temporal frame of reference of the jump as finished but the jumper in action. This is the focus of our attention.

The jumper is active here and now, and it is in the present that he jumps from here to there. Through this "in the present" and this "here" the jumper is embodied in his actual situation. Accordingly, we may say that, to comprehend the jump, we need an analysis in terms of position; to comprehend the jumper, we need an analysis in terms of situation. These are very different things, and one cannot be derived from the other.

Another reflection will also show how very different these two ways of seeing are. In jumping, I face from here to there; I am directed at the *other* place across an intervening distance toward the spot where I have not yet arrived. None of these circumstances—the actual direction, the intentional relation to the *other* place, the intervening distance, the "over there" where I have not yet arrived, the "not yet"—can be understood in terms of common objective space or common objective time. One need only reflect that the place to which I direct myself in jumping—say, the other bank of a stream—lies at this very moment before my eyes. Nevertheless, it appears to me as something in the future. In jumping, the jumper orients himself toward depth, which we must not consider as merely spatial. Depth, as we shall see, is just as much depth in time, anticipating future. "Over there," the place to which I aim myself in jumping, is a place distant from me in both time and space. Space and time are inseparable in lived movement.

Everyone here has jumped at one time or another. During childhood, there were times when we preferred jumping to simply walking. Jumping is familiar everywhere as a form of locomotion. We don't have to begin by producing it in the laboratory. Still, hasn't it become too familiar, so taken for granted that we have lost sight of the problems involved? It is very easy for us to make a dog jump by tempting it with a piece of meat.

I have already discussed some of the particular features of the jump. Now let us examine what is happening during the moments preceding the jump while we are teasing the dog with the meat.

It is only the lack of something which incites us to acquire it. This is not a complex phenomenon, but there are unanticipated difficulties when we try to understand it better. Let us not avoid the paradox that we possess something we do not yet possess, just as the dog somehow possesses the bit of meat that attracts it to overcome the intervening distance. The attractive phenomenon acts on the senses. Yet, it is evident, at the same time, that it would not be able to attract if we were not attractable, i.e., capable of self-movement or drawing nearer. This is what I mean by the intrinsic connection between sensation and movement. Whatever affects our senses derives its attractiveness solely from the simple fact of our motility.

As Ulysses neared the island of the sirens, he was filled with dread at their overpowering song; he filled the ears of his companions with wax and had himself tied to the ship's mast. Although he was immobilized, his capacity for movement remained unchanged. Ulysses learned the power of the sirens even though he was bound. Conversely, a schizophrenic patient remains immobile in his catatonic state, even though he is neither bound nor paralyzed. He remains immobile because he has been affected by a basic disturbance of his entire motor sphere. His illness involves the primary levels of his personality. We, on the other hand, although occasionally immobile, continue to be motile. Motility is basic to and constitutive of our existence. It enables us to make connections with the surrounding world and, through this, affects all of our sensations as well.

The problem of how we can have a perception of depth is one that has busied scholars for years. These controversies have dealt exclusively with sensation and perception while ignoring movement; and they have emphasized the problem of space but not that of time. This long-standing debate about how we can perceive depth has never been brought to a clear or satisfying conclusion. It could hardly turn out otherwise, since situation has always been treated as a position. But an analysis in terms of position only allows for an understanding of relationships of contiguity and propinquity. That we can perceive depth, as we say, and that, when moving, we direct ourselves into depth shows that we find ourselves over against the world in its totality. This integral relationship cannot be understood as a composite or even as a series of many propinquity relations. It cannot be brought under any system of kinematics. We discover it originally, in the realm of animate life, as a relationship we all know and are obliged to recognize, characteristic of both animals and men, i.e., all living beings with self-movement.

An analysis of situation is necessary for an understanding of lived movement and is obligatory for psychology. We cannot replace it through a physiological analysis, just as we cannot replace the latter through psychological studies. These two realms of discourse are not opposed but are complementary. There is still a need for psychology after physiology has had its say. The psychology of movement has its own aims and its own method. In the evolution of science, these have been only temporarily neglected, a neglect which must now be remedied.

Let us imagine a physiological research project on the movement of jumping that had reached the point where the physiologist was able to describe every factor: the attitude and position of the jumper; his center of gravity and equilibrium; the functions of the agonist, antagonist, and synergic muscles; the inhibition and modification of special movements; the direction of movement indicated by proprioceptive and exteroceptive stimulation; the outputs of energy, work productivity, and fatigue; c.n.s. coordination of movement; vegetative control; tonus, action currents, and chronaxie—in short, every physiological detail. All this accumulation of knowledge would not throw light on the problem of jumping as a particular mode of moving oneself. Of course, it is necessary for all these processes to be in working order if we are to move ourselves at all. *Without* muscles, it is obviously impossible to move ourselves at all. But we are not entitled to turn these words around and say that self-movement is the execution of a movement or a process *in* the muscle. Perfect functioning of the motor apparatus is a *sine qua non* of movement, but it is not the full story of lived movement. Positively stated, the meaning of "we cannot move ourselves without muscles" would be "we move ourselves *by means of* muscles." Historically, however, the means has been taken for the thing itself. It was Descartes who initiated this development. Today, everyone who believes, wittingly or not, that it is possible to understand the structure of lived movement as a combination of higher and lower reflexes follows in his path. This program, often regarded merely as a working hypothesis, now, since the publication of Pavlov's swiftly popularized observations, seems about to be realized, i.e., since the notion of the conditioned reflex has been added to that of the reflex.

It is generally accepted that Descartes was the first to advance the doctrine of the reflex. It is not so well known, however, that Descartes was also the first to describe what we now call a conditioned reflex and that he has left us a theoretical account of it. It is given in *The Passions of the Soul* (I, 50) where he writes:

And it is useful to know, as previously remarked, that although each movement of the gland appears to have been linked by nature to each one of our thoughts from the beginning of our life, we can nevertheless join them to others by *habit*. . . . It is also useful to know that although the movements of the gland as well as of the cerebral spirits which represent certain objects to the soul are naturally linked with those objects which excite certain passions in the cerebral spirits, they can nevertheless be separated by habit and linked with other very different passions. This habit can be acquired *by a single action*; it doesn't require extended practice. Thus when one unexpectedly comes across something in his food that is very unclean while eating it with relish, the surprise of this discovery can so change the cerebral disposition that it is subsequently impossible to look at such food without disgust, whereas it was previously eaten with pleasure. The same thing can be noticed in animals. For even when they are without reason or any kind of thought, all the movements of spirits and gland which excite the passions in us are continually active in them, maintaining and strengthening, not the passions, as is true for us, but those movements of nerves and muscles which are wont to accompany them. Thus when a dog sees a partridge it is naturally sustained in running towards it, and when it hears a gun fired, the noise naturally excites it to run away. Nevertheless we ordinarily train pointers so that the sight of a partridge brings them to a halt, so that the noise they hear when the bird has been fired on makes them run towards it. Now it is useful to know these things in order to encourage everyone in the reflective study of his own passions. For, since it is possible, with just a little bit of effort, to alter the cerebral movements in animals without reason, it is clear that one can do it even better in human beings; and that even those who have the weakest souls could acquire a near complete command of all their passions, could they but bring to bear a sufficient effort on their training and direction.

I have not quoted this passage to diminish the luster of Pavlov's fame since I am quite sure that he made his discovery and arrived at his theory alone, without the inspiration of this passage. He probably never laid eyes on it. On the other hand, I have not quoted this passage to do historical justice to the greatness of Descartes. I have simply intended to show that our modern doctrine of the conditioned reflex is a late blossom of Cartesian philosophy.

It is generally assumed that the doctrine of the conditioned reflex is an uncomplicated theory systematically developed in close adherence to the facts. Such an assumption is incorrect. Actually, the theory is complex and filled with contradictions. Despite its accumulation of hypotheses, the theory is unable to account for the facts; or, rather, it cannot do so except by contradicting its own assumptions. Pavlov, it seems to me, has failed in his aim of bringing psychology under the aegis of physiology. It is exactly from a phenomenological analysis of his own observations, which I accept *in toto*, that I am obliged to recognize the impossibility of understanding lived movement as the execution of motions, becoming as temporal sequence, or situation as position. The phenomena referred to and explained by Pavlov as conditioned reflexes are not explicable as processes *within* the organism but only as the ways in which animate beings behave in encountering the world; in short, they have nothing to do with *reflexes*. A corollary implication of this is that it is just as impossible to understand the fact of sensing in terms of a process of sensation as it is to understand the fact of self-movement in terms of muscular functions.

The psychologist who chooses to base his understanding of movement on the principles of motion in physics needs to consider how the space, matter, and movement referred to in these principles have been constructed. If he does this or, even better, if he simply reflects on the principles themselves, he must begin to wonder how they can be of any use to him as a psychologist. The remarkable achievements of theoretical physics and the daily confirmation of its findings have served to obscure for us the problematic nature of its axioms.

Like the physicists, we in psychology need to return to the foundations from which we can then begin to freshly consider special problems. Faced with the enigma of the physicists' concept of movement, we find the courage and confidence to develop an independent psychology of movement.

I am realistic enough to know that I have not affected the views of those who believe in a universal method which is valid for all the sciences. But I am sure that, were I to invite some of my most confirmed opponents to watch a basketball game with me, it would not be long before it became clear that the proponent of the universal method suspends his theoretical biases in the world of everyday life.

As spectators at a basketball game, we are all quite aware that the ball and the players move in different ways. The physicist is no exception. When a basket is made, he, like us, applauds the player who made the shot and not the ball that actually went into the basket. Similarly, if an opponent succeeds in blocking an almost certain basket, we do not applaud the ball but *the man* who made the block—if he is on our team.

In this case, we all draw the distinction between mechanical movement and movement that is lived. This is rather remarkable. For when we ask someone to define the difference between mechanical and lived movement, we ought not to expect a very exact answer. Some answers would use the active–passive antithesis, others would refer to the presence of purpose, while others would emphasize accommodation of movement to the actual situation. But, whatever answer was given, there would still be this striking contrast between the confidence of our judgment in the particular instance and our uncertainty about the reasons for our judgment.

In everyday life, the individual does not experience his own decisions as those of a being with objective cognition. He brings to bear a judgment that is perspectival—not an objective judgment. He decides whether things are moving themselves on the basis of his own relationships with them. He judges the situation in its entirety, without specific reflection on the form of his own movement.

In everyday life, the difference between lifeless movement and lived movement is an extremely meaningful one. Whatever our theoretical convictions, we—and I mean everyone of us—experience lived movement as one of the most important characteristics of *living beings*. For example, imagine that you are crossing a dark field at night and something huge and black looms up ahead. You haven't the least idea what it is and have no idea of its intentions. You take a closer look and discover with a shock that it is moving by itself. But no, you were mistaken, and a wave of relief floods over you as you see that it doesn't move by itself, that it is, in fact, lifeless.

In the course of such an experience, you do not reflect that the difference between lifeless and lived movement is analogous to the difference between rectilinear and circular movement. Lived movement is perceived as expressive of a particular mode of being and is accepted as such, as basic evidence, without reflection. Our understanding of lived movement is validated in everyday life, just as the physicists' doctrine of movement has been validated in technology. We may go even further and say that the conduct of social life is rooted in this comprehension of lived movement in all its variations and nuances.

The contrast between our confident judgment and our uncertainty about its bases is a striking one. Even though we are unable to understand ourselves, we are able to understand one another. Language has a twofold function; it is for social *understanding* and *objective* knowledge. There are many words that enable us to understand one another without difficulty, even though we may not have understood the matter itself clearly. Such words as "here," "now," "there," "toward," "between," "relation," and "direction" belong to this class of expressions. It is difficult for us to see the real problems involved in the use of such words because we understand them so easily. Then we take these everyday words, so well known and familiar and at the same time so obscure, and use them in science. Subsequently, these expressions borrowed from ordinary language, without awareness of their essential meaning, often turn out to be in sharp contradiction with the system of ideas into which they have been introduced. But the contradiction and, with it, the inadequacy of the theory as a whole often remains concealed, simply because the ideas are considered to be clear and distinct.

Experiencing movement in terms of the phenomenal spatial order is also a feature of the prescientific conception of lived movement, well validated in everyday life. For example, when the basketball player with the ball tries to avoid his opponent, when he attempts a pass to a fellow player down the court, our completely naïve view of this situation is that movement is directed by the phenomenal sequence "one next to the other" or "one behind the other." Or assume that a forward tries to score by passing around or shooting over the guard. As the forward advances with the ball, his opponent remains *between* him and the basket, and the basket is *behind* the guard. Although the optical projections on the retina are undergoing continual change during the action, as are the patterns of excited and nonexcited portions of the nervous system, the relationships "between" and "behind" remain invariant in meaning. And these relationships are decisive for action.

But this sketch of prescientific impression must suffice for now. I am not going to examine the pros and cons of its validity at once because the physicist has been kept silent too long. He is burning to riposte: "All that is well and good. I will even concede that I act as you say in everyday life. But that isn't a really serious objection to my conception of movement. What you have described may be valid for a movement macroscopically observed but not for microscopic observation. The microscope makes it possible for us to know truth. What you call 'lived movement' has been shown by microscopic examination to be composed of innumerable distinct motions. What you consider to be the qualitative antithesis between lived and mechanical movement is disconfirmed by microscopic examination. There are only mechanical movements, and so-called live movement, I repeat, is nothing but a compound of innumerable distinct motions."

But let us interrupt this exchange of remarks and return to our topic. I would like to begin with this reflection. If I intend to go from here to there, I must take a certain number of steps. The path is one, my action is one, and I myself am one in my attitude toward the world. Now, if we follow the procedure of the physicist and allow the identification of the lived movement with the performed motion, what can we adopt as the basic unit? Where do we stop in this progressive division? Should we use the shortening of a single muscle as the basic unit or even the single tetanic contraction? Should we take, as the unit of a thousand different motions, the action of one whole muscle, a single muscle fiber, or an even more elementary unit? Should our subdivision stop at the microscopic structures of anatomy or at the elementary particles of nuclear physics? But it scarcely matters where we stop. If we follow the physicists' principle, there is nothing like a unit of movement or an experienced change of place; there is simply a summation of distinct events in the motor apparatus that displace the body from one point to another in space. Now we are no longer speaking of self-acting as a unity in the presence of the world. This problem of unity is the same for movement as it is for sensation. Just as the narrow doctrine of association has proved inadequate to account for sensation, perception, and thought, we have also discovered its shortcomings for understanding lived movement. Even more, if we are to do justice to the self as a unity, we cannot conceive of lived movement on the same level as the execution of motions; we must acknowledge that we move ourselves *by means of* our organs.

There is nothing we can discover in muscular contractions and extensions or in colloidal changes that corresponds to lived movement and the feeling of this movement. If we were to take the explanation of lived movement as a summation of motions executed by the motor apparatus to be correct, the fact of our actual walking along a path or lived movement in general would be nothing but appearance and illusion.

Movement generally has been accepted in psychology as an independent entity. Actual movement has been transformed into something capable of entering into progressively more complex structures. To account for the higher forms of movement, new elements, like representations, are added to those required for reflex motion. In this way, the subject of voluntary movement is assumed to be identical with the subject of reflex movement—a radical error! The subject of reflex motion is the muscular or sensorimotor apparatus, while the animal or man is the subject of animate movement. Muscle is put into motion; man moves himself. It is self-contradictory from the outset to start from reflex motion and—by a progressive series of complications due to the addition of new elements—to arrive at voluntary movement, simply because we are concerned with different subjects in mechanical and in animate movement.

The objectification of movement has resulted in the atomistic approach to lived movement, in the form of the doctrine of reflexes, which dominates our understanding of lived movement and the learning of movement. Let us look at this conception a little more closely. William James begins his account of "voluntary actions" by claiming that "Desire, wish, will, are states of mind which everyone knows, and which no definition can make plainer." A few lines later he remarks,

We may start with the proposition that the only *direct* outward effects of our will are bodily movements. The mechanism of production of these voluntary movements is what befalls us to study now. . . . The movements to the study of which we now address ourselves, being desired and intended beforehand, are of course done with full prevision of what they are to be. It follows from this that *voluntary movements must be secondary, not primary, functions of our organisms* (1952, p. 767).

But it would seem that, if we can perform voluntary actions that are *determined*, we ought, *in general*, to be able to perform voluntary actions. To will something that is determined, we ought to be able to will generally. To move myself in a particular way, I ought to be able to move myself generally. The determination comes from experience. But experience is capable of determining a movement only because self-movement is open to determination. It is open in the sense that each immediate perception has its own immediately perceived limit and direction. The immediate perception is open to determination in its being limited and in its being directed to the whole in terms of the circumstances. This relationship between openness to circumstances and the totality of the situation makes possible order and agreement, defined measure and defined limits.

Learning of movements follows an internally consistent pattern. The would-be student of the violin must have a good ear, for it is the acoustical form of sound, its aesthetic quality, that is to direct the activity of his hands. He must learn a new kind of *action*. His movements never occur in an isolated manner but in the form of a sequence, an alternation, or a transition. That we speak of single movements, using the plural, tends to obscure the fact that no movement originates absolutely. We are never at the beginning; the point of departure for a movement is always the last point of the just preceding movement.

If James was right when he said that once a particular movement, like a reflex, is produced accidentally it can then be performed voluntarily, it would be just as reasonable to have the violin student begin with a violin concerto as it is to have him bow the open strings of his instrument. No, it is necessary to learn every technique systematically. And, in doing this, there is a progression of steps from easy to difficult. Why is it that we consider the bowing of a violin string easy as compared with the playing of a sonata? What criterion do we use in distinguishing easy from difficult movements? This distinction does not involve isolated movements in their particularity but the *order* of movements, their shapes and measures, their sequence, and their alternation. The learning of movements does not occur through the repetition of random motor responses associated with and activated by kinesthetic representations.

Even a path retraced a thousand times requires a stepwise adaptation. But, from an atomistic point of view, the learning of movement must be explained as the formation of a combination of isolated movements and isolated sensations; each time, the same fixed pattern of movement must be repeated. How there could be any adaptation to the circumstances of the immediate situation remains a mystery. Theory remains contradicted by the humblest facts of everyday experience—experience that tells us that we do not learn the movements, but that we learn how to move ourselves.

In physics, the location of the body in movement or at rest is contingent and irrelevant. It is point A or point B, which can be exchanged for other points. Similarly, the instant of movement is a point T_0 in time, or T_x in general. But, for the animal moving itself or for the human being displacing himself from here to there, the particular time and place are of *essential* importance.

Direction, limit, and measure are not exclusively linked with either sensation or with movement. They do not correspond with excitations of either the centripetal or centrifugal segments of the reflex arc. That is why it is impossible to derive the notions of direction and limit from physiology. Only lived movement knows of direction and limit.

The pertinence of the present discussion is not limited to voluntary movement and the learning of movements. It also applies to the "inferior" forms, as, for example, "automatic" movement. Admittedly, the special features of voluntary movement—such as purpose, decision, planning, execution, starting point, path, and goal—are missing from automatic movement. But does that necessarily mean it is not self-movement? Even though it is not directed to a determined end, isn't it still a directed movement?

Let us take as an example a puppy playing in the street. A car comes racing along, and the puppy jumps out of the way. But he does this in such a hurry that he bumps into a tree, which does not give way to him as the car perhaps would have. A movement is termed "automatic" when it is not conditioned by present experience. In our example, "automatic" means that the approaching car is not experienced as a danger in terms of the possible consequences of collision and that the leap to avoid it does not occur within an adequate grasp of the present spatial order. If we grant all this, does it follow that the jumping movement has been nothing but a process in many different muscle groups, one triggered by visual sensations? Does the dog itself jump, or is it actually the case that particular muscles set in motion have the curious effect of removing the dog's body from the path of the car?

The animal's reactions are conditioned by the structure of the situation in which it finds itself. Its automatic movement, even though not conditioned by experience, by an adequate grasp of the situation, or by a definite plan, is not mechanical movement, but a directed movement. Its direction is related to the direction of the threatening object. The movement has the meaning of "avoiding" or "going anywhere to get out of here." "Anywhere," in this case, means "not here." The movement is undetermined only in the sense that the animal is not directed to a *specific* goal, but toward an immediate change of its present situation. Its place of stay changes according to its circumstances. Here we are always "in transit." Even in a quiet place of stay, the animal is alert to possible danger. At the same time, it continues to be on the move. A place of stay, initially and under all circumstances, preserves a relationship to a "there," an "elsewhere," even when it invites us to rest.

The automatic movement does not happen *in nihilo*, with an absolute beginning and an absolute end. It is a change of direction because there is always an initially given direction. It is not a shifting of location in homogeneous space but a change of the place of stay in a vitally articulated space. It is not movement from A in the direction of B but from here to there. In short, it discloses all the features of lived movement.

Lived movement is change in something itself changeable, i.e., a Becoming. If we wish to grasp it, we must consider its *beginning* as well as its end. It is surprising that hardly anything but the goal is considered in the psychological analysis of lived movement; the beginning does not seem to play any kind of role.

Here, we meet once more with the critical problem of animate movement. Again, the problem of animate movement appears insoluble for physiological psychology, concerned with processes in an isolated organism, for it is evident that we are only able to will something we do not have or are not at this instant. Any representation of the goal must be a representation of something as yet unrealized, whatever its content. Only an animate being who is in the world and yet over against it in its totality is able to realize change, to reach a place "there"; in other words, only an animate being is capable of voluntary activity and lived movement.

The problem of lived movement is involved with the basic phenomenon of change, with Becoming itself. "Willing to move oneself" is possible only for a subject who, himself implicated in Becoming, becomes different. I can only look ahead to climbing the mountain from my position in the valley. From where I am now, the mountain top is another place, for the reason that the place where I am now is in relation to it an *other* place or, more accurately speaking, is changeable. The mountain top is a place where I have not yet arrived. I cannot arrive there except when I am no longer here. Every "there" is a "not here"; every "here" a "not there." It is thus apparent that the place where I am at present is constituted with its circumstances—i.e., I am never *entirely* in any particular time and place.

Because we are never *entirely* in any particular time and place, we are in need of complementation. In this way, we are able to transform ourselves, pass from one moment to another or from one place to another, in the continuity of Becoming. The fact of *never being complete* needs to be understood in relation to the idea of the Totality. In any single moment, the Totality can only secure representation in a particular form. Thus we see how an analysis of the phenomenon of animate movement leads us back to the ontology of possibility itself.

Thus far, I have been occupied with bringing the general problems into focus, leaving the specific problems until later.

It should be clear from what I have said that I consider the specific problems of a psychology of movement to be very different from those of the physiology of movement. Such a psychology does not concern itself with the causes and mechanisms of individual movements. What it does attempt to do is to reveal, even in its special inquiries, the individual's relationship with his world. It constantly keeps in view the global action of the individual. Frequently, the psychiatrist and neurologist are asked to determine whether a motor disturbance—for example, a paralysis—is based on a localized lesion in the motor cortex or is symptomatic of an over-all behavioral change as, for example, a catatonic stupor. When an epileptic collapses at the onset of his seizure, everyone immediately realizes this is a pathological case. How is this possible?

Simply because everyone recognizes that the dropping of this body is not related to the space of immediate experience but to the homogeneous space of physics.

However, since we are concerned here with the philosophical features of these problems rather than with the details of pathology, I would like to continue with the previous inquiry. As a way of doing this, I would like to dwell on a phenomenon close to all of us and all the more so in that it evokes the happy moments of our life.

I would like to show how the dance reveals the differences between the neutral, homogeneous space of mathematical physics and the differentiated, lived space of the surroundings in which we move as living beings. Obviously, there is an intimate relationship between dance and music, one that appears to be original and essential. Sound takes hold of us to a much greater extent than optical phenomena, which remain at a considerable distance and not just in a quantitative sense. Communication with the world through sound is very different from what it is through color. Experienced sound has a spatial and temporal structure astonishingly different from that of light and color. We may say that there are both optical and acoustical modes of spatiality. In investigating the space that makes it possible for us to dance, it is the latter mode that we need to consider. We can go even further and say that acoustical space not only enables us to dance but also that it even compels us to do so. We need only recall the myth of Orpheus, in which the irresistible power of music is expressed.

Or consider an everyday happening: A lively tune carries us away and obliges us to move, if only in a very slight fashion. As long as we do not resist these motor tendencies evoked by the music, we move in a way that is neither determined by nor directed to a goal. This kind of moving is at variance with that of our actions in a strict sense. Such movements are responsive to the structure of acoustical space—its immediately experienced qualities of height, depth, and breadth. Acoustical space is different from optical space, whose structure is given in terms of the analytical, geometric categories of distance, measure, and direction. We achieve our goals, realize our life history, in optical space. In acoustical space, on the other hand, we live only in the present, forgetting past and future; we accomplish nothing concrete, and we experience only the union between ourselves and our surroundings. In optical space, we are always directed from one place to another, and movements without direction are impossible. Dance, on the other hand, is a rhythmic movement requiring no precise direction in space.[1]

[1] For a more detailed discussion of the differences between these modalities see Chapter 1, The Forms of Spatiality. (E.E.)

Even though I shall omit all the other special problems from my presentation, much, unfortunately, must remain ill defined. Perhaps this is not only a defect of my presentation of the matter but is a difficulty inherent in the matter itself.

But, if we let ourselves be satisfied with the imprecise, we risk losing sight of the real problem because of a specious, prescientific understanding. Let us, for example, consider again the phenomenon of direction. I assume that everyone agrees that, in moving, we are always directed toward something. What else does the term "direction" signify? Direction has usually been regarded as purely spatial. Is this correct? Direction is irreversible; it points from A to B. If the letters A and B are used to define a direction, I cannot reverse them at will as I can with a straight line which I may call AB or BA. Direction is, thus, both a temporal and a spatial problem and not merely a spatial phenomenon. In other words, we are no longer confined to the temporal and spatial system of classical physics when we speak of direction and directing.

The same is true for everything that characterizes lived movement. As I have shown earlier, the subject of immediately experienced movement is a subject in continual Becoming—Becoming which cannot be grasped by physics. I need only remind you that, in the Cartesian doctrine, only that which is clearly and distinctly known, i.e., only that which is statable in mathematical terms, is real.

In physics, existence is attributed only to what is measurable. To measure something, I must know the beginning and the end of what it is I wish to measure. Whatever the mathematical sciences define is conceived of as de-fined, i.e., as finite or perfective.

We are now in a position to state the essential distinction between lived movement and the execution of motion. The object of physical knowledge is the body as having been moved, while the object of psychological knowledge is the organism moving itself. It is here that we run into the antithesis between the present and the perfect.

The misapprehensions of objectivistic psychology originate principally in its efforts to comprehend the organism moving itself as if it were a body moved. Thus, it encounters the other one as an *object* and translates what is present into the perfect tense. We live in the present; we comprehend in the perfect. Physics is concerned exclusively with the perfect, i.e., with what has already become, the terminated, the outcome. This is why its notions are exact ones and why mathematics is useful to physics to comprehend even the infinite, as in the calculus, yet also for constructing the finite. Thus, physics understands the world as it would appear to an "archetypal intellect."

On the other hand, I conceive of everything for which "the present" is the most appropriate term starting from my own present; I conceive of it as something which "becomes" with me in time. It is crucial that I maintain contact with this primary situation if I am interested in accounting for sensing and lived movement. Reflection can only detach them from this primary situation after it has recognized the spatiotemporal unity that characterizes our immediate and lived rapport with the world.

References

Descartes, R. *The philosophical works of Descartes*, trans. E. S. Haldane and G. R. Ross. Cambridge: Cambridge University Press, 1931. Vol. I.

Heisenberg, W. *Philosophic problems of nuclear science*. New York: Pantheon, 1952. Published in German as *Wandlungen in den Grundlagen der Naturwissenschaft*. Leipzig, 1935.

James, W. *Principles of psychology*. Vol. 53. *Great books of the western world*. Chicago: Encyclopaedia Britannica, 1952.

Minkowski, E. *Le Temps Vécu*. Paris: Collection de l'Évolution Psychiatrique, 1933.

CHAPTER THREE

Remembering and Infantile Amnesia

Since time immemorial, theories of memory have been dominated by an idea recommending itself because of its simplicity to the scientist no less than to the layman. There are many expressions corresponding to such an interpretation of memory, i.e., "the tablets of memory," "storehouse of memory," "impressions and imprints," "to have hammered into one's head," "to stamp into," "engrave on," and "enshrine in the memory." Terms akin to these are found in most languages. All these idioms convey the same popular notion: that simple sensory impressions leave imprints which later reappear as memory images. The trope of the engram belongs, it seems, to the archetypes of interpretation. Indeed, the simile of an imprint occurs in the oldest extant treatise on the subject, Aristotle's essay *On Memory and Reminiscence* (450a #28–450b #1).

... it is clear that we must conceive that which is generated through sense-perception in the sentient soul, and in the part of the body which is its seat— ... to be some such thing as a picture. The process of movement involved in the act of perception stamps in, as it were, a sort of impression of the percept, just as persons do who make an impression with a seal.

The quality of the material receiving the imprints, Aristotle believed, could well account for infantile as well as senile amnesias. In childhood, he thought, the receiving material is too soft and pliable—it does not keep the imprint—while in old age the texture is too hard, "the impression is not implanted at all." Perhaps Aristotle would have been pleased to learn that more than two thousand years later neurosurgeons would fall in line and devise a brain operation—lobotomy—based on similar considerations.

Biological speculations occupy considerable space in Aristotle's exposition. However, in addition, his discourse is distinguished by many keen observations and profound thoughts worthy of being incorporated into any phenomenological study. To mention only one, I quote his reference to time: "All memory," he said, "implies a time elapsed; consequently, only those animals which perceive time remember. . . ." Thomas Hobbes's epigrammatic definition of remembering, "Sentire se sensisse meminisse est" (translated literally: To perceive having perceived, this is remembering), just paraphrases Aristotle's statement: ". . . whenever someone actually remembers he must say within himself, 'I formerly heard (or otherwise perceived) this,' or 'I formerly had this thought'" (449^b 23–24)—and Aristotle continues: "Thus he includes the consciousness of 'formerly'; and the distinction of 'former' and 'later' is a distinction of time" (450^a 21–22).

But, as happens in the course of history, observable phenomena have had to yield the floor to theories of acting forces that are mere assumptions, in spite of the strident enthusiasm for experiments and empirical methods. Hobbes, one of the Founding Fathers of modern science, not only failed to remember Aristotle's remarks about time and memory; he eventually forgot his own aperçu. Convinced that the whole universe was, without exception, ruled by the laws of Galilean physics, Hobbes made it his task to explain all human behavior in terms of motion and mechanical causality. He laid the foundation of psychology as a natural science, and he thereby started the chain of reductionist analyses culminating in the formula: "Nothing but." "Sensible qualities," Hobbes declaimed, "are nothing but so many several motions of the matter. . . . Imagination is nothing but decaying sense." And so is memory, because "imagination and memory are but one thing, which for diverse considerations has diverse names" (Pt. I, Chs. 1 & 2).

Memory is decaying sense. "For after the object is removed, or the eye shut, we still retain an image of the thing seen, though more obscure than we see it" (Pt. I, Ch. 2). Hobbes not only said that it was so, but he explained why it must be so. He interpreted the decay of sense as one manifestation of the universal laws of nature—and especially of the law of inertia. "When a body is once set in motion," Hobbes said, "it moves, unless something else hinders it . . ., as we see in the water; though the wind ceases, the waves give not over rolling for a long time after; so also it happens in that motion which is made in the internal parts of man, then, when he sees, dreams, etc." (Pt. I, Ch. 2). In this interpretation, patterns of motion have taken the place of the once solid structures, of the seal and its imprints. Hobbes could well afford the conversion, because to him experience was nothing but a fancy or, as we say today, an epiphenomenon somehow linked with physiological motions in us.

Memory, then, is no longer a privilege of animals conceiving time; it is a universal characteristic of events in nature, a theme of physics rather than of psychology. *Mneme* must not be limited to organic substance, as Hering (1870) later stated. Because Hobbes supposed remembering to be nothing but an after-effect of sensory stimulation, a kind of reverberating circuit, he believed it ought not command our respect; it neither deserves nor needs any detailed consideration. With one stroke, the theory of memory has been reduced to a mere appendage of a perceptual theory. Hobbes eliminated any further need for careful observation of the phenomena of remembering; a few physiological constructions appeared sufficient. To evaluate the effectiveness of Hobbes's approach, one has only to read what some contemporary physiologists (Gerard, 1953, Penfield, 1952) have to say about memory. Yet, Nemesis never sleeps and finally reaches the transgressor. If we need not wonder about remembering because, as a universal phenomenon of persisting motion, it appears self-explanatory, then forgetting becomes the central theme; for, if the original sensory excitations persisted, nothing would be forgotten. Hobbes acknowledged the problem and, it seems, felt no difficulty in finding a solution.

The decay of sense in men waking is not the decay of the motion made in sense; but an obscuring of it, in such manner as the light of the sun obscureth the light of the stars; which stars do no less exercise their virtue, by which they are visible, in the day than in the night . . . [and] any object being removed from our eyes, though the impression it made in us remain, yet other objects more present succeeding and working on us, the imagination of the past is obscured and made weak, as the voice of a man is in the noise of the day.

Hobbes presents us with a dynamic theory of remembering or, more precisely, of forgetting, or, to be still more accurate, of apparent forgetting. Remembering is held to be a direct function of interacting intensities of prior and present stimulations. This dynamic theory leads to certain consequences, all of which clash head on with the experience we gain in everyday life and on the clinical wards.

1. If this theory was right, then we should remember a "forte" better than a "piano"; sensory deprivation should provide the best mnemonic aid.

2. If Hobbes was right, recent events should be remembered better than remote ones. However, clinical observation confirms the familiar experience that events of early years are often remembered better than those of recent date. Ribot's "law of regression" (1881) tries to account for this paleological stratification of memory, where the present is rested on the past.

3. One would experience a twilight zone where the distinction of sense from decaying sense, or, in Humes' terminology, "impressions" from "ideas" would prove difficult or even impossible; in particular, the most recent impressions would behave like eidetic images. Although, at times, we may find our memory not too faithful, we never actually confuse remembering with perceiving.

4. A memory image is supposed to resemble and to represent an original impression. On the incline of decay, an impression sinks down from one position to the next; with each step downward, some intensity, some details, would be lost. Certainly, in the last stage of decay, a memory image would be more similar to the preceding one next to the bottom than to the original. How could a trace in its last flickering resemble and represent the original in its full intensity?

5. In fact, how could a memory image welded to a trace represent anything of the past? At the moment of sensory stimulation, the impression was actual; with the activation of a trace, a memory image should become actual; impression and image each has its own particular place on the line of physical time. This certainly poses a formidable problem to any theory of traces: an engram, though generated in the past, functions in the present; and, in accordance with the theory, the corresponding memory image must be present. Taken in isolation, an engram cannot represent another thing. Belonging exclusively to the present, it cannot represent the past.

6. The distinction between perception and reminiscence rests, like all distinctions, on a comprehension in which two relata are brought together for comparison. However, an original impression and its corresponding memory image never occur simultaneously. In remembering, nevertheless, we somehow compare things remembered with things once actually seen. A memory image could never compare itself with an original which no longer exists. It could not realize its own deficiencies. Remembering, therefore, cannot be the work of individual traces and their accompanying memory images.

7. It is taken for granted that a particular impression begets a particular memory image. The organism with its brain is considered a passive recipient of stimuli impinging upon receivers; for any "conscious

experience is at the beginning of a mnemonic recording, and any trace left by a conscious state is capable of engendering it anew" (Fessard, 1954, p. 234). The engram theory proclaims the stimulus the dictator of memory. Impressions, it seems, arrive like guests in a metropolitan hotel. They come from all directions, lacking any logical connection; rooms are assigned to them just as they happen to be vacant. If this were the way impressions operated, memory would be like a warehouse where the most heterogeneous material has been stored in adjacent compartments, but there is no one keeping a record. Obviously, however, the growth of memory in the biographical order of time does not coincide with the temporal sequence of stimuli acting upon sensory organs. Otherwise, the first phase of remembering, namely, registering, would be completely detached from personal history.

Yet, it was this ahistorical interpretation of memory that dominated laboratory experiments for a long time. The nonsense syllable is the embodiment of this antihistorical spirit. The application of quantitative procedures demands such sacrifices.

While experimental research with nonsense syllables still was in its early ascendancy, Breuer and Freud (1957) wrote their preliminary study in hysteria—their publication (1893) following Ebbinghaus' monograph (1885)—in the short distance of eight years. Their famous dictum, "Hysterical patients suffer from reminiscences," opened a new era in the study of memory.

There are direct lines of contact connecting Freud with both Aristotle and Hobbes. Freud somewhere mentions Aristotle's essay; I do not know whether he was also familiar with Hobbes' writings. I am not interested in establishing any dependency; rather, I wish to emphasize a concordance in the history of ideas. There are striking similarities between Hobbes's and Freud's views, but there are also marked differences. Both men considered forgetting a central problem, and both offered dynamic explanations of apparent forgetting; but there the conformity ends. There is no need to point out how, in Freud's thinking, the content of experiences, their emotional charge, their social acceptability took the place of mere intensities; but perhaps it needs to be said that, through his libido theory and his assumption of a distribution of psychical energies in an apparatus, Freud actually renounced some of his gains and fell back on Hobbes's position. Fascinated by the problem of forgetting, he closed his eyes to the wonder of remembering. The postulate that nothing once apprehended is ever forgotten allowed and even required the re-introduction of the trace theory; note Paul Schilder's bold statement "an unchanged picture of past experiences is always present" (1942, p. 272).

Several years ago Lashley published a paper entitled "In Search of the Engram" (1950), in which he reported that none could be found. We should not be surprised that this search leads nowhere. I believe we would all agree that memory depends somehow on the brain; yet, if we hope ever to account for memory in terms of cerebral functions, we at least have to know what it is that we want to explain. Instead of indulging in physiological speculations—erroneously taken for empirical propositions—we should turn our attention back to the observable phenomena. The well-spring is everyday-life experience—the *Lebenswelt*, to use Husserl's term; there, we find remembering among the facts so familiar but so little understood.

Our first observation is simple enough: In remembering, we are directed to the past. This is a truism. "There needs no ghost, my lord, come from the grave to tell us this," a modern Horatio may object. Granted, nobody denies this observation, but does everyone respect it? Certainly not, especially when it is stated in its complete form: In remembering, we are aware of the past as past. That is to say, we remember it—the past—at present. Remembered objects, events, or persons are not present; yet, the predicate "not present" does not convey a purely negative meaning. Nonpresence is a positive characteristic. Things remembered are not present to me in my actual present, but they are present *in absentia*. They are "re-presented" in the act of remembering.

We describe our memories in the past tense. The textbooks of grammar list the present, the past, and the future side by side as tenses as if they were on equal footing. Yet the past—and the future as well—gain its meaning only through its relation to and its distinction from the present. The past tense of grammar is two-faced. Time has a double aspect. While the present is directly expressed through the act of speaking, the past is indicated, as a rule, through special grammatical forms. In such colloquial remarks as "the bus just left" or "the bus will be here in a moment," past and future cannot be separated from the actual present of the speaker and the listener; for, in a short time, the bus, expected at this moment, will already have left. The relationship "earlier" or "later" between two events remains invariant, but the great divide between past and future is my, or our, common, actual present. Past and future are temporal qualities related to the personal, historical order of time. History reaches far beyond my personal experience, yet it is past only in relation to my actual present.

Only in contrast with the present, then, does remembering gain its meaning. The present is the ground against which the past forms the figure (or vice versa). Remembrances belong to the past, remembering to the present. Therefore, remembering must be understood as a temporal relation, which implies immediate awareness of time. Awareness of the present, however accomplished, is an indispensable condition of remembering. Because remembrance is but one part of the act of remembering—one relatum only in a complex relationship—any variation of the relation as a whole, every modification of the other relatum, must interfere with remembering. Clinical observation provides ample evidence of this, but we need not turn to pathology. We all know how, in sleep, the suspension of the actual present interferes with remembering; it affects remembering in form and matter, and it affects registering as well as recalling.

Remembering occurs within the order of historical time, of one's life history. In remembering an event, I am also concerned with my own self. When I say, "I arrived in Barcelona a few days ago," I reflect upon myself. To recognize something, we do not need self-reflection; but to remember, we do. Actually, self-reflection enters in three guises: I am aware of my actual present; I reflect upon myself as the one who did this and that in the past; and it seems necessary, in order to remember now, to have known about myself doing the action or incident recalled later. Something done automatically—whatever this may mean—cannot be recalled. In remembering that I did this and that or that this and that happened to me, I see myself, as it were, from a distance. There is a kind of doubling: I, who speak now, and I, or he, who arrived five days ago, are in some ways identical—but we are also different. Still, I may say now, "I did this and that some time ago."

I still remember my first speech in Berlin. There was an old gentleman sitting in front of me, and, whenever I looked up, he always shook his head. It gave me a terrible feeling until I discovered that he had a senile tremor. At that time, I was a young assistant; I, that young man whose life was still undetermined in many ways known to me now, he and I, belong together. In remembering, I am aware of the continuity of my existence. I refer to my own historical self. In the order of physical time, a past event is gone; its reality has been cancelled out. But, in the historical order of time, the past remains, although in its own temporal position, and exerts its power. In remembering my past, I take the responsibility for him who did this and that. If I try to escape from the responsibility, I will be forced to accept it. In every court action, responsibility is related to historical time. Not only guilt is carried over; certain merits, too, are brought forward. An examination I passed more than forty years ago is still booked to my credit today.

Now, let us turn to the content of remembering. I said I arrived here a few days ago, and I still remember my way from the station; yet, my remembrance is far from being an exact copy of the original. I remember my way and my walk, but I cannot now reproduce my steps and my movements. The object no longer permits penetration. Ebbinghaus (1885) drew a curve of forgetting and was surprised to see how much was forgotten in the very first few minutes. But this kind of so-called forgetting is no function of time at all. We have only to close our eyes and try to count the squares on a floor just seen. We simply cannot do it. No one can measure a remembered length with a remembered ruler. The transition from perceiving to remembering is not a change characterized by a loss of details but an essential transformation. If details had actually been lost, how could we ever realize the loss?

Sometimes, people complain that memory is so infrequently faithful. A truly faithful memory would be a doubtful blessing. Measured by Ebbinghaus' standard, it should reproduce events in every detail, like a speech played back on a tape. An accurate copy of all these details would also require an accurate reproduction of the temporal order and extension. The remembering of affairs lasting an hour would require a corresponding hour's time. Remembrance of a day would last the livelong day. How unhappy an accurate memory would make any creature! He would be like King Midas, in whose hands everything turned to gold so that he starved in the midst of wealth. Our hypermnesic could never use his memory *as* memory. In remembering length of time, beginning and ending, short and long durations, we do not pass for a second time through time in its temporal extension. The concept of a year does not last longer than the concept of an hour. If time remembered is not time reproduced, the remembrance of an event cannot be the event reproduced. Therefore, remembering must differ from the original in many more of its aspects. Let us take an example: Before a plane makes a landing, the passengers go through certain tensions. At least, I do. I watch the situation. Will the plane and the pilot make it? But, in remembrance, the tension as such is gone. We know the end of the story, so that, after we have passed through a situation, it necessarily changes its emotional aspect. We still remember that we were excited, but we can hardly reproduce the excitement. Comfortably stretched on my couch, I can tell about the hard and miserable days of the past, and, at that moment, I enjoy the difference between the present and the past. I may also gain a new way of looking at my past. I may realize what mistakes I made—what a fool I was. In our search for the *temps perdu*, we learn to regret missed opportunities and mourn joys gone forever. We remember the past, but we cannot bring it back.

So, remembering cannot be understood as the activation of traces accompanied by the appearance of memory images. The subject of remembering is not a brain; neither is it a consciousness where single data follow each other in physical time. The subject of remembering is a human being who, living in time, experiences himself in a state of becoming, builds his life history in an ever changing continuum.

Our next task, then, is to consider remembering as a biographical phenomenon—as a phenomenon of the life history. Of course, I am well aware that remembering presents only one facet of the manifold problems of memory in its totality. There are such other features as the acquisition of habits, skills, and knowledge; there are recognition and repetition, learning and keeping in mind, etc.; and, accordingly, there are many forms of forgetting. But the best we can do today is to roughly sketch remembering in an outline.

In the expression "life history," both words determine the meaning of the expression. As living beings, we go on from hour to hour in the great circle of day and night, awakeness and sleep, hunger and satisfaction. In this change from need to satisfaction, each condition is limited to itself. Yesterday's meal will not satisfy me today. Every moment is swallowed up by the following one. We move in a circle. Over this figured bass runs the melody of the events which we note in our curriculum vitae. There are two profiles of time—the narrow vista of immediate needs and the wide horizon in which we realize our historical selves. We live on two levels of existence: on that of daily routine and on that of the great events—great in the perspective of the limited dimensions of our lives. While the candle of our life wanes, our historical shadow grows. The motto of daily routine is to get it over and done with. The motto of great days is to preserve it and write it into the memorabilia. A remembered fire doesn't burn, but a remembered offense hurts.

Who remembers—to start with our daily routine—all his meals of the last month, or all the bites of this morning's breakfast, or all the steps he made during this very day? Yet, at the time of eating and walking we were attentive to the job at hand; we watched the details; in fact, we must be attentive; otherwise, we would choke or fall badly. We are heedful during these activities; still, a short time later, we cannot remember any details. Must we conclude that they are forgotten?

These are banal affairs, emotionally indifferent. If they are forgotten, such oblivion cannot be the work of repression. As this universal type of amnesia is not due to lack of attention, nor to erosion by time, nor to the forces of repression, how can one account for it? Perhaps we will have to revise the presuppositions. Of course, if the stimulus is decisive, if the stimulus, so to speak, is a typist who at every single moment of our waking experience presses a key on the sensory typewriter and leaves an imprint on the white paper of memory, then each one of these letters should be readable later on. Then Schilder would be right: "An unchanged picture of past experience is always present" (1942, p. 272). Indeed, the majority opinion today follows this interpretation; it assumes that any single moment of experience is filled in with a single impression and that we proceed from singular data to generalizations. Obviously, the assumption—that impressions singular and unique are the original given—contradicts the collateral assumption that they can be repeatable and recollectable. We are able to remember only that which can be detached from the here and now of an original encounter with the world.

At this point, time permitting, we would have to probe deeper into the conventional misinterpretation of the singularity of *acts* of experiencing with the particularities of experience. An analogy may help to unravel the entangled situation.

I hope you will agree that card games may be considered experiments in remembering. Obviously, they test the individual player's capacity to recall. They do more than just this; they disclose the conditions which subserve and those which prevent remembering. Cards are made in such a way that when seen from the front they favor, and when seen from the back they frustrate, remembering. The card game is a concretization of the difference between singularity and particularity. Any card from a deck of cards is, taken by itself, a singular item in whatever position it may be—face up or face down. When cards are spread over a table face down, I may select one in its singularity and point to it: this one. But I cannot preserve the identity of this card beyond the moment of pointing. Face down, a single card does not reveal which one it is. For the player, its particularity does not coincide with its singularity. Its singularity cannot be detached from the single act and moment of pointing here and now. Shuffling frustrates all later identification. This is different when the cards are presented face up. Under those conditions we can select one, recognize it, and remember it through all the variations of shuffling and dealing. Face up, a card is identifiable beyond the moment of pointing, for its particularity is established in a lasting system, through colors, figures, and numbers. When cards are played face up, a good player can remember and reconstruct the distribution of hands and the sequence of tricks; but even the best card player could not follow and reconstruct all the transactions in a game played with cards face down.

Now I come to the application of my excursion. In the practice of life, we see things—like cards—face down. It is sufficient to know that this is *a* house, *a* stone, *a* tree, *a* person. Our relation to all of them is a general one, just as most of the moments in our routine life, in which we are confronted with a tree, a horse, etc., are general in structure; nor do we distinguish these moments in their particularities.

Suppose we arrive in a strange city. It is unknown to us. Everything, as we so often say, is new. Is this statement correct? No doubt, we see that there are streets, houses, people, cars, neon lights. The typical is known first; the particulars are gradually acquired. After the first acquaintance with a city in which we have never before set foot, we gradually learn the arrangement and order of its streets. We do not add one detail to another detail, but we descend on the ladder of differentiation.

Returning from a play, we remember the scenes and the plot, the actors and their performances, but we do not remember the lines or words. To grasp the particular demands a special effort. We have to stop; we have to find a system in order to differentiate and to know the difference. In the routine of life, we shun such efforts; we are satisfied to settle things, to get matters over with, on a general level. The indefinite article in grammar—*a* tree, *a* house, *a* person, *one*—is the way in which we handle things in everyday life. In our routine of life, one day, one hour, do not—or need not—have a particular meaning and importance. There remains nothing to remember because nothing was registered in its particularity. Nothing is disengaged and arrested.

When we cross a street, our main concern is not to be run over. As soon as we have reached the other side, the task is finished—it has no further relevance. But these steps of crossing belong also to another context. In crossing the street, I was on my way to a certain goal; a temporal position value is added to street and crossing. Yet, it is valid only for this one unfinished day. I realize and keep in mind what I did before noon and what remains to be done this afternoon. Tomorrow, this day will be linked as just another day to the long chain of days past. With the whole, its parts will lose their significance. There is, however, a third possibility: this, my visit to Barcelona, and this day of the meeting, and the way I took to this auditorium today will remain memorable to me.

We remember the remarkable. To register means to disengage and to arrest the fleeting from the continuum of confrontations with the world. Our question is: What constitutes the remarkable? First of all, it must be different and distinguishable from all other things experienced or known heretofore. The remarkable must have objective "marks of distinction," and we, the observers, must be able to discover them or must learn to detect them—or we must be taught to do so, as we are in psychotherapy. But the difference does not mean distinction in the sense of separation, nor does it mean absolute disparity. On the contrary, in and through their divergence from the affairs of days gone by, remarkable events are related to the past.

Yet, not each and every difference makes an event remarkable. More is required. A remarkable difference must be of some importance to an individual observer. In order to be of importance, an event has to satisfy certain conditions. It must indicate a significant change, an expansion— a revolution, if you like—in the curriculum vitae. In one word, it must be intrinsically "new."

My thesis is that only the new, or the *novum*, to use a Latin term, can be disengaged, arrested, and, therefore, registered, and later recalled and remembered.

The *novum* cannot be measured by intensities of stimuli. There is no coincidence between such physiological parameters and the historical meaning of situations. A slight variation of tone and gesture may make us feel thunderstruck, like Falstaff facing Prince Henry, his "King Hal," after the coronation. The *novum* belongs to a historical context. It occurs for the first time in my history or in the history of the group to which I belong. What is signal at one point, in the history of one person, is of no avail to another. The *novum* is not identical with the actual—for actual occurrences may be either familiar or strange, customary or surprising—nor with the ephemeral, such as news events pursued by reporters. They put their emphasis on difference rather than on importance. The news of today for which a reporter may risk his life will no longer be noteworthy tomorrow. The *novum*, however, is determined not only by its contrast with the past but also through its importance for the future. Emerging from the shoal current of neutral events, the *novum* is incorporated into the whole of memory. It is determined by its content, its temporal position, and its historical weight. Memory does not grow by the mere accidental apposition of single impressions, as if another grain were added to a heap of sand. It has a logical or, to be more specific, a historiological order.

The *novum* will not remain new; it will be followed by other events, similar or disparate. The *novum* is threatened by repetition which renders more and more difficult the retrospective distinction of intermediary events. Seen in the temporal perspective of later days, the *novum* stands out. A mother who has given birth to twenty children may find it difficult to distinguish the eleventh from the twelfth delivery, but she will remember all the details of her Opus No. 1. Think, too, of the impression that Hiroshima made on every one of us compared with later reports of the many A- and H-bomb tests which followed. The *novum* is specific in its own relation to the past, but it is general in relation to the future. It has the configuration of the time-god Janus. In temporal as well as in spatial perspective, growing distance makes discrimination more and more difficult until a saturation point is finally reached. As everyone's capacity for discernment is limited, so our capacity for remembering—registering, first, and recall later—is also limited.

The acquisition of a schema, a general pattern, enhances our potentiality for distinguishing and, therefore, for registering and recalling. Someone who knows neurology, for example, remembers with precision and clarity many cases which have become lost to the beginner. The experienced man has acquired a system by which he can order details and through which he can distinguish one case from the other. He possesses a mnemonic system which the beginner is wanting. Experience permits us to descend from vague and global observations to precise, refined distinctions.

An acquired schema facilitates registering and recall in individual cases; however, it also prevents us from remembering the conditions prevailing at an earlier stage. Looking at the dial of a clock or at a line of printed words, it is hard—if not impossible—for us to remember the days when we had not yet acquired the skill of reading. We can reconstruct in imagination our preschool years; we can not regain the innocence of ignorance. An established frame of reference facilitates but also blocks recall. We can recall something more or less correctly only if the system of coordinates within which we made the entry at the moment of registering remains unchanged. Notes in a diary are helpful in later days, provided that we can decipher our handwriting.

There are certain orders which persist from a certain age without basic changes—for example, language, simple arithmetic, or some spatial structures, as in geometry. Frequently, however, orders relatively stable undergo changes. This is especially true for our sets of values and emotional attitudes. There are slow changes throughout life and radical ones sometimes upon entering a new milieu. All of us know that patients frequently have difficulties remembering what happened to them in a short acute psychosis.

In recall, we bring back into the actual present what had once been registered and retained and has now to be reintegrated into the actual situation. The actual situation interferes with recall in many ways. Bright and dark days show the past in the light of the present. Repression is only one of the many factors which play a role in the intricate system of remembering.

The engram theory of memory is at variance with observable facts. A phenomenological analysis of remembering enabled us to disclose the historiological structure of memory and to correct some of the standard interpretations or—if I may say so now—the standard misinterpretations. Infantile amnesia is one example. In organic and senile amnesias, earlier experiences prove more resistant than recent ones. Yet, infantile amnesia sets a barrier which prevents the recovery of memories from our first years. In search of an explanation of this deficiency, Freud (1963) assumed—in line with tradition—that, since single, stimulus-bound impressions are preserved in memory, the earliest ones would also be available to us in later years, as long as they are not kept away from consciousness by the forces of repression. If Freud was right, one should expect that a child at the age of three would still remember well the events of his first and second years. This is not the case. Those early experiences are not preserved up to the advent of the Oedipal situation and then extinguished by repressive forces. Nothing needs to be repressed in this case, because nothing is preserved in its original form—for this reason: what is remembered is the *novum* in its particularity standing out from an invariant ground. This ground is built when the order of things (the world) is detached from the personal order. Before a child is able to remember, it has to fulfill the following conditions: (1) to detach the world from the moments of direct encountering, (2) to extend the temporal span beyond the moment, (3) to build an invariant framework into which single events can be entered, (4) to establish permanent and identifiable structures of particular things and events, and (5) to allow physiognomic changes no longer to interfere with the constancy of the invariant framework and with the identity of single events.

But the baby lives from one moment to the other in the narrowness of his temporal horizon. A baby experiences the world basically in relation to himself. The early tendency to put things into his mouth is quite characteristic of his own attitude to the world. He lacks specification. There is an obvious lack of self-reflection; yet, this is what is required to sever the order of one's own existence from the order of the environment. In short, there is a lack of a stabilized preserving order, of a schema in which events are to be registered in order to be recalled in later days. The conception of the historiological structure of memory not only states, concerning infantile amnesia, *that* it is so—which is a fact that everyone accepts—and not only explains *why* it is so—which Freud had tried to do—but also, finally, makes evident that it *must* be so.

Summary

Since time immemorial, theories of memory have been dominated by the idea that sensory impressions, simple or complex, leave imprints which, when reactivated, produce memory images that are more or less accurate copies of the original. Yet, the engram theory does not explain the "mnestic" functions; in fact, it precludes their understanding. As the difference between perception and memory supposedly is but one of degree, it is beyond comprehension how a memory image, in the fullness of its presence, could, nevertheless, be experienced as such; viz. as a remembrance representing the past.

Memory preserves the past as past but not in the original form. In remembrance, two modes of time are involved: the act of remembering belongs to the present and the remembrance to the past. Remembrance is a relatum—one part only of a complex temporal relation. It belongs to the continuum of historical time which does not grow by addenda. The subject of remembering, then, is not a brain passing from one condition to another in the objective order of time; nor is it a consciousness in which one individual experience follows another. The subject of remembering is a human being who forms his life history within the temporal horizon of personal time.

Human life evolves on two levels: on that of biological need and satisfaction in the circle of daily routine and on that of signal events, marked in the annals of the curriculum vitae. Corresponding to the two levels of existence, there are two modes of remembering and forgetting: one characterized by the familiar and the repeatable and the other by the new and unique.

The systematic order of the growing whole dominates the functions of its parts according to their ever changing retrospective and prospective values.

The organization of the "mnestic" system makes it understandable not only that there actually is an infantile amnesia but also that there must be one.

References

Aristotle. *Parva naturalia. On memory and reminiscence.*

Breuer, J., and S. Freud. *Studies on hysteria.* New York: Basic Books, 1957.

Ebbinghaus, H. *Über das Gedächtnis.* Leipzig: 1885.

Freud, S. *Three essays on the theory of sexuality.* New York: Basic Books, 1963.

Fessard, A. E. Mechanisms of nervous integration. In R. W. Gerard et al., *Brain mechanisms and consciousness.* Springfield: Charles C Thomas, 1954.

Gerard, R. W. What is memory? *Sci. Amer.,* September 1953.

Hering, E. *Über das Gedächtnis als eine allgemeine Funktion der organischen Materie.* Vienna: 1870.

Hobbes, T. *Leviathan.*

Lashley, K. S. In search of the engram. In *Physiological mechanisms in animal behavior.* Cambridge: Cambridge University Press, 1950. Pp. 454–482.

Penfield, W. Memory mechanisms. *AMA Arch. Neur. Psychiat.,* 1952, **67**, 178–191.

Ribot, T. *Les Maladies de la mémoire.* Paris: 1881.

Schilder, P. *Mind: perception and thought in their constructive aspects.* New York: Columbia University Press, 1942.

CHAPTER FOUR

Memory Traces

History of the Problem

The belief that memory retains actual perceptions and reproduces, as recollection, a reprint similar, although faded, to the original impression has exercised unusual power over philosophical and scientific thought. This is rather strange, for everyone can easily convince himself at any time that the much discussed couple—a recollection linked up with a previous perception—belongs to the world of philosophical fairy tales. If it existed in the reality of human existence, if it were, as Hume asserts, that every "idea" has its origin in an "impression," such a relationship could obviously never be grasped by us. The mother "impression" dies at the birth of her daughter "idea." Both remain strangers to each other forever. The philosophical *accoucheur* alone could tell something about their relation and the similarity of mother and daughter if his own experience were not the mere sequence of many single impressions and ideas. At least, that ought to be so if the sensualistic fundamental rule is likewise valid for the author of the *Treatise on Human Nature* as well as for everyone else. But, in this case, he would have been condemned to silence. *We* can compare an original and its copy; *we* can reflect on our perceiving and remembering. The root image (*Urbild*) and its reproduction, each taken alone, can do nothing of the kind. A single content of consciousness, "perception of mind," cannot compare itself to anything else, least of all to a perception which has passed. Sentences like "The most vivid idea is inferior to the bluntest sensation" contain two propositions that are contradictory. Literally, the sentence asserts that perceptions and thoughts are separated as two classes of things. At the same time, without being stated explicitly, it is asserted that we, whose experience is said to consist of such perceptions, are capable of comparing and distinguishing the separated data, i.e., that we are capable of uniting them. As long as the immanent contradiction remains concealed, the sentence sounds so plausible that the opinion which it contains has profoundly influenced all theories of memory, notwithstanding its logical, methodological, and factual insufficiency. A schematic construction, pleasing in its simplicity, hides the problem and blocks the way to the phenomenon. The positivistic scheme gains plausibility by the apparently sensible connection with physiological events—with the stimulus and its trace.

The simile of the engram can already be found in the oldest preserved treatise on memory. Aristotle says in his work *On Memory and Reminiscence* "Obviously one has to look on that which originates through perception in the soul and in the enveloping part of the body, as at a portrait, an affection (*pathos*), the lasting disposition of which (*hexis*) we call memory. For the act of perceiving imprints so to speak a schema (*typos*) of the perceived, as if one seals with a signet-ring" (450ª 27–30). This idea of the memory trace has been preserved for thousands of years—although with characteristic modifications. Most contemporary physiologists may agree to Fessard's formulation:

Any conscious experience is at the beginning of a mnemonic recording, and any trace left by a conscious state is capable of engendering it anew. Thus it seems difficult to suppose that the ultimate basis of "experience" in the physical world could be of another nature than that admitted for the storage of memories, i.e., a more or less durable modification imprinted on a plastic ultra-structure of the neurone (1954, p. 234).

Significant, in these views, is the naïve conviction that the trace, understood purely as a physical or physiological structure, could explain the phenomenon of memory. The question, "What is a trace, or, rather, what do we mean when talking about a trace?" is not raised. Nor is it asked whether or how far a trace could be conceived as a purely physical formation. That is taken for granted today. However, the change in the conception of the trace has come about only gradually—transforming the object of historical interpretation, as Aristotle thought of it, into a self-sufficient physical factor.

It is true, Aristotle himself had already turned the simile of the signet ring into physiological terms and used it for the explanation of infantile and senile amnesia. He believed that, in children, the receiving material was too plastic—like flowing water which does not preserve the imprint of a seal—and that, in the senile, it was too brittle (sclerotic). In children, the impression does not stick; in senile people, it cannot make an imprint. In this context, however, it was not a question of the mode of action but of the origin of traces. Aristotle explained lack of memory as a failure in the formation of traces, but, thereby, nothing was decided about the essential function of the engram. Aristotle, one could say, interpreted the function of the trace in connection with a phenomenological analysis of memory. His treatise starts with a short reflection on time. Perception, he says, is directed toward the present, expectation toward the future. Remembering grasps the past as past.

No one would say that he remembers the present, when it is present . . . only those animals which perceive time remember. . . . For whenever one exercises the faculty of remembering, he must say within himslf, "I formerly heard (or otherwise perceived) this, or I formerly had this thought" (449^b, 16, 28, 23-24).

The phenomenological content of remembering presents the fundamental problem: How can it be understood that remembering represents what is absent while the engram itself is present?

When one remembers, is it this impressed affection that he remembers, or is it the objective thing from which this was derived? If the former, it would follow that we remember nothing which is absent, if the latter, how is it possible that, though perceiving directly only the impression, we remember that absent thing which we do not perceive? (450^b 13–16).

Aristotle decides in favor of the second alternative. Here, he introduces the hypothesis of the engram as a possible explanation. He compares our relation to the engram with looking at a portrait. As we apprehend a picture as a picture, that is to say, as the representation of the not present original, so the soul looks at the traces as if they were pictures of the absent. The engram is the means by which the soul, in its understanding of time, presents to itself in a picture that which is absent, the past. Memory is, therefore also negatively defined by necessity. "Though the affection [the presentation] alone is present, and the [related] fact absent, the latter—that which is not present—is remembered" (450^a 26–27). In the modern interpretation of the engram, however, the reader is eliminated. Mnemonic properties are attributed directly to the traces as epiphenomena in which the physical-physiological structure of the engrams is believed to mirror itself. Eccles writes, "We may say the remembered thought appears in the mind, as its specific spatio-temporal pattern is replayed in the cortex" (1953, p. 256). The description of memory phenomena is more and more dominated by the physical model of the trace. The historic unfolding of experienced time is supplanted by the physical order of time. The merit or the fault of this transformation of the theory of memory has to be attributed above all to Thomas Hobbes. His terse definition of memory, "*Sentire se*

sensisse meminisse est," sounds reminiscent of Aristotle. In this definition of remembering, the subject of discussion is implicitly man, who—
within the horizon of historic time, knowing of himself (*se sensisse*)—
looks in the present at his past as past. But this belated insight was not
decisive for Hobbes' theory of memory. Fascinated by Galileo's physics,
he tried to understand all the contents of human existence as motions.
In order to demonstrate the universal validity of the laws of motion,
Hobbes thought out a dynamic trace theory. In memory, he discovered a
manifestation of the law of inertia. Idea and memory are "decaying
sense."

When a body is once in motion, it moveth, unless something else hinder it,
eternally, and whatsoever hindereth it, cannot in an instant, but in time, and
by degrees, quite extinguish it. And as we see in the water, though the wind
ceases, the waves give not over rolling for a long time after: so also it happeneth
in that motion, which is made in the internal parts of a man, then, when he
sees, dreams etc. (1909, p. 13).

Analogies force themselves on one's mind with modern physiological
hypotheses, e.g., with self-maintaining excitation circuits. However, it
would be unfair to value Hobbes in retrospect as a forerunner, to whom
it was granted to anticipate—more intuitively than knowingly—ideas
the importance of which could be grasped only by a later epoch. Actually, Hobbes was one of the pioneers who categorically determined
for centuries the leading ideas of later research. A new style of psychological inquiry is manifest in Hobbes' frequent use of the formula "nothing else but." It is a clear sign of the psychology of enlightenment. It
warns the reader to give up all illusions. At the same time, it encourages
him and invites him to enter the temple of Psyche without awe, confident that no god resides in the temple but that neither does a soul.
Everything occurs quite naturally, regulated by simple mechanisms.
The trivial is the true. In the light of psychophysical interpretations,
psychic phenomena lose their mysteries. When it is taken for granted
that memory is a universal characteristic of all events in nature, there is
no longer any reason to ponder over the phenomena of remembering.

However, to the same degree to which remembering has become a
matter of course, forgetting now becomes enigmatic. Because every motion of the sense organs is accompanied by a sensation, there should be
present a "phantasm," as long as the agitation continues. But daily experience is not in accord with such a postulate. Hobbes was not at a loss
for a physical-physiological explanation:

The decay in men waking, is not the decay of the motion made in sense, but
an obscuring of it in such manner as the light of the sun obscureth the light

of the stars. . . . The predominant only is sensible, and any object being removed from our eyes, though the impression is made in us to remain, yet
other objects more present succeeding, and working on us, the imagination of
the past is obscured and made weak, as the voice of a man in the noise of the
day (1909, pp. 13–14).

In this way, forgetting is revealed as a seeming forgetting. Certain correspondences between Hobbes and Freud are evident. The lasting influence of the psychophysical foundation is manifested in Freud's notion that it is necessary to give to the meanings which determine repression the new interpretation of libido quantities.

Hobbes taught that all real happening is physical motion. In the entire realm of nature, there is only a narrow range for which this basic
principle is not valid without reservations. Sensations are coordinated,
in a mysterious way, with the excitation of the sense organs of men and
animals. The connection of sensory qualities with the "basic physiological processes" remains completely inexplicable. The sensations are
mere epiphenomena. Hobbes calls them "appearance," "seeming,"
"fancy," "apparition"—words referring to their unreality. In his theory
of memory as "decaying sense," Hobbes believed he had discovered a
possibility for bringing physiological events and "appearances" into a
conceptual correlation. This was, if correct, an important discovery, for
it permitted him to go beyond the offensive fact of mere contiguity of
excitation and impression and to construe a psychic mechanism in analogy to the mechanics of bodies. Hobbes postulated a kind of isomor-
phism—not between physical and psychic forms but between the
intensity of excitation and the clarity of the phenomena. The physical
properties of the trace determine the characteristics of the memory images.

A fading sensation is said to correspond to the ebbing wave of excitation. In the decrescendo of the motion, the sensation (the perception
image) turns into a recollection (memory image). Although the change
occurs in time, it occurs without an alteration of the temporal reference
connection. The sensation itself ages. It shows the marks of decay like a
physical thing. The perceiving of the past, about which Aristotle spoke,
is interpreted by Hobbes as a passing sensation. The *genitivus objec-
tivus*—awareness of the past—becomes a *genitivus subjectivus*—passing
sensation. Hobbes says directly, obviously without noting the paradox,
"but when we would express the decay and signify that the sense is
fading, old and past, it is called memory" (1909, p. 14). Aristotle's thesis, "There is no memory of the now in the now," is turned into its opposite. Memory is explained as a decaying sensation in the actuality of
its now. According to Hobbes, remembering differs from sensing or per-

ceiving, not by a transformation of the whole situation and its temporal structure, but by degrees of clearness of the emerging images.

The psychophysicist of memory is forced to take from the discipline of physics the principle which should bring in line the physical, physiological, and psychic events. Measurability and countability of details are to him the *tertium comparationis*. Obvious objections are brushed aside, as the following reflection shows: As the "motions in us" cannot be suddenly braked but can only gradually come to a standstill by counteractions, the accompanying sensations should also approach the value of nought by a number of intermediate stages. Why, then, should the last stage of a decaying sensation point back to the remote original and not to the immediately preceding stage? How can memory find its way back to perception? How can the decaying sensation represent anything else, something that was once but is not any more? In comparison with the original impression, memory is stated to be characterized by lack of intensity and clarity of details. How can such a deficient sensation state its own defect? When, in autumn, the leaves change color, shrink, and fall, we can remember, at the sight of the withered leaves, their verdure and growing. But could anyone seriously attribute to the fallen leaf memory of its past? Strangely enough, to ask the question is not to answer it in the negative. The phenomena are subordinated to the desired explanation or sacrificed. Hobbes and his successors deduce memory from physical premises.

Hobbes's new interpretation of awareness of the past as a passed sensation was not a haphazard notion. The "appearances" have to correspond with the physical events as epiphenomena. Thus, it is decided, they can be considered only as single sensations and recollections. Hobbes's sensualistic and nominalistic theories are completely in line with his physicalistic bent. The characteristics of memory are to be found in the nature of single memory images. The postulate that it has to be so tacitly presumes that it can be so. The psychophysics of memory rests on the theory of the subjectivity of sense qualities which Hobbes took over and developed from Galileo and Descartes.

With Galileo's teachings of the subjectivity of sense qualities, the separation of somatic and psychic events had been initiated which the psychophysical theories then tried to reunite. At the same time, an objectification of experience was accomplished which was accepted as given in all later discussions on traces and their reflection in consciousness. Only with regard to such "things" as sensations, perceptions, ideas, or recollections was it possible to draw a parallel between *ordo et connectio rerum* and *ordo et connectio idearum*.

Sensory qualities cannot be treated mathematically. With them, the claim of mathematical physics to universal validity had to break down. Galileo found a way out of the dilemma by, so to speak, excommunicating the sensory qualities. They do not belong at all to the community of natural objects which the physicist is called upon to investigate.

All these tastes, smells, colours etc. are—in relation to the object to which they apparently belong—nothing more than names. They have their seat exclusively in the sensing body. . . . Fire, the thing which produces warmth in us and makes us feel warm, is a great number of very small bodies of a certain form and a certain velocity . . . but that apart from form, number, penetration, motion, and contact of these bodies any other quality still belongs to the fire: warmth,—that I do not believe (1842, IV, pp. 333 ff.).

Galileo restricted the subjectivity to colors, smells, sounds, i.e., to secondary qualities, in Locke's later terminology. As a physicist, he had good reasons not to extend the "declassification" to the primary qualities—not to light and not to space. He really wanted to prove what, in his opinion, the sensory qualities are not. He cared rather less about what they essentially are.

He was content with saying they reside in us, they deceive us, and they are mere names which we give to things. Although Galileo mentions that, "if the animal is taken away, all these qualities are suspended and destroyed," therefore the sense qualities stand in relation to "the animated and sensitive body" (1842, IV, pp. 333ff.). But he does not draw the conclusion that, if the sense qualities are relative to man, man is relative to the experienced world. He reduces the appearing world, and—without extending the reduction to man himself—he goes on to talk unconcernedly about the perceptions "in us." The notion that, in perceiving, we experience ourselves in our corporeality—that the things themselves, not their images confront us and we them—is not taken into consideration. On the contrary, the total phenomenon of perceiving is, from the start, interpreted as perception images "in us." But, while in perceiving we are in the same space with the perceived things, there is no continuity between the space represented in a picture and its environment. The frame marks the boundary between the inner space and the outer space from which the onlooker views the picture. Together with the localization of sense qualities "in us" or in our mind, the distinction between picture space and surrounding space disappears; and, with it, also the difference between picture and beholder vanishes. The mind—or, in a later continuation of the theory, consciousness—is simultaneously the room and the beholder of images immanent within it. To these images, the sensory qualities are supposed to belong. With supreme disregard for daily experience, it is maintained that the sensory qualities are never perceived as the properties of things; for instance, the lawn is not seen as a green lawn, but the green is a sense datum "in us." The perception of "green" is given the new interpretation: green perception. The entire content of perceiving could, therefore, be fully presented, it seems, in a description and analysis of the perception images.

In Galileo's arguments on the subjectivity of sense qualities, the negative and the positive statements are of a totally different order. The negative statements arise out of metaphysical reflection on the true being of things. They are, as such, clear and unambiguous. The positive statements, on the contrary, are indefinite, ambiguous, or contradictory.

Here Descartes intervened. In his metaphysics, an ontological home is assigned to the sense qualities. Although they do not belong to the reality of nature as *res extensa*, they have a reality of their own as modes of the *res cogitans*. Their deceptive character finds its explanation too. Being confused ideas, they are of a lower order. They have no legitimate claim to objective validity. Pursuing childish habits, we are tempted into assigning to them a place in the external world. The intended clarification of some of Galileo's problems led immediately to their radicalization. Hobbes, who rejected Cartesian dualism, found it necessary to extend the theory of subjectivity to the whole of human experience. The sensations, with all their supposed derivations—such as recollections and ideas—belong to the realm of phenomena as mere subjective appearances. Sense qualities—so one could now formulate Hobbes' theory—do not really exist in nature; and, as appearances, the sensations are not real. "To us," they are a ghostly shadow of true happenings. In spite of the distinction of causally determined events in nature from mere subjective phenomena, Hobbes construed just these phenomena and their connections completely according to the model of physical events. Perhaps this was not only "a naive equalization . . . of psychological data-experience with body experience," as Husserl (1954, p. 234) thought.

The dialectics of interpretation urged the application to the phenomena of the categories referring to things. The subjectivism which denies the reality of perceived things has to describe the subjective phenomena in such a way that, from their composition, at least the familiar picture of things can be regained. The objectification of experience has the result that the visible object of perception and the "subjective" perception fuse into one. The perceived is blended with the perception, like a picture woven into a tapestry. Only the sensation, which has become a thing like other things, can undergo certain alterations without losing its identity. It is the sensation which is considered to be a thing which can decay, grow old, and so change from a subjective perception image into a subjective memory image.

The objectification of experiences demanded, as its correlate, the assigning of a soul to things. This process took place from the beginning and still goes on today, usually quite unnoticed. Galileo stripped the mathematically defined physical bodies of their secondary qualities but let them keep the character of visibleness. Hobbes thought that the light of the sun obscures the light of the stars, without considering that the astronomical sun does not shine, that it is neither luminous nor gets dark. It is, no doubt, extremely difficult, if not impossible, to carry through, in full strength, the reduction of the everyday world theoretically required. The expelled qualities creep in again. For instance, Eccles' assumption "that the remembered thought appears in consciousness, as soon as its specific space-time schema is replayed in the brain cortex" (1953, p. 266) claims repetition of a physical factor. The "objective" repetition is supposed to prove and to explain the recollection. But is not the phenomenon of repetition the fundamental problem of memory? Does the "again" belong to the remembered thought, to the neural processes, or to both? Does a breath repeat those taken before? Does today's revolution of the earth repeat yesterday's revolution? The repetition, understood physiologically, is supposed to explain the recognition. But only living creatures, capable of experiencing time, are capable of grasping the "again." Memory is the condition for the possibility of repetition. Therefore, it is hardly surprising that Lashley (1950) acknowledged that his long search for the engram remained unsuccessful. Critical examination of numerous experiments, carried out systematically, compelled him to conclude that it was not possible to demonstrate the existence of a single memory trace anywhere in the nervous system.

An unsuccessful search does not prove the nonexistence of what is searched for, nor that it cannot be found. One could always retort to the unsuccessful searcher that he has not searched with the right methods or in the right place, or that he made himself a false picture of that for which he searched. Most people think that memory traces will be discovered one day. In contrast to their belief, I wish to question whether memory traces can ever be found.

The Phenomenology of the Trace

We are looking at the footprints of a man in sand or in snow. It is child's play to discover them, but it demands exacting reflection to understand the accomplished act. The theory of memory traces—a result, probably, of the deceptive easiness of the observation—has not taken the trouble to make this effort and has been satisfied with the vague definition of the concept of a trace. Strictly speaking, it gives up all claim to any definition, and instead it appeals to the popular understanding which works and is confirmed again and again at the discovery of a trace. The question what is meant by the word "trace" can easily be answered by pointing at it and raising the counterquestion "Do you see the footprints in the snow there?" Certainly. "Well, all together, they form a trace." One could, therefore, erroneously conclude that a trace consists of a number of impressions, and, consequently, the single impression is the essential part of a trace.

In continuation of our observation and in retrospect of what happened before, we can reconstruct a past event with some certainty. Path and motion, event and past event, are in close verbal and objective connection. Path and motion, the course of past events, is manifested in the trace. But what do we actually see when looking at the footprint? "Nothing but" certain hollows in an otherwise virgin expanse of snow. The hollows, arranged in rows and separated from each other by more or less regular intervals, show the outline of a shod human foot. We can measure the length, breadth, and depth of the impressions and—if we enjoy playing detective—can draw the conclusion from our measurements that probably a rather tall man walked from his house to the garage last night.

We say that the footprints are the trace of a man. But nothing of him can be seen any more. The trace is not the image of the man who passed. The impressions of his feet alone are left. If a quick generalization of this simple observation is allowed, it yields us the first characteristic of traces: They are fragmentary. They preserve only a fraction of the whole event. It has to be considered whether the fragmentary character belongs to all kinds of trace or, just by chance, to footprints. This objection will have to be examined. Our tentative assumption is expressly confirmed by the usage of language, which abounds in expressions where the word "trace" points to a small amount, a hint, a mere allusion. One talks about trace metals; one says traces of violent interference were found; the food contained traces of arsenic; or he disappeared without a trace, and not the least trace of vegetation could be discovered. In all these positive or negative expressions, the word "trace" has always the meaning of the fragmentary.

Our initial observation of the footprints led us to the conclusion that they presented the trace of a man who passed here yesterday. Thus, the trace is the sign of a past event. True, the sign is of a very peculiar kind. The trace is no conventional sign. It is no symptom, no signal. It is an immediately compelling indication of a past event. The trace signifies a *Verweisungszusammenhang*, in Heidegger's sense—namely a temporal, historical connection. But the original event has been transformed in a peculiar way. A man passed, whose footprints alone the snow preserved as reprints. The man went yesterday, and his action belongs to the past; but his trace is visible to us now. The man walked, he moved; the trace, however, is at rest. We see the trace together with the surroundings, with the blanket of snow, the trees, the fence, the houses. The trace is the residue, the deposit of a past event in a receiving material. But the essence of a trace is not given in the same way as the outline and the different measurements of length, breadth, etc. We do not look at the footprints as the orthopedist looks at the impression of a foot in plaster of Paris. The patient's foot, the plaster cast, and, perhaps, even the shoe made from the cast belong for him to the present. He compares foot, plaster cast, and shoe without the imprint in a historical perspective. In contrast, the footprints are remaining road signs of a past event.

The production of a trace requires a suitable material. It must lend itself to being stamped by the event—it has to be plastic—and it has to retain the alterations produced in it beyond the time of the generating event. The receiving material must compensate for the transitoriness of the event. A baker can pour and repour the soft dough into many forms, but the cake can only be baked once. The heat of the oven expels the plasticity for good. The loss of plasticity, caused by exterior interference, is a much more drastic alteration than the original shaping which suited the material. With the loss of plasticity, a structural change occurs and, dependent on it, a change of function. At the making of a gramophone record, the plastic surface layer is allowed to harden. In a complete change of roles, the receiver becomes a sender. An ideal material for traces would be one which up to the moment of impregnation is "ultraplastic" but which would lose its plasticity immediately with the impregnation. It is questionable whether such ideal material exists at all. A sensitive photographic film, for instance, fulfills the first but not the second condition. Therefore, it has to be protected from a second exposure and has to be fixed in the process of development. Snow is far from being an ideal material. It can be too hard or too soft; it can melt; a later snowfall can cover a trace and obliterate it. Whatever the receptive material may be, at every formation of traces, the producing event and the receiving material act together. During a thaw, the traces of kings and beggars alike disappear. The peculiarity of the event and of the material and their relation to each other determine the result. The trace is not a copy of an event on neutral ground.

Since a trace preserves the perishable and retains the past, its temporal structure deviates characteristically from the structure of the producing event. At the reception into the plastic material, the original event undergoes a kind of Bergsonian transformation. In walking, we put one foot before the other; our steps follow one after the other. In the trace, the one-after-the-other of the steps is changed into the side-by-side and one-with-the-other of the footprints. While the walker moves from one spot to the next, always exchanging one place for the next, the trace shows all his transient positions simultaneously. While the walker moved forward from a starting point to a goal, the starting and the endpoint of the trace are visible at the same time. While the walker traversed a distance which separated the start and the end from each other, the trace extends over a stretch which connects the beginning and the end. In the actuality of walking, the walker was on his way. The virginal field of snow lay in front of him. We see the trace he left behind as a resting whole. In the actuality of walking, the result was still uncertain. We can lose our way. We can be compelled to turn back. In contrast, the trace shows a way, which was still untrodden and open to the future, as completed. From a trace, we can read off the efforts of the walker, whether or not he succeeded in his intention. A trace, therefore, contains less but also more than the original event. In each case, it presents the happening in a peculiar transformation, like the printed page reproduces the fleeting sounds of spoken words in a finished composition. In reading, we restore the original temporal order, following the lines word by word.

Traces must be read. In order to understand a trace as a trace, we cannot simply leave it as it presents itself. The trace does not talk by itself; we have to make it talk. For this end, we have to apprehend what is visible at present in connection with the history of its origin. Our understanding of a trace is guided by a specific insight. We discover a trace as an artifact, as something which, by nature, does not belong to the material into which the trace is imprinted. Nobody is in doubt that footprints do not drop down simultaneously with the snowfall. A trace cannot have occurred at the same time as its matrix. A footprint appears as a figure—alien to the ground and not belonging to it. It is forced upon the material. The strangeness points to this: Something has happened to the snow, something which does not belong to it. The strangeness points to a past interference with the integrity of the trace-preserving material. The strangeness endows the trace with the character of past happenings.

Not all traces, of course, can be noticed as easily as footprints in snow. It needs the practiced eye of the hunter to discover the traces of an animal in such slight changes as characteristically bent branches or slightly damaged bark. Sometimes a trace can be demonstrated only by special procedures. The chemical or microscopic proof of a trace is, however, always guided by the preceding understanding of the essence of the trace. Whether blood as a spot is clearly recognizable to everyone or only shown with the aid of a microscope is a purely technical question, determined by the special circumstances of the particular case. The problem is not simply that of the possibility of discovering traces but one of the confirmation of a supposition—namely, the hypothetically already-discovered trace. Always, the character of an artifact is maintained. This does not mean that only human interferences in natural structures are to be understood as artifacts. Wind and weather leave behind their traces on fences and houses. The character of being artificial or even ingenious is not decisive; but the circumstances of the trace's origin, which are indicated through the strangeness of the fragmentary formations, are decisive. A preceding familiarity with the new formation is not needed at all. Enigmatic imprints of objects which we have never seen before strike us no less than the familiar configuration of a footprint. The necessary condition is always the same—namely, that the receiving material and the trace do not belong together by nature and are recognizable in their objective disparity and, thereby, in their temporal stratification.

In our paradigm of the footprint, a more differentiated configuration is impressed into a nondifferentiated material. But the relation between trace-preserving material and trace-producing event is not always that between *hyle* and *eidos*. The receiving material can possess the richer form: inkspots on the page of a book are traces of inconsiderate use. Also, in that case, the trace is an artifact inasmuch as the original material suffered slight changes from an alien force operating from outside. The influence should not surpass certain limits. If the receiving material was transformed completely, then it could not retain any trace. Water is not the trace of melted snow; a growing seed is not the trace of sperm and ovum. We do not interpret a ruin as the trace of a castle, but we are able to discover, in the wreckage, the trace of a conflagration or a bombardment.

Each artifact tells a story. But, for good reasons, we do not regard the essentially constructive parts of a work like nuts and bolts which hold together the steel frame of a bridge as traces of past hammering and screwing. The actions of making, determined by the *telos* of the future form, enter into the completed product and last together with it. In contrast, a footprint reaches its end with its beginning. It does not serve a future whole. The trace is a residue; it is effect and not work.

In understanding a trace, we surpass the present and the given. We interpret the trace in conjunction with its history. Discovery and reading of traces is an achievement of historical interpretation. It presupposes the possibility of an interpretation which grasps and reconstructs the past as past. The visible impression of a foot signifies a trace only when we read the alteration which lasts into the present as a rune of past happenings.

The trace in the snow gave us the certainty that a man had passed the spot. The certainty was founded in the contingency of the change. By its nature, the field of snow is a homogeneous plane. We understand the trace as an interference and destruction of the snow's original condition. In our understanding of the trace, we are reconstructing the yet intact state as it existed before the step which produced the impression. In our thoughts, we fill up the shell of the foot impression again, and we return to the beginning—the earlier state of the still untrodden field. We follow the trace back, therefore, into the pluperfect past. We undo the trace-producing event in order to let it then "occur" again.

All this happens implicitly and so little expressively that an exact explication sounds almost strange. The self-evident is, as usual, the least understood. In order to be understood, it has to be first removed from self-evidence. Therefore, it remained almost unnoticed that always a historical reconstruction of the observed by the observer is at the root of a scientific "statement" of a movement. In every observation—with or without experimental controls—we pursue an event from its beginning to its end as a movement completing itself. Then we describe the event, in retrospect, in such a way that we divide it into three phases. First of all, the beginning of the event is defined against a phase "I" which preceded it. Then, a second phase follows which lasts to the end of the movement. It is separated from our present by a third phase. We return from the end to the beginning and follow the event experienced as being completed again, from beginning to end. As a matter of fact, we do the same thing every day in telling a story of a past event by going back to the pluperfect without pointing it out directly. The report, "Mr. X visited us last night at eight o'clock," points beyond the moment of Mr. X's arrival and back to the time when the visitor was not yet present. Likewise, eight o'clock is understood as a time between seven and nine. All this is simultaneously understood although not specially expressed, because it is evident in a certain way. In experimental examinations of memory, it is frequently overlooked that an impression becomes a trace only by an interpretation of the present which goes back to the past.

The reading of a trace, such as the footprint, demands—for and with the historical interpretation—a spatial extension of the field of vision. It is evident that only the snow crystals at the bottom of the footprints are directly affected by the physical force—so to speak, by the stimulus. They alone have been pressed together by the weight of the stepping foot. The outline of the footprint separates the infield from the outfield. Nothing has happened to the snowflakes outside this wall. The trace-producing process did not involve them. For our observation of the trace, however, the single footprint stands out clearly against its environment. As in every drawing of a boundary, we have to go beyond the limited space into the enclosing field. The environment, which is not at all affected by the trace-producing force, has, nevertheless, to be considered in its untouched entirety. We, the readers of the trace, view the footprint as a figure on a ground; but, while figure and ground are visible simultaneously, they are still comprehended in their temporal stratification. What happened stands out against what remained untouched—against the environment which did not suffer any alteration. The snowflakes which were under the stamping foot, however, do not stretch beyond themselves. They do not stand out as figures on a ground to which they have no physical relation whatsoever. The single particles are not parts of a macroscopic field.

From a physical point of view, therefore, the trace in the snow is "nothing but" the transposition of snow crystals in narrowly restricted and spatially separated areas. In soft snow, the foot of the walker sinks in until it eventually meets resistance from firmer ground. The high snow cover becomes for us deep snow. In a field deeply snowed under, every tread produces a shaft, the bottom of which is separated by a considerable distance from the original level, the surface of the snow. The trace-producing occurrence begins on the uppermost plane and is completed on the lower level. The alteration started in the past; but, with the transition from the initial position to the end position, the original situation has gone and disappeared. Therefore, in a foot trace, the imprint corresponds with the impression, but only with two essential reservations:

1. the footprint is a negative of the stepping foot;
2. the trace is the end result of the generating process.

The trace begins at the moment that the trace-producing event ends, and it subsists there where the process found its conclusion.

The footprint does not reproduce the stepping. The trace is not a facsimile of the trace-producing event. The engram reproduces the stimulus as little as the writ reproduces the movements of the writer. A graphologist is able to draw conclusions from handwriting with regard to the act of writing and the state of the writer. Traces must be read; they do not read themselves.

Apologetic, Critical Discussion

The observation of footprints led to the conclusion that the trace is an object of historical interpretation of fragmentary residues of past events in a preserving material, as far as these relations, in their temporal interlacing, can be comprehended on the basis of certain indications. The physiological theory of the engram is less exacting. It has no need and no place for interpretation. On this theory, the phenomenon of memory is deduced directly from the function of engrams themselves, from the mnemonic properties of the nervous substratum. The engrams—the theory says—are reactivated; the traces read themselves. If our interpretation is correct, then the basic axiom of the physiological theory has to be abandoned.

Perhaps we made it too easy for ourselves by the choice of our example. An organism does not remain passive like snow and sand; it reacts actively to the entering stimuli. The simple schema of traces that was at the bottom of the old association theories has been abandoned long ago. Instead, it is assumed today that both fresh impressions and alterations in the life and the drives of the individuals influence and change the memory traces (Rapaport, 1950). "In every single memory act literally millions of neurons are in action" (Lashley, 1950). After all, the foot trace is only one of many other kinds of trace. In the world of man and animal, there is the smell trace. Among the technical products, perhaps the photograph or the sound tape has to be considered. The physiologist who long ago relinquished the antiquated ideas of the trace by impression reaches "full of good courage into the sky" of electrophysics and field theory.

Two roads are open to meet such objections. One can examine critically the opposing examples, one after the other, without hope of ever killing the hydra. Or one can try to show how far the result that we gained from the example of the footprint is necessarily valid for all kinds of trace. This proof should not be too difficult if one keeps in mind that, in a trace, the past is preserved in the present as past. By this fundamental relation, all other determinations are laid down at the same time.

As past, the past itself is not present. The ground, trampled by horses waiting impatiently, becomes a trace only when horses and riders have disappeared. Since the past itself cannot be present, it cannot be preserved whole and in the fullness of its possibilities. The preservation of the past is necessarily fragmentary. The lightning does not flash in the split oak tree any longer, the fury of the storm does not rage any more in the broken trees and the roofless houses—in the traces of their destruction. Of course, it is not necessary for a trace to develop at all; but, if a trace is formed, event and material must fulfill certain conditions, given by the historiological structure of the trace. Whether the trace is impressed into the preserving material, as a footprint, or adheres to the material, as in the droppings of an animal, or destroys the material, the trace is always a residue of past happenings and not an image or sign of an object. Ashes are the trace of fire—not of firewood. Whether the trace-producing event was a mechanical, a chemical, an electrical, or a biological event does not matter in principle. The trace is always the end result of past influence. In an engram, the "stimulus" is not copied. Through the action of the stimulus, the ultrastructure of the nervous tissue has been altered; it is not the same as it was at the beginning of the stimulation. The "mnemonic" properties of the material cannot be identical with its plasticity. Plastic material—be it snow, shellac, or brain tissue—is ready to take any kind of form. But it is likewise ready to give them up again. If an impression is to be preserved, then it must either be made "air tight" against all later influences, or the plasticity has to be removed from the material.

The trace, which preserves past events in the present as past, appears in the iridescent light of bitemporality. But is it seriously possible to talk of bitemporality? The expression sounds strange or meaningless. Such a manner of speech can apparently be easily disposed of by pointing to elementary logic: Either, one may argue, something is past or it is present. It cannot be both at one and the same time. But this objection already contradicts itself, because it can be said and because it can be thought. What is valid for the stated is not valid for the saying nor for him who says it. For, in such a statement, we talk about the past in the present. The past is meant as having passed. Only from the present can the past be grasped as past.[1]

Each tale, each "once upon a time," recalls the past as past into the present. Linguistically, only the past is expressed by a grammatical

[1] The present itself—for instance, this very moment in early morning—on the other hand, is only ascertainable as one moment in the completing whole of this day (see Heidegger, *Being and Time*). Our discussion here has to be restricted to the aspect of bitemporality.

tense: I went, I did, I was. The bitemporality has no linguistic representation of its own. But that is not at all necessary, for the present is always expressed through the act of speaking. It can be stated expressively, as in such sentences as "I tell you [now, in our present talk] I was not in the theater yesterday." "I went yesterday" implicitly means "I, who am talking to you now, I, who stand in front of you here, I am the same who went yesterday." The English usage "I was walking" makes the bitemporality still clearer. With the bitemporality of "I did" or "I was" corresponds a duality of the "I." I, who stands here today and who does not go, I am the same who went yesterday. I am the self-same, but still I am not the same. Yesterday I was tired, today I am tired no longer. I am not as I was, I was not yesterday as I am today. In everything that I was or am, that I did or do, I experience the *possibilities* of my being. But the bitemporality is no privilege of the speaker; it is valid for all our statements, for the "you were" as well as for the "he (she, it) was." We grasp the factual—as far as we grasp it—against the background of its possibilities. We experience the factual as an "adumbration," a limited realization of possibilities. The possibilities exist together; the realizations exclude one another.

In looking back at past happenings, our relation to things is not different from what it is in predicting the future. In a bet, we gamble on possibilities. We dare to predict an event, the future occurrence of which is unascertainable at the present moment. We do not know, in advance, how the coin thrown up in the air will fall. The statisticians say: There are two equivalent chances—heads or tails. For us who predict, there are two chances indeed, but the coin itself does not predict. During its course up and down, it is always in one position, changing one for the other in quick rotation, while the betters are in agreement that the toss could end in one position as well as in the other.

In reading of traces, the condition one meets is grasped as factual realization of past possibilities. A footprint is impressed in the snow. It need not be so. The artifact signifies to us that it has not always been so. In the interpretation of the trace, we project the actual, the visible, on the grounds of its invisible possibilities. The physical trace is incapable of achieving just that. This also shows that the trace preserves that which has passed in the present, that it must be read, and how it can be read. At the same time, it is proved that the search for the engram can come to nothing.

A discussion should be concluded with a *q.e.d.* But there remains one doubt which cannot be easily silenced. Everyone is familiar with the behavior of dogs who, with their noses deep to the ground, appear to study eagerly the local information of the smell newspaper. Can one say of them and of other animals that they accomplish a kind of historical interpretation? The question seemingly leaves us only a choice between two evils: the curse of absurdity and the confession of failure. Before we give up, we want to examine once more whether a positive answer is really so devious as it may appear at first glance.

Every modality is a variation of the fundamental theme of the I–world relation. The transition from seeing to smelling permits and demands modifications which do not need to call the principle in question. Let us, therefore, postpone our decision and consider shortly the world of smelling and the phenomenon of smells.

Smells can be experienced as properties of something. The roast smells good, the rose emits sweet fragrance, the bad egg stinks. As properties, smells are comparable to surface colors to a certain degree. The verbal expressions of smelling, scenting, or stinking indicate, however, that smells present themselves as an activity, as an emanation. The smell comes from the objects; it detaches itself from them. Smells are not qualities attached to things, such as red or green. We see the rose, but we sniff at it in order to find out how it smells. As the tactile impression is tied to the touching movement, smell is tied to the breathing movement. Yet the correspondence is not complete in these cases. The touching hand glides over the surfaces of things themselves and discovers their roughness or smoothness. In contrast, smells are breathed in and incorporated with joy or with disgust. While language assigns sound to hearing and light to vision, the word smell designates both the act of perceiving and the action of the perceived. Even in direct approach, the sense of smell functions as a sense of distance. Finally, one can compare smells with sounds, and one finds again a certain concordance.

As the sound leaves the sounding body, smell leaves the odorous body. Therefore, they can become atmospheric smells which fill a room, a barn, a stable, a fir forest, or a mountain meadow. Such smells belong to the whole region and not to the single parts. When entering a bakery, a hospital ward, and a railway station the typical smell meets us.

Smells come toward us. Borne by air currents, the kitchen smells reach us. Now, one does not say, "The roast smells good," but "It smells of . . . ." Smell announces something which is not present itself, something which is nearby. Floating smells also signify something not present to an animal. The not present is not absolutely absent, not an empty nothing; the smell announces its nearness. The not present is at arm's length or, rather, at smell length. Wafting smell attracts the dog; it moves against the current of smell toward that which it smells of.

The dog runs to the kitchen, the dustbin, or the bitch in heat. Sense impressions guide mobile creatures within an open horizon to possible goals.

Trace smells also point to something else which is not present. But trace smells are stationary, not wafting. They are tied to a spot, adhering to a place, but, at the same time, are alien to it. The dog sniffs at the tree, and there, in a narrow zone, it smells not the tree but a dog. It sniffs at the ground, and there, in a narrow spot, it smells a cat, a man, or perhaps something unknown. The fresh smell of excretion contrasts with the dull smell of the tree. It is different; it is added, in the true sense of the word, accidentally. It is something left behind which does not belong there by nature. As the agent is not present itself, it must have been present before. It points to the past as past. It must be so. The conclusion is compelling. Unfortunately, we do not smell in syllogisms, but perhaps that is just as well. The senses achieve—each in its limited zone—with one stroke that which has to be taken apart in discursive thinking and then reassembled again. In looking at a footprint, it is immediately obvious to us what—in reflection—has to be developed from its involved conditions. No less directly, the dog on the track responds sensibly to a situation without comprehending abstractly the situation and its own behavior. When studying the smell tabloid, the dog does not sit still like the human reader of a newspaper. It is on the go; it moves forward in a zone of things that are subject to gravity, resting and present: of visible and smelling roads, of houses and trees. There it finds, in its movements, spots which are marked by accidental smells, overpaintings, which "forerunners" left behind there. Like a low accidental sound which stands out against the permanent roaring of the engine and draws the attention of the driver, so, for the dog, the important accidental smell stands out against the tenuto of the permanent ground smells. The dog follows the accidental smells; it goes after them. The forerunners are not present any more. The dogs grasp their past presence still in the present residues.

The discovery of historical talent in the dog which searches for traces ought not to lead to the assumption that the past is always preserved and grasped as past, as if the words "as past" might be an unnecessary amplification. The preservation of the past in the present as past is to be distinguished from the continuation of the past in the present. This distinction is expressed in the different past tenses of the verb. The imperfect tense denotes the past as passed: "He quickly grew up." The perfect tense denotes the continuation of the past in the present: "He is handsomely built." The perfect tense denotes that a form has matured, i.e., that it has been brought to its definite completed form. To the imperfect tense, one can add in one's mind "at the time" but not to the past tense. In the perfect tenses, the participle is assimilated to the adjective; the "is" gives up the connection with the "has become." One is how one has become. One has what one has acquired. The in-the-past-acquired becomes what one has got. Although the later is always partly determined by the earlier, the relation of earlier–later does not suffice to grasp the becoming of something to something—e.g., the growing of the germ to the mature organism—or the originating of something out of something—e.g., of a building out of the building materials in planning. The continuation of the past in the present is restricted to the spheres of natural growth, artificial manufacture, and the acquisition of skills and habits. Geological formations, to be sure, developed in the past, too. In viewing a valley, a mountain, or a lake as an individual, we talk about their history. But, as they lack a *telos*, each state is only a station on the road. The past has vanished; the relation of earlier–later is a sufficient schema of consideration. In growing, forming, and learning, however, the begetting is "contained" in the begotten, the producing in the product, the learning in knowledge and skill. Therefore, we are inclined, in the aesthetic attitude, to extinguish traces of the making in the completed work. When the framework of a house is completed, the scaffolding is decorated; but, before the opening ceremony, when the last touches have been completed, the scaffolding is dismantled. For a short hour, the new is entirely of the present. The smooth surface of the new car should show neither traces of manufacture nor traces of use.

The preservation of the past as past signifies recollection. The acting of the past in the present of organic forms is the theme of the *mneme* (Hering, 1890; Semon, 1904). An organism is transformed by mutation, under the influence of the environment, or by the acquisition of "conditioned reflexes." It is not any more as it was previously. Synapses of the nervous system which were transformed in the past, under the influence of practice, function in the actual present later on. They cannot be the basis of the "again."

As the theory of traces ignores the peculiarity of temporal order, it needs to level all temporal characteristics or to reduce them to the empty formula of the earlier–later. In a paper entitled "What Is Memory?" Gerard (1953, p. 118) mentions the "memory of the linseed oil." Short exposure to light effects an alteration of the oil, at first unnoticeable; but, on repeated exposure to light, the previously exposed oil changes quicker than oil which was not exposed before. The oil "remembers" its past experience, Gerard writes, "and shows therefore changed behavior."

The pebble smoothed by the water rolls differently from the originally angular stone. Experience has modified its behavior, and the past is stored in the altered structure. In analogy to these examples, one could say the ashes in the fireplace remember the firewood and the fire or the broken pieces remember the pitcher which was carried too often to the well. In brief, each later state would be the recollection of all the earlier states. In Gerard's discussion, the colloquial usage which attributes experience to stones and memory to linseed oil is surprising; still more surprising is the choice of his examples, because they illustrate just the opposite of what he wants to prove. Gerard finds in such events "a clear indication how memory—by means of material (physical) traces of the past—can work" (1953, p. 181). If memory behaved as Gerard describes, then he could not describe how it behaves. The pebble has lost one particle after the other in the course of years. The past is not preserved but has vanished. The exposed oil has passed from one state to another. In the transition, the earlier state has disappeared. An exposed film cannot be used a second time. It is not the same as it was originally. We, however, remember how it once has been. We are aware in the present of the past as past.

The theory of traces claims that a dormant trace is awakened to new life. Here we enter into the sphere of physiological and physical miracles. The Bible reports miracles of various kinds. Many refuse to believe them just because they are miracles. The believers, however, know very well that, if poor Lazarus was awakened from death, it could have happened through a miracle alone. The theory of traces demands from us a still higher degree of belief. It reports miracles but asserts they are natural events. A trace, the more or less lasting alteration of the nervous tissue, it is maintained, can be re-awakened. What has happened is undone. Simultaneously with the reactivation, the second miracle occurs. "Every trace which a state of consciousness leaves behind is capable of producing it again" (Fessard, 1954, p. 234). The misinterpretation of the phenomena misleads to a magical physiology—namely, an effect is held capable of reproducing its cause; the children are capable of begetting their parents. The seal supposedly reproduces the sealing, the footprint the stepping foot. Actually, nothing of the kind occurs. The footprint, generated as it is in the mechanics of pressure and counterpressure, becomes visible for the observer in a light which was not produced by the trace. It would be most amazing if the trace, which was formed in the plastic ultrastructure of the neuron, could, in principle, accomplish something else.

As Fessard emphasizes, the trace is a more or less lasting modification of the tissue. If that is so, how can a reactivation of the trace take place? Just as under the influence of the footstep an imprint occurred in the snow, the nervous tissue passed from state A into state B under the influence of a stimulus. However one may imagine the reactivation of a trace, it can only begin to have effect where the impression had ended, i.e., to stay with the example of the footprint, deep at the bottom of the impression. A trace, from the physiological or physical point of view, cannot return to the starting position by itself. Muenchhausen's tricks are denied to it. Reactivation is not capable of filling up the stamped shaft again—as the reading of traces demands—and then sinking the shaft a second time, now without external influence. A trace is the negative end result of the effect of the stimulus. Its reactivation needed a preparatory process by which the "more or less lasting changes" would become erased, so to speak, and had then to reproduce themselves by themselves. Had one stuck to the expression "stimulus–effect," nobody would have conceived the idea of reactivation. The enticement is given only by the word "trace."

The change of name takes place at the end of a long chain of misinterpretations of the physical and physiological happenings, which occurred in about the following stages:

1. Perceiving is reduced to a perception image which appears in the consciousness of the perceiver.

2. The reduction, however, is not complete. The observer reserves to himself a privileged position. He remains in the natural attitude. From the environment accessible to his sight, he selects some visible objects which he relates to another object—the body of a man.

3. In progressive reduction, the objects, which are visible to the observer, are re-interpreted as stimuli in relation to another individual.

4. The invisible stimuli produce in the retina photochemical and photoelectric reactions which, after conduction through the afferent system, are followed by demonstrable electric effects in the brain cortex.

5. This effect in the cortex is thought to be accompanied in consciousness by a perception image.

6. As perceiving is reduced to an image of perception, remembering is reduced to an image of recollection.

7. It is assumed that perception image and memory image are alike, like the first print and a later print from the same plate. (According to

the present-day theory, the memory image is more similar to an over-print of several different plates.)

8. However, since the perception image is not considered to be a print from the completed plate—since it is thought of as coordinated not to the stimulus–effect but to the effecting stimulus, not to the engram but to the engraphein—the memory picture has to be related to a process of anengraphein. The analogy demands the reactivation of the inactive engram.

This means: The physiological hypotheses are actually formed in accordance with the interpretation of perceiving and recollecting. This interpretation, however, is guided by mechanical ideas, so that the confusion increases more and more in this Ping-pong game of misinterpretations. Consequently, the distinction between stimulus and object is not carried through at all. The idea of the trace as an effect of a stimulus is linked, in a vague way, with the idea of the image of an object. This image can then re-appear through a kind of phosphorescence.

The difficulties arising from the conception of reactivation do not even then disappear, if one assumes that the reactivation is brought about by new stimuli or the intervention of other brain regions. In each case, the task remains to explain how a trace ever could find back from its end state to its original state and, still in this original state, remains tied to the end state so that it swings back there. Through physiological restitution, a tissue is rendered susceptible to a new stimulation. In contrast, in the reactivation of a trace, the previous effect should have been erased and preserved at the same time. Even if—in spite of all the mentioned objections—a reactivation of traces could occur, the reactivation would have to be an active process like all other cerebral events. They have all the character of the now.

The reactivated trace cannot comprehend itself as repetition. For, in that case, it would have to be capable of comprehending the original and past activity of the trace-producing process. Although we can play again a gramophone record, the "again" is not a physical characteristic of the happening. The second performance is a second one only with regard to the earlier one, but the second playing does not alter physically in any way the record played earlier. Each of the two happenings is and remains singular, limited to its position in time. The repetition can be grasped only by the hearer, who might perhaps recall the first occasion. A "conscious experience," corresponding to a reactivated trace, would also be limited to the actual now, like the reactivated trace. It would not be a repetition, not a recollection. The "once before," the "earlier," or the "again" does not belong to a single memory image. The reading of traces presupposes memory rather than that the function of traces founds memory.

Conclusion

The fiasco of the theory of traces will not deter the clinician from searching for a connection between function of the brain and experience. He never doubts that there is a coordination or even a dependence of memory performance on somatic events. He demands a substitute for the shattered theory of traces. If the theory of traces does not give you satisfaction, can you offer anything better? The answer is: Not yet. But perhaps one can consider the criticism as the first step in the right direction. It makes it clear that long preparatory work has to precede a new physiological theory of memory. Meaning and possibility of psychophysical coordination must be examined anew. Human experience, the attitude of man toward the world and to himself, should not be assimilated to events within an organism. The dogmatic assumption of the coordination of one conscious datum to one physiological process rests on many suppositions. All of them, the openly declared as well as the concealed and evident ones, must be rendered accessible to historical reflection. Only if the phenomenon of perception is freed from the traditional reduction to a perception image, the problem of the relation between perceiving and remembering can be really comprehended. After many years of being accustomed to a scientific terminology, we have to relearn the mother tongue of human experience. We must practice grasping correctly the meaning of such expressions as the wondrous "I was" and the "again." That will make it possible for us to critically repeat the discussions of the problems of time that have occupied the last decades. The contrast between the experienced and the physical world will remind us that all body–mind coordination can be only a coordination of "my experience" with "my brain." New problems force themselves upon us at every step. The familiar meaning of "mine" is suddenly estranged. If the meaning has been regained on a new level, then it becomes doubtful whether the egocentric position of the experiencing man in his world can be at all fitted into the objective impersonal world of the physical space and time systems. Must we follow physics and biology in their descent to the microscopic? Which meaning remains to the macroscopic order—to the natural size of things in the world of living—in which the work of the physicist and the physiologist takes place? All determination of physical processes is always a personal action. It happens in a horizon open to the future. But the discovered determinations, as such, are finite and complete. They are a text in which the temporal order of becoming is replaced by objective symbols of extended time. Therefore, it is doubtful whether the functions of "my brain," as the organ of an experiencing being, can ever be comprehended as a special case of the brain—that brain which is the object of physiological studies. Should we ever regain the clearing in this forest of problems, then we will have returned from our long wandering not with a new answer but with a new kind of questioning.

References

Aristotle. *Parva naturalia. On memory and reminiscence.*

Eccles, J. C. *The neurophysiological basis of mind.* New York: Oxford University Press, 1953.

Fessard, A. E. Mechanisms of nervous integration and conscious experience. In *Brain mechanisms and consciousness.* Springfield, Ill.: Charles C Thomas, 1954.

Galilei, G. *Il saggiatore.* Florence: 1842.

Gerard, R. W. What is memory? *Sci. Amer.*, 1953, 118–126.

Hering, E. *Über das Gedächtnis als eine Funktion der organischen Materie.* Wien: 1870.

Hobbes, T. *Leviathan.*

Husserl, E. *Husserliana.* Vol. 6. Haag: Martinus Nijhoff, 1954.

Lashley, K. S. In search of the engram. In *Physiological mechanisms in animal behavior.* Cambridge: Cambridge University Press, 1950. Pp. 454–482.

Semon, R. *Die Mneme als erhaltendes Prinzip im Wechsel des organischen Lebens.* Leipzig: Engelmann, 1904.

Rapaport, D. *Emotions and memory.* New York: International Universities Press, 1942.

CHAPTER FIVE

Awakeness

All work done by man is accomplished in state of awakeness. Growth and metabolism, respiration, and circulation go on even during sleep; but, in order to eat and drink, to find food and shelter no less than to write papers and to read them, we have to be awake. Awakeness is taken as a matter of course; the phenomenon, accordingly, appears self-evident. It seems unnecessary—even superfluous—to speak about awakeness. In court, judge, jury, defendant, and attorneys are expected to be awake. A witness reports while awake what he has once seen with eyes open, wide awake and watchful. Yet, legal codes, although they frequently refer to conditions of clouded consciousness or of dream-like and amnesic states, do not bother to define awakeness. Psychological and philosophical dictionaries also contribute nothing. The literature dealing with dreams and dreaming is immense. The number of references in the bibliography of a recent monograph (Von Sliebenthal, 1953) on dreams exceeds one thousand, but there is hardly any word on awakeness. Even language appears biased; for the nouns "sleep" and "dream" and for the verbs "sleeping" and "dreaming," there are no direct antonyms. Obviously, in practical life, no need is felt for a special word to describe a mode of being that, in any case, is the indispensable condition of all description and ·conversation. Freud (1949), who had so much to say about dreams and the unconscious, states that consciousness, as such, is familiar to everybody and that nothing more can be said about it. True, awakeness is not synonymous with consciousness, for we are also conscious of dreams; they also are experienced. Nevertheless, in the effort to define, wakefulness does not fare much better than consciousness. The distinction is simply taken for granted, at least in the practice of everyday life.

Among philosophers, there are some who do not share the conviction of the man on the street and who find the distinction far from indisputable. Descartes, as is well known, pretends, in the first of the *Meditations*, not to be sure whether he is asleep or awake. Hobbes (1909) calls the sensible qualities fancies, the same waking as dreaming. Freud (1950, p. 129) praises the dream as a "perfectly valid psychic phenomenon."[1] However, such evaluations originate in general methodological and systematic considerations. Eager to obliterate the borderline between sleep and awakeness, all three thinkers, while denying either the disparity or the distinctiveness or the difference in "validity" between the two, make the diversity of dreams and awakeness their theme. They all, just like Sigismund, the hero in Calderòn's *Life Is a Dream*, speak about dreaming while awake. According to Freud, the dream is the *via regia* to the unconscious; but, on this royal road, only those who are awake can travel; and they have to double their vigilance, turning their attention simultaneously to the manifest content and the hidden meaning of the dream. The interpretation of dreams, as all scientific endeavor, is a task and accomplishment of waking men.

Although we may find it difficult, because of the lack of a *genus proximum*, to give an exact definition of awakeness, it is no Herculean task to make a practical distinction between it and dreaming. Indeed, it is easy, and the distinction is most reliable. We are confident that here is an area where we will not make any mistake. In some way, we must have already understood awakeness whenever we distinguish between dreaming and being awake, but, as so often, we find ourselves embarrassed in trying to give a full account of the conditions and actions most familiar to us. We discover our ignorance where we have felt most secure. St. Augustine's famous dictum[2] is not applicable to a definition of time alone.

In any case, while awake, we have more to say about dreams than about the waking state itself. We know that dreams come during sleep, that in sleep the sensory contacts with the environment are suspended, that the motorium is in abeyance, and that the dreamer is excluded from communication with others. He is quartered in his private world.[3] He

---

[1] Freud (1950, p. 129) says, "The dream is not comparable to the irregular sounds of a musical instrument, which, instead of being played by the hand of a musician, is struck by some external force; the dream is not meaningless, not absurd, does not presuppose that one part of our store of ideas is dormant while another part begins to awake. It is a perfectly valid psychic phenomenon, actually a wish-fulfilment; it may be enrolled in the continuity of the intelligible psychic activities of the waking state; it is built up by a highly complicated intellectual activity."

[2] "What is time? When nobody asks me, I know; if I want to explain it to someone inquiring about it, I do not know" (Book XI).

[3] See Heraclitus' Fragment 89 (in Bakewell, 1939).

does not see, but he has visions; he does not leave his bed, but his dreams carry him away to the most distant regions; he does not communicate with us in a common world, but he talks to the people in his dreams. The dreamer does not realize that he is the creator of his dreams; he is a captive of his own creation. We are all overpowered by the reality of the dream world. Waking experience, repeated day after day, does not help us; it is not continued into dream and sleep. Only after awaking is the dream that overwhelmed me turned into a dream that I have had. During sleep, the dream was not mine; I was a part of the dream world, which I could not recognize as mine. Sleep and dream interfere with the possibility of establishing and realizing primary Mineness.

With all this, we measure the dreamer by standards alien to his experience. We describe the dream, so to speak, from outside, but we cannot look at awakeness from outside. There is no further retreat possible. The understanding of awakeness must be intrinsic to awakeness itself. Yet, perhaps the deficiencies of the dream state could help us to discover the characteristics of awakeness. What dreaming lacks should be significant for an understanding of awakeness.

Awake, we distinguish between dream and awakeness; we know that we are awake. Sleeping, we dream of being "on the job"; we do not know that we dream. The capacity to distinguish may then be taken as the second criterion, for the manifest dream, which alone interests us here, is not merely lacking in such particular distinctions as those between red and green, Jones and Smith, New York and New Orleans. Even if the dreamer were to make distinctions, they would not "stay put"; all demarcations are in flux. Dream visions are lacking in weight and substance. There is no selfsame "subjectum" which binds the sequence of views in a systematic order. There are adumbrations, but there is no identifiable What. The dream does not condense, as Freud assumed, many "elements" into one; the dreamer is incapable of stabilizing discriminations. Awake, we are able to distinguish; we not only discriminate while awake but also we distinguish, first of all, between dreaming and being awake. The distinction of the *two regions*—dream and awakeness—in general, is fundamental to all others.

In making this distinction, we know about ourselves; we know that we are awake and thereby know about the possibility of being in a different state. On waking up, I discover that I have slept, namely, during the night just past. Together with the particularity of my present, I know its limitations. I experience my present as my being thus-and-so, together with my being not this-or-that. The distinction is not simply one between dreaming and awakeness: I distinguish between my being awake and my dreaming—to be more explicit, between my being awake and my having dreamed. The distinction is, therefore, a biographical one, related to my life history and its temporal order. With the distinction between dreaming and awakeness, I comprehend the well-ordered temporality of my existence. I notice that I move every moment from one phase to another. Awake, I know about myself and thereby about my today and yesterday. I comprehend the continuity of my existence, lasting through sleep and dream into the present.

In our waking existence, each day is connected with the past and prepares the future. Our "days" consist of days and nights, but only the days are entered into the context of our life history. The events of the day carry the legend "to be continued," but dreams are not delivered as serials. A dream of one night does not follow up the dream of the preceding night. We do not pick up the thread of a dream where we left off the previous night, as, at the beginning of a day, we resume the theme of our life history where we laid it down. Even if the same theme should last through the dreams of several nights, the dreamer is not aware of this connection. While he is dreaming, he does not remember the dream of the preceding night; he certainly does not remember it as a dream. There are the so-called repetitive dreams; as often as they recur, however, the dreamer experiences the same situation as a new event, actual and present—a kind of *jamais vu*. He does not experience it as repetition. Only in the continuity of the waking state can one, as the same one, return to the same spot. Awake, we remember our dreams, but we separate this remembrance from all memories of our waking state. These memories belong to the continuous text of our life histories; not so the dreams. The dreams are different from all that has actually once happened and, furthermore, from everything that could have actually happened. Indeed, we never reproduce a dream as it occurred to us during sleep, for, just when we comprehend it as a dream, we already have performed a basic change.

One may object that the dreamer also remembers, that the manifest contents of dreams are memories which are distorted, to be sure, but still memories. This may be so, but, in dreaming, memories are not experienced as memories; the dreamer drifts in memories that do not occur to him as such; they occur as present, only to make way for others also present. Dream images are not timeless; much happens in dreams, but the order of time dissolves; it withers away. Moments following one another are no longer in a manifest, meaningful context; *sequence is without consequence*. There rarely is unity of time, of space, or of action. While the stage and the actors undergo the most amazing metamorphoses, the dreamer is not in the least surprised. He experiences only the momentary, actual "being thus" of the dream landscape, incapable of actualizing any possibility of its being different. Dreams are anacoluthic and anachronistic.

On waking, we realize that we have slept; in dreaming, we do not realize that we were previously awake. On waking, we realize that we were carried by our dreams to distant countries while we actually lay in our bed; in our dreams, while visiting such countries, we do not realize that we went to bed and fell asleep. Yet, the dreamer does not "assume" that he is awake. He has no choice between various possibilities, like being awake or not awake. Such a choice—the necessary condition of assumption and belief—is open to us only when we are awake. The dreamer is overwhelmed by the actuality of the dream world.

Greeting the new day after a restful night, I identify myself, now awake, with the one who slept. The identification, however, is not complete; it is limited to the biological level. I take cognizance of the fact that my life, running through a cycle of wakefulness and sleep, was extended through the silent hours of the night. In a statement like "I slept well," the pronoun "I" has a dual meaning. It signifies me, the speaker who is awake (whoever makes such a statement is awake; a sleeper may talk in his sleep, but he does not speak about sleep), but it also signifies me as the one who slept.[4] Obviously, the speaker does not mean to say that he was awake while he slept but that he passed through different modes of being without losing his identity. He integrates sleep and dreams in his vital existence; at the same time, he eliminates them from his actual life history where day is welded to day.

Waking, we experience the beginning of a new day. Waking has its place in the order of world time. There is no corresponding experience in sleep and dreaming. Although dreams may have a temporal arrangement of their own, no clock announces to the sleeper the beginning of sleeping and dreaming. Dreams are not recorded in the continuum of time; but the moment we arouse from sleep, when we "come back" to ourselves and to the world, we are concerned, more often than not, with the question "What time is it?" Through this question, I relate the ac-

---

[4] In grammar, the tenses of the verb are enumerated side by side; yet, there is always a double aspect of time hidden in the usage of past and future. The words "I wrote" express the fact that I performed an act of writing some time in the past, although, at present, I am not writing but speaking about myself. The past must be related to and distinguished from the present. Language, through the grammatical form of the past tense, expresses only one term of that relation, while it leaves it to the very act of speaking to express the other—the present—by implication. This typical formal difference between past and present approaches, with reference to sleep, a degree of disparity.

tual present—this moment Now which always is my own personal Now —to the embracing order of the world. The answer to the question "What time is it?" assigns to this moment Now its place within the framework of the twenty-four hours of the day. Question and answer are related to the current day comprised as a whole, i.e., to a day still incomplete and unfinished.[5] We try to locate the actual moment as a point in a temporal continuum extended beyond the present. Whatever the question may be, it singles out one moment on the dial in its totality. We determine our now and here descending from the whole of time and space. At dawn, "early" and "late" are qualifications of the actual moment in relation to the time ahead. Six o'clock determines "on the clock" one point in relation to hours past and hours still to come.[6] Six o'clock has a meaning only through its position between five and seven, between dawn and sunset, morning and night, and, ultimately, between the preceding and the following midnight. The familiar word "today" signifies a day as a whole, although no one has ever directly experienced this or any other day as a whole. Whenever we ask for the time, we do it, say, in the morning or in the afternoon, always limited to the present; nevertheless, we relate our question to a continuum, a whole, which is potentially accessible to us although it is actually incomplete. In the continuum of time, we realize the continuity of our existence. Waking marks for us the beginning of a new day, because, awake, we experience our existence within the horizon of the future and the past—because we are able to reach beyond the borders of the actual moment.

As daybreak, or any other beginning, is the first in a series of events still to come, we must be directed to the future—ahead of ourselves—in order to comprehend a start, an opening, a prelude. Science determines events in relation to the past; they are understood as the last in a series.

[5] We deem it redundant to say "What time is it today?" but this is what we actually mean. The corresponding French idiom *Quelle heure est-il?* more precisely asks the question: What hour is it, namely, of this day?

[6] We may well remember that clocks and watches are human artifacts, that hours and minutes are established by convention. But neither should we forget that the experience of time is not a human invention and that the possibility of articulating the continuum is not due to any convention, whatever the arbitrarily chosen unit of measurement may be. Watches made in these days are far superior to the old sundials and hourglasses; there is no progress in the anticipation of the future and in the remembrance of the past. A "primitive" man will have little difficulty in familiarizing himself with our method of chronometry. Most of the patients whom we call, in psychiatry, "disoriented in time" still comprehend what the words "today" and "tomorrow," "morning" and "night," "week" and "month" signify, although they may be unable to tell their age, give the date, or report the chronicle of their life. Chronological information and chronometry suffer under conditions other than the experience of time in the various aspects of its continuity.

The role that anomalies of time refraction plays in the pathology of speech and memory will be discussed elsewhere.

Yet, in the practice of experiencing and observing, the scientist watches a development from its beginning to its end. He turns his attention to the future. When the horizon of the future is suddenly "blacked out," as happens in accidents, the present itself can no longer be apprehended; as a rule, amnesia caused by a head injury is retrograde. Sleep, contracting the temporal horizon, produces a mild retrograde amnesia. Hence, the transition from sleep to wakefulness is clearly marked; the transition from wakefulness to sleep is not.

The conviction shared by everybody in the practice of life, our habitual conviction that we are able to distinguish with all desirable accuracy between dream and waking experience, seems not unfounded, notwithstanding Descartes' professed bewilderment "that there are no certain indications by which we may clearly distinguish wakefulness from sleep" (1955, pp. 145-146). In the search for criteria, Descartes compared the illusions of dreams with the hallucinations of the insane and found them alike. He compared both with details of his actual situation[7] and found all of them equally deceptive. He did not compare dreaming with being awake; he did not compare the transition from dream to wakefulness with that from wakefulness to dream, but he focused his attention on singular "thoughts" cut off from the context of experience and claimed that "all the same thoughts and conceptions which we have while awake may also come to us in sleep" (1955, p. 101).

The dream argument, repeated with slight variations in the *Discourse on Method*, the *Meditations*, and the *Principles of Philosophy*, was, in Descartes's opinion, a necessary step on the way to the pronouncement of the first principle of philosophy. It helped him to destroy man's confidence in the natural world through an apparently irrefutable evaluation of everyday-life experience. Although the dream argument precedes and prepares the *Cogito*, it presupposes, nevertheless, the validity of Descartes's metaphysics.

At the start, Descartes acknowledges that dreams and waking states are different; although he insists that he could not find any certain marks for distinction, he must have found some indications sufficient to discriminate between the two. Yet, instead of defining the difference, he tells a story: "How often has it happened to me that in the night I dreamt that I found myself in this particular place, that I was dressed

---

[7] Descartes said, "For example, there is the fact that I am here, seated by the fire, attired in a dressing gown, having this paper in my hands and other similar matters" (1955, pp. 145–146).

and seated near the fire, whilst in reality I was lying undressed in bed" (Descartes, 1955, p. 145).

Here Descartes spoke in the vernacular, like one who still has confidence in the world which, as Descartes hurried to say, might have been created by an evil demon. This example taken from everyday life was used to show that, while in dreams we are spellbound by our "thoughts," awake we discover their illusory character. Awake, we are able to gain an insight inaccessible to the sleeper. Descartes, at first, did not deny that the waking state is superior to the dream; but then he reversed himself and used the discovery made in wakefulness to discredit the reliability of all sensory experience. He resolved "to assume that everything that ever entered into my mind was no more true than the illusions of my dreams" (1955, p. 101). Even so, there remains a decisive difference: Descartes was sure that his dreams were illusions, but he forced himself to assume that the same could be said about "everything that ever entered into my mind." Descartes was very cautious: "My astonishment is such," he wrote, "that it is almost capable of persuading me that I now dream" (1955, p. 146).

To support this assumption, Descartes introduced the theorem that "all the same thoughts and concepts which we have while awake may also come to us in sleep" (1955, pp. 16–21). However, in the example chosen from everyday life, he did not use the "same thoughts" but let the dreamer dream that he was seated by the fire to discover on awakening that he was lying in bed. At this point, he did not reveal why the thoughts of one who awakens in his bed should belie the thoughts of his dreams. Indeed, if both dreams and waking experience consisted of congeries of single thoughts and if the "same thoughts" occurred in both conditions, none of these single thoughts would prove its superiority. Following each other in time, the illusory character of one group of them could not be demonstrated. As there is no mark which allows a distinction, all of them may just as well be true as illusory.[8] There would be no chance even to conceive of an illusion. The victim of illusions is not aware of his condition; only one who stands on safer ground is able to clear up an illusion. The observation that I dreamed of sitting near the fire while, when awake, I found myself lying in bed demands that I remember the images of my dream. The thoughts of the dream are still

_____

[8] Descartes wanted to treat dreams and awakeness as peers. However, if they cannot be clearly distinguished, we may just as well assume that we are awake when we dream as that we dream when we are awake. Descartes "wondered whether all life was not a permanent dream" (1955, p. 148). While Hobbes and Calderòn followed suit, Freud preferred the other alternative.

present in waking states, but they are present as memories. They have a temporal character different from actual sensory experience. To distinguish—even in a superficial manner—between dream and awakeness, dreams must be carried over into the waking state. Memory—or, better, remembering—mediates between dreaming and being awake. When we recall a dream, we are aware that the "dream thoughts" remembered at present belong to the past, and we also realize that we dreamed when we experienced these thoughts. The redistribution of "thoughts" to the two regions of dream and waking states follows their synopsis in wakefulness where "there are three times: a present of things past, a present of things present, and a present of things future" (St. Augustine, Book XI). Sleep reduces the temporal tones; accordingly, the articulation of time vanishes in dreams.

In full agreement with everyday experience, Descartes noticed that, when awake, we discover the illusory character of our dreams, but, in his interpretation of this discovery, he assumed that thereby the epithet "illusion" was to be fixed to a thought that came to us in sleep. Such thoughts—as, for instance, the "thought" of the fireplace—acquire, in Descartes' presentation, a strange resemblance to material things. Should we later on actually see the fireplace again, this would mean, according to Descartes, that the "same thought" came to us while awake. Although, when awake, we are not aware of the label "illusion" fixed to that thought, there it is—and the mark is indelible. To detect it, we have to turn things upside down, like a piece of china which carries its stamp on the bottom.

In the original version, an actual experience of the fireplace preceded the dream experience; but, in the interpretation following the example, Descartes inverted this natural order—the dream thought was given priority over wakefulness. Supposedly, it returned as the same—although stamped "illusion"—to the realm of wakefulness. Yet, the one who awakens in his bed and recalls his dream actually compares two different memories: the fireplace once seen in the room nearby and the one appearing in his dreams. He realizes that the condition of the actual sight of the fireplace agrees with his present situation in general, while the dream appears to him to be deficient. The label "illusion" attached to the dream thought gains its meaning only in relation to the state of wakefulness. Descartes presented, however, the illusory character of the dream as if the relation to awakeness could be severed without erasing the stamp "illusion." He ascribes to the dream thought, with its stamp, a kind of independent existence. The illusory character of the dream proves contagious and infects the experience of the waking state. The initial lack of absolute certainty has been turned into absolute uncertainty.

Our life runs through a circle of wakefulness and sleep. In general, we believe that these two modes of being cover the whole of our existence. Therefore, if we cannot "with certainty distinguish whether the thoughts that come to us in sleep are as false as are the others" (Descartes, 1955, p. 220), how could we ever discover and ultimately avoid all the illusions? Is there a third condition, besides dreaming and being awake, that enables us to judge both of them? Descartes claimed that such a state existed. It is the *res cogitans* that alone can and must be entrusted with that task.

The Cartesian system did not allow its author to acknowledge a relevant difference between dream and wakefulness, for they are biological phenomena; they are connected with the body. The thinking substance always thinks; it never rests. If the body goes to sleep, dreams present themselves to consciousness; if the body is awake, sensations appear. As consciousness *(cogitatio ipsa, cogitatio sive natura cogitans)* comprises the various *actus cogitandi* (knowing, wanting, perceiving, etc.) as its modes, the relation of consciousness (or *cogitatio*) in the wider sense to the individual *cogitationes* remains one and the same, whatever the actual modifications may be (Descartes, 1955, p. 222). Consciousness, confined to its *cogitationes*, searches for certain indications by which to distinguish the ideas which come while the body is asleep from those which come while the body is awake. Considering them in their isolation, it fails to discover definite marks. However, in considering them in their context, it succeeds in judging that some of them are real and others not. The attribute "real" means that, in the so-called outside world, something corresponds more or less directly to some "thoughts" occurring in consciousness. "Reality" cannot be experienced immediately.

The theorem "that all the same thoughts and concepts which we have while awake may also come to us in sleep" has no basis in the experience of everyday life; it presupposes the Cartesian transmutation of the natural world. It presupposes that one could doubt the reality of things seen without doubting the reality of seeing. It presupposes that sensory experience must be reduced to sensory data—to thoughts (perceptions) that enter and leave the mind on different occasions and under varying conditions. It presupposes that one could reduce the experiencing, living person to an incorporeal mind—a thinking substance—and, nevertheless, continue to speak about awakeness and dreams. However, justified doubt of the reliability of everyday-life experience does not silence the senses. Descartes could conceive of himself as a thinking substance; but, while pretending to have no hands, no eyes, no flesh, no blood, nor any senses, he could not actually transform himself into a *res cogitans*. The writer of the *Meditations* is not an incorporeal Cartesian ego but remains René Descartes, the man, who, while making himself an object of his reflection, expresses his findings through the medium of human language that will say, also, through bodily motion and sensation. In meditating, in doubting and arguing, in denying any valid distinction between dreaming and waking, Descartes did not speak from his dreams but wrote fully awake and alert.

Toward the end of the sixth day, when Descartes had re-created man and saw that he had accomplished his task "to build anew from the foundation" (1955, p. 144), he was willing to concede a limited degree of trustworthiness to the old creation.[9] He rejected the doubts of "bygone days" as hyperbolic and ridiculous, especially the general uncertainty concerning sleep, which he did not distinguish from the waking state.

And, as a matter of fact, if some one, while I was awake, quite suddenly appeared to me and disappeared as fast as do the images which I see in sleep, so that I could not know from whence the form came nor whither it went, it would not be without reason that I should deem it a spectre or a phantom formed by my brain, rather than a real man. But when I perceive things as to which I know distinctly both the place from which they proceed, and that in which they are, and the time at which they appeared to me; and when, without any interruption, I can connect the perceptions which I have of them with the whole course of my life, I am perfectly assured that these perceptions occur while I am waking and not during sleep (Descartes, 1955, pp. 198-199).

Although Descartes finally referred to the "whole course of his life," his demonstration was not yet convincing. Since the irregularity of appearance and disappearance, in his first example, did not lead him to the assumption that he was asleep but persuaded him that something was wrong on the side of the visible object, the regularity of visible events could not establish the certainty of being awake. An experience such as the one mentioned by Descartes is, in our day, not unfamiliar to the many people who enjoy television. There, it can be that a young man, putting his hands around the neck of his sweetheart to choke her,

---

[9] Descartes provides the reader with several clues that the fiction of six days' meditating was chosen as an allusion to Genesis, rather than dictated by the natural articulation of the text.

disappears all of a sudden while a young lady singing the praises of some soapsuds takes his place, only to vanish just as miraculously as she entered, permitting the young man to finish his noble task. Being awake, we are able to distinguish and to separate the imaginary space of stage and screen from the space of our corporeal existence and action. The stable order of space and the continuity of time precede the determination of the consistency or inconsistency of events. The moment we open our eyes, rousing ourselves from sleep, we are once again "there" in a world with firmly established orders of time and space, with objects opposite to us upon which we can act. The stability of our waking state is not founded in the realm of logic and judgment; in the stillness of a dark night, while nothing happens, we are able to realize our being awake.

Descartes used seeing and visible objects as examples. Had he written about hearing and sounds, which are in the habit of coming and going haphazardly, he might have realized that awakeness provides for logical operations but is not itself established by inference. It is not from the context and consequences of events that we conclude we are awake; on the contrary, being awake we expect consequences. I have only to look and there are the surroundings, solid and lasting in themselves. Even the unforeseen appears in a field of foresight. If, after awakening, I am unable to orient myself, the question "Where am I?" arises immediately; the place of my existence, still undetermined, is found determinable.

Waking, we are "back again"; we need no scientific apparatus, no footnotes, and no commentaries to realize that we are awake. We do not watch the coming and going of percepts in our minds to cry out at the end: Behold, this is real! We do not look on an "outside world" from which we, conceived as mind, intellect, or consciousness, are in turn excluded; we do not project sensory data, which first occurred in our mind or our brain, into an "outer world." We do not use our eyes and other sense organs like binoculars to watch events on a distant stage; we ourselves are on the stage. Awake, we find ourselves within the world; we experience ourselves in the world, together with the world, in relation to the world. Self-awareness does not precede awareness of the world; the one is not before the other; the one is not without the other. We are not distant observers who, through a curious process of reality testing, scan neutral sensory data and arrange them into two groups—real and unreal. Awake, we experience the power of reality in our action and the world's counteraction—in its resistance and our suffering. We do not wait for science to give its approval. The choice is not between two predicates, real or unreal and true or false. Experienced reality is not the theme of a theoretical proposition. Its counterpart is not unreality but destruction and death. The question is to be or not to be. We experience reality in a personal relationship; it is not detached from us; as a living creature, I am a part of it; it affects me in its dramatic actuality; I am seized and caught. The one who awakens is not a "mind" making judgments—not a "consciousness" attending to an outside world—but a human being experiencing the world in his corporeality. The experience of reality is prelogical; it is not mediated.

That we experience the world and ourselves in our corporeality does not mean that we are aware of our body as an object or consider it as a "body image"; still less does it mean that we add proprioceptive and visceroceptive stimuli to exteroceptive ones. Physiology distinguishes and separates organs, sensorium and motorium, receptors and effectors, afferent and efferent pathways. In a reflex movement, sensory stimulation precedes motor contraction. However, in our actions, we are directed to objects which, in their visibility, lie ahead of us. The motor response can never reach a stimulus, but we, as experiencing beings, move toward a goal. Reflex movements occur within an organism, depending on events in the adjacent space, but you and I sense and move within an environment. The relation "experiencing beings–environment" does not copy the relation "stimulus–nervous system" (see Straus, 1963, pp. 175 ff.). Sensory experience and motility cannot be separated and localized in direct correspondence to sensibility and mobility. Only a motile being, capable of disengaging itself from the ground, can face objects and can meet, in sensory experience, the Other; only a sentient being, to whom an environment is opened, can move spontaneously. (See Buytendijk, 1956.)

Physiology relates the transition from sleep to awakeness to events within the organism—and rightly so. Beyond that, however, awake, we find ourselves in the world. We are there in our corporeality and motility. The physiological and the phenomenological problems of the state of awakeness must be kept clearly apart. The scientist who studies the physiological conditions of sleep is awake. This he takes for granted. He has not had to wait for the results of his experiments to establish the difference between being asleep and being awake. Observing, during his waking hours, the phasic variations of communication with others—men and animals—and interpreting the expressive character of their behavior as symptoms of biological processes within their bodies, he gradually builds up a physiology of sleep and awakeness. Should he succeed in his research, should he acquire the fullest insight—a virtually complete knowledge of everything that goes on in the brain—this information would not add one iota to his personal awareness of being awake. The phenomenology of awakeness, however, may furnish him with meaningful questions in his physiological studies.

Awaking from sleep, we are ready to get up. To arise means to rise against gravity. Experiencing in our corporeality, we find ourselves bound—but not chained—by heaviness; in our ponderosity, we long for levity and buoyancy. In waking and arising, upright and motile, we meet the Other—things as our objects, i.e., ob-jecta, gegen-stände. In opposition to the ground and to the Other, I experience myself and that which is most truly mine—my body. Partial conquest of gravity, lifting us from the ground, assures us of our monadic existence and gives us freedom for action. Yet, all locomotion remains motion in a field of gravity. In our lofty thoughts, we travel in weightless bounds through ages and space; in fantasy, we mount Pegasus and are carried away. In the sensory experience of the waking present, we are pedestrians who can move only step by step, held back by the ballast of corporeal existence. Through our heaviness, we are confined to the Here; through our motility, our ability to conquer gravity and to move, we are potentially over there. The Here, always my here and now, is a mere stopping place en route to other places. The actuality of the present moment is experienced as limitation—as a phase in the continuity of our existence related to a segment of the world. Proceeding continuously from horizon to horizon, a border rather than an end, we, in our heaviness, meet things in their own weight. There is nothing that we can skip; awake, we are held within the cumbrous continuum of the here and now, where the pendulum has to swing through the seconds and minutes and where sequence implies consequence.

Dream and fantasy have been compared not without reason. Notwithstanding some similarities, there is this fundamental difference: As a dreamer, I enter into the dream world, while, in fantasy, I remain master of the situation. Someone indulging in fantasies, submerged in memories, or lost in thought is but detached from the continuity of his corporeal existence. Against this background, fantasies and memories are always contrasted; it constitutes the continuum from which all experience starts and to which it returns. Thus far, sensualism is right; thus far, common-sense opinion is also right when it interprets as real that which we meet in the continuity of our corporeal existence between life and death.

The answer to the question why the dreamer is lost in the dream world is no longer difficult. In sleep, we lie down. The sleeper does not withdraw his interest from the world, as Freud said. Going to sleep, we completely surrender to the world; we abandon our stand opposite to it. Therefore, the sleeper is no longer free and able to conduct himself toward the world, to assert himself and to stand his ground, to hold his own. The primary nonconceptual experience of What is Mine can be realized only while we are awake. The sleeper who disengages the sensomotorium, who renounces the conquest of gravity, has suspended the reality in contrast to which he could conceive of dreams as his dreams. In contraposition to primary experience alone can thoughts be experienced as thoughts, images as images, dreams as dreams. The dream world overwhelms the dreamer; it appears real not in opposition to the unreal but in default of any unreality. A system of invariants is needed if distinctions are to be made and retained. Musicians must tune their instrument to the same pitch and preserve it as the invariant acoustical base. The ghastly noise produced by a victrola when, in its early states, the tension of the spring prematurely faded well illustrates the point under consideration. Intervals can be kept only if an invariant ground permits discrimination. Awake, we are able to recognize an invariant order with and by virtue of change. Being motile, the world appears to us in its persistence. In relation to the permanent, we can change our position.

Not until our sight and the seen have been separated can "the same" persist through many different sights. Not until this happens can we distinguish appearance from the appearing thing and thereby separate the real from the unreal, insight from deception, truth from seeming. When we are awake, we can linger with something, we can repeat an action, we can return to the starting point. Through the perspectives we discover the constancies and through the adumbrations the What. In dreams, we cannot accomplish such a separation. The dreamer, for whom the appearing is not separable from the appearance, lacks the possibility of distinction between reality and sham. The Other, which only as an *ob-jectum* shows itself persistent, does not grow in its own right. This possibility is realized in wakefulness. Awake, therefore, we reach—in the prelinguistic and prelogical sphere of sensory experience—the inchoation of verbal explication and of the logical modes. Corporeality and motility are conditions for the primary, sensory apprehension of the world, as well as for its secondary, scientific interpretation.

Sensory experience opens the world to us and places us in its order, i.e., in a situation where we begin to think and where we progress in our thoughts beyond the boundaries of the initial situation without leaving it completely. The second step could not be made were it not prepared by the first. The universe that is opened up in prescientific and scientific interpretation is not altogether alien to sensory experience. In the order of space visible to us in awakeness, we can establish places and, after having determined them, relate them to each other. In this spatial structure, we can mark borders and discover the equality of distances with the reversibility of the direction of our sight. As we approach an object or see it from a distance, the proportions remain constant. In the world we experience while awake, geometry—the identifiable relation of lines, angles, and proportions—becomes possible. We are not mathematicians solely by virtue of being awake, but, in the world experienced under the conditions of awakeness and in our relation to it, geometry can be built up. Awakeness, physiologically understood, is a condition for mathematics, because mathematics is an interpretation of the world accessible to us while awake, begun with the emancipation of the view from the visible.

In the waking state, we can communicate with ourselves and with others. The dreamer is alone in his dream world. No one else can enter it, nor can the dreamer leave it. The relation of the sleeper to one awake is unilaterally negative. The sleeper cannot place himself in contact with the one awake, as the latter can do with a sleeper. He can watch the sleeper and take care of him, or he can attack him and destroy him. Thieves come during the night. The sleeper is powerless; he is at the mercy of the one awake. Only after "coming back" out of sleep, regaining power over himself, can he retaliate, approach, or evade. All communication, it seems, is based on being together in the synkinetics of meeting and fleeing. We do not discover the alter ego by either inference or empathy; the Other is not a thing of peculiar characteristics marked against a neutral background. I discover the Other as a fellow creature, as a partner in waking intention of motion, as a being who, within the world, may approach me or leave me alone in a meaningful counteraction.

The traditional definition of man as a rational animal has frequently been interpreted to mean that one has to conquer the animal in order to be rational—that rationality has to be severed from animal existence. Considering awakeness, one may find that rationality originates in and issues from the animal nature, i.e., from corporeality and motility. While man transcends the boundaries of his here and now, he remains bound to the original situation.

References

Bakewell, C. M. *Source book in ancient philosophy.* (Rev. ed.) New York: Charles Scribner's, 1939.

Buytendijk, F. J. J. *Allgemeine Theorie der menschlichen Haltung und Bewegung.* Berlin, Göttingen & Heidelberg: Springer-Verlag, 1956.

Descartes, R. *Meditations on first philosophy. Discourse on method. The principles of philosophy.* E. S. Haldane & G. R. T. Ross (Trans.) New York: Dover, 1955.

Freud, S. *An outline of psychoanalysis.* New York: Norton, 1949.

Freud, S. *The interpretation of dreams.* (3rd ed.) New York: Macmillan, 1950.

Hobbes, T. *Leviathan.*

von Liebenthal, W. *Die Wissenschaft vom Traum.* Berlin, Göttingen & Heidelberg: Springer-Verlag, 1953.

St. Augustine. *Confessions.*

Straus, E. W. *The primary world of senses.* New York: The Free Press, 1963.

CHAPTER SIX

Objectivity

The balance and the sword are the traditional emblems of justice. To these, the artists of the thirteenth and fourteenth centuries added a third symbol. In their allegorical representations, Justitia, carrying sword and balance, appears with her eyes covered by a bandage. The bandage over the eyes did not symbolize an unconscious wish to use the sword blindly, without looking at the scale. Rather, it was thought that the judge, as guardian of equality before the law, ought to deliver his judgment without regard for person; he must close his eyes to the status, the power, and the wealth of the parties. With slight changes, present-day clinical research could adopt this allegory of justice as its own. It would need only to replace the sword with the pen, keep the scale, and reinforce the bandage with a second layer. "Double blind" has become a password for good experimental planning. But there is a pregnant difference between the past and the present. The bandage of Justitia indicates an ideal rather than a real situation. No one doubts that it requires almost superhuman efforts to satisfy the ideal of impartiality—this sublime form of objectivity. "Double blind" is no symbol of human effort. On the contrary, it is the name of a technical safety device to make up for human weaknesses. A machine or a machine-like arrangement is expected to reduce the moral demands made on the researcher and, finally, to do away entirely with the human factor which threatens the results of observation and research. We might well ask whether and how far such expectations are justified.

The word "objective" characterizes and evaluates a statement. It points, accordingly, regardless of where it applies, to the speaker's attitude of objectivity. The logical form of a statement, the linkage with exact measurement, or the use of mathematical expressions are no guarantee of objectivity. Consider the following report: "At 18.20 hours I switched on the electric crucible; thirty-one seconds later the manometer showed the pressure increasing rapidly. An explosion threw me to the floor. I escaped from the inferno with the greatest difficulty. . . ." Such a report by no means excludes the possibility that the speaker himself started the conflagration. Truthfulness on the part of the observer is, thus, the first and indispensable condition of objectivity. Although the claim is made that there are lie detectors available, there are, at the moment, no truth detectors on the market. Only they who are liable to err can find the truth; only they who are able to keep the truth silent are capable of sincerity. Without such inner freedom of judgment and expression, no statement would have significance.

In everyday life, in politics, business, and society, rectitude does not always reach the saturation point. Advertising occasionally exaggerates the virtues of the articles being praised. The scientist, on the other hand, is supposed to act as a "professor," i.e., as someone who makes known his observations and conclusions without regard for his personal advantage and ambitions. In the tournament between truth and fame, fame is not always the loser. Scientific findings and views at times threaten established interests. The profession of science occasionally demands personal commitment and courage.

With the best of intentions to integrity, it is impossible to prevent particular expectations from coloring observation. The investigator is faced with a personal dilemma: Objectivity requires that he renounce all personal interests; but he cannot do research without being personally engaged. Inescapably, he foresees certain results and prefers one outcome to another; if he were completely indifferent and nonpartisan, he would be virtually unable to find any problems. With the formulation of a problem, he has already taken the side of a particular answer. He cannot remain a neutral observer. The schema of isolating a single variable, formulating a hypothesis, and testing it by statistical means is a robot ideal, rarely realized by a human being. Scientific reliability demands, nevertheless, that one presents himself with the arguments of both parties, appears as the advocate of both sides, and, further, plays the role of the judge who weighs the pros and cons in sovereign fashion.

To make progress at the same time one does justice to the nature of the problem depends, in no little measure, on the knowledge of the investigator. The novice is not in a position to make the same observations as the person with experience. Furthermore, the results depend on a talent for observation and a gift for happy formulation. But, even so, we have not yet finished enumerating the factors which can compromise personal dependability. The exactness of observations is controlled by the personal equation. Experiments are jeopardized by the Heisenberg principle of indeterminacy. Even in the macroscopic sphere, the experimental activity can alter the situations whose characteristics are to be investigated.

It is not surprising that a strong need for automatic controls has made itself felt. The steadily growing number of investigators and their publications motivates the search for methods to neutralize human weaknesses. "Double blind" is only one among many methods serving to increase the factor of dependability. The one-way mirror that owes its popularity originally to the primitive delight in secret observation finds methodological justification in the expectation that, by using it, it may be possible to limit the power of the Heisenberg factor. The manifold tests from whose application one hopes to secure material for quantitative and statistical evaluation are well known. Mechanically drawn up protocols simplify the task of the observer; he will ultimately be limited to the reading of pointer indices, and the observational "lag," as expressed in the personal equation, will be eliminated. Nevertheless, success is never realized without sacrifice. The proverb *"Naturam expellas furca tamen usque recurret"* also holds for our case. Human nature does not allow itself to be excluded from human undertakings. While it is doubtlessly true that many circumstances endanger objectivity, the exclusion of these circumstances does not yet add up to objectivity. The factors that endanger objectivity are more likely to be covered up than controlled by mechanical preventive measures.

In our attempt to explicate objectivity in an objective manner, we are moving in a circle. But that is unavoidable. Just as the investigator of language is compelled to make use of language in his researches, so the logician is unable to dispense with logic in his analysis of logical forms. Still, we may be able to improve our position by taking a look at objectivity from the vantage point of a neighboring sphere. Since objective methods have become very popular today, we can take up an observation point close at hand. At the race track—perhaps because of lack of trust in the absolute impartiality of the judges or from doubt of their ability to grasp minimal differences in rapid change with the unaided eye—an electronic photo device has been introduced. Photo-finish photography makes it possible for the judges to determine the winner when he wins merely by "a nose." While such precision reduces the number of dead heats, there are, from the standpoint of philosophical hippology, serious problems that lead us back to the question of objectivity. A somewhat odd story—it sounds almost like a fairy tale—may clarify this situation.

Horse and Trainer: A Fable

There was once a Derby winner by the name of Rocketpower. One day, on the beautiful race track of Keeneland in Lexington, Kentucky, he met with his great opponent, Happylegs. In the opinion of all those who were able to closely observe the finish, it was a dead heat. The judges, however, decided, after a thorough study of the finish-line photos, that Happylegs had won by a nose. When the horses had been returned to their stalls and their saddles removed, Joe, who was Rocketpower's trainer, patted his horse on the neck and said, "Rocky, if you only had a longer nose."

The horse turned around to him, looked at him silently for a long time, and then—then it suddenly began to talk.

"What do you mean by that, Joe?"

For the first moment, the trainer was baffled, but he quickly recovered from his surprise. He had spent his whole life with horses and had talked with them every day. He never doubted in the least that they understood each word. Deep within, he cherished the conviction that they could answer but that they refrained from speaking out of wisdom and pride. So, without further ado, he took up the conversation.

"The photo-finish picture showed that you lost by a nose length," he said.

"What," said the horse, "I, Rocketpower, the son of Rocky Mountain out of Panacea, I'm supposed to have lost? By a nose length? That's a laugh! Above all, the hoofs and not the nose ought to decide."

When we talk with animals, we all have the tendency to talk with a certain condescension. Joe was no exception. In a pedagogic tone, as if speaking to a fourteen-year-old boy, he observed:

"One can compare a race with an experiment in which the speed is to be determined. The distance is the independent variable; the time is the dependent variable. Consequently, we simply measure the time."

"But a nose length is not a unit of time!"

"Not directly, but since you horses all gallop over the same distance, we let your position count as an indicator of time."

"But we haven't all run the same stretch. You should know that! At the start, Happylegs, the lucky dog, naturally had the number-one position, and where was my place? Way on the outside! That makes more than a nose length, doesn't it?"

"I would guess a couple hundred nose lengths," Joe said.

"So you agree that, at the start, a few hundred nose lengths don't matter, but, at the finish, one nose length decides the whole race."

"You're not so far from right. And, still, it's not so; we look at the whole thing *as if* all horses ran exactly the same distance."

"I don't understand what you mean by this 'as if.' "

"I mean, we simply posit the equality. It's a convention."

"A convention can't change the facts."

"You *are* old-fashioned!" Joe retorted. "It's certainly true that horses don't belong in the age of the automobile. Conventions don't have to alter facts; they make them."

"Maybe I'm old-fashioned, but it's still an unfair method. When a nose length doesn't count at the start, then it shouldn't be counted at the finish line."

"There's something to that," said Joe, and then solemnly, as if he were reciting, he continued, "In the evaluation of a work, the measuring instrument must be commensurable with the achievement."

"Stop using such big words, Joe, you're only making fun of me."

"I'm not making fun of you. I'm taking you as seriously as a talking brute deserves to be taken."

"Am I a brute?" Rocky asked.

Rocky really didn't know whether he should feel himself flattered or insulted. His education was spotty; self-taught, he was limited to the little that he was able to pick up from the conversations in his immediate surroundings. Still, the trainer's friendly glance instilled trust in Rocky.

"Joe, can you tell me how long Happy's nose is?"

"I would judge four inches."

"And what was the distance of the race?"

"A mile. Why all these questions? Oh, I think I see! You want me to compare the length of the race course with the length of a nose."

Then, as if to himself, he said, "I've got to find a common denominator. A mile has 1,670 yards, a yard has thirty-six inches. The race," he said, concluding his calculations, "covered a distance of more than 62,000 inches. A nose length is approximately 1/16,000th of the whole."

"16,000?" repeated Rocky with a blank expression.

"Not 16,000, Rocky, I am talking about 1/16,000th. Listen closely. You have four legs; one of them is a fourth of the total number. The flies that bother you so much have six legs; one of these is a sixth of the total number. A spider. . . ."

Rocky broke in impatiently. "Are there any animals with 16,000 legs?"

"You mustn't think only about legs. We use mere numbers as pure forms so to speak."

"Have you ever counted to 16,000?"

"That isn't necessary. We can work with numbers because we know exactly how they are constructed. You don't have to count them beforehand. Everyone knows that 16,000 is larger by one than 15,999, that it is smaller by one than 16,001, that we divide 16,000 in four equal parts of 4,000 parts in each one, and that we cannot divide it in three equal parts."

"Can numbers be seen?" Rocky asked.

"No. Groups can be seen and enumerated. The numbers themselves can't be seen."

"If they are invisible, how can one apply them to what is visible?"

"Perhaps I can get across my meaning better this way," said the trainer as he pulled some hairs from the horse's mane. "Now look! If I put 16,000 such hairs on top of one another, that would just about reach to the height of your shoulders. Naturally, I mean in terms of its thickness and not of its length. Therefore, one might say that you've lost by a hair's breadth."

Joe smiled, gratified by his own joke, but Rocky didn't leave him much time to enjoy himself.

"Why should a hair's breadth make Happylegs the winner and me a poor second? Are humans accustomed to handling their affairs with such precision? Are your races also decided in terms of nose lengths?"

"Good Lord!" Joe cried. "After all, there are differences!"

Rocky, like many animals, had a sensitive ear for nuances of tone. He sensed that the trainer spoke of equines with a certain contempt. His long-restrained anger erupted. Whinnying and stamping, Rocky worked himself into a wild and growing excitement.

"I'll never run a race again in my life!"

Now it was the trainer's turn to lose his composure. He was only too well acquainted with the sensitive temperament of the thoroughbred. Rocky had to be soothed.

"Of course you're right," he said. "You are the fastest horse in the world. To let these four inches decide is nonsense. But you must understand that a race track must have winners. A dead heat brings in less to the parimutuel; it scares away the betters. If it should happen repeatedly, the track would lose money, and the breeders would ultimately stop breeding horses. Under such circumstances, there would probably never have been a Rocketpower. We turf people adhere to this basic principle: All horses are created unequal. So, we agree to accept a few more inequalities into the bargain. Short and sweet, photo-finish photography, even if it isn't fair, as you've observed, is nevertheless utilitarian or, as one also says, pragmatically justified."

Joe's friendly words softened Rocky's anger. After a short pause he said, "Can I see such a photograph?"

"Glad to show you," said the trainer, drawing a photograph from his pocket.

The horse eyed it, sniffed it, and nibbled it. Then he shook his head and said, "I don't know what that is. Perhaps it's paper, but one thing is sure—it isn't a horse. Look at me—my flanks, my chest, my whole form."

"You've got to understand," Joe said, "this is a photograph, a picture; see, that's your nose."

"What are you talking about! That's my nose?" Rocky gently bit the trainer on his arm and said, "Now you know where my mouth and my nose are."

The trainer laughed a bit embarrassedly and repeated, "Please try to understand. I'm showing you a picture that only represents you and the other horses."

"All right. I see the picture now, here with my own eyes. How can you insist that I am, at the same time, seeing what took place an hour ago? I can't see both at the same time. Can you?"

"Yes, I think I can," Joe replied. "If I study this photograph or, as you term it, this paper, then I see you and the other horses in a certain way."

"Look at me," Rocky said, "can you see me now?"

"Yes."

"Do you see any of the other horses?"

"No."

"But you've just asserted that you've seen me and the other horses in this picture. Do you mean to say that you've seen it with your own eyes?"

"Certainly. Exactly."

Since the trainer had nothing further to add, Rocky shook his head incredulously and continued with his questions.

"What I still wanted to say was that it was burning hot during the race. But, on the paper, I don't feel that at all."

"Heat can't be represented on a photograph."

"And how about hay?"

"Yes, that's possible. It can be photographed."

"Can one eat it?"

"No."

"So in the picture you can set forth things seen. Smells, tastes, heat you can't reproduce. Why only seen things?"

"I don't know," Joe answered. "But let's go back a little bit. When a cook tries a dish, then he takes a bit—that is, a bite, a tiny part of it. That gives him a foretaste. Similarly, with odors and materials; it is always a test or a sample of the entire stuff. With a photograph, it is different. It isn't a sample or a test nor anything taken from the figured object. A picture is a representation that speaks directly to the eye. There is nothing that resembles a picture for the taste, smell, or feeling."

"Why is that so?" Rocky asked.

"I can't tell you," said Joe. "I haven't studied. You must ask a psychologist. They have certainly reflected about it."

Joe's words had an unexpected effect. Rocketpower grabbed the photograph from the trainer's hand, let it fall to the ground, and stamped around on it.

"What are you doing, what's the idea?"

"Don't you see?" Rocky said. "Now I'm ruining your picture."

"What, by the way, do you hope to gain by destroying this single photograph? There are many, many more copies of it."

"Now how am I supposed to understand that?" Rocky asked. "After all, we only ran one single race. Are there *many* pictures of one race? And does every one show the same event?"

"An event cannot be duplicated," Joe explained. "But you can preserve it in an image and then reproduce it as often as you like. One can, as I've said, make many copies, and each one is objective in the same way."

"How many all together?"

"As many as you want. A couple of hundred more or less doesn't make any difference. A race like this one will probably be shown in one of the picture magazines; thousands, even millions, of people will see it."

"And each one of them will be looking at another copy?"

"Finally you've seen the light!" Joe exclaimed. "The people can be miles apart from one another, or they can be in the same room; they can look at the picture together, or someone will examine it today and another one tomorrow. But, in each case, they all see the same picture. I mean, each of them goes over one of the many representations of the single unique event. Excuse me, I'm using such long words again. I'm not doing it to annoy you."

"Joe, the people who wanted to see our race had to come to Keeneland on a certain day, but you can carry a picture with you wherever you go."

"A creature of flesh and blood like yourself is tied down to a definite place. When I want to see you, then I have to come to you here in the stall. I don't have any other choice. With a picture, however, we are completely unrestricted, completely free."

"Many people, spread over the entire world you say, will see this picture," Rocky said. "Do they all know then that it shows me and Happylegs?"

"Yes; at least, the caption will make it clear to them."

"Caption? That's a word I've never heard."

"Rocky, you're an unusually clever horse, but you've still lots to learn. Long ago, humans invented a way of representing and storing up spoken words by means of visible signs. Such written or printed signs are even used to replace talking; they express something without anyone speaking."

"That's too much for me."

"You must simply believe me—a caption explains what is to be seen in a picture."

"Without it, people wouldn't understand what a photograph depicts?" Rocky asked.

"Not exactly. Every normal human being would naturally see that in our case it had to do with a horse race, but he couldn't say which one."

"Please, move slowly, Joe. During the race, one exposure is made, one picture is taken."

"Right."

"Then many copies are made. When someone looks at such a picture, he sees it's a race, but he doesn't know which race it was."

"That's right."

"You make an exposure of a single definite race; but the picture that comes out of it shows any race."

"No, it doesn't show any race," Joe said, "but only a definite one. But the picture alone doesn't make clear which race it is. Finally, each single race is, of course, also a race in the general sense."

"Even though it was run right here just an hour ago?"

"An artist can paint a horse race simply from his fantasy," Joe explained. "Such a picture doesn't need to depict a definite horse race in a definite place. A photograph, however, is, as everyone knows, a rendering of an actual happening and nothing else."

"Then a photograph is a picture of something that is past."

"What should I say? Really, I believe you're right. A photograph is always the past preserved in a picture. While you look at it in the present, you must realize that it is related to the past. The photograph presentifies the past."

"Can one make photographs of things that take place in the future?"

"Naturally not! It sounds funny: 'a photograph of the future!' But, perhaps, it isn't so funny. The architect projects figures of buildings that do not yet exist. He shows how such a building will look in the future. He constructs a blueprint—a work schedule that shows the worker what he is to do at a definite hour in the future."

"Now you have completely confused me," Rocky said. "I don't understand what you mean by a blueprint. I think I was able to follow you when you said that every one of many persons is able to study a copy of this photograph and that he will then see a picture of a race, without knowing exactly what race it was."

"What a bright fellow you are, Rocky! If someone were to find this photograph someplace in twenty years, he would even then be able to recognize it as the picture of a horse race. The yellowed paper would show him that it's an old picture and must, therefore, represent an event that occurred way back in time. The photograph ages, but the pictured occurrence stays tied to its place in time. Someone who picked it up would be completely uncertain which race it depicts."

"And how do they know today?"

"I've already told you. The printed words that have been attached to the picture make it clear."

"Then words add something to the picture: information that the picture itself cannot give. And the picture improves the direct observation. Direct observation is, therefore, the poorest of all."

"You have a chip on your shoulder, Rocky. As soon as your tongue is loose, it begins to wag."

"Now you're sore and scolding me," said the horse. "I'm only trying to make clear to myself what seems obvious to you but which is so difficult for me to comprehend. I can't understand that someone in New York and someone else in San Francisco can observe a picture and that both know it depicts an occurrence in Kentucky. The two persons certainly can't see each other."

"Certainly you aren't serious in asking that, Rocky. You remember, don't you, how long it took for us to go from New York to San Francisco."

"Oh, now I understand. They were all once in Lexington, and they have memories of it."

"Of course, many have been here but, by no means, all of them. Nor is that necessary. The name 'Lexington' designates a place that they know how to determine in the whole of the United States."

"How can they be familiar with something without ever having become acquainted with it?" Rocky asked. "Isn't it necessary to travel to every place in order to know a country?"

"Nobody knows the United States in the way a mailman knows the houses on his route. If anyone should get the idea of traveling around for many years to place his foot on every little piece of earth, then he would know the country no better in the end than someone who stayed in his own town all his life. On the contrary, the longer he remained on the road, the more his impressions would become confused. Finally, he wouldn't even be sure whether he had carried out his plan. As long as he is en route, he would never know where he actually is located."

"How do you know where you are located?"

"Because I can make myself a picture of the whole."

"Now you are talking about a picture again. Are you thinking of a photograph of the United States?"

"No, there isn't one or, anyway, not yet. I'm thinking of another kind of representation—for example, a map."

"How long does it take to go on a map from New York to San Francisco?"

"What do you mean? How long does someone need to go from New York to San Francisco on a map? No time at all! On the map, you can see both places at once with a single look."

"Joe, do I have to remind *you* how long it took us to move from New York to San Francisco? Three days! But, on a map, you say, one doesn't need any time. So there are no distances on a map?"

"The map only represents distances," Joe answered.

"And then they disappear? Can one be in two places at the same time?"

"The distance doesn't disappear, it is only transformed. On a map, you aren't in two places at once. For a bug that crawls around on the map, there are also distances. He needs time in order to get from the spot designated as San Francisco to the spot named New York. We, on the other hand, look at the map in using it and are nowhere on the map, even when our own place is indicated there. In our bodily existence, we find ourselves in a definite place. The map only *sets* the country there *before* us. Looking at the map, we are opposite to it."

"Is everyone able to use a map?" Rocky asked.

"Most everyone. Still, there are a few exceptions, such as people who have never learned to read."

"Reading must be learned, but how is it with the seeing of pictures?"

"We don't have to learn that," Joe said. "Everyone, at least every normal human, can recognize a picture as such. If someone is unable to read the text himself, then he can have someone else read it to him."

"So, finally all the many individual persons will understand from the observation of the many individual copies that the photograph depicts a particular race at Keeneland. All will understand one and the same thing. How come?"

"That must be so because we all live together in one and the same world."

At that moment, a stable boy brought oats and hay. Horse and trainer interrupted their conversation. Both were completely exhausted. For the first time in his life, Rocky showed no sign of appetite; he murmured something to himself that sounded like, "A race . . . one thousand pictures . . . one thousand people . . . one and the same thing. . . ." As soon as the stable boy had left the stall, Rocky resumed the conversation:

"The many copies all represent the same thing; do they, in turn, represent one another?"

"No, but a person can replace the one copy by another one. They are all like one another and similar to the original."

"Didn't you say before, Joe, that the photos are used to make a better decision than direct observation allows? Are they like the original and at the same time superior?"

"Certainly, in a certain way, they're better. The camera reacts more quickly than the human eye. Therefore, it's useful for objective observation."

"The photograph shows something that one could never see in direct observation. How do you know then that the reproduction is correct?" Rocky asked.

"It must be so. We can prove it."

"What does 'prove' mean?"

"Look, we know the mechanism of the camera because we built it."

"You've built it with your own hands?"

"No, not I. Other people in a factory have produced it. Therefore, I say that *we* know. I know it only as a member of a group. I have read about it and know how the apparatus functions. You, yourself, set it in motion, precisely at the moment you crossed the finish line."

"Can't the apparatus ever fail?"

"Everything made by human hand can fail," Joe sadly replied.

"How do you know, then, that it actually functioned?"

"The result, the picture, proves it. It confirms our predictions."

"Can you see the mechanism work?"

"Not directly. But, after the race, the film is taken from the apparatus, and the negative, as we call it, is developed by a photographer."

"Can't he, perhaps, deceive and smuggle in another photograph in its place?" asked the horse.

"There's always someone who's watching."

"Couldn't all of them be in a plot against me?"

"It seems to me as if you're getting paranoid now. Ultimately, you've got to trust those who do the work; they're upright and dependable people. Quite apart from the fact that I would always recognize your nose, Rocky."

"Have you ever seen it before in such a picture?"

"No, I looked at the photograph for the first time on my way here."

"How can you recognize my nose then?"

"I can't explain that to you; I simply do it. What's the sense of continually asking how and why?"

"So you put your trust in the picture because you believe in the manufacturer," Rocky said, "because you rely on the apparatus, because you are certain that you can recognize something that you have never seen in such a way before."

"Don't treat me like a fool!" Joe retorted. "That can all be proved; it must be so."

"The proof, whatever that may mean, comes first of all?"

"Of course, why not?"

"Up to today I've always believed that you humans were much smarter than we horses, but today I am having grievous doubts. Didn't you say that the picture is similar to the original and could, therefore, reproduce it?"

"That's right!"

"Now listen, Joe. During our race, everything was moving, and here, in this picture, everything's at rest—nothing changes. Do you really insist that this picture depicts movement and shows the movement more clearly than you, yourself, could observe it in the race?"

"One must naturally understand the right way to observe and interpret a picture. I've already told you it only presents one phase of the whole occurrence. In this special case, it is the last moment of the race."

"And what about all the leaps that we made on the way from start to finish? Aren't they shown?"

"Oh my, I'm afraid it's hopeless," Joe said. "You've got to add it in your imagination, your fantasy. Do you understand?"

"Do you understand it?"

Rocky noticed the angry look of the trainer and said, "Excuse me, Joe. Naturally you know it, but all this is hard for me. It is, after all, my first day of reasonable talk, and I still have difficulties in understanding the meaning of several words, for example, 'representation.' "

"Is that all!" Joe cried happily. "You, and Happylegs, and the other horses, the judges, the audience, and many other things were actually present this afternoon. This thing here, the photograph, represents all that."

"Joe, you've just called this photograph a 'thing.' Earlier you spoke about many other things. Is there any other word for 'thing'?"

"One can also speak about objects."

"An object represents another object then? How remarkable!"

"Rocky," said the trainer, "I think we ought to stop; it's getting late."

"Please, wait a moment. I've never had the good luck to talk with you. Perhaps it will never happen again."

"All right, what else?"

"What about this? On the race track, I carry you or one of these kids you call jockeys on my back. If it should ever occur to one of them to want to carry one of us, then we would die whinnying. But you have just taken this photograph out of your pocket and this little thing, weighing nothing, depicts us and other things that you could never lift."

"You must forget about the weight."

"And how about the size? You need the photograph in order to find out the winner. The difference was a nose length, that is, four inches, you said. And how big is this picture?"

"Two and one-half by four inches."

"So you claim that one can establish by means of an object that measures less than three inches, a thing much larger in size?"

"One could enlarge the picture three or ten times; it doesn't depend on that," Joe answered.

"So the actual size of four inches can be represented by a picture that measures two or six or twenty inches, and this all doesn't make any difference?"

"Just so. The size of the picture doesn't matter; it depends only on the proportions, on the ratio."

"This afternoon at the race, four inches were actually of decisive importance. But when you presentify that which was once present, then one can afford to ignore it."

"You are fast in running, Rocky, but, in thinking, you may be a bit slow."

"Why don't you help me then? Once, when I turned around in the middle of the track and ran back to the start instead of to the finish, you struck me. But here, during our chat, you've walked back and forth and looked at the picture first from this position and then from the opposite one."

"The race course is given on the picture within its own space. That is, it is completely independent of its relation to its present surroundings."

"Isn't the photograph also a part of my surroundings?"

"Sure, but there's a fundamental distinction. For example, a picture of you hangs on the wall in my room. But it doesn't really belong to the wall. A frame separates the space of the picture from the actual space. But even the frame is not necessary."

"Then, you could hang my picture in any other place."

"In any place whatsoever, without it the least affecting the imaginary space of the picture."

"What happens when I turn the photograph around?"

"You're not supposed to do that; then you would lose sight of the picture."

"So this whole piece of paper is not a picture; it is only a picture on one side. How deep does it go then?"

"I'd really prefer to say it has no depth at all. It is pure surface—two dimensional, as we term it."

The trainer looked around in every direction, as if to reassure himself that nobody was secretly listening. "Rocky," he said softly, "one could actually say it's immaterial. Perhaps 'abstract' would be the right word. But I'm not certain because I hold this thing here in my hand and carry it around with me. You're right, it's amazing that this thing whose weight, size, volume, place, position, direction, and time do not count, that this fragment, this excerpt from our surroundings, serves to objectively determine the size and direction of other things in the fullness of their real existence."

As so often happens, confidence was repaid with confidence.

"Joe, I must tell you something. I can't see any picture at all, no matter whether you turn it this way or that. This side is all white; the other one is a bit brighter here, a bit darker there."

"Don't give it a second thought! That probably happens because your eyes are situated more to the side. Thereby, you have a better eye for things that approach you, even from behind—things you shy away from. You are always in a sort of contact with things—always poised and ready. A picture, on the other hand, demands a certain distance from things, a suspending of their actuality. For you, it is difficult to find the right posture to put yourself at a distance from things. In this, you are like all other horses. That probably is the reason, too, why horses usually do not speak."

"That was bitter medicine. Allow me one last question. You said this photograph is objective. Is that because, or despite, all the alterations that the original suffered in being counterfeited?"

As one can readily imagine, the trainer felt very uncomfortable.

"Rocky, you're a thoroughbred. You purebreds have lost all your healthy horse sense. Why these questions? I hate to say it to you, but you talk almost like a professor of philosophy."

To trainer Joe goes my thanks for giving me this authentic account. He considered it necessary to apologize for having to adjust himself to the horse's level when it came to talking about numbers. In his opinion, we don't apply numbers to things but project the things onto the rational system of numbers.

"How could I hope," he told me, "to explain to a horse the enigmatic duality of the spatial and temporal orderings with which we are concerned in the contemplation of a picture? I believe that you psychiatrists encounter similar problems in the study of time curves, like those in the EEG. There, you see lines without motion, but you interpret them as registered movement. You represent time by an extension whose beginning and end are simultaneously visible. You study an electroencephalogram for weeks and months after it has been taken, and reproduce it in your publications. You even compare an earlier with a later record, as you transport past events into the present and unite happenings separated by a wide interval of time so that they are accessible to simultaneous observation. With such a free disposition, you search for an objective judgment."

"For me, it was a great experience," Joe concluded his report. "The naïveté and stubbornness of the horse made me realize the naïveté of our own attitude. As a matter of fact, a photo-finish camera contains not only lenses and filters but also invisible components of a psychic nature that never attract our attention because their employment is so effortless."

The most recent history of the concept of objectivity shows how right Joe was.

PART II

Anthropological Studies

CHAPTER SEVEN

The Upright Posture

Introduction

A breakdown of physical well-being is alarming; it turns our attention to functions that, on good days, we take for granted. A healthy person does not ponder about breathing, seeing, or walking. Infirmities of breath, sight, or gait startle us. Among the patients consulting a psychiatrist, there are some who can no longer master the seemingly banal arts of standing and walking. They are not paralyzed, but, under certain conditions, they cannot, or feel as if they cannot, keep themselves upright. They tremble and quiver. Incomprehensible terror takes away their strength. Sometimes, a minute change in the physiognomy of the frightful situation may restore their strength. Obviously, upright posture is not confined to the technical problems of locomotion. It contains a psychological element. It is pregnant with a meaning not exhausted by the physiological tasks of meeting the forces of gravity and maintaining equilibrium.

Language has long since taken cognizance of this fact. The expression "to be upright" has two connotations: first, to rise, to get up, and to stand on one's own feet and, second, the moral implication, not to stoop to anything, to be honest and just, to be true to friends in danger, to stand by one's convictions, and to act accordingly, even at the risk of one's life. We praise an upright man; we admire someone who stands up for his ideas of rectitude. There are good reasons to assume that the term "upright" in its moral connotation is more than a mere allegory.

The upright posture distinguishes the human genus from other living creatures. To Milton, Adam and Eve appeared as ". . . Two of far nobler shape, erect and tall, God-like erect, with native honor clad. . . ."

Some biologists, however, would like to take exception to this praise, and, in slightly more prosaic statements, they indict the upright posture as a cause of hernias and flat feet. However this may be, whether the poet is right or his misanthropic opponents, whether upright posture is an excellence or not, in any case it is a distinction. It does not occur in any species other than man.[1]

Upright posture, while unique, is also essential. This is no necessary consequence. The exceptional might be nothing but a peculiarity, an accidental caprice of nature. However, there is no doubt that the shape and function of the human body are determined in almost every detail by, and for, the upright posture. The skeleton of the foot; the structure of the ankle, knee, and hip; the curvature of the vertebral column; the proportions of the limbs—all serve the same purpose. This purpose could not be accomplished if the muscles and the nervous system were not built accordingly. While all parts contribute to the upright posture, upright posture in turn permits the development of the forelimbs into the human shoulders, arms, and hands and of the skull into the human skull and face.

With upright posture, the vertebral column takes on, for the first time, the architectural function of a column. The skull rests on the articular surfaces of the atlas (which here, indeed, deserves its name) like an architrave on the capitals of columns. This arrangement makes it possible and necessary for the atlanto-occipital joint to be moved forward toward the center of the base of the skull, resulting in the typical configuration of the human skull, the extension of the base, and the closing vault, which in turn provides wider space for the orbitae. The skulls of the other primates still show the shape characteristic of other quadrupeds, in which the head does not rest on the vertebral column but hangs down from it. The foramen magnum accordingly is in a more caudal position; the clivus cuts the vertical at a more obtuse angle. The other

---

[1] F. Weidenreich (1946) discusses the relationship between man and his simian, ancestors. He enumerates the main peculiarities that, compared to the condition of the apes, characterize man in his upright posture. The human leg, which he mentions among other things, "is stretched in hip and knee joints to its maximum extent and adduced toward the midline, so that the knees touch each other, while in anthropoids, even if the latter succeed in standing and walking upright, the legs remain bent in hip and knee joints and are held in abduction, so that anthropoids always stand stooped, with their knees crooked and turned outward" (p. 6). In the so-called normal attitude of man, therefore, the lines connecting the centers of hip, knee, and ankle joints are all located in the same frontal plane. The plumb line passes through this plane. Furthermore, the center of the hip joint is, for each leg, vertically above the center of the knee and ankle joints.

primates—as has been said—are built to stand upright but not for upright posture.[2]

Because upright posture is the leitmotiv in the formation of the human organism, an individual who has lost or is deprived of the capacity to get up and keep himself upright depends, for his survival, completely on the aid of others. Without their help, he is doomed to die. A biologically oriented psychology must not forget that upright posture is an indispensable condition of man's self-preservation. Upright we are, and we experience ourselves in this specific relation to the world.

Men and mice do not have the same environment, even if they share the same room. Environment is not a stage with the scenery set as one and the same for all actors who make their entrance. Each species has its own environment. There is a mutual interdependence between species and environment. The surrounding world is determined by the organization of the species in a process of selecting what is relevant to the function cycle of action and reaction (von Uexkuell, 1926). Upright posture pre-establishes a definite attitude toward the world; it is a specific mode of being-in-the-world.

Relating the basic forms of human experience to man's upright posture may well be called an anthropological approach, if that term is used with its original connotation. It was not until the middle of the nineteenth century that the meaning of "anthropology" was confined to zoological aspects, to a study of man as an animal in his evolution and history as a race. The nineteenth-century view aimed to see man exclusively and understand him completely as an animal. It was motivated by an antagonism to theology. Instead of seeing man created in the image of God, it wanted to see man as the descendant of the monkey. This antitheological view remains theological because of its concern with refutation. However, one can and should consider man in his own right without either theological or antitheological bias. Anthropology can be developed, indifferent to both the Biblical account and the evolutionary theory of genesis.

This writer's interest is in what man is and not in how he supposedly

[2] The comparison of man and other primates is a time-honored topic, widely discussed among pre-Darwinian zoologists. Most of the characteristic differences enumerated by Weidenreich (1946) were known to the anatomists of the eighteenth century, who also considered the possibility of a common origin. Daubenton published, in 1764, a paper about the different positions of the foramen magnum in man and animals (Herder, 1778). Even the sentence passed on upright posture because of its inherent evils is old enough. Moskati (1771), comparing the essential differences of man and animals, came to the conclusion that upright posture disposed heart, circulation, and intestines to many defects and diseases.

became what he is. Paleontology tells what man or what his ancestors once were but not what man actually is. Even if one concedes to paleontology that it has discovered the living or extinct ancestors of man, it has little to say about how the change to modern man came about or about what its final result was. Looking from man to the hominids[3] or the other primates, we see what man no longer is. Looking from the other primates to man, we see what the other primates are not yet. Any explanation of the causes of evolution demands a knowledge of both the old and new forms. No designer of an automobile would try to explain its present form and shape by mere reference to its forerunners. It is true that a modern car has some basic traits in common with the old buggy, but just that which gives an automobile its characteristic shape is not learned from the old form. It is the automobile's own function and dynamic structure that determine its shape.

Paleontologists are inclined to exaggerate their gratitude to the ancestors of humans. In a very illuminating survey of the development of the humerus from fish to man, Gregory (1949) states that man has inherited the basic pattern of locomotion from the earliest vertebrates and that he owes the modeling of a potential humerus and a potential ulna to the crossopterygians of the Devonian age. Still, man's gait and behavior seem slightly remote from the Silurian ostracoderms.

With all due respect for the accomplishments of those early ancestors, we should not forget to investigate our own situation. Man is not only the end of a long development; he also represents a new beginning. One may doubt if old rocks will reveal all the secrets of human existence.

Human Kinematics

Acquiring Upright Posture

Upright posture has a delayed beginning in the life of an individual. The heart of the unborn beats in the mother's womb. Breathing starts with the first cry at birth. Upright posture keeps us waiting. Even when the physiological conditions—e.g., the maturation of fibers, the development of postural reflexes, or, later, the elongation of the legs—are ful-

---

[3] The early Darwinians were searching for the "missing link" connecting modern man with the living anthropoids. Today, the opinion prevails that the human branch parted from the modern anthropoids "much earlier than we ever dreamed." Weidenreich (1946) believed that this separation occurred in the Miocene period or not very long afterward. Portmann (1944) placed it in the late Cretaceous period. From there on, a fragmentary line of hominids, documented by fossils in Europe, Asia, and Africa, leads toward modern man. There is also another line, still more hypothetical, leading to the living anthropoids: chimpanzee, gorilla, orangutan.

filled, the child will not master upright posture at once. He has to learn it, to conquer it. The acquisition will pass through several phases, which, although not completely separate, are sufficiently distinct. Progress is slow; it takes a number of years. This development will be followed here from the getting up, to standing, and, finally, to walking.

The origin and the beginning of upright posture do not coincide, just as the first cry, the beginning of the functioning of breathing, does not mark the origin of breathing. The conditions surrounding the beginning of a function, whether it be breathing, speaking, or standing, do not at all give an account of the structures of breath, speech, upright posture, or of their origins. As long as one speaks about breathing and walking, the distinction appears banal and not worth mentioning. There are, however, situations where the distinction is less obvious but not less true. This writer wonders whether genetic psychologists sometimes actually do confuse beginning and origin.

Upright posture characterizes the human species. Nevertheless, each individual has to struggle in order to make it really his own. Man has to become what he is. The acquisition does not make him an "absentee landlord." While the heart continues to beat from its fetal beginning to death without our active intervention and while breathing neither demands nor tolerates our voluntary interference beyond narrow limits, upright posture remains a task throughout our lives. Before reflection or self-reflection start, but as if they were a prelude to it, work makes its appearance within the realm of the elemental biological functions of man. In getting up, in reaching the upright posture, man must oppose the forces of gravity. It seems to be his nature to oppose nature in its impersonal, fundamental aspects with natural means. However, gravity is never fully overcome; upright posture always maintains its character of counteraction. It calls for our activity and attention.

Automatic regulation alone does not suffice. An old horse may go to sleep standing on its four legs; man has to be awake to keep himself upright. Much as we are part of nature with every breath, with every bite, with every step, we first become our true selves in waking opposition to nature. In sleep, we do not withdraw our interest from the world so much as we surrender ourselves completely to it. We abandon ourselves to the world, relinquishing our individuality. We no longer hold our own in the world, opposed to it. Awakeness and the force of gravity are mutually interdependent. While awakeness is necessary for upright posture, that is, for counteracting gravity, gravity determines waking experience. The dreams of one night are not related to the dreams of another night, but days are related to one another. They form a continuum where every hour, every moment, anticipates the next and prepares for it. Held back by gravity to a precise point, we can overcome distance only in an orderly sequence. During our waking hours, sequence means consequence. Gravity, which holds us in line, imposes on waking experience a methodical proceeding. In sleep, when we no longer oppose gravity, in our weightless dreams, or in our lofty fantasies, experience becomes kaleidoscopic and finally amorphous. Sequence, then, no longer means consequence. Awakeness is no mere addendum, still less an impediment, to an otherwise happily functioning id. The waking man alone can preserve himself, and he alone can help drives to reach their goal.

In the Hobbesian philosophy, man, haunted by fear of violent death, creates the commonwealth to keep disruptive natural tendencies in check. A permanent, never resolved discord ensues between man in the state of nature and man as a member of society. Locke, Rousseau, Freud, and many others took up the theme and added to it variations of their own. If only these many descriptions of man's state of nature were more than historical fantasies! Yet, one need not invent prehistory; we can make use of a very concrete experience. We can read man's natural endowment from his physique. Considering man in his upright posture, we do well to envisage the possibility that not society has first brought man into conflict with nature, but that man's natural opposition to nature enables him to produce society, history, and conventions.

The direction upward, against gravity, inscribes into space world-regions to which we attach values, such as those expressed by high and low, rise and decline, climbing and falling, superior and inferior, elevated and downcast, looking up to and despising. On Olympus, high, remote, inaccessible, and exalted, dwell the Homeric gods. On Mount Sinai, Moses receives the Ten Commandments. Below, in the depths, is Hades and the world of shadows. There, also, is the Inferno. However, such evaluations are not unequivocal. "Base" (adjective) and "base" (noun) have, in spite of their phonetic resemblance, different etymological roots and opposite meanings. "Base," the adjective, is derived from the Latin root *bassus* with the connotation "short" and, later, "low"; "base," the noun, originated in the Greek root *baino*—"walking" or "stepping." The earth that pulls us downward is also the ground that carries and gives support. The weighty man signifies, by his dignified gait, that he carries a heavy burden but sustains it well. Upright posture as counteraction cannot lack the forces against which it strives.

Standing

In getting up, man gains his standing in the world. The parents are not the only ones who greet the child's progress with joy. The child enjoys no less the triumph of his achievement. There is a forceful urge toward the goal of getting up and of resisting, in a state of dangerous balance, the downward-pulling forces. There need not be any other premium, like satisfaction of hunger, attention, or applause. The child certainly does not strive for security. Failure does not discourage him. He enjoys the freedom gained by upright posture—the freedom to stand on his own feet and the freedom to walk. Upright posture, which we learn in and through falling, remains threatened by falls throughout our lives. The natural stance of man is, therefore, "resistance." A rock reposes in its own weight. The things that surround us appear solid and safe in their quiet resting on the ground, but man's status demands endeavor. It is essentially restless. We are committed to an ever renewed exertion. Our task is not finished with getting up and standing. We have to "withstand." He who is able to accomplish this is called constant, stable.

Language expresses well the psychological meaning of standing, with all its facets. The coupling of the transitive and the intransitive meanings "to stand" and "to stand something" characterizes them as resisting and, therefore, enduring against threat, danger, and attack. The etymological root of standing—sta—is one of the most prolific elements not only in English but also in Greek, Latin, French, and German. It may suffice to mention only a few derivatives of an almost exhaustible store. Besides such combinations as "standing for," "standing by," and "making a stand," there are many words where the root has undergone slight changes but is still recognizable: e.g., "state," "status," "estate," "statement," "standard," "statute," "institution," "constitution," "substance," "establish," "understand," "assist," "distant." This entire family of words is kept together by one and the same principal meaning. They refer to something that is instituted, erected, constructed, and, in its dangerous equilibrium, threatened by fall and collapse. Falling is not always tragic. Clowns, modern and old, primitive and sublime, all have made use of falling as a reliable trick to stir up laughter.

With upright posture, an inescapable ambivalence penetrates and pervades all human behavior. Upright posture removes us from the ground, keeps us away from things, and holds us aloof from our fellowmen. All of these three distances can be experienced either as gain or as loss.

1. *Distance from the ground.* In getting up, we gain the freedom of motion and enjoy it, but, at the same time, we lose secure contact with the supporting ground, with Mother Earth, and we miss it. We stand alone and have to rely on our own strength and capacities. With the acquisition of upright posture, a characteristic change in language occurs. In the early years, when speaking of himself, a child uses his given name. However, when he has reached the age when he can stand firmly on his own feet, he begins to use the pronoun "I" for himself. This change marks a first gaining of independence. Among all words, "I" has a peculiar character. Everyone uses "I" to refer to himself alone. "I" is a most general world. At the same time, it has a unique meaning for every speaker. In using the word "I," I oppose myself to everyone else, who, nevertheless, is my fellow-man.

Because getting up and standing are so demanding, we enjoy resting, relaxing, yielding, lying down, and sinking back. There is the voluptuous gratification of succumbing. Sex remains a form of lying down or, as language says, of lying or sleeping with. Addicts, in their experience, behavior, and intention, reveal the double aspect of sinking back and its contrast to being upright. A *symposium* found the ancient Greeks, a *convivium* the Romans, stretched on their couches until, after many libations to Dionysus and Bacchus, they finally sank to the ground. *Symposium* means "drinking together," or "a drinking party." It could be well translated by the characteristic German word *Gelage*. Plato's dialogue first helped the word *symposium* to reach its modern connotation. The old and new are not so far apart as one might assume. Their relation can also be expressed—Plato clearly indicates this—as the difference between being upright and sinking.

2. *Distance from things.* In upright posture, the immediate contact with things is loosened. A child creeping on his hands and knees not only keeps contact with the ground but is, in his all-fours locomotion, like the quadrupeds, directed toward immediate contact with things. The length-axis of his body coincides with the direction of his motion. With getting up, all this changes. In walking, man moves his body in a parallel transposition, the length-axis of his body at a right angle to the direction of his motion. He finds himself always "confronted" with things. Such remoteness enables him to see things, detached from the immediate contact of grasping and incorporating, in their relation to one another. Seeing is transformed into "looking at." The horizon is widened, removed; the distant becomes momentous, of great import. In the same measure, contact with near things is lost.

Thales, the philosopher and astronomer, fell into a ditch while watching the stars. A young child is close to the ground; to him the stars are far off. He does not mind picking things up from the ground; but, growing older, he will learn to accept our table manners, which remove even food to a distance. We set the table; we serve the meal; we use spoon and fork. Our feeding is regulated by a ritual, which we like to discard at a picnic. Artificiality and tools interfere with the direct satisfaction of hunger. The mouth is kept away from the plate. The hand lifts the food to the mouth. Spoon and fork do not create distance; tools can only be invented and used where distance already exists. In the early months of life, hands hold on to things in a grasping reflex. Not until the immediate contact of grasping is abandoned is the use of tools possible. This development is not simply the result of motor maturation. An imbecile may never learn and a paretic may unlearn manners, not so much because of failure of the motorium as because of the loss and lack of distance. Pointing likewise presupposes distance. It appears to be a human activity. Animals do not easily, if at all, understand pointing to distant things.[4] Pathology reveals an antagonistic relationship between grasping and pointing. There are cases where pointing is distorted while grasping either remains undamaged or is later intensified and becomes forced grasping (Goldstein, 1931).[5]

3. *Distance from fellow-men.* In upright posture, we find ourselves "face to face" with others, distant, aloof—verticals that never meet. On the horizontal plane, parallel lines converge toward a vanishing point. Theoretically, the vanishing point of parallel verticals—to which we are comparable, standing vis-à-vis—is in infinite distance. In the finiteness of seeing, however, parallel verticals do not meet. Therefore, the strict upright posture expresses austerity, inaccessibility, decisiveness, domination, majesty, mercilessness, or unapproachable remoteness, as in catatonic symmetry. Inclination first brings us closer to another. Inclination,[6] just like leaning, means literally "bending out" from the austere vertical.

Dictators, reviewing their parading troops, try to show by their rigid

---

[4] It is the hunter who understands and interprets the dog's aiming as pointing. The "point" is the natural outgrowth of the dog's pausing previous to springing the game.

[5] Experimental ablations of cortical areas indicate that grasping is under the control of Brodmann's area 6.

[6] The root is Latin, *clino*, to bend. It is interesting to see how greatly language is shaped in accordance with expressive phenomena. Not only does the English language have two words of the same structure from different roots; but there is the German word *Zuneigung*, with still another etymological derivation, which, however, expresses the same meaning with the corresponding space experience. All this points to the fact that metaphors do not simply carry over a meaning from one medium to another. There is a much more intimate relation—that between expressive motion and emotional attitude.

poses their imperturbable and unshakable wills. Formalized attitudes and pantomimic, signifying gestures follow the pattern set by spontaneous expressions. When we lower our heads or kneel in prayer, when we bow or bend our knees in greeting, the deviation from the vertical reveals the relation to it.

So it is with expressions of reverence, of asking and granting a request, and many others. The formalization and shortening of social gestures sometimes make it hard to recognize their origin; but even the stiff forms of military greeting may, with a slight courteous bending of the head, be revitalized by spontaneous expression.

There is only one vertical but many deviations from it, each one carrying a specific, expressive meaning. The sailor puts his cap askew, and his girl understands well the cocky expression and his "leanings." King Comus at the Mardi Gras may lean backward and his crown may slip off-center. However, even the disciples of informality would be seriously concerned if, on his way to his inauguration, the President should wear his silk hat (the elongation and accentuation of the vertical) aslant. There are no teachers, no textbooks, that instruct in this field. There are no pupils, either, who need instruction. Without ever being taught, we understand the rules governing this and other areas of expression. We understand them not conceptually but, it seems, by intuition. This is true for the actor as well as the onlooker.

One may argue that these are cultural patterns with which we grow up and that our final attitudes are the result of many infinitesimal steps. To support this view, one may point to the fact that gestures of greeting were different in the old days from ours and are different in the Occident and the Orient. Yet, in spite of their divergences, they all are variations of one theme. They are all related to the vertical; they are all modifications of the upright posture. Exceptions only confirm the rule. We give our assent by nodding the head, which is obviously also a motion that carries the head downward following gravity, away from the vertical. It has been observed that this gesture is not universal, that there are peoples to whom the same vertical motion of nodding means negation or denial. However, these two forms of expression, which indeed resemble each other, are not identical. Our mode of assertion, as well as their negation, consists of a two-phased motion—the motion downward and the movement up and backward. While in assertion the accent is on the downward motion, negation chooses the opposite direction. The head is moved from the position of inclination back to the vertical, expressing inaccessibility and denial.

Cultural patterns do not arbitrarily create forms but, within the given framework, formalize a socially accepted scheme valid only for its group and period. With upright posture counteracting gravity, the vertical, pointing upward and away from the center of gravity, becomes a natural determinant. The vertical is a constancy phenomenon. Its apparent position does not change, even if the head is tilted, and, therefore, its projection on the retina varies. At an early age, children are able to draw a vertical or a horizontal line, to copy a cross or a square, but they fail when asked to copy the same square presented as a diamond.[7]

Walking

With getting up, man is ready for walking. The precarious equilibrium reached in standing has to be risked again. A quadruped rests with relative safety on his four legs, which inscribe an appropriate base on the ground. The center of gravity does not leave its position above this base even when the animal walks or trots. The human situation is different. The center of gravity is elevated high over the small base of support. This provides for greater flexibility and variability of movement, but it increases instability and the danger of falling. Man has to find a hold within himself. Standing and walking, he has to keep himself in suspension.

The legs support the body like columns; in the hip joint, the trunk rests on the femur bones as on pillars. At least, it seems to. The appearance is convincing enough for a hysterical person to use it as a model for his astasia-abasia. If one tries, however, to carry through the comparison in detail, one sees immediately the striking contrast to the architectonic principles of column and pillar. Many old temples have collapsed, leaving their columns still standing erect. The stone pillars of a bridge are constructed from the foundation upward. Each lower section really carries the upper one, which can be removed without unbalancing the lower ones. Neither the skeleton nor the legs will stand of their own power. The legs could not do it, even if the muscles could still contract and were not severed from their origin on the pelvis. The legs have to be held in suspension by the counteraction of the trunk muscles and by the counterweight of the trunk. A column, a pillar, or a tower taper off. Their bases are broader than the top. Human legs also have a conical shape, but the bulk is high. The origin of the muscles and, therefore, their main volume is on top. The muscles extend with their tendons downward

[7] Gibson and Mowrer (1938) assumed that our orientation in space is determined by postural factors, while visual stimulation is of secondary importance. Asche and Witkin (1948), however, in their more recent experiments, came to the opposite conclusion.

from pelvis to knee and again from knee to ankle. Their contraction, however, is directed upward.

With the circumference of the thighs near the hip joint considerably larger than the circumference around the ankle, the leg resembles an inverted obelisk more than a column. This leg-obelisk cannot support itself on its tip. There is a gyrostatic system of balance, holding the legs as much as being carried by them. The old anatomical names of muscles and the traditional signification of their functions are often misleading. The bicepts femoris and hamstring muscles, the so-called flexors of the leg, bend the lower leg in one position only, while in another they extend the knee and the hip. The erector trunci and the muscles of the legs cooperate—with gravity as their invisible partner—as synergists, originating in adjacent areas of the ilium and the sacrum. They act on the pelvis in opposite directions. They turn the pelvis around an axis, connecting the centers of the hip joints. There is a second balancing system between the right and left that keeps the pelvis and trunk in balance in a sagittal plane. From clinical observation of dystrophies and paralyses, we learn which individual muscles—e.g., the gluteus maximus, the iliopsoas, the quadriceps femoris, the sacrospinalis—contribute to upright posture; from physiological experiments, we come to know how they are correlated. Through the combined work of observation and experiment, we gain information about the means of locomotion. At this point, a new horizon of problems is opened up—the question of how a being equipped with such motorium will experience the world and himself in this world.

Human bipedal gait is a rhythmical movement whereby, in a sequence of steps, the whole weight of the body rests for a short time on one leg only. The center of gravity has to be swung forward. It has to be brought from a never stable equilibrium to a still less stable balance. Support will be denied to it for a moment until the leg brought forward prevents the threatening fall. Human gait is, in fact, a continuously arrested falling. Therefore, an unforeseen obstacle or a little unevenness of the ground may precipitate a fall. Human gait is an expansive motion, performed in the expectation that the leg brought forward will ultimately find solid ground. It is motion on credit. Confidence and timidity, elation and depression, and stability and insecurity are all expressed in gait.

Bipedal gait is, in fact, a balance alternating from one leg to the other; it permits variations in length, tempo, direction, and accent. In a polka step, even the rhythmical sequence of right and left and left and right is interrupted and exchanged. The symmetry of rhythmically alternating locomotor reflexes is thereby broken. Steps varied in many ways can be united in a scheme, in a meter. It is not poetry alone that moves on "metrical feet" in an anapestic, iambic, or trochaic meter. In marching or in dancing, we perform a great variety of set patterns. "Per-forming" means that we follow a given form, that we are able to conduct ourselves in accordance with a scheme set beforehand, that we can use our limbs like instruments. Everyone who drives a car uses his legs and feet as tools. No one, however, outdoes the organist, who plays one pedal with his feet. Such an instrumental use of the limbs, obviously not limited to the arms and hands, demands a centralization of functions, demands a dominating hemisphere. For symmetrical alternating movements, bilateral, segmental, and suprasegmental structures may suffice. Instrumental use depends on an interruption of symmetry followed by higher integration.

A breakdown of this integration should result in kinetic apraxia of trunk and legs. There are indeed some cases recorded (Nielsen, 1946) that confirm this expectation. Their number is small. It probably would be greater if, as Sittig pointed out, more attention were given to this symptom. Even then, it might escape observation for two reasons: first, paresis may cover the apraxia of the legs; and, second, gait and other symmetrical motions may still be found intact when actions based on less symmetrical motions, such as jumping and dancing, have already failed (Kleist, 1934).

Upright Posture and the Development of the Human Hand and Arm

The Hand as a Sensory Organ and as a Tool

In upright posture, the frontal extremities are no longer asked to support and carry the body. Relieved from former duties, they are free for new tasks. The anterior limb develops into the human arm and hand and acquires multifarious new functions. For this development, upright posture is not only the genetic condition but also continues to dominate the functions of hand and arm.

Opposition of the thumb has been frequently mentioned as the most essential innovation. This statement is not completely true or completely correct. It is not correct because the hands of other than human primates are not entirely lacking in opposition of the thumb.[8] It is not completely true because one detail is singled out. With the same justi-

[8] The proportions of their hands, however, especially the length of the metacarpus, prevent the formation of the finger–thumb forceps with its characteristic effect (Revesz, 1944).

fication, or lack of it, the index finger has been honored as the specifically human acquisition. Those who say this think, of course, of its function of pointing. The index finger, however, could not point if the hand were not joined to the arm and if the hand and arm were not related to upright posture.

In upright posture, the hand becomes an organ of active gnostic touching—the epicritic, discriminative instrument par excellence. As such, the hand now ranks with the eye and the ear. Anatomy that describes the eye and the ear as sensory organs does not grant the same privileged status to the hand. Anatomy dissects. It divides the hand into different layers and, "in a systematic order," describes the skin as a part of the integument and places the bones in the osteological, the muscles in the myological, and the vessels in the cardiovascular system. Not to call the hand an organ seems strange in view of the fact that "organ" originally meant "tool." For Aristotle (432a 12–4), the hand was "the tool of tools." Anatomy has good reasons for its procedure; they are not, however, simply of a pragmatic order. The hand is a tool in relation to the living, experiencing being—to the man who stretches out his hand, touches, and grasps. The anatomical description that attributes the tissues of the hand to different systems is an analysis of the dead body. The wholes that function as frames of reference differ widely.

The hand as an object of anatomy and the hand experienced as a part of my body are not exactly the same object. The moment the anatomist takes up his scalpel, he behaves, in regard to his own hand, like anyone who has no knowledge of anatomy. This change of attitude is not simply a relapse into naïve, primitive, prescientific behavior, unavoidable as a kind of abbreviating procedure. The anatomist, like everyone else, does not innervate the opponens, the interossei, the flexores digitorum. He does not use *the* hand but *his* hand. The possessive relation expressed by the words "my," "yours," "his," familiar and simple as it appears, contains, in fact, one of the most difficult problems for our understanding. It indicates the transition from physiology to psychology.[9]

Anatomy and physiology relate the body as a whole and its parts to neutral space—as the frame of reference. In experience, however, I experience my hand as an organ in relation to the world. The space that surrounds me is not a piece of neutral extended manifold determined by a Cartesian system of coordinates. Experienced space is action space; it is my space of action. To it, I am related through my body, my limbs, my

---

[9] Sherrington (1947) emphasizes this gap between physiological and psychological approach and method. Although he does not directly mention the problems posed by the possessive relation, he obviously is fully aware of them.

hands. The experience of the body as mine is the origin of possessive experience. All other connotations of possessive relations are derived from it. "Mine" is a distinction that has its place only in the experienced relation of myself and the world. Severed from this basic concept of experience psychology will lose its specific theme and content.

Discussion is necessarily discursive. Analysis cannot avoid dividing into parts that which exists as a whole. When the dissection is completed, synthesis sometimes will be found difficult. It depends on the preceding methods of dividing. They may be so radical as to prevent the restitution of the whole. Adding part to part does not give a full reintegration of the whole. The parts have to be understood from the beginning as parts of that specific whole to which they belong. With attention focused on details, the human arm and hand appear as just one other variation in the development of the forelegs. For every part, one can find a homologue in other species. However, "homologue" means difference as well as similarity. If one gives due respect to both and considers the arm in its entirety within the entire framework of upright posture, one can hardly deny that, through the peculiar structure and function of arm and hand, a new relation between the human organism and the world has been established.

Only in relation to action space, then, will the hand be understood as a sensory organ. It is true that the microscope does not reveal any tactile receivers specific to the skin of the hands. Meissner's corpuscles and Pacinian bodies are most numerous, but they are also found elsewhere. Their number alone would not justify our speaking of the hand as a sensory organ. There is a better reason for doing so than the mere frequency of corpuscles. It is their distribution over the multiplex, mobile structure of the fingers, which, in their diversity, form a motor-sensoric unit. It is not the individual finger that, in feeling, recognizes but all the fingers together, combined in a group. It is not the resting finger that feels but the actively moved digits. Tactile impressions result from motion; nevertheless, we do not experience our motion so much as the quality of the things touched (Katz, 1925). We feel the smoothness of a surface by letting our fingers glide over it.

While motion is indispensable for tactile impressions, the impression-guided fingers function as working tools. This intimate interpenetration of sensorium and motorium is well expressed in such words as "handling," "fingering," "thumbing," "groping," each of which combines the transitive and intransitive meanings of touching into one. The hand has, it seems, an insight of its own. In an ataxia of the legs, seeing may partially compensate for the sensory deficiencies. However, in a posterior root deficit of the hands, seeing is of little help; neither is it an aid in finger agnosia and right–left disturbances.

The epicritic-discriminative functioning of the hands depends on still another condition. There is an inner distance necessary—a remoteness experienced in spite of the proximity of contact. A physician, in examining (palpating) a body, is expected to remain a neutral observer. He should be neither attracted nor disgusted by what he observes. His goal is not closeness nor unification. His action resembles that of a wine-taster who takes a sip but spits it out again, avoiding swallowing and incorporation. The gnostic function of touching depends on the uprght posture, which through its permanent distances produces a hiatus in the immediateness of contact.

"Experienced distance" (Minkowski, 1930) cannot be expressed in geometrical terms. It cannot be defined as the length of a straight line connecting two points in space. The geometrical consideration of distance is completely indifferent to time. The concept of a vector adding direction, and thereby time, to distance would be more adequate. Still, it lacks any conative character. Geometrical distance relates two points in space, both detached from the observer. Experienced distance is that which unfolds between an experiencing being and another person or object. It can be experienced only by a being who aims at unification or separation. The modes of unification and separation vary. The spatial relation is only one among others. While experienced distance cannot, therefore, be expressed completely in spatial terms, it never lacks a spatial element. The space to which it is related, however, is not the conceptual homogeneous space of mathematics but perceptual space, articulated in accordance with the specific corporeal organization of the experiencing person.

The role of distance is not limited to the hand as a sensory organ. It also dominates manual expression, communication, and contact. Distance is ambivalent. Sometimes we want to preserve it; sometimes we want to eliminate it. The hand is instrumental in both cases. When our equilibrium is out of balance or disturbed, the hand grasps for a hold. In darkness, it functions as scout and sentry, warning against collision and searching for contact. Sometimes no hold is found, no contact is made. Searching hands stretch into the void. It is as if emptiness were localized in our hands. Indeed, only the empty hand, like the beggar's hand, can receive. Emptiness is the condition by which our hands can be filled. Only because of remoteness can it make contact.

We understand that the phobic patient feels somewhat more comfortable by carrying something in his hand, maybe no more than a cane, an umbrella, or a bag. Does not each of us, if he alone is exposed to a group—e.g., as a speaker or an actor—like to put his hands on a chair or a desk or to fiddle with a pencil or notes? Finally, we may even surprise ourselves with gesticulations which help less to clarify our thoughts than to fill emptiness and cover distance. In such situations, we are only one step ahead of the embarrassed child who pulls his fingers, as if in doing this he could fill his empty hands.

All the variations of the expression of emptiness are related to upright posture. They are, it seems, a universal language. When Darwin prepared his book on expression (1910), he sent questionnaires to missionaries abroad in order to find out the distribution of gestures familiar to us in the western world. He was interested, among other things, in the gesture of shrugging the shoulders, an expression of the incapacity to advise or to help. Here, one again meets the empty hands. With the lifting of the shoulders, we also supinate our arms and demonstrate the empty hands. Shrugging the shoulders is an expression of fruitless endeavor. Darwin learned through his questionnaires that this expression is indigenous everywhere, not imported from other civilizations, not formed by more or less local conventions and customs. Its universality proves it to be autochthonous with the human race. It is a universal and spontaneous gesture of man, wherever and whenever he, with upright posture, experiences a distance from things and fellow-men.

Expansion of the Body Scheme by the Arms

In upright posture, the arms expand the body scheme. The arm motion circumscribes a sphere which surrounds the body as territorial waters surround the shores of a country. This constitutes a section of space that, like the three-mile zone, belongs to the central body and yet not completely. It is not an indisputable property but a variable possession. My intervening space is a medium between me and the world. As such, it has the greatest social significance; it mediates between the other and me. In this space, which is not completely my own, I can meet the other as the other, join him as my partner, arm in arm or hand in hand, and yet leave him in his integrity. Through this space, I hold the other at arm's length or let him come toward me and receive him with open arms. It is the space of the linking of arms or of embracing[10] but also of crossing the arms, a motion in which we keep distance, "circumwalling" ourselves in an attitude of defense or of fortification. It is also the space of handshaking. There are many nuances of handshaking, such as warm

---

[10] The etymological root of "embrace" is *brac*, as in *brachium*, the Latin word for arm.

and strong or cool and hesitant. There can be spontaneous advance or a no less spontaneous containment—as by the hand of the schizophrenic. In a farewell, the hands hold each other, press each other, move on together; they will not part. In a handshake that seals a bargain, the hands meet each other halfway in a mutually firm grasp in which the motion is arrested, expressing final agreement. Even the formalized gesture signifies social acceptance. We pass through a reception line, and the hands stretched out toward us tell us that we are welcome and received into the group.

The "three-mile zone" is not static. It is a border with fluctuating frontiers. It expands or shrinks. The body scheme is not so much a concept or image that a person has of his own body as it is an ensemble of directions and demarcations—directions in which we reach out toward the world and demarcations that we encounter in contact with the world (Schilder, 1935). The body scheme is also experienced, therefore, as an I–world relation. Corresponding to our conation, space itself loses its static character, opens endlessly before us, and expands or represses us. The "de-pressed," with his head bent, his shoulders lowered, his arms fallen to his sides, and with his slow, short steps succumbs to the pressure that pushes him down. The Christian attitude of kneeling in prayer, of bending the head, and of interlacing the hands expresses humility, surrender to a higher power. The hands, withdrawn from the territorial space and joined at the midline in full symmetry—taking no sides— have renounced all action. The Moslem, in his pious prostration, goes to the extreme of fatalistic submission. The ancient Greek attitude of praying—upright, arms lifted and extended—opened and widened the body space in an enthusiastic gesture—"en-thus-iastic," indeed, because *en-theos-iastic* means "to receive the God" or "to be possessed by him."

> Ah, but a man's reach should exceed his grasp,
> Or what's a heaven for?—Robert Browning

In pointing, also, man's reach exceeds his grasp. Upright posture enables us to see things in their distance without any intention of incorporating them. In the totality of this panorama that unfolds in front of us, the pointing finger singles out one detail. The arm constitutes intervening space as a medium which separates and connects. The pointing arm, hand, and finger share with the intervening space the dynamic functions of separating and connecting. The pointing hand directs the sight of another one to whom I show something, for pointing is a social gesture. I do not point for myself; I indicate something to someone else. To distant things, within the visible horizon, we are related by common experience. As observers, we are directed, although through different perspectives, to one and the same thing, to one and the same world. Distance creates new forms of communication.

The organization of action space is deeply imprinted on the memory. Even after the loss of a limb, it persists in the "phantom." As long as there is a phantom, there is also intervening space through which the illusive arm stretches to a distant world, with the illusive hand in a terminal position. It is a common experience that the phantom arm shrinks, that the phantom hand moves closer to the trunk, but it never disappears completely; it is preserved in its terminal position. The loss of the limb reduces the reach. It modifies the intervening space but does not annihilate it altogether.

The human arm owes its specific mobility to upright posture. Many factors contribute to its development and functions, but through all of them upright posture is at work. First to be mentioned is the change in proportions of the sagittal and transverse diameter of the chest. In quadrupeds, the sagittal diameter is relatively long, the curvature of the ribs flattened, the motions of the humerus in the shoulder joint restricted, and the flexibility of the elongated scapula limited. The humerus is kept in close contact with the trunk. The basic function of supporting the trunk prevails, and this imprints one definite general mark on the structure of the shoulder girdle, in spite of all the variations to be found in different species. With upright posture, the transverse diameter is increased. This change, together with the corresponding sharp, angular curvature of the ribs, gives to the human thorax its characteristic shape, which in turn permits the development of the shoulder girdle into a kind of superstructure. This superstructure, which tailors like to emphasize, moves the root of the arm upward very high and markedly to the side. Far from supporting the human body, the arm and the shoulder are themselves supported or, better, held in position by muscle action, especially by that of the trapezius. The arm, separated from the trunk in its full length, can swing from its elevated hub with the widest angle of excursions in the greatest variety of motions.

The arm, not designed for one specific task, has acquired the potentiality for a wide range of performance. The principle of growing indetermination, one of Hughlings Jackson's criteria of functional evolution (1932), is applicable to the comparative anatomy of the shoulder girdle.[11] One should not forget that the human arm neither supports the

---

[11] The highest centers of the brain are, according to Jackson, the least organized, the most complex, and the most voluntary. Evolution is a passage from the most to the least organized, from the simple to the most complex, from the most automatic to the

trunk nor has to hold up the body, a function still assigned to the fore-limb of tree-inhabiting primates. Small but still significant changes en-sue in the shape and position of scapula and clavicle, in the origin and insertion of the shoulder muscles, and in the configuration of the acro-mio-clavicular and the sterno-clavicular joints. All this together pro-vides for maximum flexibility of the arm, aiding the display of the mechanisms of the scapulo-humeral articulation, where, because of the looseness of the capsule and the shallowness of the glenoid cavity, the humerus can move with great ease in all directions. In the hip joints, on the contrary, the head of the femur is deeply set in the socket of the acetabular cavity and the capsule is tight and reinforced by strong liga-ments. While the primarily tectonic formation of the neck of the femur also somewhat extends the range of excursions, the emphasis in the hip is on stability, in the shoulder, on flexibility.

Language, obviously inspired by phenomenological observation, takes the arm as the prototype of the articulation of a limb and of its motions from the joint, for the root of the word "arm" is $\sqrt{ar}$ with the meaning "to fit, to join," the same root from which the Greek ar-thros and the evenly Latin ar-ticulatio stem.[12]

Within the totality of the new spatial dimensions acquired with up-right posture, lateral space is perhaps most important. Through the mo-bility and action of arm and hand, lateral space becomes accessible and relevant for man. In this sector, most of the human crafts originated. Hammer and ax, scythe and sickle, the carpenter's saw, the weaver's shuttle, the potter's wheel, the mason's trowel, and the painter's brush all relate to lateral space. This list could be extended ad libitum but prob-ably would never come to an end, for lateral space is the matrix of primi-tive and sophisticated skills: of spinning and sewing, stirring and ironing, sowing, and husking, soldering and welding, fiddling and golfing, batting and discus-throwing.

The crafts of peace are followed, accompanied, or preceded by the techniques and weapons of war: club, sword, spear, bow, sling, and

---

most voluntary (Jackson, 1932, pp. 46 ff.). The highest centers were not, or were little, accessible to direct experimentation in Jackson's time. Their functions were found by inference, reasoning backward from the observation of peripheral perform-ances. The diverse functions of finger, hand, arm, and shoulder would tell something about the organization of the corresponding highest centers. Complexity of the brain centers must have and does have its exact counterpart in the organization of the limbs.

[12] In this paper, the writer has made frequent use of etymology, although it is not customary to introduce "linguistic evidence" in a biological discussion. However, because the history of a word represents the sedimentation of general psychological experience, it appears to the writer to be justified to refer to etymology as an auxiliary discipline.

boomerang, to mention some elemental forms only. Lateral space makes action at a distance possible, as David successfully proved to Goliath.[13] Superiority has not always belonged to the light forces. Even so, the importance of action at a distance, for which throwing is the primordial and perennial model, remains undiminished and, with it, the importance of lateral space.

The development of primitive and elaborate weapons makes one wonder whether "arm" (the limb) and "arms" (the weapons) may have the same etymological root. To this question, the linguists answer both "yes" and "no." Their answer is "no" because arms, arming, and armament are historically related to the Latin root *arma*. The Romans' word for "arm" (the limb) is *brachium*, with another derivation and meaning. However, the root for *arma*, "weapon," is also $\sqrt{ar}$.

In considering the phenomenon of throwing, one cannot pass over the remarkable difference in the manner of throwing of the two sexes. It seems the manifestation of a biological, not an acquired, difference. Gesell (Gesell *et al.*, 1940, pp. 85-89) illustrates the familiar facts with some good photographs. They show little girls of five and six and two boys of the same age throwing a ball. The girl of five does not make any use of lateral space. She does not stretch her arm sideward; she does not twist her trunk; she does not move her legs, which remain side by side. All she does in preparation for throwing is to lift her right arm forward to the horizontal and to bend the forearm backward in a pronate position. In the final motion, action is limited to the triceps and flexors of the hand. The excursion of her motion in the elbow joint does not exceed an angle of about 90°. The length of the lever from the fulcrum at the elbow to the palm of the hand coincides with the length of the forearm. The ball is released without force, speed, or accurate aim. It enters almost immediately the descending branch of a steep parabola. At the age of six, the girl tilts her right shoulder slightly and moves the

[13] In this Biblical legend, a situation permanently repeating itself is told as a unique event. The Bible takes great pains to describe Goliath's heavy armor (Sam I: 17). It also tells that Saul offered David his own sword, a "helmet of brass," and a "coat of mail." However, David, not trained in the use of these weapons, laid them down. We may not go far wrong if we assume that the Bible, in a poetical condensation, describes as a duel what is really a conflict of two civilizations and of two types of military tactics. Goliath, the Philistine, belonged to a settled, seafaring nation, advanced in the techniques of metal forgery; David, described as a shepherd, belonged to a small nomadic tribe that invaded the Philistine territory from the interior. The conflict of the two coexistent types of military tactics is this: Goliath, heavily armed—the Philistine "Maginot Line"—almost immobilized by the weight of his armor—someone has to carry his shield before him—can move only directly forward to a close fight, while David, a kind of guerilla fighter, finds his advantage in mobility, in dodging, and in sudden attacks. This conflict between fortified defense and mobile attack is found in all military history up to our own time.

left foot forward one small step, but shows no further progress. A boy of the same age, when preparing to throw, stretches his right arm sideward and backward; supinates the forearm;[14] twists, turns, and bends his trunk; and moves his right foot backward. From this stance, he can support his throwing almost with the full strength of his total motorium. The excursion of his final motion reaches an angle of 180°. It moves around the left standing leg as its central axis. The radius of this semicircle exceeds by far the full length of the arm. The ball leaves the hand with considerable acceleration; it moves toward its goal in a long flat curve.

As this difference appears in early childhood, it cannot result from the development of the female breast. While the legendary Amazons had the right breast removed to allow the use of bow and spear,[15] it seems certain that Nausicaa and all her companions threw a ball just like our Betty's, Mary's, and Susan's. How can we explain the difference? The little girl has no more difficulty in keeping her equilibrium than the boy. It is true that she is weaker in muscle power, but, therefore, one should expect her to compensate for this lack of strength with added preparatory excursion. Instead, we find her avoiding the turn into lateral space. Maybe the masculine way of throwing corresponds to masculine "eccentricity," while the feminine attitude reveals a deep-seated restraint and an inclination to circle around one's own center. The difference, then, would belong to the area of expression; it would not be a difference of strength and build but of a general psychological attitude in relation to the world and to space.

Thus far, lateral space has been discussed as if it were a unit, a single whole. Indeed, in many motions, we lift our arms symmetrically in surrounding space. However, even simultaneous movements need not be actually symmetrical. They appear symmetrical; they are not so in their intention. The arms can be stretched and the hands can point in opposite directions, to the right and to the left, at the same time. It is this contrast of directions that divides, articulates, and organizes lateral space, producing heteronymous, unequal parts. These can be reunited into an ordered whole where one half dominates the other. Spatial syntax cannot deviate from the general principle of taxis, which always demands a leading part to which the others are subordinated. The pair, right–left, is the true embodiment of unity, unfolding itself into opposites or, if we begin with the opposites, the unity of a contrasting manifold. Both

[14] Supination reaches its fullest and freest excursion with the horizontal abduction of the arm.
[15] Amazon means a-mazos, without breast.

aspects belong together. Practical discrimination between and coordination of right and left precede their conceptual distinction. The amazing cases of autotopagnosia demonstrate to what extent the organization of the body scheme, as a manifold of directions, dominates recognition. In the Gerstmann syndrome, we find (1) finger agnosia, (2) agraphia, and (3) acalculia, besides a right–left disturbance. Searching for a common denominator, we may find it in the loss of the capacity to organize opposite directions into one or to break the unit into opposite directions:

1.   The fingers of the hand repeat, so to speak, the right–left scheme for one side. Thumb and little finger point in opposite directions. This maximum of divergency (the direct opposition) sets the pattern for the intermediary positions.

2.   Writing, the spatial construction of letters, presupposes the same capacity to differentiate a scheme of varying directions and to establish them simultaneously in advance. The shape of the printed letters *b* and *d* illustrates this well.

3.   Numbers follow the same principle. Two, the model of all numbers, is a unit of one plus one, which, while they become united, remain separate: one and one, or two. The figure "one" is unity, the "two," a unit. It should therefore not be surprising that a child learns cardinal numbers a considerable time after mastering the ordinals. While he knows the series of numerals and enumerates the fingers of one hand, he is not able to sum them up into one unit of five. When he has reached the age when he can conceive of cardinal numbers, he is usually able to distinguish right and left.

Neurophysiological Considerations

The highest skills are contingent on the unification of opposites—the coordination of relatively independent parts that are not bound together by symmetry, homology, or synergy. A good violinist in a fast spiccato run coordinates the motions of his left hand and fingers with those of his right shoulder and arm. He has to combine into one pattern the action of distal muscles on one side with that of proximal ones on the other. His movements should be speedy, accurate, well-timed in tempo and rhythm, and with the appropriate accentuation and phrasing. Playing from parts, his motions will be directed by seeing and controlled by hearing. Here, "seeing" does not mean simply response to optical stimuli but comprehension of symbols which express pitch, time proportions, and dynamics; "hearing" is not merely the reception of acoustical stimuli but the anticipation and perception of sounds ordered in the various aspects of music. The necessary flexibility and versatility of motion of the upper limbs could not be accomplished without the compensatory movements of the trunk and leg; in other words, postural adjustments are continually necessary, and—perhaps not yet satisfied with all this— we may have to allow our artist to tap the basic meter with his foot, in this way setting one mechanical, repetitive motion against all the variations. Finally, a concert recital will vigorously activate the autonomic system.

Such a performance, which involves the functions of the whole body, depends on the capacities of the nervous system for differentiation and integration. The highest forms of integration are proportionate to the available divisions of labor. Lateral space, the development of handedness, has brought about the highest forms of integration. While considerable knowledge has been accumulated relative to the cooperating parts, the organization of the whole is still inadequately understood. Neuroanatomy and neurophysiology have rarely envisaged the diverse mechanisms related to lateral space as one functional unit. In a short survey, one may enumerate its major components, their connections, and their ways of interaction.

Clinical experience, more than experimental observation, points to the inferior parietal lobule (gyrus supramarginalis and angularis) as the highest level of integration concerned here. It has been found involved in cases of right–left disturbances, finger agnosia, agraphia, alexia, and constructive apraxia. As the highest level of coordination, it should be supplied with tactile impulses, both exteroceptive and proprioceptive, and with acoustical and optical stimuli. If neighborhood relations mean anything, the inferior parietal lobule may well be looked on as a center, surrounded by and connected with the somesthetic areas of the postcentral gyrus, the optical areas of the occipital lobe, and the receptive acoustical areas of the temporal lobe. It is not to be expected that any motor activity would start from here but that motions would be integrated, directed, and controlled from this area. Neighborhood relations also indicate that the inferior parietal lobule receives impulses from Brodmann's area 22, the acoustical adversive field, and from area 19, the occipital eye field, both areas serving adaptation of the body to events in lateral space. The superior parietal gyrus, Brodmann's area 7, has not yet been mentioned. Foerster (1936) believes it to be an extrapyramidal field, more important than precentral area 6 with its subdivisions. Like areas 19 and 22, area 7 is also supposed to be in the service of motions related to lateral space. It closes the circle of the areas surrounding the inferior parietal lobule, which, therefore, is in close relation to an extrapyramidal field, initiating synergistic motions, and to the central gyri with their specified focal organization. If areas 39 and 40 function as a field of integration, bilateral representation of sensorium and motorium is indispensable. Commissural and association fibers, which, it seems, provide the main connections, could well serve this purpose. With the commissural connections of corresponding areas, a time differential may become effective through which the minor hemisphere may be subordinated to the dominant one.

Action in lateral space is, to a great extent, directed and controlled by vision. The oculomotor apparatus, on all its levels from the periphery to the cortical eye fields no less than the central optical pathways, is intimately related to motion in lateral space. The homonymous division of visual fields and retina which cuts through the macula is a most appropriate device for the control of lateral space, perhaps even more so then for binocular frontal vision. In lower vertebrates, all retinal fibers cross. The reason may be, as Ramon y Cajal (1909) assumed, that in the absence of crossing, the optical projection would be completely incongruent with the visible objects. The new acquisition in mammals with overlapping visual fields is that the temporal fibers remain uncrossed. The twofold cortical representation of lateral eye movements demonstrates their great importance. The frontal eye field probably regulates voluntary movements of the eyes; the occipital field controls lateral gaze induced by the sight of moving objects.

In the brain stem, the cortical nuclear fibers reach the pontine center of conjugated lateral gaze, which is also influenced by acoustical and vestibular stimuli. The final section of this pathway has not yet been fully established. The cortico nuclear connections add conscious and voluntary control to the mesencephalic automatic regulations of gaze and posture. In this group, the Moro reflex has special significance for the present problem. The functions of the superior colliculi seem limited, in man, to the control of vertical movements, while the wide cortical eye fields chiefly direct rotation of the eyes to the contralateral side. Some tracts, descending from the midbrain and ending in the cervical cord, integrate the functions of the accessorius, of neck and shoulder muscles, into the complex sensory motor system in control of lateral space. On the most peripheral level, the plexus formation seems to serve the coordination of proximal and distal muscles.

Upright Posture and the Formation of the Human Head

Upright posture has lifted eye and ear from the ground. In the family of senses, smell has lost the right of the first-born. Seeing and hearing have assumed dominion. Now, these really function as senses of distance. In every species, eye and ear respond to stimuli from remote objects, but the interest of animals is limited to the proximate. Their attention is caught by that which is within the confines of reaching or approaching. The relation of sight and bite distinguishes the human face from those of lower animals. Animal jaws, snoot, trunk, and beak—all of them organs acting in the direct contact of grasping and gripping—are placed in the "visor line" of the eyes. With upright posture, with the development of the arm, the mouth is no longer needed for catching and carrying or for attacking and defending. It sinks down from the "visor line" of the eyes, which now can be turned directly in a piercing, open look toward distant things and rest fully upon them, viewing them with the detached interest of wondering. Bite has become subordinated to sight.

Language expresses this relation in signifying the whole, the face, through its dominating part—the eyes, as in the English and French word "visage," in the German *Gesicht,* and in the Greek *prosopon.* While the origin of the Latin word *facies*—and therefore, also, of the English noun "face"—is uncertain, the verb "to face" reassumes, in a remarkable twist, the original phenomenological meaning: to look at things straight ahead and to withstand their thrust. Eyes that lead jaws and fangs to the prey are always charmed and spellbound by nearness. To eyes looking straight forward—to the gaze of upright posture—things reveal themselves in their own nature. Sight penetrates depth; sight becomes insight.

Animals move in the direction of their digestive axis. Their bodies are expanded between mouth and anus as between an entrance and an exit, a beginning and an ending. The spatial orientation of the human body is different throughout. The mouth is still an inlet but no longer a beginning, the anus, an outlet but no longer the tail end. Man in upright posture, his feet on the ground and his head uplifted, does not move in the line of his digestive axis; he moves in the direction of his vision. He is surrounded by a world panorama, by a space divided into world regions joined together in the totality of the universe. Around him, the horizons retreat in an ever growing radius. Galaxy and diluvium, the infinite and the eternal, enter into the orbit of human interests.

The transformation of the animal jaws into the human mouth is an extensive remodeling: mandible, maxilla, and teeth are not the only parts recast. The mark of the jaws is brute force. The muscles that close the jaws, especially the masseter, are built for simple, powerful motions.

Huge ridges and crests, which provide the chewing muscles with an origin appropriate to the development of power, encompass the skull of the gorilla. They disappear when the jaws are transformed into the mouth. The removal of these pinnacles permits the increase of the brain case while, at the same time, the reduction of the mighty chewing muscles permits the development of the subtle mimic and phonetic muscles.

The transformation of jaws into the mouth is a prerequisite for the development of language but only one of them. There are many other factors involved. In upright posture, the ear is no longer limited to the perception of noises—rustling, crackling, hissing, bellowing, roaring—as indicators of actual events, like warnings, threats, or lures. The external ear loses its mobility. While the ear muscles are preserved, their function of adapting the ear to actuality ceases. Detached from actuality, the ear can comprehend sounds in the sounds' own shape—in their musical or phonetic pattern. This capacity to separate the acoustical Gestalt from the acoustical material makes it possible to produce purposefully and to "re-produce" intentionally sounds articulated according to a preconceived scheme.

Just as the speaker produces his words—articulated sounds which function as symbols or carriers of meanings—these should be received and understood by the listener in exactly the same way. The articulated sound, the phoneme, has an obligatory shape. The phoneme itself is a universal. The relation which connects speech and speaker can be held in abeyance so that speech as such can be abstracted, written down, preserved, and repeated. Speech, while connecting speaker and listener, keeps them at the same time at a distance. The most intimate conversation is bound to common, strict rules of phonetics, grammar, and intended meanings. A spontaneous cry can never be wrong. The pronunciation of a word or the production of the phoneme is either right or wrong. The virtuosity acquired by the average person in expressing himself personally and individually in the general medium of language hides the true character of linguistic communication. It is rediscovered by reflection when disturbances of any kind interfere with the easy and prompt use of language or when the immediateness of contact does not tolerate linguistic distance, and the word dies in an angry cry, in tender babble, or in gloomy silence.

In conversation, we talk with one another about something. Conversation, therefore, demands distance in three directions: from the acoustical signs, so that the phoneme can be perceived in its pure form; from things, so that they can be the object of common discourse; from the other person, so that speech can mediate between the speaker and listener. Upright posture produces such distances. It lifts us from the ground, puts us opposite to things, and confronts us with one another.

The sensory organs cannot change without a corresponding change in the central nervous system. No part could be altered alone. With upright posture, there is a transformation of sensorium and motorium, of periphery and center, of form and function. While upright posture permits the formation of the human skull and, thereby, of the human brain, the maintenance of upright posture demands the development of the human nervous system. Who can say what comes first and what comes last—what is cause and what is effect? All these alterations are related to upright posture as their basic theme. "In man, everything converges into the form which he has now. In his history, everything is understandable through it, nothing without it" (Herder, 1784, p. 129).

The phenomenon of upright posture should not be neglected in favor of the lying man, or the man on the couch. To do this is to ignore facts that are obvious and undebatable, accessible without labyrinthine detours of interpretation, facts which exact consideration and permit proof and demonstration. It is true that sleep and rest, lying down and lying with someone, are essential functions; it is no less true that man is built for upright posture and gait and that upright posture, which is as original as any drive, determines his mode of being-in-the-world.

"The upright gait of man is the only natural one to him, nay, it is the organization for every performance of his species and his distinguishing character" (Herder, 1784, p. 128). Human physique reveals human nature.

Summary

The wound cut by the Cartesian dichotomy of mind and body is covered over, but not yet healed, by mere reference to the mind–body unity. This term is useful only if it is filled with definite meaning and classified in its presuppositions as well as in its consequences. The idea of a mind–body unit demands, first of all, a revision of those traditional concepts of psychology which are shaped in accordance with a theory of a mind–body dichotomy. Experience can no longer be interpreted as a train—an accumulation or integration of sensations, percepts, thoughts, ideas, and volitions occurring in the soul, the mind, the consciousness, or the unconscious for that matter. In experiencing, man finds himself always within the world, directed toward it, acting and suffering.

This study discusses the mind–body relation from one well-defined point of view. In analyzing upright posture, it points out in detail the correspondence between human physique and the basic traits of human experience and behavior. It also sets forth how some expressive attitudes of man are related to his basic orientation in the world as an upright creature.

Upright posture, which dominates human existence in its unity, makes us see that no basis exists for claiming any kind of priority for the drives. The "rational" is as genuine a part of human nature as the "animal."

References

Aristotle. *De anima.*

Asch, S., & H. Witkin. Studies in space perception. *J. exper. Psychol.*, *1948*, **38**, 325–337, 435–477.

Browning, R. Andrea del Sarto.

Darwin, C. *The expression of the emotions* (1872). New York: Appleton, 1910.

Foerster, O. Die motorischen Bahnen und Felder. In O. Bumke & O. Foerster, *Handbuch der Neurologie.* Vol. VI. Berlin: Springer-Verlag, 1936.

Gesell, A., *et al. The first five years of life.* NewYork & London: Harper, 1940.

Gibson, E., & Mowrer, O. Determinants of the perceived vertical and horizontal. *Psychol. Rev.*, 1938, **45**.

Goldstein, K. *Über Zeigen und Greifen.* Vol. 4. Berlin: Der Nervenarzt, 1931.

Gregory, W. K. *The humerus from fish to man.* American Museum Novitates, January 31, 1949.

Herder, G. W. *Ideen zur Philosophie der Geschichte der Menschheit.* Riga: 1784.

Jackson, H. *Selected writings. . . .* Vol. 2. London: J. Taylor, 1932.

Katz, D. *Der Aufbau der Tastwelt.* Leipzig: Engelman, 1925.

Kleist, K. *Gehirnpathologie*, Leipzig: 1934.

Minkowski, E. Les notions de distance vécue. *J. de Psychol.*, 1930, **27**, 727–745.

Moskati. *Vom Koerperlichen Wesentlichen Unterschiede der Thiere und Menschen.* Goettingen: 1771.

Nielsen, N. J. *Agnosia, apraxia, aphasia.* (2nd ed.) New York & London: Hoeber, 1946.

Portmann, A. *Biologische Fragmente zu einer Lebre vom Menschen.* Basel: 1944.

Ramon y Cajal, S. *Histologie du système nerveux de l'homme et des vertébrés.* 1909.

Revesz, G. *Die menschliche Hand.* New York & Basel: Karger, 1944.

Schilder, P. The image and appearance of the human body. *Psychol. Monogr.*, 1935, No. 4.

Sherrington, Ch. *The integrative action of the nervous system.* (9th ed.) Cambridge: Cambridge Univ. Press, 1947.

Sittig, O. *Über Apraxie.* Berlin: S. Karger, 1931.

von Uexkuell, J. *Theoretical biology.* New York: Harcourt, Brace, 1926.

Weidenreich, F. *Apes, giants and man.* Chicago: Univer. of Chicago Press, 1946.

CHAPTER EIGHT

Man: A Questioning Being

It is a questioning being that faces the world when man looks at things, turns to his fellow men, or reflects upon himself. Whether he asks for counsel and information regarding his everyday needs, or, far beyond any practical considerations, strives for insight, whether his concern is with the first or the last questions, he does only what he cannot leave undone. He can inquire into things, he can question himself, he can direct his questions to others or be interrogated by them, or he can run away from perplexing situations or turn his inquisitiveness to the uncovering of problems. In so doing, he only demonstrates and fulfills a basic mode of human existence. When he attempts to evade painful questions, to withdraw from "re-sponsibility," questions follow and pursue him—even into sleep. They emerge from his past, they threaten him from the future, they haunt him in the present. Questions themselves never disappear because questioning never ceases. Although particular questions can be transmitted to others and accepted by them as their own, the act of questioning cannot be taught. Nor does it require a teacher. The first question arises early in the life of every healthy child, from the very roots of its existence. We are able to ask single questions because we are questioning beings at our very core.

We must therefore distinguish but not separate the relationship of the questioner to the world (and to himself) from the relationship of the questioner to the person questioned and, finally, from that of the question to the answer. The *psychological* relation of the questioner to the world, the *logical* one of the question to the answer, and the *sociological* one of the questioner to the person questioned are intimately connected. The ability to formulate questions and to seek answers as well as the possibility of putting questions to others for an answer must be inherent in the relation of the questioner to the world.

In questioning, man has passed the threshold between mere animal existence and human life. At this point, he did not have to wait for Aristotle's guidance. The syllogism in its various forms, the laws of contradiction, and other rules of logic had to be discovered and formulated; questioning is man's natural endowment. Questions are as revealing as dreams, or even more so. Since their selection depends on historical, social, and cultural conditions, a full inventory of the questions that have animated and agitated or failed to disquiet a person, a nation, or an epoch gives us deep historical insight. With all such knowledge, however, we have not yet reached the center of our inquiry, for the problem first in order is not what questions a person asks but that he is capable of asking at all. Among the empirical sciences, none is more interested in this problem than psychiatry. Confronted with psychotic patients, the psychiatrist faces—at least in a great number of cases—persons who are impaired in that basic capacity.

Questions and answers are dependent on language. Gaze and gesture serve only as substitutes for speech. The ability to question, to speak, and, it should be added, to think point to a common source. An investigation of the act of questioning necessarily leads on to an investigation of thought and speech. The act of questioning is the beginning and the origin of thought. The psychology of thinking starts—or should start—from an examination of the questioning act.

This was not the opinion of the earlier experimentalists in psychology. The assumption of some sensory elements, ideas or images, connected in accordance with the "laws of association," seemed to satisfy all requirements for a theory of thought. Since the turn of the century, the psychology of thinking has moved far away from this simple form of associationism, in spite of Pavlov and his many followers who were eager to translate the older concepts of the mechanism of ideas into physiological terms. Nonsensory elements, "awareness," have been added to the traditional sensory elements; "tasks" and "determining tendencies" have replaced the older "reproductive tendencies." The Gestalt psychologists have coined the expression "system under stress" to deal with the motivation of thinking. Psychoanalysis has added the hypothesis of unconscious dynamics to conscious or experienced motives. One may even speak about problems and problem situations. Nevertheless, the phenomenon of questioning in the complexity of its psychological, logical, and sociological relations has hardly come into sight. While everyday-life conversation is made up, to a large extent, of questions—starting with "How are you?"—while the columns of every newspaper are filled with questions and problems, while the country is flooded with questionnaires of every kind, and while the future is "but one big question mark," psychological textbooks, dictionaries, and monographs have little to say about questioning; philosophy, too, offers no logic of questioning.

And yet, in actuality, one might well consider every statement as an answer to a question implicitly posed. Predication, which is the primary form of assertion, bears direct evidence of this. In all sentences of the form S is P the subject S is determined essentially or in an accidental respect by the predicate. S, the undetermined but definable term, could be this or that. From among the many possibilities, the predicate selects one as actually defining the subject. "The weather is fair" refers to other possibilities, like cold, rainy, stormy, etc.; "The door is open" says something, because the door could be closed or locked. The statement, "It was a brick house," does not mention other material, e.g., wood, stone, or aluminum; however, it silently alludes to the other possibilities, for otherwise it would be a mere tautology. Even apodictic statements like $(a + b) (a - b) = a^2 - b^2$, just in positively excluding any other possibility, take cognizance of them. As a logical proposition, the sentence is confined to its established meaning; as a psychological judgment, it encompasses many other possibilities. From the point of view of mathematics, there is only one correct answer to the question, "How much is 7×18?" From the point of view of the one who asks the question there are many possibilities. Otherwise, he would not have "to find out," namely, among the many possible answers; otherwise, he could not err. The psychology of thinking comprises truth and error, wisdom and madness, insight and delusion. The process of thinking reaches beyond the logical relations of thoughts. Therefore, if a statement's implicit question is not comprehensible, the statement itself remains unintelligible. We cannot follow a conversation when we do not know "what the others are talking about." Introductions and commentaries of great works frequently serve no other purpose than to elaborate the questions which have once moved the author but which have not been stated in so many words. Maybe the author took them for granted in the historical situation or purposely concealed them; maybe the questions were hidden from him or, for aesthetic reasons, he preferred to pass over them. After all, it is the question which links the single steps of thinking into a train of thought.

The question proffers possibilities to the answer and demands that the who or what, the when and where, and the how and why be defined. The unequivocal and the obvious exclude the question or make it superfluous and senseless. It is meaningful to ask, "What day is today?" Today may be the twenty-second of August or the tenth of September or some other calendar day. It is meaningful to ask, "Are you back already?" only if one tries to express surprise. This is undoubtedly how the question will be understood. Taken literally, it would be a meaningless question—either a joke, which feigns to treat the meaningless as if it were meaningful, or folly, which actually treats the meaningless as meaningful. The limit of determinable possibilities is reached in questions that can be answered with a "yes" or "no."

There are other kinds of senseless questions—the paradoxical and the absurd ones. A question is paradoxical when it demands the determination of unlimited and, therefore, actually undeterminable possibilities. In meaningless questions, the answer is superfluous; there is nothing to decide. In paradoxical questions, the answer is impossible; nothing can be decided. Absurd questions miss the area of possible decision entirely. It would be absurd to ask, "Is red heavier than green?" or "In what key is 2 : 2?" A prerequisite of meaningfulness is that a question must move within a given area of possible decisions.

From this short consideration of the logical relationship between question and answer, we may learn something about the psychological state of the questioner. The questioner is amazed or confused; but he is not simply confused—he is also aware of his confusion. Further, the possibility of clarification is anticipated in the answer-directed question. The lack of knowledge of the questioner is not total ignorance, not complete lack of knowing; his lack of knowledge is qualified and is in itself a kind of knowing. The confusion of the questioner, after all, has its source in his discovery of possibilities which offer the opportunity for deciding. The questioner becomes confused because he does not simply accept things as they appear and is no longer oriented toward them in terms of direct action. The individual begins to realize the questionable character of phenomena once he suspends direct action, achieves distance from objects, and reflects upon himself. The questioner is amazed, as Aristotle says, that things are the way they are. They could be different; the questioner has discovered the possibilities of things behaving differently. He breaks through the horizon of sensory phenomena; he transcends the immediate present. In this transcendence, he "comprehends" the phenomena as parts of a greater whole. The phenomena themselves have become transparent to the questioner; through their transparency, he begins to see the order that holds the parts together. The questioner "knows that he does not know"; his ignorance is preknowledge about a possible order. Through the mediation of an order already discovered—or yet to be discovered—the question directs itself toward a decisive answer.

The driving force behind occidental astronomy was the attempt to "save the appearance," that is, to understand the apparently confusing and irregular movements of heavenly bodies as an expression of an inviolable order. The confusion of the questioner originates from and with his expectation of an anticipated order. One and the same existential attitude manifests itself in question and answer, in questioning and understanding. The disquietude fermented with the question would not cease with the dawn of insight if the same situation did not persist. For just this reason, we are right in pointing to the act of questioning as the origin and the beginning of thought. Thinking is a movement from question to answer. In order to understand man as a thinking being, we must grasp the initial state and the closing situation as well as the path which leads from the question to the answer.

The difference between the psychology of thinking and the logical order of thoughts was not unknown to the "father of logic." "All men by nature desire to know," states Aristotle in the opening sentence of the *Metaphysics* (980a #1). An indication of this, according to Aristotle, is the delight men take in sensual phenomena, even apart from their usefulness. Man, however, is not satisfied with sense impressions alone. He is pushed forward by amazement, wonder, and admiration. "As a result of his amazement, man begins now, and first began to philosophize. Originally he wondered about the obvious difficulties; then, in his step by step progress, he discovered more magnificent problems, e.g., in the appearance of the moon, the sun, and the stars, in the origin of the universe" (982b #12-17). Later in the same chapter, Aristotle again repeats, "Man begins by wondering that things are as they are" (983a #14-15). Amazement then interrupts the matter-of-fact acceptance of things around us. The wondering person asks, "Why this way and not another?" He asks for reasons, after previously having discovered the possibility that things could be different. In his confusion and amazement, he discovers at the same time his own ignorance and seeks an answer; he philosophizes, says Aristotle, in order to escape from his ignorance. Once having gained understanding, however, he would wonder more if things were other than they are. The striving for understanding comes to rest in the answer. Thinking appears as a movement from the question to the answer—as a process which leads from a dissatisfied, worse state to a satisfied, better one.

The *Metaphysics* presents this idea without detailed elaboration. Even though Aristotle in a few lines has said much of great significance, this introductory passage had no lasting stimulating effect. It has been embalmed as a quotation; it may be that, just here, the Aristotelian logic, being limited to the proposition and its relationships, exerted an inhibitory effect. True, Aristotle mentioned other forms of speech, but he relegated their consideration to poetry and rhetoric. He returns to the problem, although only tangentially, in the *Analytics*. In the *Categories*, i.e., the possible mode of addressing objects, Aristotle used words which ask questions like why and where and how and how much? Nevertheless, the organon of logic was probably the most important single factor contributing to the shift of interest away from the act of questioning as a central theme.

Let us attempt to disentangle the complex, intertwined relationships of question and answer, questioner and person asked, and questioner and questioned object through an analysis of some typical question situations.

1. We begin with a trivial example, trivial in the etymological sense.[1] Assume that someone, a stranger in town, wants to find out the way to the railroad station. He turns to a passerby with the words, "Pardon me, sir, could you tell me the way to the Union Station?" The man gives the requested information, and our man arrives at the station, having taken the suggested route.

In this simple process, we have to distinguish (a) the initial situation of the questioner, (b) the turning to the man questioned (i.e., the relation between questioner and person questioned), (c) the relation of the question to the answer, (d) the relation of the answer to the question, (e) the final situation of the questioner.

At the beginning of this little rencontre, the questioner is confused. Several conditions contribute to this confusion.

First among them, one would think, is that the questioner finds himself in strange surroundings. He would not, however, become at all confused in a village which stretched out alongside one single street, leaving nothing for decision. The confusion sets in only in the network of streets of a larger town which, because it cannot be dealt with in its entirety from one location, offers many possible paths and directions. Such an abundance of possibilities constitutes a necessary but not sufficient condition. If the questioner only wanted "to look around a little," he could turn in any direction, and any direction would be right. In strolling

[1] Trivial = tri-via = three ways; something to be found at the crossroads, i.e., everywhere, common. Commonplaces and trivialities invite our attention because they show the average man in typical situations, while an analysis of these situations reveals how complex these facile achievements actually are. Once aware of this complexity, we are better prepared to anticipate the possible forms of disturbance and to deal with pathological manifestations.

around, we are at leisure, in a kind of vacation mood.[2] It makes no difference where we are or where we go. We are spared the necessity of making decisions and of relating our position to the whole, taking every part as it comes along as a part only and not considering how it is related to other parts. A certain mood corresponds to certain attitudes toward the environment and vice versa. In strolling around, we permit ourselves to behave for a while like hoboes; carefree, living in the moment for the moment, we have no goals and no questions—an enjoyment, a happiness, which some addicts try to produce permanently by means of drugs to lead them into their "artificial paradises."

The wish to reach the station puts an end to the state of casual wandering. With the wish, a goal is set and therefore a direction preferred. The wish divides the region into "farther" and "nearer," "welcome" and "unwelcome" areas. The region is perceived in terms of values, an aspect which then limits the realm of free arbitrary movements. The spot where our man finds himself is no longer an "anywhere" but a "here," a place which has now entered into a determined or determinable relationship to other places. The location of the questioner achieves meaning in the still unknown whole of the city's geography; although the stranger is ignorant of the specific structure of the whole, he thinks of it, nevertheless, in terms of a whole.

The questioner's wish to reach the station can be fulfilled only as he regulates his steps in line with the existing objective order. The request for the proper direction is, after all, a verbal short cut. Actually, the question about the route asks for the best—frequently understood as the shortest—route. Other motives may guide the question—for example, the desire to miss heavy traffic or to avoid steep climbs or to elude certain persons. The question assumes a standard for a comparison of possible routes, e.g., with regard to length or steepness. The correct choice—that is, one emancipated from the idiosyncrasies of the wishing person— guarantees the fulfillment of the wish. "Wishful thinking" fails in its purpose. To gain distance is the first condition for a successful procedure of questioning in a particular case. In the practice of everyday life, we frequently fail to find the right answer because we are unable to gain the necessary distance from the concrete situation and from ourselves.

The wish, then, determines a task which leads to a question. Of course, here we are not dealing with the psychologist's "tendencies which deter-

---

[2] These words have a characteristic etymology, since "leisure" means permission— from *licere*, to be permitted—and thereby freedom, followed by exemption from occupation or being free from engagement; "vacation," with its root, *vacare*, likewise means to be empty and thereby free from duty and service.

mine the sequence of ideas in consciousness" but rather with the thinking behavior of a person—the actions of a real being who, in questioning and answering, experiences the world. The subject, the "who's who" of questioning, is not "mind" or "consciousness," nor is it a brain or a nervous system. Questions arise from a human being. We attempt to understand questioning as his mode of finding-himself-in-the-world.

The motivation determines a question, but it does not, as such, create the "situation" of questioning. It is not altogether superfluous to stress this point, since not infrequently the actual or assumed uncovering of motives is felt to give the genetic explanation of a situation. George Humphrey, in a monograph on thinking, defines a problem as a "situation which for some reason appreciably holds up an organism in its efforts to reach a goal" (1951, p. 312). This definition, in encompassing too much, determines very little; it is so broad that it seems applicable to nearly any situation and, therefore, also to problems of thinking. However, while it determines a "problem" in some of its aspects, it leaves essential characteristics undetermined. This definition could not be applied without bias—to say the least—to the efforts of those men in Babylon and Egypt, for example, who tried to determine the orbits and movements of the sun and stars. Granted that they were acting as astrologers rather than astronomers, the assumption that the sublime order of the celestial bodies may influence and predestine the human scene in its turbulence and fragmentary aspects did not arise as a result of dammed-up desires; it did not originate with a direct attack on the environment. Humphrey insists—and rightly—that the psychologist should consider the organism and environment as correlates. Yet, the essential point for an understanding of human inquisitiveness is that man is able to suspend all direct action toward his environment; to reflect upon himself; to see himself within his environment; still more, to see himself together with his environment; and, finally, to relate the unit of this particular situation to the structure of the whole to which it belongs. Only such detachment from the environment and the observer's reflective consideration of himself with his environment could enable an astronomer to conceive of a heliocentric system where he understands himself, together with the earth as spinning around, against the direct testimony of sensory experience. At the opposite extreme, there are organisms appreciably held up in their efforts to reach a goal, who never "think" of solving their problems by thinking. We are familiar with the behavior of a dog who, visiting a tree, twists his leash around its trunk. Eager to follow his master in the original direction, he pulls straight forward, thereby only fastening the leash around the tree more tightly. Thinking demands gaining distance—in this case, suspension of the immediate tendency to walk on in the old direction, understanding the entanglement in a detached manner, and, finally, solving the problem by adapting oneself in accordance to the complex order understood in its demands. In the first case, the problem is not related to a natural goal; in the second, the denied satisfaction of a desire does not produce thinking. Even the simple and seemingly transparent example of the question about directions leaves no doubt that the possibility for questioning—whatever the particular motivation may be—points to a much more comprehensive context.

Lost in the labyrinth of streets and not knowing to which of the many possibilities he should give preference, the stranger turns to someone whom he considers to be familiar with the locale and willing to give the required information. His question is a "re-quest" for information.

Readiness to help cannot always be taken for granted. Therefore, the questioner will clothe his question in a form that makes it clear that the question is a request: "Pardon me, sir, could you tell me . . ."; of course he is not actually interested in whether or not the other has such knowledge; he would be startled by the laconic answer, "Yes." The circumstantial formulation (i.e., a formulation, polite because corresponding to the complexity of the circumstances) attests to the fact that the questioner leaves the decision (whether or not to comply) to the person questioned and that he appreciates the answer as a favor. He does not demand or threaten; he requests information. Sociological relations govern the appropriate mode of expression.

In our example, the questioner is the receiver and the one questioned, the giver. This is not always the situation of questioning. If we divide questioning into three large areas, depending on whether the questioner is directed toward things, toward himself, or toward others, then in the third area we may distinguish informative, catechetical or ascertaining, inquisitive, or Socratic or stimulating questions as possible forms —among others—of questioning. It may well happen that the same question is posed in all these different situations. A curious patient, for example, may ask the doctor how the presence of sugar can be demonstrated in urine; as a teacher, the doctor may ask that very question of a medical student; the question may emerge in a malpractice suit; it may appear in ordinary conversation, and—as with all Socratic questions—first arouse the wonder accompanying not knowing and establish the questionability of things. Depending on the circumstances, the same question has a different function and calls forth varied reactions. The sociological relation connecting questioner and the person questioned does not, therefore, directly coincide with the logical relation connecting question and answer. The former determines the verbal style in which the question is put. The curious patient will not approach his physician in the same direct fashion as the latter will question a student. In the question for directions, the introductory formula expressed the questioner's feeling that he was imposing himself on the passerby, that he was breaking through a distance that existed between them.

As a rule, we are not reluctant to ask a stranger for information, but we would have serious doubts about asking him for money. Anticipating that such a request would be little appreciated, we would have to decide whether to appeal to the other's pity or to frighten him into submission —whether to beg or to threaten. In asking for directions, in the request for information, we expect a certain readiness to help. If we treat the modest request for directions as a symptom through which we are able to diagnose existential relationships, then we may discover a meaningful law of behavior in the expected and demonstrated willingness to help. Its *raison d'être* is this: In giving an answer, the person questioned gives nothing away. The act of answering is a special kind of giving; the receiver gains without the giver's losing anything thereby.

The consequences of this relationship, that is, giving without giving away or giving without loss, are of the greatest significance in the formation of human societies. This may be seen in the ability to teach and in the enthusiasm and pleasure of teaching; it may be seen in the possibilities of verbal communication and participation—possibilites which exceed all forms of nonverbal behavior. At a meal, each participant receives a "portion"; no one receives all, and each one's portion differs from the others'. At a lecture, however, everyone receives all and each receives the same as every other person. If unexpected guests come to a meal, then the host becomes anxious that there "may not be enough"; if unexpected participants come to a lecture, then the group is enriched. It is for this reason that the great and lasting human societies are not constituted primarily as economic groups—as hunting, grazing, or herding societies—but as lingual-cultural societies. That is to say, they share an interpretation of the world, an interpretation which is lived out historically. What makes such a shared interpretation possible is, as in the request for directions, the immateriality of language through which the What of things is thematically grasped. The questioner and the person questioned direct themselves, in their question and answer, toward the order of things. This order is understood by each one as one and the same for all of them and, therefore, valid and obligating, tying and binding. This truly generic order, detached through language from the concrete individual things, is capable of unlimited reproduction; the questioner and the person questioned refer to it as something common and identical to all. They understand each other through the order in that they communicate with each other about it. This also applies to the request for directions. The words "How can I get to the station?" actually are substitutes for a longer series which, were it completed, would probably go somewhat as follows: "Which of the possible directions shall I take at this point? Where should I go then? How long should I keep on in that direction?" The person questioned comprehends the full meaning of the abbreviated question and answers accordingly: "Go straight ahead until the third street, then turn left, etc." The conversation refers to the possibilities of designating locations precisely, to the totality of possible directions, to the network of streets, and to the regularity in the diversity of the city plan which makes it possible to count street blocks. The answer, then, in order to satisfy the requirements of the question, requires a comprehensible, determinable order as well as a determining factor that may be applied to this order—for example, the number series in relation to the network of streets.

The question points ahead to the answer, and the answer points back to the question; together, they form a meaningful whole. An answer may consist of a single word: "yes" or "no," a number, a direction, "there," etc. The word "five" said alone is not meaningful; as an exact answer to a question, however, it has a very precise meaning. The answer becomes understandable through the question. Question and answer, therefore, differ from stimulus and response; their temporal Gestalt contrasts sharply with the sequence of starting and stopping of the big computers, which are so often interpreted these days as duplicating in their operation the functions of thinking (Wiener, 1948).

The possibilities presented in the question are determined by the answer; the specific confusion of the beginning state has thereby been cleared away. The questioner is satisfied. For the sake of simplicity, we assume that the answer he received was correct. It could have been wrong and still have satisfied the questioner. Here, too, the logical relationship between question and answer is not equivalent to the psychological factors involved in the act of questioning.

Our traveler has accepted the answer and is finally on his way to the station. With all this, he has not learned much, however. He received directions for reaching the station but not information about where to locate it within the plan of the city. He remains bound to the one route; he would be able to repeat the walk with certainty only from the one spot where he originally met the passerby—very much like a rat trained to follow a path in a maze.

The mere putting of oneself in motion and finding a way to a goal does not by itself imply that one has a method at one's disposal. A method emerges only from an understanding of the whole, together with its parts, of a certain order which permits a determination of the single case or, depending upon the circumstances, an ascent to a more inclusive order.

Our questioner, too, has gained no insight. All he has learned is the sequence of the parts of the route; he can plan to make the correct turns at those points which have been indicated to him. The informant could not transfer his knowledge of the city to the questioner—understanding must be gained; there are no short-cut procedures—but, like a specialist using his own knowledge, he was able to direct the questioner toward practical action. He accomplished this by drawing a kind of system of coordinates over the city within which it was then possible to designate directions and to figure distances. The applied geometrical-arithmetical scheme reveals nothing of the uniqueness of the city. The answer assumed in our particular case is useful only if the layout of the city permits such a schematization. Otherwise, different modes of information would have to be applied; the native could offer himself as a guide, or he could be replaced by a system of signs or guideposts sufficient to indicate the desired directions at the various intersections.

In this manner, we can follow the highway numbers from the Atlantic to the Pacific without ever knowing "where" we are. In this manner, we may act with things that we have "learned by heart." We go from verse to verse, from formula to formula, without a view of the whole and without understanding what we are doing. In this manner, we use water faucets, radios, electrical switches, political slogans, and a thousand other practical things. In this manner, we cover large stretches of our journey through life, until an unforeseen obstacle forces us to learn better the road that we have been following. In psychotherapy, through the process of a Socratic searching into the past, we attempt to re-open possibilities that have been bypassed to a person who has been going through life on a "single track," in the hope that they have not been irrevocably lost to him.

2. The next example has been chosen to illustrate and elucidate the biphasic aspect of the movement leading from question to answer.

Let us imagine an engineer to whom the task has been assigned not of finding an existing road but rather of constructing one in an as yet undeveloped area. His question, too, is "Where?" but the answer will not be available to him without much effort. There is no one whom he can ask for information. He himself must inquire into the state of affairs; that is, he must first survey the area in order to prepare for himself a determinable system, a certain order. Not before he has completed the survey and inscribed the results into a general ground plan (a map), can he, in the second phase of his work, apply determining factors. In the first phase, he has to achieve a general view of the existing possibilities so that he may decide, in the second phase, which one among them is to be preferred. He makes his choice, taking geographical, geological, technical, economic, and legal factors into consideration. Each of those causes the hitherto neutral map to become differentiated in terms of a specific order of values. The individual factors used in determining the answer come into competition with one another. An area which is better from the point of view of one evaluation has disadvantages when other values are considered. Only a careful comparison of the advantages and disadvantages of each of the single determinants will bring about the decision. This decision, representing an attempt to balance the many conflicting demands, can never be wholly unequivocal or totally satisfying.

In order to keep our analysis within bounds, let us assume that our questioner has at his disposal all the tools and skills required for surveying. Even so, his work compels him to make many excursions—he can't take it easy. He has to brave the elements and deal with the rugged terrain. The question obliges him to shoulder burdens. It is not, however, an austere superego which forbids him to stretch out somewhere at ease. The engineer does not give up his comfort in order to comply with some of the conventions considered necessary by human society; he toils, not without pride, because the question provides an opportunity for achievement and his endeavor promises a meaningful existence as a reward. This attitude is not obliterated by the fact that he acts under economic pressure—that he also works in order to earn a living. The decisive factor is not that he *must* assume burdens but that he *can* do so— that, as a questioner, man is able to surmount the boundaries of mere biological existence, of survival and adaptation, going far beyond the so-called superego's sphere of frustration and denial. Motivation unfolds its strength within the realm of possibilities which it encounters rather than creates.

The capacity to reach beyond oneself is manifested by the results of the first phase of seeking an answer—in the map drawn after the original survey. A map, just like language, does not simply reproduce something that would, in the same way, be available to us without it. The map is more than a merely mnemonic device, more than an illustrated symbol of an absent object, more than a summary. With its aid, we take control of the territory in a new way; a transformation has taken place that had its start in the questioning attitude of surveying.

In front of me is a map of the United States. At one glance, I can see the mighty expanse of the entire country between the two oceans. Here I see the United States in a way that neither I nor any one else has ever seen it or ever will see it. If I look around in my room or out of the window, then my sight is blocked by the nearest wall. A horizon constantly confines our natural vision; on the map we transcend every horizon. Questioning, breaking through the sensory horizon, makes cartography possible; in transcending the boundaries of what is directly visible, we are able to place the immediate data into an encompassing order comprehending that which is *not* immediately available to the senses. A map is, therefore, not merely a shorthand reproduction. Even if it were possible to lift a person to such a height that he could look over the entire hemisphere, he would, nevertheless, see it in perspective, just as a person looking down from an observation tower finds himself closer to the area vertically below than to any other section in the panorama. The perpendicular drawn from the apex of a cone to the center of the base is shorter than any other line connecting it with points of the base's periphery.

Not only are all sensory horizons eliminated on a map but the perspective, too, is wiped off. While he walks around and measures the area, the surveyor always moves at the center of a horizon which is differentiated in terms of perspective; now the forest is nearby, now the meadow, now the valley, now the mountain top. The map makes all modifications and distortions caused by perspective disappear. In the process of surveying, the questioner grasps what is measurable and what has been measured in such a way that he is able to represent it in a homogeneous, neutral, spatial scheme. The actual operations of measuring do not appear in the final delineation of the map. Even the simple floor plan of a house does not show the spatial relationships as we actually see them. That is to say, the plan shows them as we actually do not see them; it presents them totally divorced from our individual actual existence and, therefore, as fitting into a general geometrical pattern. All abstractions begin with an abstraction from one's own individual existence, with an abandonment of the perspectives that confine the individual. For this reason, those moments when we are challenged in our vital existence and bound to our perspective (whether through fear, pain, or hunger) are moments which do not favor the questioning, thinking approach to things.

Cartographic representation erases the horizons with a sovereign disregard for natural size. It must do it! A map on a scale actually coinciding with natural size would be of little use. Only the reduction of the scale together with the ablation of the horizons permit us to get a synopsis, to get a total view of contours and boundaries and to determine distances and the relation between locales. Nevertheless, within a narrow range, considerable variations in scale are permissible. The map of the United States may be reduced to the size of a postcard without losing its familiar outlines—the same outlines that we would recognize on a panel covering an entire wall, that we would think of as "immense." The natural size of the presented objects is of little importance; what counts is the adaptability of a map to the natural size of man, for whatever the map reveals to the spiritual eye must be apprehended by the corporeal eyes within the narrow range of reading distance. In its own material structure as a physical thing, the map must be a handy tool, corresponding to man's direct physical reach; as representation, a map rests on the possibility of dematerializing the represented structures, just as with any geometrical design the actual, natural size of the object is a matter of indifference as long as the proportions, i.e., the ratio or *logos*, are maintained. By means of the map, we are able to represent landscape, not as it appears in its physiognomy, but transformed into pure spatial, geographical relations.

Our assumption that the construction engineer has at his disposal, not the map of the region but all the necessary figures and tools to construct the map is equally remote from two extremes—that maps made by others were available to him or that he first of all had to invent the mathematical procedures necessary for the solution of his task. Limited space excludes the discussion of the many problems that well up. Let us say only that in the second case we recognize the necessity, basic to all questioning, of ascending to more and more comprehensive orders—the necessity of the *inductio* in the Aristotelian sense. For this, the recent, as well as the older, history of physics has magnificent examples to offer. From the opposite possibility mentioned before (i.e., the use of maps already available), we can briefly extract the following: Whoever uses a map and thereby translates the geography represented in it back into the actual terrain must have understood the essence of the original transformation in a radical sense, for the transformation needs to include the questioner. Suppose the driver of a car stops to consult the map and demonstrates to his companion, "We are here"; the Here pointed out on the map is a tiny area, easily covered by the tip of the pointing finger. The Here on the map, however, is understood as representing the real Here (the city of Louisville, for example), which totally surrounds the speaker as a physical being. A process of decorporealization corresponds to the process of dematerialization. In order to construct and to use a map, the individual is required to understand how he fits into and is subjected to these new relationships and their lawful order. In asking questions and in discovering the means of answering his questions, man emancipates himself from the confines of the immediate here and now; he knows where he stands, he understands his own particular position, he actualizes his freedom, but, at the same time, he enters into a new dependency. Now he can plan; now he must plan. Before the surveyor—man as a questioning being—made his first move, long before he came to know his position exactly, he knew one thing: that he was a part of a whole, the order and structure of which he could comprehend.

Here, the gates to many psychiatric problems are being opened. There can be little doubt that some so-called disturbances of thinking are actually existential disturbances of questioning, impeding the achievement of a questioning transcendence of the self.

3. The objection might be raised that the example of the surveyor and his task presents a very special case; the analysis, moving on too high a level, could contribute nothing typical to the problem of the questioning act. Therefore, it does not seem inappropriate to turn in the opposite direction and to focus attention on the simplest forms of questioning.

Beginning at a tender age, before they come to grief with Oedipus, children exhibit an insatiable curiosity and inquisitiveness. Their development progresses in a frequently described and easily understood series of steps. Among the earliest forms of questions appears the quest for the name of things—the question "What is that?" We may well be expected to demonstrate whether, in this case, too, one is justified in claiming not only that the child is confused but that, in a certain sense, he is aware of his confusion; that, anticipating knowledge, he is directed toward a presented order of things; and, finally, that, in the primitive manner of his questioning, the child "transcends himself."

The initial situation is clear or, at least, seems to be clear: the child sees many different things around him; he hears adults calling these things by their names; he wishes to emulate the adults; perhaps he wishes to conjure up missing objects by means of name magic. Such an evaluation, niggardly with the factors that can be described more exactly, is too liberal with pure conjecture.

No one would deny that a child who asks for the name of an object must have scanned the object as such. More specifically, he has grasped This One as different from other This Ones and as different from the background. Beyond that, it has also become clear to him that the particular This One is a What; in other words, he has realized not only that things are separated from one another but that they differ from one another in kind—that they differ in their Whatness. Finally, he must have recognized that the various This Ones are in a certain sense constant, that they remain what they are although they appear to him in continuously varying aspects throughout the day. With this act of comprehension, with this subjective creation of things, the child has reached the starting point for the "What is that?" question.

In the two dozen or more months that precede this first period of questioning, an infinite number of ever changing impressions crowd in on the child. Impression follows impression, but, piercing through their temporal succession, the continuity of the world manifests itself; or we could say that the world shows itself as continuous in the ever changing sequence of impressions. The concept of time has its source in the experience of duration in change. Each instance, with all its impressions, is experienced as a phase of becoming; as a momentary, actual aspect of the world; as a unity unfolded into a manifold of opposites and finally organized into a multitude of things. Each one of them appears in a diversity of views, perspectives, or illuminations; the many views, however, are held together by the What, which is maintained through all perspectives. The What is seen only in "adumbrations" (Husserl's *Abschattungen*). Right through them, we aim at the What that never completely emerges as such, yet, pervading all appearance, determines their context and their constancy. The form, size, and color constancies are modifications of the time constancy. In the visual sphere, things are perceived as basic *Gestalten* which do not covary with the physiological changes in perspectives; the intended What of things so overshadows the perspective views that "perspective" had to be discovered. Similarly, in our familiar world of stable (i.e., time-constant) things, it requires special reflection to bring time perspectives to awareness. But such an effort is indispensable to determining the starting point at which the child begins his questioning. If we start with the assumption that, at the beginning of the individual life history, the "givens" consist of an amorphous mass of single data which in the course of objective time appear, one group after another, then the problem of constancies, of the comprehension of things, or of their Whatness assumes the form in which it presented itself to Mach, Helmholtz, and many others. But, if we have learned to understand that the experiencing person in the continuum of his becoming comprehends the world in its spatial and temporal continuity, then it is obvious that the continuum of the world unfolds itself in opposites; something appears as such a thing always in opposition—that is to say, in a meaningful relation—to something else. This One is that which maintains and asserts itself in time within the framework of meaningful, spatially distributable opposites.

The child asks for the name of that which fastens appearances into things or groups having a meaningful unity; he wants to know their What. He does not ask for the proper names of individual things but for their generic designation. He calls his animal toys by proper names which he uses as vocatives, but, as far as things are concerned, he wishes to know what they are. He seems to share the point of view of those who adhere to the doctrine of *universalia in rebus*. What is overlooked by the nominalists appears to be known by every child, namely, that even individual things are apprehended as universals. If nominalism wished to carry its point of view to its logical conclusion, then it should not stop with the individual thing; rather, it would have to demand that names be applied as designations only to each of the individual perspectives, to the unendingly changing aspects of the individual thing—if one could even speak of individual things any longer. Neonominalism has actually begun to tread the path leading from individual things to individual occurrences. The paradox here, however, is that the word, as *phonema*, must share the fate of things. What could be more singular than the transient sound, the *flatus vocis*? If articulated sound is to serve as word, then the *phonema*, independent of time, place, and intonation, must in its sound configuration be identifiable as "the same." When a child hears a word spoken, he repeats it with childish modifications and mutilations. The actual sound is not repeatable. The child is able to repeat nothing but the sound configuration, which emerges with the matter of the tone only to disappear again immediately. Whenever a word is spoken as a carrier of meaning, the temporal—actually, the timeless—permanence of the sound configuration must have been grasped in the brief moment of its duration.

With the question "What is that?" the child gives us to understand that he has discovered the universality of language at the same time as the *universalia in rebus*. He does not ask his mother, "What do you call this?" but, rather, "What is this?" Things and their names, which, after all, appear as immanent attributes of things to the child, all belong to a general order. The child's parents did not create this order. They are familiar with it and know it, but—and this is just what the child's question proves—they are also subject to it. The order, arrived at through the name, is universally valid and universally obligatory. Parents become teachers and mediators; their authority is no longer based exclusively on their being bigger and stronger and on their providing food and shelter but, from now on, on their also being wiser. It is also thereby understood that they are not creators but creatures. They are familiar with a world that exists independently of them. To this world, both the child and his parents can direct themselves together. The child has no doubt that the thing whose name he wants to know is seen by the mother as the same thing and in exactly the same manner as he sees it. The orientation toward one universal, all-encompassing world common to all makes communication in it and about it possible. The child demands to know the *real* name; he demands to know things as they are in themselves and not as they are in terms of a wish-fulfillment relationship to himself. The private language of childhood ends in the course of the first questioning period.

This interpretation of the immanent content of the "What is that?" question seems to make an adult out of the infant. But we are dealing here with the interpretation of the immanent content, of intentions that the child has without comprehending them in a reflective sense. We do not claim that the child knows this content in all its implications. Nevertheless, we are justified in stating that, with his questions, the child is oriented toward an anticipated, determinable order and that, in questioning, he requests its determination.

With the name, the child acquires power over the What of things; things become graspable through being named. The period of the vocative is replaced by that of the nominative. This is a big step. While we are in immediate contact with things, we are able to see, touch, and move them only as these concrete, particular objects; our reach is limited to the here and now. Even if we were able to aim at the What, without speech we could not handle it; we could not sever it from the object. Only through the mediation of linguistic symbols are we able to deal with things in terms of their Whatness. From this What we are then able to isolate attributes—color, size, weight—and to manipulate them. Freshmen in high school Latin are given the practice sentence "The table is round." Notwithstanding its simplicity, something is accomplished in this sentence which cannot be equalled by any physical force, no matter how great: the divorcing of the "roundness" from the table. With his first question regarding the What, with the slow building of his vocabulary, the child attains entry into an area that extends far beyond the horizon of physical existence. He reaches beyond himself into a sphere of order that permits him to shape his own life, but also commits him to doing it.

The enthusiasm of youthful questioning has its reverse in the aversion of the aged to everything new and in their dogmatic rejection of all questions that threaten their security. Old nations like to build a Limes, a Chinese wall, or a Maginot line; they sit behind their walls, which they pass off as impregnable, often against their better judgment. Their irritable rejection of new questions betrays their secret uncertainty. We can evade single questions, but we remain, nevertheless, questioning beings. For this reason, it has been found more effective, instead of closing one's ears to new questions, to drown them in a flood of banal questions or to surrender oneself to routine and to activity for its own sake. The theoretical and moral justification for this purports to be that, in the last analysis, all questions are pragmatic and serve the fulfillment of our daily needs. It is claimed that questioning begins and ends as a search for the useful or as a wondering about the unusual; "admira-tion," it is said, is directed not toward the *mirum*—the wonderful, the marvelous, the great cosmic order—but rather toward the *miraculum* —the exceptional, the curious, and the strange.

The claim that all questioning is but a special type of seeking can be supported by such phrases as "to seek an answer" and "to find a solution." It also must be admitted that, of our three examples, at least the first one suggests a comparison to the seeking–finding process. The traveler in the strange city, without asking anyone, could have looked for the station on his own and finally would have found it. Furthermore, in spite of the differences of topics, of initial and final states, and of frames of reference, the "What is that?" question is similar to the question regarding the correct way, insofar as both are directed toward a third person who, because of his knowledge of matters, is able to answer. Since both questions belong to the group of informative questioning, it is necessary to test the questioning of the child and see whether we should not also permit its inclusion into the scheme of "seeking." Yet, here we immediately discover marked differences. The traveler could have found the station accidentally, but the child must learn the precise name; the traveler needed information, but the child required instruction; the traveler would have been able to make out on his own, but the child is dependent on others. The next objection will then be that just this last distinction really proves the difference to be secondary, caused only by the child's helplessness; no basic difference supposedly exists between finding and learning, information and instruction. Arguments of this sort could be continued indefinitely.

Since a certain similarity between seeking and questioning cannot be denied, we are faced with the following alternatives: Either questioning is a special form of seeking, or the type of questioning illustrated by the first example is a special form of questioning similar to seeking. And this it is indeed! If we favored the first part of the alternative, we would be embarrassed to have to account for the mere question "When?" Suppose someone wishes to know when a train will arrive. He cannot find the When, but he can *find out about* it. He need only go to the station and wait for the arrival of the train. This arrival, however, presents him only with the Now and not the When. The question about the When is related to objective time somehow articulated by clock and calendar. In this order alone, one can designate a point of time which will serve as an answer to the question "When?" This question can be asked only by a being who is able to go beyond the moment and who can orient himself in objective time and avail himself of it; that is, it appears in a questioning, thinking, speaking being.

A searching animal is limited to finding a way toward food, a mate, or shelter; it is limited to locomotion, to the approaching toward a concrete thing that it can incorporate or in other ways take possession of. In simple "where" questions (e.g., "Where is the station?" or "Where is my hat?") our attitude corresponds most nearly to this type of seeking, because in seeking we are likewise after something with the intention of using it for ourselves in some way. However, there is this difference: The Where in the seeking of animals is path-goal determined; the Where of human questioning is a designation of a location in the whole of the geographical relationship. A question may be put in the service of seeking, but the question does not itself thereby become an act of seeking. Seeking food ends with finding it; hunger ends in satiety, only to return, within the cycle of need and satisfaction, to the initial state. Questioning which, with the answer, ends in knowing, does not return to the beginning state. The process of questioning and answering results in a movement forward, in an ascent to a new level. As questioning, understanding beings we enter, individually or in groups, the realm of history. The insights gained through questioning are transmittable; they are possessions bequeathed from one generation to the next. The younger generation starts from a new point. In the sphere of searching, on the other hand, the same cycle repeats itself without end.

Whether the movement from one level to another may be considered as progress, we are unable to say, since the goal is unknown to us. The events of the last fifty years have shaken nineteenth-century optimism and faith in progressive social evolution. But, apart from all historical facts, a consideration of the essence of questioning leaves little room for such optimism. It is man—not a soul, a mind, or a consciousness—who orients himself questioningly in the world—man bound to the here and now in the reality of his physical existence. As a questioner, he breaks through the confines set by his senses. In the act of thinking, he reaches through perspectives to the What, through the time-bound to the timeless, from the fragments to the whole, from confusion to clarity. The pleasure inherent in understanding has its source in the transition from the limitations of sensory experience to the view of the comprehensive order. Nevertheless, in breaking through the horizons of the senses, man, regardless of color and creed, is held in his place. He is forced to express the whole through parts, the What through perspective images, and the timeless through the time-bound—a bottomless well of errors and confusion. The representation of the comprehensive order, therefore, requires both humility and courage: humility, patience, and self-denial in the striving to understand the order in itself; courage in the attempt to represent the whole with particular means.

The order understood through questioning enables *us* to order and to regulate. Comprehended order makes possible a technological civilization. The *homo faber* can produce only in obedience to the laws of nature. Comprehension of the authentic order allows him to use things according to their nature and yet for his own purposes. Therefore, his achievements can be measured by objective standards; they can prove themselves good or bad, masterly or faulty. When man breaks through the sensory horizon, the moment becomes subordinate to the future and to the past in the whole of time. Activity can follow a plan. In the accomplishment of his acts, man actualizes his own self. In freeing himself from the constraint of immediate experience, man can give meaning to his own existence, and he becomes responsible to himself. Self-realization breaks the boundaries of self-preservation. The questions "What is that?" and "What should I do?"—the theoretical and the ethical questions, science and con-science—both rise from the same source.

References

Aristotle. *Metaphysics.*

Humphrey, G. *Thinking; an introduction to its experimental psychology.* New York: John Wiley, 1951.

Wiener, N. *Cybernetics.* New York: John Wiley, 1948.

CHAPTER NINE

Descartes's Significance for Modern Psychology

The author of the *Meditations*—he who reports of himself how many falsities he had been willing to accept as true in his youth, he who decides to doubt everything previously taken for granted, he who shuts off all his senses—is an erring man.

Error is a *fact;* we know from experience that we are exposed to innumerable errors. But how can there be error?

Descartes accounted for the possibility of error in various ways. Best known is his presentation in the "Fourth Meditation," where he derives error from a tension between the bounded character of knowing and the boundlessness of willing. Our errors are consequences of an extravagance of our will. However, we are able to bring ourselves to confine the will, i.e., affirmation and negation, within the boundaries of clear and distinct knowledge. Even if erring has been implanted by the Creator as a possibility in the *res cogitans*, this possibility does not necessarily have to be actualized. Thus, the "Fourth Meditation" closes with the triumphant words: "After all, I have learned today what I must guard against, so that I may never err again . . ." (1931, p. 178). Likewise, he says at the beginning of the *Principles* (I, 6): "But provided that he who created us is all-powerful, and even though he would take pleasure in deceiving us, we will not fail to discover a freedom in ourselves, such a freedom that we can refrain from giving assent to things we do not understand well, whenever it pleases us, and thus we can avoid ever being deceived" (1931, p. 221).

So even if God wished to deceive us, He would be unable to do so, if we did not agree. Our errors are shortcomings in our ways of acting, not shortcomings of our nature (*Principles* I, 38). Error could be eliminated, at least in actuality.

But, at the beginning of the same "Fourth Meditation," Descartes establishes another basis for erring that, as Hobbes already demurred, is not altogether in agreement with the subsequent, more detailed presentation. "But if I turn back to myself afterwards," says Descartes, "I have the experience that I am nevertheless exposed to innumerable errors, and if I seek for their original cause, I observe that I have been placed as it were intermediate between God and Nothing, i.e., between the highest Being and Not-Being, so that insofar as I also participate in a certain fashion in Nothing, and I am lacking in extraordinarily much, it is not surprising that I err" (1931, p. 172).

The *Meditations*, then, are more reserved than the *Principles*. In the above passage, at least, it seems as if error were inseparable from finite substance.

In the *Passions*, we find a new, third establishment of a basis for the possibility of error and the most radical one. It is easy to show that it is new. In deriving error from the tension between knowing and willing, error is located solely in the essence of the *res cogitans*. And where Descartes says that he has been placed midway between God and Nothingness, there, too, the assumption is still permitted that he is not speaking of himself as a human, this human being, but of himself as *res cogitans*. In the *Passions*, on the other hand, error stems from *human nature*; we all err because we are composed of a soul and a body.

The close tie between body and soul makes the perceptions obscure and confused. Although Descartes, in this work, emphasizes complete freedom of the will, he cannot help but concede that the passions push the will in a definite direction. To be sure, the will cannot be forced by the passions to any sort of action; yet, we read that the passions are in opposition to the will. The will must first of all secure and assert its freedom against the passions. By acting on the pineal gland, the will can move the vital spirits in a direction opposite to the one in which they have been impelled from without. Therefore, it is not surprising when Descartes remarks that the passions pull the weak soul now in this direction, now in that direction, and the will, obeying first one and then the other passion, continually puts itself in opposition to itself (*Passions* I, 48).

Although there are remedies against the passions, these remedies originate in the same sphere as the ills they ought to remove. The soul is unable to do anything directly against the passions. Its only way out is to represent to itself those things that are usually linked with the particular antipathetic passions. So, again, in the last analysis, only passions avail against passions (Passions I, 45). And even this maneuver finally fails before the stronger emotions, so that the soul is ultimately unable to achieve mastery of the passions (Passions I, 46).

Accordingly, given the passions, to err is irremediably human. Therefore, it seems to me that the Passions presents the most radical kind of basis for the possibility of error. Corresponding to this, we read toward the end of the "Sixth Meditation": "The nature of man, insofar as it is a composite of mind and body, must occasionally be at fault and deceptive" (1931, p. 198). With regard to practice, Descartes even makes the significant concession that the consequent pursuit of false judgments and postulates can have a certain usefulness (Passions I, 49) and that even a mistaken joy (fausse joie) is often better than a grief whose basis is true (Passions II, 142). The human being, then, by his very nature, is wedded to error.

Man who errs is the theme of the Passions and, therefore, of Cartesian psychology.

This basic characterization is retained in detail throughout the work. All the varieties of passions, their hierarchical order, their usefulness, and their usage are all derivable from the nature of man as a being of body and soul and, hence, as an erring being. The primary passions are the best illustration of this. Five of them—desire, love, hate, joy, and sadness—are, as it were, modes of the same anthropological situation. They disclose the relationship of man to other human beings and to things in the world as a being of spirit and body. The sixth basic passion, wonder (admiratio), which Descartes puts first, is the most powerful of all. But it, too, is constituted only as a passion of erring man.

As far as our experiencing is passion, in the most general sense of the term, it is determined by the nature of our being human. The psychology of Descartes is an anthropological psychology in the sense that he shows how our actual experience, in terms of its content, and our being, in terms of its nature, are linked together, and he also shows the kind of linkage there is.

To be sure, Descartes made it explicit, in defining the passions (Passions II, 27), that they were caused, supported, and enhanced by a certain movement of the vital spirits. But, when this idea is further developed, a remarkable correlation between the bodily causes of emotions and the experience of them is discovered. Only this enables us to understand why a purely intellectual joy should usually be accompanied by a passion of joy and why, to use another example, thinking about a love object results in movements of the blood and vital spirits exactly like those caused by the passion of love *(Passions* II, 102; II, 107).

The *Passions,* like all of Descartes's work, has had many followers. The ideas of Descartes have become so much a part of everyday thought in Europe that later centuries took credit for the discoveries prepared for or actually made by Descartes.

Just because European thought was so deeply suffused with Cartesianism, those who came later were unaware of repeating the great thinker; they were ignorant of the sources on which they depended. In keeping with this anonymous Cartesian tradition, system-bound, problem-laden theories have been presented as truths of common sense. While this anonymous tradition links modern psychology with the philosophy of Descartes, it also stands between the two. It has prevented the thought of Descartes from being transmitted as a meaningful yet imperfect whole but has caused it to be disintegrated into its parts. By themselves, however, the parts are no longer the same as when fitted into the whole.

Descartes himself wrote that his explanation of the passions was to be neither rhetorical nor moral philosophical. He wished to write about the passions as a "physicist." Yet it was only from his anthropological position that he could write as a physicist of the passions; the two were inseparable for him. Descartes, however, has influenced the development of modern psychology solely as a physicist of the passions. Psychology has completely neglected his anthropology. Psychology ignores man who errs. But what else is the subject matter of psychology if it is not this?

Definitions of psychology by Brentano, James, or Froebel show where psychology has followed Descartes and where it has turned away from him, for they have nothing to say about man and still less about man who errs. The task of psychology is given as the description and explanation of psychic appearances or states of consciousness. There is a complete abandonment of the inner tie between human being and consciousness.

A multitude of states of consciousness, separable from one another, are supposed to be in one-to-one correspondence with similarly distinct physiological events. However, it makes little difference whether one applies this isolating view to sensations, states of consciousness, or *Gestalten.* In each case, the inquiries are directed to repeatable events in an isolated, worldless subject.

For Descartes, the human body is a particular bodily thing among other things, even while at the same time it is "my body." Although the passions are caused and sustained by movements of the vital spirits, they are not merely events in an isolated and worldless subject. The disintegration of the Cartesian system has simplified the original conception to the point of caricature. Yet, if Descartes is the victim of this development, he is at the same time its originator.

Since perceptions were considered both as bodily processes and psychic impressions and since it was held that movements of vital spirits could stimulate the will and that both of these affect the pineal gland and the will can direct the movements of the vital spirits—in short, that bodily and psychic events form a unity of opposites—all this seemed to justify extension of the psychophysical mode of explaining the passions to man's entire psychic life, including thinking and willing.

Descartes, however, repeatedly emphasized the unity and indivisibility of the *res cogitans* and was opposed to the separation of the soul's faculties that occurs in ancient and scholastic philosophy. At the same time that he speaks of the will, he also refers to plural volitions (*les volontés*). These volitions have been shaped into a variety of fixed matrices so that certain kinds of movement of the vital spirits naturally correspond to each of the various particular volitions. The will is on the verge here of breaking down into a pluralism of reflex events. Already, the motifs are visible that will continue to be effective for centuries to come, motifs which have relegated the problem of lived movement in psychology to complete oblivion. The dividing line between the reflex in the body and movement of the will as conduct toward the world breaks down, and mechanistic physiology suppresses psychology.

One obstacle slowed down such a development. Descartes had said of the human mind, in his synopsis of the *Meditations*, that "though all the accidents of the mind suffer change, though, for instance, it thinks of some things, wills others, and senses still others, it always remains the same mind" (1931, p. 141). Psychic being is, thus, always presently incomplete, the moment having a temporal relationship to the whole so that the latter can only be understood as becoming. But this conception of the *res cogitans* was opposed by another, one that required the support of God from moment to moment to maintain the finite substance, the equivalent of a continually renewed creation. It was the latter of these two contradictory conceptions, temporal atomism, that finally prevailed.

Descartes's analysis of wonder (*admiratio*) is a striking example of this. While it still remains possible to understand five of the basic passions in such a way that the extramundane soul observes the temporal relationships to which the body is subject, time itself becomes constitutive in the case of wonder. Wonder can only occur for a being who him-

self becomes, in the course of his history, one who knows of his becoming, since it is clear that the new is the object of *admiratio*.

Descartes, however, overlooked the problem that emerges at this point.
He misconceived it to such a degree that, in the grip of tradition, he
wrested the new out of its polar tie with the old, and set the new up to
stand alone. The old and familiar excites no passion; indifference is absence of emotion. Wonder is without an opposite. Now, the way was
open to the strange notion that the new is both the cause and the occasion of wonder.

Descartes opens his treatment of the particular passions with Article
53, entitled "L'Admiration." Here, and in Article 70 where he discusses
the definition and cause of wonder, Descartes adopts the position that is
to characterize mechanistic psychology: He fails to discriminate the conditions of performance from the actual performance itself.

The development in psychology that remained linked with some features of Descartes's thought has produced a crisis about which there has
recently been much discussion. Many remedies have been proposed.
Anthropological psychology, fed by many different sources, reappears
as one of the remedies. It is the crisis itself that has given rise to it and
not merely reflection on the crisis. Anthropological psychology, however, does not have a dogmatically formulated program. It simply at-
tends to the solution of concrete tasks wherever it discovers them. At
the same time, however, it presses in the direction of rethinking the
foundations of psychology. It holds the anthropological standpoint in
common with Descartes; it, too, is concerned with man as erring or,
more broadly, as questioning, although at the same time without returning to Descartes.

In anthropological psychology, man is seen as questioning, i.e., as
becoming, incomplete from one moment to the next. This psychology
conceives every moment as a differentiation of what is less differentiated; it knows that psychic functions are never to be met with *in nuce*
and so it does not fall into the error of supposing that simple thought is
the product of simple thinking. Nor does it attempt to pair off in some
linear fashion biological functions or types with forms of culture or
spiritual forms of life. In this way, it guarantees the freedom within
which the psychic forms of spatiality and temporality can be discovered,
without reference to the spatiotemporal concepts of natural science. It is
on the way to such elementary formations of psychic becoming that we
gain the perspective from which a deeper understanding of pathological
features in the psychic life, like sensory illusions, delusion, and compulsion, becomes possible.

At root, it holds man to be erring and considers the tension between *koinos kosmos* and *idios kosmos*, between universe and individual, to be irreducible. It knows that man remains limited to existence in perspective and that the world *pros hēmas* is not the world per se; it knows that, in psychology, the knower can only be understood in relation to one who errs, even though we can *tē physei* eventually realize our error only from knowledge as such.

References

Descartes, R. *Philosophical works*. New York: Dover, 1931. 2 vols.

CHAPTER TEN

Human Action: Response or Project[1]

The term "psychomotor" was coined by Wernicke (1900) more than fifty years ago. Serving a dual purpose, it carried a double connotation. On a descriptive level, it was used to label a peculiar kind of behavior, which—in Wernicke's opinion—could neither be explained as a strictly neurological disturbance nor understood as pathology of action; but the word "psychomotor" also signified a cerebral mechanism, a section of the "psychological reflex arc" in its function and dysfunction. As Wernicke saw it, such duality of purpose was not charged with the danger of ambiguous meaning. Indeed, the two aspects had to be complementary if it were true that

there is nothing else to be found and to be observed but motions and that the whole pathology of mental diseases consists of nothing but the peculiarities of motor behaviour. . . . Motions alone are observable. From these we infer events which occur in consciousness (the organ of consciousness) of another person. The symptomatology of psychoses has for its topic motions insofar as they reveal the functions of the organ of consciousness; that is to say the organ of association.

Wernicke's belief in a strict parallelism makes it understandable that he should have named a cerebral pathway "psychomotor." Experience, to him, reflects processes within the nervous system as an epiphenomenon in a step-by-step correlation. The clinical method of psychiatry, therefore, requires the study of the final result—motions—in order to infer the neurological processes from which it proceeds. Wernicke attempted

[1] Extended version of a paper read at the annual meeting of the Amer. Psychiat. Assn., San Francisco, May 1958.

to subject the whole of psychic life and its disturbances to the concepts of neurophysiology and neuropathology. In a meeting such as the Laurentian Symposium, where neurophysiologists and neuropsychologists discussed the relations of brain mechanisms and consciousness (Fessard, 1954), Wernicke would not have considered himself as an outsider. He was convinced that, in his day, even before further investigation of details, the general pattern of cerebral functions, i.e., of the "psychological reflex arc," was already sufficiently well established to construct— even to deduce—psychiatric symptomatology from neurophysiology. In this enterprise, the Lichtheim-Wernicke diagram of aphasia served him as a model.

In 1874, at the age of twenty-six, Wernicke published his paper on sensory aphasia. Under certain conditions, he found, patients were unable to understand spoken words, although they heard well and could as a rule discriminate articulated sounds, the phoneme, from other acoustical data. In spite of their lack of understanding, these patients were able to speak. Wernicke concluded that one had to distinguish a concept center (C) from a sensory center (s) and a motor center (m). The afferent impulses would reach an acoustical projection field, an area of "primary identification" where memory images of articulated sounds, the sound images of words (Helmholtz, 1870), were stored. From this area, impulses would be conducted over transortical pathways (sC) to the concept center, the locus of "secondary identification," i.e., of the meaning of words. In speaking, efferent impulses initiated in the concept center would reach the Broca area over the transcortical pathway (cm) (see Figure 10–1).

The diagram permitted Wernicke to localize the various forms of cortical, subcortical, transcortical, and conduction aphasia observed or postulated by him and the other "diagram makers," to use Head's disparaging term (1926). While the idea of a cortical center suggests precise localization, Wernicke emphasized that the hypothetical concept center must be understood as extending over wide areas of the hemispheres. He therefore had little difficulty in modifying and expanding the diagram of aphasia with its focal disturbances to a diagram of psychoses with, as he assumed, diffuse disturbances of the association organ. He divided "the concept center" into two different zones: one of sensory images (A) $(Anschauungs-Vorstellungen)$ and another one of goal images (Z) $(Zielvorstellungen)$, as indicated in Figure 10–2.

In this expanded diagram, the section $sAZm$ represents the psychological reflex arc. The part Zm is the psychomotor pathway. Under normal conditions, Wernicke speculated, Zm is under the control of Z. Under

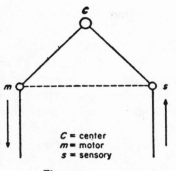

Figure 10–1

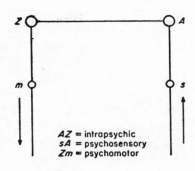

Figure 10–2

pathological conditions, through a process of "sejunction," the trans-cortical pathway Zm is broken loose from Z. It is blocked in cases of apraxia; it enters into uncontrolled—hypo-, hyper-, and parakinetic—activities of its own in cases of motility psychoses. Because of the patho-logical sejunction, psychomotor manifestations are experienced by the patient as movements not intended by him.[2] To an observer, they may look like spontaneous movements, but they are dissociated; in Wernicke's terminology, they are pseudospontaneous.

Although Wernicke's speculation was to some extent confirmed by clinical and pathological observations in cases of apraxia, his bold at-tempt to build psychiatry on the basis of neurophysiology failed. With the collapse of his system, the term psychomotor lost its home. The name was kept on the books while its meaning became more and more obscured. Finally, this traveler without passport found refuge in the realm of epileptic equivalents. The idea of pseudospontaneity was the link between the recent and the older usage of the word.

If psychomotor behavior is a kind of dyspraxia characterized by pseudospontaneity, then it would seem that normal behavior, eupraxia, must be considered as spontaneous action, dependent on "the capacity to carry out purposive movements." But who or what is the subject of purposive movements? Is it the experiencing being, or is it the nervous system? Or will an ultimate analysis prove the two to be identical? Pur-posive movements are directed toward a goal. A change is anticipated and realized through movements subserving a plan. In action, we reach beyond a given situation into the realm of possibilities; within a tem-poral horizon, open to the future, we busy ourselves producing a new

---

[2] Wernicke's psychomotor symptoms are more or less identical with catatonic mani-festations. Actually, the clinical observation of "induced movements," of waxy flexi-bility, posturing, etc., led Wernicke to assume sejunction as their pathophysiological basis.

situation. We do not simply react to things as they are, but we act on them—i.e., we move with the intention of modifying things from an actual to a desired condition. We see things as they are and visualize them as they could and should be. However, if " 'mind' can only be regarded, for scientific purposes ... as the activity of the brain" (Hebb, 1949, p. XIV), action must be identified with muscle contractions controlled by stimuli and traces. Physiology studies neural events *within* an organism, between "input" and "output," substituting stimuli for objects and muscle activity for action. Obviously, the motorium cannot anticipate any goal, nor do afferent impulses foresee any change. Neurophysiology, it seems, cannot acknowledge purposive movements or action as real. At best, it may accept them as subjective phenomena. We are faced, therefore, with the question of whether the system of neurophysiology can provide even a niche in which to place purpose and action as legitimate concepts; if not, can we find an interpretation which will make them fit into the system? Finally, will we have to modify the system itself (Straus & Griffith, 1955)?

These are serious questions; for, if purpose and action are not acceptable, success and failure, satisfaction and guilt, and hope and despair must also be abandoned. In order to find at least a tentative answer to these problems, I devised experiments in which one indispensable presupposition of the neurophysiological theory of action was put to a test.

No one, it seems, ever doubted that purposive movements must be acquired. Wernicke, although he distinguished pseudospontaneous from spontaneous actions (*Initiativ-Bewegungen*), defined the latter category as "re-actions" to stimuli from the outer world mediated through memory images. Liepmann (1905), in his studies of apraxia, related action to extrakinetic and kinetic engrams working together with actual perception. Wilson (1908) spoke about the "severance of ideational and kinetic memories" in apraxia and thereby referred to their integration in eupraxia. Russell Brain believes that the fact that "normal individuals can frequently carry out mirror writing with the left hand ... without previous training" should be explained through the assumption of an "unconscious education of the left hand [simultaneously with] the education of the right hand in normal writing" (1955, p. 146). As a final witness, we may call up William James who claimed that voluntary movements are secondary functions of an organism. Indeed, he not only stated that this is so but also declared in the most categorical fashion why it must be so. "If in voluntary action properly so called the act can be foreseen, it follows that no creature not endowed with divinatory power can perform an act voluntarily for the first time ..." (1918 p. 487). Yet, in spite of this apparently irrefutable argument, our experiments demonstrate that many nonoracular creatures are able to perform an action voluntarily for the first time.

The setting is simple. No elaborate equipment is required. All that is needed is a blackboard and a piece of chalk. However, we eliminated the habituated performance of writing. We did not allow our subject to face the blackboard but asked him to turn his back to the writing plane. When standing in this position, we put chalk in his left hand—if he was right-handed—and ordered him to write in the lower left quadrant of the board behind his back a group of capital letters, as, for instance, USA. This must be a simple task, for all of our normal subjects succeeded after a fashion. True, the resulting letters were not samples of calligraphy, but they were sufficiently clear and distinct. As our subjects assured us they had never written before in this or a similar manner, we think the claim is justified that they performed a voluntary action "for the first time."

While the task appears to be simple, the motor performance is highly complex, and the whole action is beset with theoretical problems. In its simplicity, the structure and the performance are as transparent as could be desired. We can analyze it without taking premature refuge in the thicket of neuronic pathways. Here, then, is a purposive movement, new in its organization, and performed, nevertheless, on the first try—quite in contradiction to James's reasoning and prediction.

This act of writing was not guided by a specific pre-established physiological organization. There was neither an innate nor an acquired assemblage of kinetic engrams, no recorded tape of synaptic links that, when replayed, could have coordinated the muscle contractions and ordered them from phase to phase in a sequence prescribed by the whole of the purposive performance. The learned skills of writing could only counteract the new achievement, for in the habitual act of writing, according to Brain's description,

nervous impulses must pass through those extensive areas of the parietal and occipital lobes concerned in the evocation of ideas and then through the left temporal lobe . . . and then to Broca's area. . . . The expression, if it takes the form of writing, must continue by the evocation of graphic word-schemas depending upon the left angular gyrus and these in turn must arouse the graphix motor-schemas organized in the neighborhood of the hand area of the left precentral convolution (1955, p. 1453).

Yet, in our experiments, the expressive process, instead of releasing efferent impulses to the right, i.e., the habituated writing hand, must be carried over from the left to the right hemisphere. The task of writing with the left hand demands a suppression of the habitual performance. An activation of suppressor areas could not account for this change, because suppressor areas, when in function, supposedly silence cortical activities in general. In our experiment, however, one habitual performance alone is suppressed and replaced by another one never heretofore learned. The new performance is not a simple extension of the existing repertoire of movements, comparable to the acquisition of a painting which is added to a museum collection; rather, it resembles the procurement of a picture of unusual size that forces a rearrangement of the total display. The left-handed writing in our experiment is not a mere addition to acquired habits but is in opposition to them. It is radically new.

The same is true for the "information" reaching the brain through tactile, proprioceptive, and kinesthetic stimuli aroused in the left arm during the process of writing. The assumption that our subjects had undergone an unconscious education of their left arm and hand would indeed be farfetched. There is no symmetry of movements between the performance with the left arm and the habituated act of writing. Instead of abducting and moving the right upper arm forward in the shoulder joint to a comfortable middle position between inner and outer rotation, our subjects had to adduct the left arm and to move it backward in a maximal inner rotation; instead of bending the right forearm and holding it in a comfortable middle position between pronation and supination, they had to stretch the left elbow joint and turn the left forearm into maximal pronation; instead of extending the right hand comfortably at the wrist, they had to bend the left hand to the utmost. One might well expect that, under such circumstances in a system of neuronic circuits and feedbacks, the deviant incoming messages would profoundly disturb the activities of the occipital, parietal, and frontal senders. Yet synaptic connections established in decades of writing experience and reinforced through countless repetitions did not interfere with the new, unlearned performance. Obviously, the circuits were not "jammed."

To say that the movement of the left hand was not guided by sight would be an understatement. In writing, we are used to moving our arm forward into a section of illuminated space. Together with the writing pad, we see our hand in motion and watch the lines resulting from our writing activities. There is a spatial concordance between exteroceptive and proprioceptive information. In our experiment, however, the optical and kinesthetic sectors do not overlap. The subject turns his arm into an optical vacuum, but, as the EEG would faithfully attest, optical stimuli are by no means absent. They are plentiful and much more intense than usual. The room is flooded with light reflected from walls, floor, and ceiling, because photographic recording demands strong illumination. Our subject, one may argue, is aware of his environment and its topography. He knows that a blackboard is placed behind him. He keeps his right arm at rest and uses his left arm instead. However, in line with those psychologists who "have perfectly succeeded in developing a coherent science, based on behavior, taking no account of consciousness" (Fessard, 1954, pp. 200 f.), must we not discard knowledge of the environment, awareness of one's own body, and anticipation of results. All subjective phenomena must be explained in strictly objective terms. The living and experiencing organism must be understood as a highly complex apparatus. But such a theoretical transformation—should it be feasible at all—would help us little toward a solution of our problems. A photosensitive apparatus, while hit by optical stimuli, does not *see* (any reference to seeing would have to take account of consciousness). As it does not see, it had no relation to objects *qua* objects. The apparatus reacts to changes in adjacent space, but it is not aware of them; it cannot relate one thing to another; it cannot determine a position in the environment. Consequently, it cannot conduct its own behavior so as to produce any foreseeable changes. Yet, our subjects, following a verbal instruction, proved capable of suspending acquired habits, of ignoring intense stimulation, and of manipulating the environment according to a plan. An instruction contained in less than twenty words has the profound effect of evoking purposive movements never before enacted, at the expense of well-established habits. How does the instruction work? How can it work?

Our experiments, which demonstrated the fact and thereby presented the problem, also provided some clues for a solution. For the second step of our experiment, we instructed our subjects again to face away from the blackboard and to use the left hand; but this time they were to invert the letters—either turning them around a horizontal axis (as though reflected in a stream), or around a perpendicular axis (as in mirror writing), or twisting them in a double turn. Such demands did not overtax our subjects, although there was some slowing down of action. The performance was clearly divided into the two phases of deliberation and of the execution of movement. The expression of contemplation was quite characteristic and revealing. Once the right order was achieved in imagination, the motor act was usually prompt and decisive. The action was guided by the projected design, by the product to be achieved. Motor function followed anticipated form.

Here the term "design" is not used as a pseudonym for the term "schema," although it occurs in a related context. The schema is understood as a physiological organization of neurones capable of being excited by a wide variety of stimuli. Visual word schemas supposedly play a dynamic part in exciting the motor mechanisms used in writing. The schema does not appear in consciousness, although it may be used to evoke a conscious image. In responding uniformly to a variety of stimuli, the schema makes possible recognition of similarity among differences.

In our experiment, however, the task was not to recognize similarity among differences but to adapt a general pattern to a specific orientation in space. Our subjects do not move from the particular to the general but proceed from the general to the particular. A schema, if it exists—and there are good reasons to doubt its existence—cannot determine in its unspecificity the very specific performance accomplished by our subjects. Needless to say, no graphic motor schema is inverted when a subject flips the graphic signs into an abnormal position; the designs are turned upside down but not the movements producing it. If the schema could be used (by whom?) to evoke a conscious image, such evocation still would not enable one of our subjects to perform his task. He has to manipulate and to orient the design in a free play of imagination. He has to reflect on himself—his actual and possible position—and, finally, he has to present—one might almost say re-present—in reality the products of his imagination.

The sign USA is promptly recognized when heard or read; its parts form a unit. One might expect that the physiological impulse of inverting a schema would turn the group of letters as one whole. Our results did not confirm such expectations. The subjects divided the unit into its component parts and treated each one individually. Faulty orientation of one or two letters appeared together with a correct representation of the others.

While all normal subjects were able to comply with the instructions, they committed errors. Mistakes, present from the beginning, occurred more frequently when figures had to be drawn in abnormal position. We soon learned to distinguish two groups of errors: those resulting from faulty motor performance and those caused by a misconception of the design. The capital S proved most vulnerable—for obvious reasons. The three letters—U, S, and A—although equally well "imprinted" and equally familiar to everyone, present a variety of graphic patterns. The differences in their spatial organization made themselves felt the moment any unusual motor performance was required. The U and the S can be drawn in a continuous motion. The A has to be dismantled and reassembled. The loop of the U balances on the line; it opens up toward the tip while the little pyramid of the A opens out toward the base and its two legs meet in the tip of the angle. The physiognomy of the A is that of architectonic stability; the U appears in a labile equilibrium; the S suggests inner motion. The U and A, built symmetrically in relation to a vertical axis, have a vectorial character. The S is symmetrically divided by a horizontal axis. The contrary turn of its upper and lower part prevents a vectorial tendency, but, even so, the S has a horizontal orientation. The S is tricky insofar as its performance runs counter to our custom of writing from the left to the right. Without guidance of sight, quite a few of our subjects succumbed to the habitual tendency and inadvertently drew the S in the mirror shape. Motor habits proved stronger than the projected design. Many even failed to recognize a faulty drawing of the S or did not feel certain whether the design was correct or not when, after completion of the tasks, they were allowed to turn around and examine their productions. But deviation from the normal or required abnormal position of the A and the U never escaped notice.

Detection of a misprint demands comparison of the actually visible figure with the standard design. The well-known, although usually not visible, paradigm determines whether a specimen in sight can be acknowledged and accepted or must be rejected and replaced by a better one. The invisible standard decides the validity of the reproduction. In the case of the letters A and U, detection of a mistake was usually followed by prompt correction; in the case of the letter S, a third and sometimes a fourth trial was required—first, to turn, in imagination, the standard design into an unusual position and then to break the motor habit.

The result obtained in the initial stages of the experiment made further elaborations desirable. We devised additional tasks with the intention of either increasing the difficulties of motor execution without increasing the complexity of design or, vice versa, making the task of design more difficult without adding to the motor requirements. We gradually reduced and finally eliminated all unorthodox positions and movements from the designing tasks.

To increase motor difficulties, we asked the subjects to continue writing behind their backs, but this time we instructed them to use the right hand and to write above their shoulders. In this new and unrehearsed performance, the arrangement of body and limbs is still more awkward than it was in the first one. The subject has to raise his arm at the shoulder to the horizontal in maximum adduction. He then has to bend the forearm backward to the extreme and to supinate it fully. Even this was not sufficient preparation for the task. In order to make contact with the board, the subject had to twist his trunk and, if he was of good size, he had to spraddle his legs and bend his knees.

Thus, the whole performance had to pass through three stages: adaptation of the body to the blackboard, "shouldering" the right arm, and execution of writing movements producing the desired letters or words. The last phase directs the preceding ones as a means to an end. In our experiments, the adaptation was not acquired through prior conditioning. Our subjects had been instructed—in general—what to do but not —in detail—how to do it. Each one had to discover for himself a practical mode of procedure. The unhandy and unrehearsed second act was not a reward for the odd stance achieved in the first set. In the sequence of movements, the first one served as preparation for the second one which, in turn, prepared for the final action. The anticipated result dictated the necessary preparation.

Preparatory actions of varying complexity play a great role in human affairs. For us, who, as experiencing beings, can visualize a design, anticipate a result, and reflect on our own position in space, the task appears simple enough. To find an adequate explanation within the traditional framework of neurophysiology is quite a different proposition.

In the situation of our experiments, efferent impulses must reach the muscles of trunk, hip, and legs to evoke an attitude never before linked with the action of writing. This new attitude only prepared for other ones, culminating in the finished product. The trunk was lowered so that the arm could be brought into a position suitable for the writing movements to follow, ending in the production of letters. This whole array of movements directed toward a goal belongs to the macroscopic world of visible, tangible objects—of things which can be manipulated by experiencing creatures. The scale of the macroscopic world is graded according to "natural size." Neurophysiology, however, turns its attention to microscopic structures and expects to find on the molecular level an answer for most, if not all, of its problems. The question is whether science must reduce the macroscopic to the microscopic level and whether, in the course of this transaction, the phenomena demanding explanation can be preserved.

"The mission" of an efferent impulse terminates at the end-plate with the activation of a muscle fiber. An impulse traveling its way to a filament of the ileopsoas does not prepare the advent of any other impulse, nor does the activity of a muscle as an integral unit—signified by the anatomical name—anticipate the function of any other muscle. When we speak about purposive movement, we consider the elementary physiological function as part of a larger whole. Contractions of muscles serve the motion of parts of the skeleton and thereby enable an organism to change—purposefully—its position in space, to act on the stage of the environment. Only at this point have we finally reached the level of preparatory action. Afferent and efferent impulses, activation of fibers, and motion of skeletal parts and their joints are studied as processes within an organism dependent on events in adjacent space. Only the experiencing being has a relation to an environment as the scene of his operations. In writing, the final product becomes a part of the environment severed from any direct contact with the writer. Looking at his work, the writer sees—at present—something he did in the past. If we equated seeing with stimulation, then we would have to say that the writer's organism is activated by another series of afferent impulses provoking another volley of responses. "Looking back," however, the subject is able to revise, correct, or improve his production through additional movements.

Events within a body are related to the chronometric order of physics; actions of an experiencing being are related to the chronological order of history, where the present is determined by the future and reaches back into the past as past. The physiologist, who relates data observed by him to physical time, orders his own actions within the frame of historical time. He plans his experiments, anticipating a possible outcome, and reports the actual findings looking back at his observations. Action is directed toward a goal. Preparatory movements are made for the benefit of others still to come. The present is determined by the future; actuality is directed by possibilities—an action not yet done— and, in our experience, an action never done before demands and guides the preceding ones.

In the next section of our experiments, the motor requirements were modest but the design was made more difficult. The subjects, sitting on a chair facing the camera, had to draw on the reverse side of a little blackboard which they held in one hand. The instruction was e.g., to write four digits and then to turn the blackboard around its proximal axis by 90° so that the figures written would appear in normal position to an observer looking at it from the opposite direction. Another subtest was to write the numerals so that they would appear in normal position to the subject when he turned the blackboard 90° around its distal axis toward himself. Let us suppose a subject had to write the numerals 5376 and could see them through a sheet of transparent plastic; a correct solution would present the four digits in the first case ƆƔƐƧ and in this arrangement ƧƷ\ℚ in the second case. In the first case, a correct drawing corresponds to mirror writing. This can easily be seen when the problem and its solution are presented side by side, i.e., after the solution has been achieved. Our subjects found themselves in a different situation. In the experimental arrangement, there was nothing suggesting such a solution. The subjects were told what numeral to write; they had to start from scratch. They had to abandon in imagination the actual situation and to figure out how things would appear to someone looking at them from the opposite direction.

The task of the subject was not to identify himself with one single person but to understand how the environment must be seen by any counterpart. The first step a subject had to take in the process of re-orientation was to realize that the act of writing had to begin from the right-hand margin and not from the left, as in the orthodox procedure. Following this point of departure, the numerals had to be brought into the required position. In a free play of fantasy, we find no obstacle in turning weightless images in any direction. Even if we have never actually seen the digits 5376 arranged in the manner required by this experiment, we can design them in the order set by the instruction. The actual performance was a reconstruction of the completed design. The design had to satisfy two conditions: it had to be correct in relation to the fictitious counterpart, and it had to be in a correspondingly abnormal position in relation to the writer. The subject had to play a double role. The design, first oriented in relation to the counterpart, had to be adapted to the actual position of the subject. There is little wonder that our subjects spent considerable time in deliberation, seldom accompanied by conative movements of writing. Corrections, however, after a false start were not so rare. Because of the capricious shape of the Arabic numerals, a correct beginning would not guarantee correct continuation, and neither would a wrong start prevent a correct ending.

The second subtest is not much less involved; even so, the motor execution in this case is also actually a reproduction of a design made in a free, although exact and logical, play of fantasy. On the way to a solution, the subject first had to visualize the end product. He had to turn—in imagination—the required numerals 5376. In the last step, the imagined blackboard with the imagined numerals inscribed upon it had to be turned back into a horizontal position so that the blackboard as seen in imagination would coincide with the real one. Returning from his excursion into the realm of imagination, the subject was now able to actually follow with the chalk the outline of the figures conceived before; just as in remembering, the past is brought back into the present but as past, so in planning, the future is pulled forward into the present, although as possibility. One may ask whether our subjects did not use their past experience, so that their movements were conditioned by the past and not determined by the future. If "past experience" refers to a particular event similar in structure, the answer to this question is in the negative. If, however, past experience refers to the general truth that blackboards, books, and writing pads may be turned in many directions and that numerals small and large may be read from diverse material, the answer must be in the affirmative. However, knowledge of this kind refers to possibilities. With our subjects, it was not a memory of something that actually happened but an understanding of what could have happened—be it in the past or in the future. In any case, our subjects had to jump ahead of the actual situation. They had to reach a hypothetical goal and to return from there to the starting point. The temporal configuration of planning cannot be shaped within the framework of clock time, with its irreversible sequence of earlier–later and its dimensions of one-after-the-other and simultaneity.

Even the motor performance of the task, the execution of the design, taken by itself, has an involved temporal organization. The act of writing or drawing is extended in time no less than that of talking and listening. In print and script, however, acoustical sequence is transformed into optical simultaneity. On a printed page, letters and words are at rest; they do not follow one another. We, the readers, moving from word to word and line to line, restore sequence. A sign like USA certainly appears as one unit where all three letters seen at one glance are simultaneously present. In a written letter or numeral like 3 or 5 or 7, no part has a temporal priority over the other; yet, in printing a U on the blackboard, the writer must begin at one end and follow the loop to the other end. The horizontal stroke of the 5 may be made before or after the other parts, but the very act of producing ends in a visible product where all temporal differences are finally eliminated. Some forms of dyslexia, agraphia, acalculia, and constructiva apraxia probably are related to disturbances of the required functions of de- and retemporalization.

The movements of our subjects are comparable to those of a copyist and, for that matter, to those of a student who learns the skill of writing through imitation of patterns. They all agree, insofar as the hands are directed by an established pattern—invisible and inverted, in the case of our subjects and visible and given to the copyist and student. Even a child who learns how to print a letter must understand, at least in practice, that the letter A can be mobilized, i.e., divided into three parts and reconstructed by three strokes. The child learns to conduct the pencil so that lines comparable with his model in length, direction, and angulation are produced by his movements. The action of our subjects, of a copyist, and of a student are directed by a *vis a fronte*. The translation from the present position to the next one is determined by the goal to be reached; yet, when a technique like writing or typing has been learned, the *vis a fronte* has been replaced by a *vis a tergo*.

Casual observation gave us an opportunity to test this hypothesis and to extend our studies to problems of habituation. One of the few patients included thus far in our list of subjects, when confronted with the simple task of writing USA right-side up behind his back, to our surprise made the letters upside down. Although his mistake was pointed out to him, he was unable, even with repeated trials, to correct his initial error. It made no difference whether he used his right or left hand. Since this patient was a man of low intelligence, Dr. Lyons, research psychologist in my laboratory, suggested that his performance could be considered a "minus" rather than a "plus," a failure due to the persistence of a motor habit. If this assumption were correct, we argued, it should be possible to arrange situations in which even normal subjects would find the more or less automatic reproduction of a habitual sign in an abnormal position easier and more convenient to execute than the intended and planned inversion of its pattern.

We proceeded as follows. Once again, we stood the subject with his back to a large, upright blackboard. In this position, he was first asked to move his right hand as if signing his name rapidly on a small blackboard held in front of him. We then lowered the small blackboard to the horizontal plane, while the subject continued his feigned performance of writing his signature, and finally turned it another 90° to a vertical position behind him. The subject now received a piece of chalk with the instruction to write his name on the large blackboard behind him but without changing the direction of his movements. Under these conditions, the signature appeared with all its familiar characteristics but in double inversion, just as though it had been written by someone who leaned over the top of the blackboard from the other side. In this position, following the instructions we had given, the subject had executed the habitual act of writing from left to right but had identified his up and down strokes with the extension and flexion of the wrist. In some cases, the deviation of the product itself, in relation to the gravitationally determined field of the environment, escaped notice. It may be worth mentioning that, among our volunteer female subjects, one married woman, to her own astonishment, wrote her maiden name, and another, also to her great surprise, wrote her given name in Gothic script which she had not used since her school days.

In the final phase of this test, we asked the subject to face the blackboard and to repeat his signature in the same—but now obviously abnormal—position. It made little difference whether his original production was covered or left open to his inspection, whether the subject had realized he had deviated from the normal position, or whether he was unaware of this and was surprised on discovering it. In every case, the reproduction, performed now under the guidance of sight, was inferior to the original. The execution was slow and was preceded and interrupted by periods of deliberation; mistakes in the order and orientation of letters were not infrequent; and the characteristic traits were less marked. The behavior of our subjects demonstrated, first, that, under certain conditions, the execution of habitual skills may be paralyzed and, second, the way in which the execution can be replaced by actions new in design and performance.

Once again, we are confronted with William James's dictum that "voluntary movements must be secondary, not primary functions of our organism" (1950, p. 487)—that only a creature endowed with divinatory power could transcend such natural barriers. Yet, our experiments show that no supernatural gifts are required. The capacity to perform an act voluntarily for the first time is not limited to a few privileged beings. Anyone can do it, and everyone does it—and first of all those who conduct experiments and write books about their observations. It behooves us, therefore, to answer two questions: What is wrong with James's statement? How is a new performance possible? However, a theme like this cannot be presented adequately as an appendix to an experimental study; available space sets the limit and confines us to a mere sketch (the interested reader will find a profound discussion of these problems in F. J. J. Buytendijk (1956, 1957).

James, like so many others who today share his view, claims that his statement is a fruit picked from the tree of experience. Actually, it is the application of an obsolete metaphysical dogma which interdicts experience from speaking for itself. In the *Principles of Psychology* James postulates "a blank unmediated correspondence, term for term, of the succession of states in consciousness with the succession of total brain processes." Although James conceded that "this is certainly only a provisional halting-place, and things must some day be more thoroughly thought out," he believes that through "a mere admission of the empirical parallelism . . . psychology will remain positivistic and non-metaphysical"[2] (1918, p. 182). Yet, empirical parallelism is a late and distorted paraphrase of Spinoza's proposition, "The order and connection of ideas is the same as the order and connection of things" (Ethics Bk. II, pr. op. VII). In this statement, ideas *(cogitatio)* and things *(extensio)* are understood as two attributes of the one infinite substance. Spinoza's pantheistic philosophy enabled him to heal the wound set through the Cartesian dichotomy of mind and body—or, to be more specific, to reunite in some way *extensio* and *cogitatio*, which Descartes had conceived as being two radically different substances. Severed from Spinoza's metaphysics and applied as a scientific hypothesis to individual organisms, parallelism—far from being empirical and positivistic—is a totally arbitrary supposition eluding any attempt at verification; nevertheless, it has far-reaching consequences.

Psychophysical parallelism transcribes a geometrical concept into a temporal one. The succession of conscious data is supposed to run parallel with the sequence of brain processes, insofar as an event in the first series occurs simultaneously—term for term—with one in the other. It follows, then, that one and the same order of time must be applicable to both groups. Time has taken over the role and function of Spinoza's infinite substance. If parallelism would remain consistent with its own basic assumption, it should allow for two orders of time—one corresponding to the succession of physical events and the other, to the sequence of states of consciousness. But then the idea of an "empirical correlation" would become completely meaningless. Parallelism, therefore, proclaims—without any qualm—the chronometric order of physical time as the only one. This first step actually eliminates any possibility of understanding action, thought, or memory—in short, it effaces all psychological phenomena.

In order to force experience into a framework of physical time, the data of consciousness must be assimilated to physical objects. Sensations, perceptions, emotions, and volitions are considered as a multitude of separate entities. Such integers—to use James's own term—follow each other in time; they appear and disappear. If they are only transitory moments in the flux of time, how is it then possible to experience present, past, and future—to conceive of time and to measure it? In the famous chapter entitled "The Stream of Thought," with its emphasis on

---

[2] It makes sense to single out James as the outstanding representative of a whole group—for obvious reasons. His presentation, although by now advanced in years, is by no means antiquated. Indeed, while James moved on to new positions, many contemporary psychologists are entrenched at his provisional halting-place as shown by the following quotation from Eccles: "In general, it may be postulated that any thought pattern in the mind has a counterpart in a specific spatiotemporal pattern of neuronal activity" (1953, p. 266).

continuity and flux, on the transitive parts and the fringes, James (1918) provides some answer to these questions. Yet, these great contributions to psychology contradict rather than justify his basic assumption. Strangely enough, in his analysis of action and of imagination, James was not able to do likewise and to emancipate himself from the fetters of psychophysiological theory.[3]

In line with Spinoza's philosophy, psychophysical parallelism emphasizes the strict separation of the two series of events no less than their exact correlation. Both kingdoms are of equal sovereignty: The mind does not determine the body's behavior, nor does the body determine the mind. Yet there is, it seems, an unavoidable distinction to be made, a difference which gives a privileged status to the body. The body of an organism is related to other bodies; it is a part of the physical universe. The mind, however, is related to one body only; it is not directly related to the world, nor to other bodies, nor to other minds. "The mind which the psychologist studies is the mind of distinct individuals inhabiting definite portions of a real space and of a real time" (James, 1918, p. 183). Mental events must, therefore, be depreciated, debased to mere epiphenomena of cerebral events which they accompany. The mind shares domicile with the brain, as a sort of sublessee. "All sensa are identical with parts of the brain and not with the surface of the external physical objects" (Price, 1950). The data of consciousness, it seems, form an inside world, brought into indirect contact with the "outside world" only through hypothetical secondary acts such as projection (Fulton, 1943), reality testing (Freud, 1915), or unconscious inference (Helmholtz, 1866). Consciousness appears to be a superfluous duplication of physiological processes. It makes little difference whether conscious data do or do not accompany events within the nervous system. Supposedly, they do not add anything new to the situation of a body directed by physiological mechanisms; they do not extend its reach. In other words, psychophysical parallelism isolates the experiencing being from its environment.

Indeed, James's proposition that voluntary actions must be secondary was not derived from a psychological analysis of action but was based on a physiological reconstruction of motion. James reduced action to an event within the body, to a combination of efferent impulses and muscle

---

[3] There were, as McDougall said, two Jameses: "James the physiologist and sensationalist psychologist, and James the author of the purposive psychology which was the root of his pragmatic philosophy." To this quotation Müller-Freienfels adds, "There were many more Jameses than that" (1935, p. 237). Indeed, empirical parallelism was hardly reconcilable with James's attack on atomism, the "domino psychology," and the "passivism" of traditional psychology. It was still less in agreement with the voluntaristic, tychistic, pluralistic philosophy of his later years.

activities released and steered by afferent impulses. A nervous system, of course, is not aware of any relation to the environment nor of its own position within an environment. It reacts to stimuli; it does not conduct itself in relation to objects. Purposive movements cannot occur for the first time in a nervous system, because this would imply the new synaptic connections were made by choice, in anticipation of a meaningful adaptation to the organization of the environment. Action cannot be explained in terms of neurophysiology alone, for, in every action, the present condition is relinquished in favor of a future one; that which is not yet or is not yet so is realized, in exchange for that which is. Actuality is replaced by possibility. In acting, I operate within an extended spatiotemporal field, proceeding from a given start toward an intended goal. I experience (myself)—though not conceptually—as essentially motile. I also view the objects in my surroundings as alterable, contingent on a shift from an actual condition to one anticipated in imagination.

The actual situation is but a limitation of possibilities. The goal to be reached thereafter, the possibilities to be realized, inhabit the present potentially. When I move from my desk toward the door of my office in order to open it and finally to step out into the hall, my future position at the door is already present to me while I am still sitting at my desk. I see the door now, at this very moment. Nevertheless, I see it as a potential goal; I see it from here over there. Capable, within limits, of overcoming the power of gravity, we, as motile beings, find ourselves *in* the world yet lifted off from the ground and opposite to things, which thereby are transformed into objects, the Other. As an experiencing being, I am at the center of my environment. My position here and now is the hub of my spatiotemporal orientation. The actual moment, my now, is the divide between future and past. Future and past are personal tenses of time that are always related to the present of an experiencing being. From this center, the surroundings are opened to me as a field of action and observation. Were man but another particle drifting in the stream of events in their spatiotemporal contiguity, he could not act and he could not observe. Only in opposition to things are we able to observe objects; only from an egocentric perspective can we measure space and time. Acting is personal; it requires the I–world relation, it occurs within an egocentric environment, it is performed within a temporal horizon open to the future, it is directed toward objects susceptible to change, and it is not triggered by stimuli.

Natural science and all the dependent disciplines which study man primarily as a body cannot account for action. They are forced to deny its reality or to eliminate the problem through a biased interpretation. Objects must be replaced by stimuli and meaningful connections by synaptic links; anticipation of the future must be interpreted as the aftereffect of events which occurred in the past. For, stimuli and their traces work only in the present; stimuli have no relation to possibilities; they do not occur in the mode of "not yet."

Yet, if an organism cannot perform an act "voluntarily for the first time," the observer cannot do it either. Nay, in accordance with his own theory, he himself could not even conceive of a first and second time. The concepts of first time and repetition are historical categories of time. They have no place in the realm of physical events; their home is in the world of the physicist. In the universe of physics described by the physicist, events occur but once. They have a unique position somewhere on spatiotemporal world lines. Physical events are never repeated; only their form is repeatable. The observer alone, who, in his experience, reaches beyond the individual moment, can comprehend repetition. It would be more appropriate, therefore, to say that voluntary movements cannot be secondary, because physical events happen but once. In James's theory, the physical and the historical aspects of time and the concept and the experience of time are mixed up.

The neurophysiologist is forced to exempt himself from the rules applied to his objects, men or animals. This inconsistency is unavoidable; otherwise, the observer could not give any account of his activities. In accordance with his own doctrines, he must consider himself as an organism responding to stimuli which cause certain events within his nervous system, events located in the observer's skull and brain—and in no other place. Although observer and observed play a different role in a psychological experiment, they are—in principle and in practice—exchangeable. The basic rules of the game are obligatory for both. If the behavior of a subject can be fully explained as manifestations of events within a nervous system, then the behavior of the observer must be submitted to the same process of reduction. But this would eliminate all possibilities of observing and experimenting.

The physiologist substitutes—and rightly so—optical stimuli for the objects visible to him. Stimuli are constructs; they are never directly observable. Optical stimuli produce a photochemical reaction; they are not characterized by the qualities of brightness, color, visibility, and horizon. Yet, in an almost tragic confusion, many psychologists speak of stimuli as if they were objects. They speak about mastering stimuli and manipulating them. They refer to an animal approaching a stimulus, obviously without realizing that such statements are in absolute contradiction to their own basic assumption. One cannot manipulate a stimulus, because stimuli are physical agents which have acted upon a receiver and have been absorbed into an organism. The moment a physical agent becomes a stimulus, it has lost its independent existence outside of an organism. Stimuli always operate as particular agents causing particular events within a particular nervous system. Stimuli are private; they cannot be shared. Nervous systems do not communicate with one another. But, to experiencing beings, a world of visible and audible things is opened; about such objects, we can communicate with each other. Objects—whether in the practice of everyday life or in a physical or psychological experiment—exist only in relation to experiencing beings conscious of the Other.

There cannot be two psychologies, one for the subjects observed and another reserved for the observer. What is sauce for the goose is sauce for the gander. If scientific methodology requires the reduction of all observable behavior to neurophysiological processes, the behavior of the observer cannot be spared. There is no reason to grant him immunity in an asylum where all inquiry must be stopped. We cannot place the observer, like a dictator, above the law valid for everyone else. Indeed, he should be the first one to be investigated, for propositions about the observer's behavior are the very foundation of all other propositions. In his statements, the observer refers to visible objects, he relates one object to another, he manipulates variables, he changes conditions, he anticipates results and verifies his expectations, and he establishes facts in relation to possibilities—in one word, he acts. Putting it the other way around, we say, what is sauce for the gander must be sauce for the goose. If we are compelled to consider the activities of an observer as action, we have every right to consider the behavior of our subjects as actions.

In the experiments conducted in our laboratory, we observed the behavior of fellow men, not of nervous systems; we watched the conduct of an experiencing creature, not of an apparatus. We met our subjects as partners in an environment common to all of us. We placed the subjects next to a blackboard, a thing visible to them just as it was to us. We gave them instructions, convinced that they would hear and understand our words, just as we ourselves spoke, heard, and understood them. The subjects of our experiments we made the objects of our observation. Yet we studied their performance and achievements as the actions and productions of experiencing beings.

As a consequence—and our experimental results only serve to emphasize this—we will have to reconsider the basic assumptions of psychophysiology. Such re-examination may, perhaps, lead from a physiological psychology to a truly psychological psychology—a psychology of human beings and of the human world as the basic science of the humanities.

Summary

The term "psychomotor" signifies, in Wernicke's neuropsychiatric system, a section of the "psychological reflex arc" (1900). Psychomotor symptoms are considered as manifestations of a "sejunction" through which the psychomotor pathway acquires a pathological autonomy. Psychomotor behavior is regarded as pseudospontaneous. It seems to follow that spontaneity is characteristic of at least some forms of normal behavior. Neurophysiology, however, cannot acknowledge the possibility of spontaneity. In neurological interpretation, actions must be reduced to stimuli- and engram-controlled movements. It is postulated that all meaningful behavior must be learned behavior.

Experiments were devised to put this postulate to the test. Subjects were required to write on a blackboard, behind their backs and using their nonhabitual writing hand, various words and letter combinations in various orientations—that is, right side up, or as in a mirror image, or as though the letters were reflected in a stream, or in a double twist compounded of the first two turns. All twenty-one normal subjects participating in the experiments were found able to carry out, without previous training, these tasks which demanded completely new motor integrations of various degrees of complexity. To distinguish further between difficulties of motor execution and complexity of design, two additional kinds of tasks were introduced: (1) subjects were required to write familiar words in script, behind their backs and above their shoulders, thus executing a task of completely novel and anomalous motor integration but with minimal demands in terms of design; and (2) they were given problems in which motor requirements were modest but problems of design were paramount, such as writing sets of Arabic numerals on the underside of a blackboard that had to be turned to appear in various orientations to an onlooker.

Results of these studies make it plain that action depends on and follows a design correctly planned and anticipated in imagination.

The demonstrated fact that voluntary actions can be performed without previous training leads to the problem of how such achievements are possible. A preliminary answer to this fundamental problem is given with a comparison of the relation of an experiencing being to his environment and that of a nervous system to stimuli.

References

Brain, R. Aphasia, apraxia and agnosia. In S. K. Wilson, *Neurology*. Vol. 3. (3rd ed.) Baltimore, Md.: Williams & Wilkins, 1955.

Buytendijk, F. J. J. *Allgemeine Theorie der menschlichen Haltung und Bewegung*. Berlin, Göttingen, & Heidelberg: Springerverlag, 1956.

Buytendijk, F. J. J. Das Menschliche der menschlichen Bewegung. *Nervenarzt*, 1957, **28**, 1–7.

Eccles, J. C. *The neurophysiological basis of mind*. Oxford: Clarendon Press, 1953.

Fessard, A. E. Mechanisms of nervous integration. In *Brain mechanisms and consciousness*. Springfield, Ill.: Charles C Thomas, 1954.

Freud, S. Instincts and their vicissitudes (1915). In *Collected papers of*. . . . Vol. 4. New York: Basic Books, 1959. Pp. 60–83.

Fulton, J. F. *Physiology of the nervous system*. (2nd ed.) London: Oxford University Press, 1943.

Head, H. *Aphasia and kindred disorders of speech*. Vols. 1 & 2. Cambridge, Eng.: Cambridge University Press, 1926.

Hebb, D. O. *The organization of behavior*. New York: John Wiley, 1949.

Helmholtz, H. *Handbuch den physiologischen Optik*. 1866.

Helmholtz, H. *Die Lehre von der Tonempfindungen*. (3rd ed.) 1870.

James, W. *Principles of psychology*. Vols. 1 & 2. New York: Henry Holt, 1918.

Liepman, H. *Über Störnsungen des Handelns bei Gehirnkranken*. Berlin: Karger, 1905.

Müller-Freienfels, R. *The evolution of modern psychology*. New Haven: Yale University Press, 1935.

CHAPTER ELEVEN

Shame as a Historiological Problem

The term "historiological" has not yet been accepted as a naturalized citizen by psychology. Nevertheless, I have used it to define my subject, first, because I do not know of a better word and, second, because it denotes that the immediate experience of shame can only be understood with the help of historical-psychological categories. This is so because the experiencing person understands himself historiologically, i.e., as continuously emergent (*Werdend*). Of course, this kind of self-understanding is not a conceptual knowledge but a more elementary form of self-disclosure.

One may think that I have chosen a poor subject to demonstrate the importance of historical categories in psychology, for, as far as psychology has been concerned with the problem of shame at all, it has attempted to interpret it statically. The definitions given by Lipps (1907) and others illustrate in a striking way this nonhistorical way of looking at things in psychology. Therefore, if we can demonstrate the necessity for a historical method in this instance, we will have gained two points: a more intimate acquaintance with the phenomenon itself and, at the same time, a clarification of the problem of method in psychology. While normal psychology, and particularly experimental psychology—with its formulations so alien to everyday life—have been able to treat the problem of shame as trivial, pathopsychology, especially in the treatment of neuroses, urgently requires development of our theme, if only to avoid the errors of psychoanalysis. Our position forces us to fight on two fronts: against the static interpretation of shame in normal psychology and against the genetic interpretation of psychoanalysis.

I shall begin by contrasting my view with the theory of Freud (1963). Freud often speaks of the barriers of shame and disgust and how they have been set up by the disciplinary measures of those to whom the child's education has been entrusted. This genetic interpretation of shame and disgust rests on a group of significant assumptions and leads to remarkable consequences.

1. Shame and disgust merely inhibit the actualization of innate drives and demands. The actions prevented by shame and disgust stem from more primary drive impulsions.

2. Shame and disgust are acquired modes of behavior. They do not originate at the same level as the drives whose actualization they block. Shamelessness or unashamedness is primary according to Freud; shame is secondary.

3. Shame and disgust are basically prohibitive. They call for abstention from certain *specific* actions.

4. From such *specific* abstentions, with the help of the Unconscious, feeling-toned attitudes and chronic traits gradually develop.

5. Shame and disgust are peripheral activities. Basically, they represent an abstention that is demanded and imposed but one that is no more able to affect the continuity and character of the original attitude than any forced renunciation or confession is able to modify one's real character. Man would be happy only if he could live without shame or disgust.

6. There are certain partial drives whose actualization is interfered with by the barriers of shame and disgust. But, in the perversions, the partial drives are active in an unmodified way, showing themselves without disguise. In shame, it is the drive to consume by looking (scoptophilia) that has suffered a painful restriction. Therefore, in Freud's view, we ought to be most successful in explaining shame genetically by relating it to voyeurism. But this certainly needs testing.

Freud does not consider perversions as deteriorations or distortions of human existence. On the contrary, the original drive impulsions appear in them nakedly. The psychoanalytic theory of perversions, so closely tied to the doctrine of partial drives, assumes and must assume the ultimate aim of all libidinal drives to be the gain of pleasure. All the various partial drives agree in this aim; thus, they can function vicariously for one another, and, thus, there is a quantitative equilibrium among them. In each instance, the world is but an object, i.e., a means toward the end of drive gratification. Man has no real and actual relation to the world; the world is a source of disturbances from which man turns away to himself. Psychoanalysis not only makes use of a mechanistic terminology out of a historically contingent accident but is, in its basic concept, a mechanistic psychology. Its object is the individual viewed in isolation. All experiences are to be understood, in the last analysis, as events in an isolated organism. Psychoanalysis is a solipsistic doctrine; it is not a solipsistic theory of knowledge but—and this has even farther reaching implications—an anthropological solipsism.

Yet, the perversions are pervasive modifications of and disturbances in man's communication with the world. The concept of *communicative mode* is of fundamental importance for anthropological psychology. The voyeur does not become a voyeur out of an exogenous or endogenous heightening of his "urge to look." Anyone who draws his sexual gratification from looking at another lives continuously at a distance. If it is normal to approach and unite with the partner, then it is precisely characteristic of the voyeur that he remains alone, without a partner, an outsider who acts in a stealthy and furtive manner. To keep his distance when it is essential to draw near is one of the paradoxes of his perversion. The looking of the voyeur is of course also a looking at and, as such, is as different from the looks exchanged by lovers as medical palpation from a gentle caress of the hand. In viewing, there is a transition from the immediate I–thou encounter, i.e., mutual participation, to a unilateral intention—a transition from the I–thou relationship to the subject–object relationship proper. All looking and being looked at is a lapse from immediate communication. This is demonstrated in everyday life by our annoyance and irritation at being observed. The psychotic experience of being looked at is also based on a change in communicative mode. "Looking at" objectifies. Objectification is the second and essentially perverse action of the voyeur, along with his keeping his distance. Both are closely linked together. Objectification is only possible with a keeping of distance, and, conversely, it is only the keeping of distance that makes objectification possible. The peculiar mode of existence of the voyeur directs his curiosity toward the sexual organs, the sexual function, and the sexual word, continually in search of both clarity and closeness, whereas lovers search for concealment, half-light, and silence.

Thus, the voyeur does not participate in reality in any direct sense but only by way of the objectifications, i.e., reflected knowledge. He makes the Other into an object in and for itself. His objectification, then, permits arbitrary re-enactments in fantasy. The behavior of the voyeur is not an inherently meaningful surrender to fate, like that of lovers. The perversion of the voyeur, like all perversions, reveals a fundamentally different kind of attitude toward the world, toward himself, and toward his partner. The voyeur reveals, in his objectifying attitude and in his furtive entry into the Other's most intimate experience, the antinomy of two modes of being—the public mode and that of immediate being.

These two modes of being, the public and the immediate, are separated by shame, which, at the same time, protects immediate experience from invasion by the public sphere. We will call this latter form of shame, our main interest at present, protective shame. We may now define our subject very generally as the antithesis between public and immediate experience. It is our aim to give an adequate understanding of this antithesis and, from this, to show how immediate being could be threatened by the public.

The public sphere is only found among humans. We cannot speak of "the public" in the plant kingdom or among other animals. The public emerges simultaneously with language or the production of symbols. From a functional psychological point of view, it is linked with perceiving, thinking, and thoughts. Incidentally, what we call the private sphere is a delimited public sphere and not the polar opposite to "public," which we call "immediate."

We belong to the public in the ways we are described—e.g., by our name, title, position, status, profession, etc. Everyone is assigned a particular role in the public sphere, but this role is not merely "played." Both the assumption and performance of the role assigned to the individual is linked to a certain way of being human. If we meet a stranger in public, we usually ask two questions: "Who is he?" and "What is he?" The name identifies someone in the social space of the family, of the birthplace, of the chronicles. To the question of the What of his being, we answer by stating his profession, position, etc. The specification points to something general and repeatable. (*Le roi est mort. Vive le roi.*) These are general and repeatable functions that the individual assumes in public. The intimate person is always initially concealed by his public figure. It is possible to participate in the public figure with a noncommittal, one-way kind of general interest; but the intimate person opens and reveals himself to understanding only in mutual and immediate participation.

The public originally constitutes itself through objectification, i.e., reflection. The logical features of identity, generality, and repetition here assume an anthropological significance. What is conceived as definite in a logical sense has the significance of finite and, thereby, finished in an anthropological sense. Conceptual determination, rationality and the past, and completion and accomplishment are closely and reciprocally related. Now, to the extent that a man becomes identical with his public position, i.e., to the extent he is what he has become—and no one is exempted from this fate—he loses the possibility of immediate becoming. As a man ages, he tends increasingly to turn toward the past and live in repetition.

Public being is characterized, as we have seen, by objectification or reflection, generality, repetition; the outcome is noncommittal, one-way participation. Immediate being, on the other hand, is not objectified, it is singular, unique becoming and calls for reciprocal sharing.

Shame divides what is immediately becoming from the finished outcome and protects whatever is in becoming from violation by the completed. The temporal and historical moment, an important feature of any anthropological approach, is implicit in this antithesis between immediate becoming and completion. This antithesis between *natura naturans* and *natura naturata* should make clearer our reference to shame as a historiological problem.

Shame is basic to human existence and is continuously active; it is not made up of many isolated occurrences of shame separate from one another in time. Shame is not merely active at certain times and under certain circumstances. When someone is ashamed, it is a sign that the permanent safeguard of shame has been breached, that immediate experience has been jeopardized by the entry of public experience. But the need for protection in immediate becoming is still imperfectly explained by the antithesis between the two modes of being. It is conceivable that the two modes of being could alternate. Experience, however, shows that immediate becoming—whether erotic, religious, or spiritual—generally seeks protection against the profane and safeguards against the presence of the nonparticipating stranger. The stranger is of necessity an observer. He is, thus, at odds with the shared unity of the group, and his mere presence tends to introduce some objectification into every immediate relationship.

The phenomenon of the comic will help to elucidate the peculiar linkage of the stranger with objectification, one-way participation, repetition, and the destruction of immediate becoming. We will state this as several theses:

1. What is strange tends to be comic, e.g., that which is old-fashioned or the customs of other countries and peoples.

2. Only the strange is comic. The traditional figures of comedy—the stutterer, the dullard, the cuckold, etc.—are comic only as long as sympathy is denied, i.e., when communication is in one direction only. We suffer with the hero, but we laugh about the clown.

3. What is different beyond all comparison is not strange; there is always similarity in what is strange. Neither the plant nor the worm are comical, but the ape is.

4. Repetition, or the element of parody, is essential to the comic. Repetition, repeatability at will, annuls the seriousness of a word, an act, or a person. Hence, the comic effect of children's miming and aping of adults, the comic effect of twins, and the uncanny effect of the double. Note, in addition, the repeatability of the comic figure in contrast to the singularity of the tragic hero: a joke can be repeated, while a word is serious only at a particular time.

Repetition, sacrilege, or profanation; the comic; the strange; one-way participation, and outcomes are all linked together on the one hand; on the other are singularity, seriousness, decision, mutual participation, and immediate becoming. To the stranger, our doings seem just so much to-do, even in the cool detachment of historical perspective. In the presence of the detached observer, we are in danger of experiencing our own doing as so much to-do. For this reason, we are inclined to keep strangers at a distance.

Whatever is in becoming must gradually emancipate itself from what has already become. The terminated prevails in tradition, the family, language, and knowledge; they are with us everywhere. To come into our own immediacy, we must unloosen ourselves from the outcomes, as in crisis, revolution, solitude, or *Wanderjahre*. Maturity, like all coming to oneself, requires a break with what has been inherited. We come to ourselves only in confrontation with the other. The incest prohibitions that prevent the individual from lingering in the sphere of the terminated enounce the essential laws of becoming as positive injunctions. Shame is a safeguard for immediate experience against the world of outcomes. It does not constrain the erotic, as is assumed in psychoanalysis, but makes the erotic possible for the first time. Shame is a protection against the public in all of its forms. The stranger, of course, is a perfect expression of the public threat of invasion to immediate experience, but it is not the only one. The word, in the form of "dirty joke," vivid representation as pornography, and self-observation in the mirror shows the objectifying character of a self-representation. Those who are in love have no use for the "dirty joke," pornography, or the mirror, for these all belong to the shrunken existences of persons no longer capable of being immediately touched. Words of affection tend to exclude the language of everyday life, giving rise spontaneously to an idiom that is personal and jealously guarded, one that names rather than describes. The secret that shame protects is not, however, as prudery makes the mistake of believing, one that is already in existence and only needs to be hidden from outsiders, for those who are in becoming are also hidden from themselves. Their existence is first made explicit in their shared immediate becoming. Youth keeps its secret still, while age has become knowing. Thus, youth is impelled to youth. Here, again, incest prohibitions are to be understood as essential laws of becoming.

One of the important forms of shame, in addition to the protective, is that of concealing shame. Most writers on shame have mostly chosen examples of concealing shame while claiming to treat the topic generally. Concealing shame judges the individual in terms of the group ideal, primarily attempting to conceal the deficiencies and deviations from the group ideal before a third person. The power of concealing shame diminishes as distance from the group increases. While protective shame safeguards immediate becoming, concealing shame acts on behalf of social prestige. It addresses itself directly to the onlooker and is oriented to the objectified public image. Thus, honor and disgrace, like medals of honor and stigmata, are both thing-like; like any possession, they may be transferred or inherited.

The group ideal changes in time and varies also according to country, people, class, and generation. And the form taken by concealing shame varies according to the prevailing group ideal.

The essential character of shame, preservative and concealing, discloses itself in a variety of ways, just as the idea of justice finds its situationally valid actualization in positive legal norms. While language does not provide us with different terms for distinguishing protective from concealing shame, it actually does for the privative forms of shame. The negative of protective shame we term "shamelessness," and the negative of concealing shame we term "unabashedness."

Psychology has limited itself for too long to an analysis of the contents of experience in terms of objective states. In so doing, man has been turned into a rubber-stamp subject, much like a thing. But a phenomenon such as shame can only be fully revealed within a perspective in which man is understood in terms of becoming or being actively engaged with his world, a perspective which grants sufficient significance to temporality and historicity in experience. Only a historiological psychology suited to such phenomena can comprehend and clarify the antitheses between singularity and repetition, immediate becoming and outcome, and temporal character and points on a time coordinate. Such a psychology reveals shame as an original feature of human existence and shamelessness as acquired behavior.

References

Freud, S. *Three essays on the theory of sexuality.* New York: Basic Books, 1963.
Lipps, T. *Vom Fühlen, Wollen und Denken.* Leipzig: Barth, 1907.

CHAPTER TWELVE

Rheoscopic Studies of Expression

In the fall of 1949, a laboratory dedicated to the studies of expressive motions was opened at the Veterans Administration Hospital, Lexington, Kentucky. The first tasks were to disentangle the skein of problems, to find a theoretical basis, and to develop adequate techniques. Now, as we begin to see results, it may be fitting, before publishing details, to give a general review of the situation.

The importance of expressive motions in the practice of everyday life and in medical activities in general can hardly be overrated. Actual knowledge of expression, however, is far from being commensurate. Paradoxically, everyone in his understanding of expression is at the same time expert and ignorant; as Saint Augustine said about time, "As long as no one asks me, I know the answer; the moment I want to explain it to an enquirer, I do not know."

It is through expression that we comprehend another being as a living and experiencing creature. It might be claimed, therefore—and with good reason—that expressive phenomena are the true marks of objects of psychological research that distinguishes them from all other things. Even if we hesitate to accept these views as axiomatic, we cannot deny that expressive motions direct interpersonal relations to a very large extent. Age, sex, group, race, color, epoch, and language do not constitute obstacles. We take it for granted that a mother realizes how her baby feels long before he is capable of pronouncing the simplest words. But also—and this is more startling—long before he is capable of distinguishing a circle from a square, the baby responds to the expression of the mother, e.g., whether she is friendly or angry, cheerful or sad.

Guided by expression, mother and child form in their reciprocal understanding a synkinetic group.

Expressive understanding even transcends barriers separating species from species. We can talk to a dog in many languages; he understands all of them not because he is polyglot but because he responds to the expressive values of intonation. These facts present an interesting but also a perplexing problem. We will not ascribe to the baby "inference by analogy" nor to the dog reaction by empathy. In order to give an account of the phenomena of expressive motions, we may well be forced to revise the principles of psychology.

Verbal communication is limited to those who speak the same language—a language that they once had to learn. Expressive communication is *universal*; it does not have to be learned. There are no schools that offer instruction in expressive motions; if they did, they would do more harm than good, for expressions are not intended as such. Intention usually interferes with their performance. Although highly communicative, they are not, or need not be, produced for the purpose of communication. This spontaneous production is paralleled by an equally *spontaneous comprehension* of expression. There is no doubt that we can, to some extent, acquire control over our expressions. We can also hope to improve our understanding of them—otherwise such research as this would be meaningless. However, we can travel a long distance without ever having to reflect on expressive motions.

This spontaneity of expression guarantees its *reliability*. Expressive deception is much more difficult to accomplish than verbal falsification. How often do our expressions reveal our true feelings against our intentions! In case of a discrepancy between words and expressions, we rely upon the expressions rather than the words. Through an ironical contrast of content and expression, everyone instantaneously grasps the true intention. "But Brutus says he was ambitious; and Brutus is an honorable man." By veiling, irony reveals.

The psychiatrist, in his endeavor to lift the mask of insanity, finds in expressive motions salient clues. Expressive motions dominate psychiatric judgment to no less a degree than in everyday life. No psychiatrist aware of the melancholic expression of a patient will trust his words that deny his depressive mood. Gait, voice, breath, and gaze betray the patient. Anticipating an impending suicide, we may even double our measures.

Although, in psychiatry, we depend so much on our observations of expressive motions, we have very little precise communicable knowledge. We have impressions, intuitive impressions; but, even if our impressions are correct—as they sometimes are—we rarely can give a clear account of them. We cannot demonstrate, and we cannot prove. The psychiatric situation does not differ from that of everyday life. However, our predicament is more serious because we are limited to opinions where we are entrusted with judgments.

In the search for a remedy, one first has to make clear why such a wide gap should exist between practice and knowledge. There are many reasons:

1. Our very familiarity with expressive motions prevents us from seeing them as problematic. Why should we bother about expressions as long as they serve us well in our need for orientation, for adaptation, and for cooperation with others?

2. Our understanding of expressive motions is a kind of performance, an acting more than a knowing. Expressive motions flourish in the immediateness of personal contact. They seem to evanesce the moment we make them an object of observation; they fade when the I–you relationship is switched to an I–he, when observation takes the place of partnership. Experimentation, therefore, threatens to destroy the very object we want to study.

3. Expressive motions are frequently fleeting, transitory. They are gone with the wind, leaving no trace and giving no opportunity of ascertaining them; once gone, they are not repeatable at will. Also, for this reason, expressive motions seem to defy experimentation.

4. Knowledge is directed toward what is regular; expressive motions are unlimited in number. While, in many cases of psychological research, we can be guided by language, here it is of no direct help. Our vocabulary has only too many words that signify nuances of expression.[1] The situation resembles that of some African languages, which have fifty or more words to name shades of one color, especially of brown. The reason here is the same as there. Practice is interested in particulars and in their discrimination, while knowledge looks for the basic structure—the one in many.

5. Our understanding of expression is a global reaction. This is in full agreement with the fact that expressive motions are a unity into which many single motions are integrated; we are not sad on the left side and cheerful on the right. Our expression is *uno tenore* and, accordingly, it is expressed by the whole organism. We may realize at first glance in what mood our partner is; however, when asked to ex-

---

[1] The same can be said of emotions, a coincidence that points to the kinship of expressions and emotions.

plain why we think so, we may find it difficult to give any detailed answer.

6. A satisfactory theory of expressive motions is still lacking. Without an adequate theory we cannot expect to order the multitude of expressions into a finite group of basic attitudes, or natural dimensions. A mere collection of facts, a wholly empirical approach, will not yield meaningful results.

Obviously, then, the problems found in research on expression are manifold and of differing weight and dignity. They may be grouped into three main divisions: theoretical, technical, and experimental.

Theoretical Problems

Since observations are answers to questions, pertinent observations depend on reasonable questions provided by theory. There are no plain facts open to disinterested inspection, certainly not in a field where observation so closely borders on interpretation, as in the study of expressions. Research is always directed by theoretical assumptions, whether we are aware of them or not. The theory, therefore, has to be formulated —at least tentatively—when or before experimentation is started. The results obtained under the guidance of theory will, in turn, confirm or refute its validity. If valid, the theory should also enable us to survey and to chart the accumulated facts; in other words, a valid theory should contain a prescription for a systematic order of observations.

While a theory is indispensable, it need not be new. However, there are strong reasons that recommend a revision of the existing theories. In the past, many attempts have been made to arrange the multitude of expressions into a systematic order. None of them has been fully successful. Although their failure may be partly owing to the lack of adequate technical devices, the blame has to be laid primarily to the deficiencies of the theories.

The history of theories of expression reaches far back. As in so many other fields, the recorded history of them begins with the work of the great Greek thinkers (Pollnow, 1928; Buehler, 1933; Allport and Vernon, 1933). All through the ages, down to Darwin, Wundt, and Klages, the theoreticians were inclined to see in expressions outward, physical signs of inner, psychical conditions. They took it as their task to explain this relation between the *sign* and the *signified*, which here obviously is one aspect of the mind–body relation. Everywhere in psychological research, the mind–body problem is present; in some areas of expression, the theorist cannot evade the mind–body problem. He is, therefore, forced to go beyond the frontiers of psychology and psychopathology.

The mind–body problem is not answered simply by denying its existence. Psychological thought has become deeply ingrained with the Cartesian dichotomy of mind and body. We can renounce all allegiance to it and still remain bound by it; it reappears under many guises—as epiphenomenon or as sensory data; it operates in the aliases of stimulus–response or of reality-testing. Under its influence, psychological science has drifted further and further away from everyday-life experience. In the process of analytical reduction, the phenomena themselves have been obscured and distorted. The study of expressions urges a reevaluation of phenomena; this will lead to a rehabilitation of *experience*. At this point, we shall find a tenable solution of the mind–body problem that contains—still enveloped—a theory of expression. In unfolding it, we shall also obtain a method of discovering the basic categories of expression.

A thorough discussion of these complex problems must be given elsewhere.

Technical Problems

Compared with former days, we are in an advantageous position. The modern laboratory has devices that facilitate research in expressive motions. Early investigators were limited by inadequate technical equipment. Indeed, the raw material of their studies was not so much the original phenomenon of expressive motions as some derivative; they had to be content with either the physiognomic mask (Porta, 1650), portrayal by an actor (Engel, 1783), artistic painting and drawing (Bell, 1843), the imitation of expression by electric stimulation (Duchenne, 1876), the collection of diversified observations (Darwin, 1872), or such expressive precipitates as handwriting (Klages, 1924). Today, we can study under experimental conditions in a wide range of controlled variations facial expression, posture, carriage, gesticulation, voice, and intonation, shifting our attention from one manifestation to the other as we please. With the camera, the motion picture, and sound recording we are able to arrest the fleeting, repeat the unique, analyze the global, and reintegrate the parts into a whole.

The term "rheoscopic"[2] was selected to signify such applications of

[2] The word "rheoscopic" is coined in accordance with "microscopic" and similar terms. As the microscope makes accessible to critical sight (*scopein*) the minute (*micron*), rheoscopic procedures open to vision the fleeting (*rheo*). If it is permissible

film-recording techniques, which have already been used to some extent by such psychologists as Buehler (1933) and Lersch (1932).

New methods bring new problems, obstacles, and handicaps. Progress is never a pure gain. Photo floodlights and camera produce an artificial situation, irritating and bewildering, which induces shyness in two forms. In a photo and studio, light has an almost corporeal character; it does not seem to emanate from a source that illuminates the room in spheres of diminishing brightness; it fills space equally everywhere, not sparing any friendly area of claire-obscure; in its penetrating obtrusiveness, it cuts off all retreat into privacy. Plunged into this mercilessly revealing light of the laboratory, the patient finds his innermost being exposed to the scrutinizing eye of the camera. Certainly, these are not surroundings conducive to unguarded behavior—just the opposite; the patient becomes self-conscious and feels isolated. Sound-recording, if done openly, adds its share to the denaturalized environment of the studio. Sound-recording interferes with the casual, informal, noncommittal frankness of conversations, which are not phrased for deposition and re-examination.

If lens and recorder disturb naïve production, the next thought may be to move the recorder out of sight and to hide the camera behind a screen. First thoughts seldom are final solutions. Hiding the equipment would preserve the naïveté of the patient but would affect the spontaneity of the experimenter and put him into a predicament, the more embarrassing if the patient should ask point-blank whether recording is being done. While there is no great technical difficulty in camouflaging a microphone, the one-way screen does not present—not even from a technical point of view—a good solution. Absorbing a great deal of light, such a screen aggravates the lighting problem. It is hard to explain to a patient the stupendous brilliance of illumination when no camera is visible. Even if the patient remains unaware of the camera, natural contact with him suffers under the surveillance of a peeping lens.

The psychological disturbance caused by mechanical devices will not be cured by the addition of more devices. Such deficiencies must be compensated for in the sphere of interpersonal relations. If the patient is adequately informed about the character of the laboratory, if warm personal contact is maintained during the performance, and if the scenario catches his interest, he may overcome his initial amazement. Actually, only a few patients refuse to cooperate, most of them neurotics. The severely

---

to compare techniques that are rather unsophisticated with instruments brought near to perfection, one could say that the rheoscopic technique magnifies time as the microscope magnifies space.

psychotic patient, limited in the modulation of his behavior, appears less annoyed in this situation than one would expect.

The scenario sets short scenes for which the cameraman has to prepare. Even if the photographer completely understands the idea of the experiment, and his first love is not photography, he has to turn his attention to the camera, sometimes at the most inopportune moments. Under the conditions of these experiments, we are limited to "first nights"—to performances without rehearsals. Unfortunately, the protagonist does not know the part assigned to him; he has to learn it while playing. Unfamiliar with the script, the patient may display the most interesting behavior during the interludes, just at a moment when the photographer is busy measuring light and distance, focusing, or rewinding. Here, a second camera might be a valuable asset. This camera should be simple in construction, requiring less careful adjusting and needing no tripod or dolly. The disadvantage of another operator must be weighed; the more people present, the more public the performance, the greater the intrusion into the privacy of the patient.

Even under ideal conditions, the camera will never cover everything we should like to retain. It is frequently more accurate but, at the same time, less flexible than the observer; it is selective, but its selection does not always coincide with the intentions of the experimenter. The lens does not see exactly like the eye. The camera adds and omits; in focusing the figure, it neglects ground and periphery. In reducing colors to black and white, it intensifies the contrast. In projecting three-dimensional space on a two-dimensional plane, it creates a new organization which is more abstract but easier to survey.

While the camera is no computer that does all thinking for us, it is indispensable for the manipulation of time. Rheoscopic studies begin with—perhaps it is better to say, culminate in—the analysis of the finished film strip. One must not forget that the film strip is no mere copy of the original events. Taken by itself, it provides a new medium in which operations, absolutely inapplicable to the original events, become possible for the first time. On the film, action is frozen, time is brought to a standstill. The continuity of motion is dissected into temporal segments, into phases. In this new medium, one can reverse time, return to the beginning, and repeat motions unrepeatable in the original setting. Whereas, in the reality of time, one moment excludes every other moment, here earlier and later phases may be brought together for simultaneous observation. What has been extracted from the current of time may finally be returned to the temporal flux for enlightened inspection.

Shown with an ordinary projector, the presentation of the strip runs parallel to the original events. This procedure, by no means useless, is insufficient for rheoscopic analysis. The potentialities invested in the film are better actualized by a "film editor," an apparatus that, simple as it is, permits the singling out of individual frames, speeding up, slowing down, and repeating. However, because of the smallness of the screen and inadequate optics, the use of the editor is limited. It can serve only one or two observers. For demonstration and didactic purposes, one has either to reshape the film completely or to resort to a special projector, now available on the market, that satisfies all requirements except sufficient flexibility in speed.

Rheoscopic analysis is not synonymous with slow motion. The two techniques are more different than similar. In slow motion, the time enlargement does not exceed a ratio of one to four.

Slow motion has successfully been used for the analysis of motion in neurology, athletics, and industry. In all these fields, it has proved useful because the picture, which paraphrases the tempo, can be compared with the movements undistorted in speed. In industry, furthermore, the emphasis is shifted from the motor performance to a detailed analysis of the path traversed. In the study of expression, where we are not interested in the way but in the motions themselves—which usually are neither uniform nor repeatable—the usefulness of slow-motion technique is limited.

Experimental Problems

The laboratory devoted to the study of expressive motion at the Veterans Administration Hospital in Lexington, Kentucky, is still in the early phases of the program outlined. In the short time that has elapsed since its beginning, we have not been content to find out what has been done in the past, what must be done in the theoretical field, and what can be done technically; we have gone ahead and applied our principles to concrete cases. The results have been encouraging; they will be published in due course. Moreover, it has become clear that such experiments are valuable beyond the demarcation line set by the original plan, in such ways as the following:

1. The laboratory is a training ground for the physician in a special type of observation easily transferable to the ward.

2. The laboratory is also a testing ground for the patient, an addition to the general diagnostic instrumentarium that could well stand comparison with many familiar tests. The situation in the laboratory is

substantially different from the conditions of staff room, ward, and interview; one knows considerably more about a patient after he has acted out a scenario. Therefore, even discounting all interest in the particular problem of expression, a certain merit could be attributed to the procedure in itself.

3. With growing knowledge and understanding of expression, new problems come into sight. Expression may lead to an understanding of the distorted world in which a patient lives when all other means of communication break down. Modes of expression cut across the established clinical differentiations. Varying where the clinic unifies, unifying where the clinic differentiates, they urge, in their elemental nature and trustworthiness, revision of clinical distinctions. Thus, in this research, goal and end do not coincide.

References

Allport, G., & P. Vernon. *Studies of expressive movement.* New York: Macmillan, 1953.

Bell, C. *Anatomy and philosophy of expression as connected with the fine arts.* (5th rev. ed.) London: Bohn, 1865.

Buehler, K. *Ausdrucks-Theorie.* Jena: Fischer, 1933.

Darwin, C. *Expression of the emotions in man and animals.* New York: Appleton, 1910.

Duchenne, G. *Mécanisme de la physionomie humaine.* Paris: Baillière, 1876.

Engle, J. J. Ideen zu einer Minik. Vols. 7 & 8. In *Collected Works of . . . .* Berlin: Mylins, 1785.

Klages, L. *Einführung in die Psychologie der Handschrift.* Stuttgart: Seifert, 1924.

Lersch, P. *Gesicht und Seele.* (4th ed.) Munich: Reinhardt, 1955.

Pollnow, H. Historisch-kritische Beiträge zur Physiognomik. *Jahrb. Charact.*, 1928, 5, 159.

Porta, G. B. della. *De humana physiognomonia.* Bertheli, 1650.

St. Augustine. *Confessions.* Book XI.

CHAPTER THIRTEEN

The Sigh

In his book *Expression of the Emotions of Man and Animals*, Darwin praises Charles Bell, "so illustrious for his discoveries in physiology," as the one who "may with justice be said not only to have laid the foundations of the subject as a branch of science, but to have built up a noble structure" (1904, p. 1). Darwin was referring to Bell's essays on the *Anatomy and Philosophy of Expression as Connected with the Fine Arts*, published in 1806. Both authors, although sharply at variance in their theories, agreed in their estimation of expression as a subject for research. Fascinated by the phenomena and surprised by the problems involved, their interest in the matter never faltered. Bell, who had started the composition of his book on expression "before," as he said, "the serious pursuits of life began," published the first edition at the age of thirty-six. This publication marked only the beginning of a long period of renewed and intensified studies. In 1840, two years before his death, Bell, then a septuagenarian, visited the Continent. He went to Italy with the intention of verifying his principles of art criticism for a revised edition which he was preparing. In the preface to this third edition, published one year after the author's death, Joseph G. Bell says about his brother: "It was from these investigations that he was first led to make those discoveries in the system of nerves which are now acknowledged to be the most important contributions of modern times to the science of physiology" (1843).

Bell was still alive when Darwin began his own collection of data on expression. He continued and expanded his observations for a period of more than thirty years before writing the *Expression of the Emotions*. In this book, published in 1872, he mentions that his "first manuscript notes on the subject of expression bear the date of 1838" (1904, p. 18) Summing up the importance of expression, after such a long period of research, Darwin says, in the calm undramatic style characteristic of so many of his works,

The movements of expression in the face and body, whatever their origin may have been, are in themselves of much importance for our welfare. . . . To understand as far as possible the source or origin of the various expressions which may be hourly seen on the faces of the men around us, not to mention our domesticated animals, ought to possess much interest for us. From these several causes, we may conclude that the philosophy of our subject has well deserved the attention which it has already received from several excellent observers, and that it deserves still further attention, especially from any able physiologist (1904, pp. 364-366).

Bell had a more epigrammatic formulation: "Expression is to passion what language is to thought" (1865, p. 198). If this is so—and who would doubt it?—a new effort to solve the riddle of expression requires no justification; rather, we need an explanation of why so little attention is given to this subject at a time when psychiatry puts so much emphasis on passions and emotional disturbances and when psychosomatic medicine claims to be a new specialty or, at least, a new approach to many old problems.

There are theoretical and technical difficulties that everyone who studies expression must face. (See Chapter 12.) But they stopped Bell and Darwin as little as they discouraged Engel (1785), Lessing (1874), and Lavater (1794) in earlier days or Duchenne (1876), Piderit (1867), and Wundt (1912) later on. Nor is contemporary philosophy and psychology lagging in this field.[1] Psychiatry alone remains silent, although perhaps nowhere else in human affairs is expression used to the same extent as a practical guide. There must be, in addition to the general and permanent obstacles, some motive for this silence characteristic of our days that counteracts natural scientific curiosity. It should not be hard to find it. It must be disdain for what is supposed to be mere description.

Research in expression demands patient observation of manifest phenomena. It demands a phenomenological analysis which respects the phenomena as they appear, accepts them at face value, and resists the temptation to take them for coded signs which reveal their true meaning only after an intricate process of deciphering. This attitude, necessary for research in the field of expression, is met with peculiar disregard. Description, it seems to many, does not penetrate the surface; the true nature of psychological experience can be understood and explained

[1] From a rich bibliography, I mention only Klages (1921), Buytendijk & Plessner (1925–1926), and Allport & Vernon (1933).

only by methods reaching the deeper level of the operating forces that, in their dynamic relations, in action and counteraction, occasionally burst forth to the surface, producing the observable phenomena. However, one must not forget that the despised descriptive phenomena are the only ones directly accessible to us. The validity of dynamic hypotheses depends on the accuracy of descriptive observation. Whatever physicists may tell us about the structure of the universe and whatever psychologists and psychopathologists may have to say about the unconscious, in the formulation of their thoughts and in the communication of their ideas, they remain bound to the descriptive level. Concepts of irrational forces are in themselves rational concepts—or not concepts at all; terms that signify the unconscious are understandable and communicable only within the realm of conscious experience. Niels Bohr, in a paper concerned with the notions of causality and complementarity, reminds the reader that also in "dealing with the paradoxical features of quantum theory . . . all well-defined experimental evidence, even if it cannot be analyzed in terms of classical physics, must be expressed in ordinary language making use of common logic" (1948, p. 317).

The epistemological depreciation of descriptive experience is compatible only with a certain type of metaphysic. If we assume with Descartes, for instance, the existence of an incorporeal intellect, then, brushing aside sensory experience as deceptive and illusory, we still may hope to reach truth by acts of "pure thinking." However, if we understand science as a human accomplishment, we must not ignore the fact that science can never disavow its origin in the human world, from which it starts and to which it returns. Scientific truth is in direct relation to the reliability of sensory experience. Before we try to explain anything, we certainly have to make sure what it is we want to explain. Explanations which show little respect for phenomena are not worth much, even if they are labeled "dynamic."

Instead of entering into further argumentation about the epistemological and metaphysical assumptions on which the antithesis descriptive versus dynamic is based, it may be better to test what and how much can be accomplished through careful descriptions. The sigh may serve as the first example and model for our general considerations.

The sigh, like so many other expressive motions, has been observed all over the globe, among people of all races and colors and among groups very dissimilar in customs and habits. Wherever human life has been depicted, from olden days on—in the Bible or in Homer, in the *Divina Comedia* or in the *Comédie humaine*—sighing is mentioned. It is as universal, although not so frequent, as breathing; but, still, it is frequent enough. There has never been any doubt about its meaning. Milton, in writing "Nature from her seat, sighing through all her works, gave signs of woe," assumes that the meaning of sighing is obvious and understandable to everyone.

The universality of expression is a phenomenon which has puzzled practically all observers. Because sighing shares with most, if not all, expressions the character of universality—by which I mean universality of production and of understanding—the discussion of the problem posed by the universality of sighing may be postponed until a later moment.

Sighing is a variation of breathing. The sigh interrupts the flow of uniform and inconspicuous breathing. It stands out like a monolith from the plateau of regular breathing. It is a single respiration, distinguished from the preceding ones and those which follow by its length, its depth, and its sound. Deep is the conventional attribute of the sigh. It indicates that a larger volume of air is inhaled in sighing; however—and this is very peculiar—the air passages are not opened to the air pressing in. While volume and time are increased, there is no corresponding widening of space. The jaw is kept close to the maxilla; it is not pulled down by muscle action, nor is it allowed to sink down following its own weight. In sighing, the lips remain tight, or they are only slightly opened. The tongue, in its middle third, is arched toward the palate. During the sigh, the air flows through a narrowed passage. The friction with the contracted walls produces the particular sound which distinguishes sighing from other forms of intensified breathing. The air inhaled in a larger volume has to be removed if breathing is to return to its original rhythm and measure. This is effectuated through an expiration which resembles the inspiration, since it also is longer and louder than the phase of exhaling in quiet respiration; the air passages remain tightened in the exhaling phase of sighing.

The discordance between the volume of air and the caliber of the airways makes it clear that the sigh does not serve a need for increased oxygenation. Sighing is the behavior of an eupneic person. The dyspneic patient and the hyperpneic athlete cannot afford the luxury of sighing. We do not find the sigh in a person afflicted with a circulatory failure or in an athlete regaining his breath after exertion. As Cabot and Adams point out, "a sighing respiration is ordinarily not" a sign of cardiac or pulmonary disease. "Sighing respirations are most commonly found in nervous, fatigued, bored or excited persons" (1942, p. 207).

A patient in cardiac failure, gasping for air, is undoubtedly far removed from sighing. Here, the passages, jaw, lips, and mouth are wide open; the auxiliary muscles enter into function together with the diaphragm and the intercostals. The inspiration is prolonged and retarded at the turning point from inhaling to exhaling. The dyspneic patient with pulmonary edema tries to increase as much as possible the inner pulmonary surfaces and to hold the air for maximum utilization.

The hyperpneic athlete, who is not cyanotic and can make full use of the oxygen content of the air, shows a third type of breathing. Here, also, the passages are opened as much as possible; in the athlete's panting respiration, the speed is accelerated and the inspiration appears short compared with the expiration, which is accentuated and ends in a fast crescendo. If one would like to symbolize sighing by musical notation, one could do it by marking two half notes not differentiated by any accent. There is as much weight on the inhalation as on the expiration. In the forced breathing of the athlete, we would have to write a short upbeat followed by a longer downbeat, ending in an abrupt sforzando. Dyspneic breathing would have to be represented as asymmetrical, the inspiration lasting into the second half of the bar and separated from the expiration by a short rest.

White and Hahn, in one of the rare cardiographic studies of sighing (see also Baker, 1934), found that "sighing is never due primarily to heart disease but always to fatigue or nervousness or other such factors." In their series of observations "of the eight cases of organic heart disease without effort syndrome but with congestive failure, none showed abnormal sighing." Among the patients who sighed frequently, the authors did not find "any evidence of faulty action of kidneys, heart, lungs, or metabolism" (1929, p. 187). White and Hahn's observations are well documented with respiratory tracings, which also illustrate clearly the sporadic occurrence of sighs and the symmetry of inhaling and exhaling in sighing. The sighs are written as single spikes in the midst of regular breathing movements. After a sigh, breathing returns to the same level from which the sigh departed.

Statistical and experimental studies thus confirm the results of direct observation, which, simple as it seems, has far-reaching consequences. It indicates that sighing is a variation of breathing not caused by "air hunger." The sigh, obviously, has no physiological cause, or, as Darwin liked to say about expression, it "may not be of the least use," or "not of any service." Alexander and French probably had something similar in mind with their statement that expressive innervations "are not motivated by utilitarian goals" (1948, p. vi). If the sigh does not result from specific physiological conditions, we cannot avoid the conclusion that physiology does not comprehend the phenomenon of breathing in its totality. Breathing belongs in still another context. It is one of the basic experiences of an experiencing being and one of his fundamental modes of conduct. In this region, the region of experience (*Erleben*), we may, therefore, expect to gain an understanding of the sigh in particular and of expressions in general.

Perhaps someone may still try to claim a physiological purpose for the sigh. He may argue as follows: The respiration of the one who sighs, whether he is depressed, tired, or bored, is not sufficient. He stands or sits stooped, his head bent downward; subsequently, his breathing will be shallow and will bring about an oxygen need after a while that will be satisfied by the more voluminous respiration of sighing. It was on such assumptions that Darwin based the explanation of sighing. In a chapter dealing with "Low Spirits, Anxiety, Grief . . ." he remarked,

The breathing becomes slow and feeble, and is often interrupted by deep sighs. As Gratiolet remarks, whenever our attention is long concentrated on any subject, we forget to breathe, and then relieve ourselves by a deep inspiration; but the sighs of a sorrowful person, owing to his slow respiration and languid circulation, are eminently characteristic (1904, p. 177).

In his description of grief, Darwin used, besides his own observations, three passages from Gratiolet's work on expression. On one occasion, Gratiolet said,

Je ne puis m'empêcher de faire ici une remarque. C'est que l'attention est fixante de sa nature, et que pour cette raison elle n'est jamais sans quelque mélange d'effort. Cet effort suspend pour un instant la respiration. De là ce besoin urgent de respirer et de bâiller après quelques moments d'une attention soutenue. Cet état est souvent très pénible, et comme il est instinctif, la volonté ne la gouverne pas, et les personnes de travail en sont souvent singulièrement incommodées (1865, p. 232).

The assumption of "air hunger" is in conflict with the paradoxical fact that no open air passages correspond to the increased volume of air. If sighing were intended to serve any purpose of re-establishing the metabolic equilibrium, it would be a very inappropriate means to this end, for the increased time spent in sighing slows down the rhythm of respiration from a ratio of fourteen to sixteen to one of twelve to fifteen per minute. Sighing could only increase and not reduce the oxygen deficit.

Careful scrutiny of our film strips of patients studied for expressive movements brought to light an occasional sigh—or a few—in a great number of cases. Reviewing this material, we found not one case where any irregularity of breathing would announce an oncoming sigh. Invariably, the sigh, as a single act of breathing—a deep inspiration coupled with a deep expiration—interrupted a series of inhaling and exhaling regular in rhythm and volume. Sighing was less frequent when patients were active; it occurred more often during the short intervals between individual tests or tasks, at a moment when the patients were left to themselves.

The absence of any strictly physiological meaning and purpose in sighing can be further demonstrated if we turn our attention from the sigh to the sighing person. He does not increase the action of the diaphragmatic and costal muscles like the hyperpneic, and he does not have recourse to auxiliary muscles like the dyspneic; instead, he lifts and lowers his shoulders synchronously with the inspiration and expiration of sighing. One can, as in an experiment, nearly prevent sighing by arresting the excursion of the shoulder girdle. It suffices to cross the arms so that the palms grasp the humerus, a position which does not interfere with hyperpneic diaphragmatic breathing. The lifting of the shoulders adds little to the physiological function of breathing; in fact, sighing is of so little use to respiration that, if it is done at repeated short intervals, it will render a person dyspneic. In hyperventilation, intensified breathing, corresponding to an anxiety state, for example, actually leads to a disturbance of the acid–base equilibrium.

The statement that sighing is not physiologically determined needs some qualification. Obviously, sighing, like any other physical performance, depends on physiological mechanisms. When we say that sighing has no physiological determination, we take the term "physiological" in the specific sense, as it is used by physiology itself. The physiologist considers respiration insofar as it serves the exchange of gases; he is interested in the chemical and reflex controls of breathing, in the maintenance of standard solutions of CO_2 and O_2 in the blood, in the preservation of the acid–base equilibrium, and in the elimination of heat during hyperthermia.

Such physiological knowledge of breathing, admirable as it is, has no counterpart in the immediate experience of breathing. The discovery of the biochemical functions of breathing is of very recent date. Even William Harvey had not yet come to understand or to anticipate the process of oxygenation. As late as 1649 he emphatically denied that blood undergoes any initial change during its transit through the lungs (Pagel, 1951). The experience of breathing, however, is as old as mankind. It is universal and immediate; it is every man's property, as indisputably as breathing itself. It begins in the earliest phase of any individual's life. The physiological knowledge, on the other hand, is a possession shared only by a small number of scientists. It is acquired in later years through indirect methods, always open to further argument. Biochemical concepts are an abstract knowledge which can never be turned into primary physiognomical experience.

The difference between the experience of breathing and the physiology of respiration is not identical with that between prescientific interpretation and scientific explanation. The physiologist studies processes within an organism. The theme of experience is different—so radically different that its meaning and content cannot be pressed into the physiological scheme of stimulus and response. This could be done only if experience were "nothing but" an epiphenomenon accompanying nervous processes, if perceiving were "nothing but" stimulation of receivers and afferent nerves, if acting were "nothing but" contraction of muscles. The formulation of a theory of expression will lead to a head-on collision with these assumptions, which, in my opinion, delude psychology and psychopathology. A discussion of the traditional declaration of the incompetency of experience has to be postponed at present. We still have to work our way upward from a description of a special phenomenon of expression to an insight into its general problems.

Unfortunately, immediate experience is ineffable; it does not know itself not because it is unconscious but because it is unreflective. Like Sleeping Beauty, who had to wait for her prince to break the spell, immediate experience has to wait for the one gifted with the power of the word to bring it out into the light. The moment this is accomplished, however, immediate experience is threatened by another danger. Just as objective observations are answers to questions and are, therefore, determined by tradition, training, and expectation, immediate experience may be masked by the very word which enunciates it. Our personal experience also appears to us in the light of tradition, training, and interpretation. A questionnaire concerned with the experience of breathing would be of little use. The answers probably would be filled with references to oxygen and carbon dioxide. We have lost our naïveté; we are— one may say—scientifically prejudiced. Nevertheless, while the word which reflects immediate experience easily degenerates into a stereotyped formula, we can, with some effort, return to it its original vigor. We may justly expect the meaning of an experience as old and universal as that of breathing to be revealed by language, the true repository of common human experience.

In the Biblical words, "And the Lord God formed man of the dust of the ground, and breathed into his nostrils the breath of life; and man became a living soul," breath is conceived of as the principle of life.

Breath is the deity's gift to the creature. It "animates" the organism and transforms the shaped matter into a living being. The breath blown into Adam's nostrils becomes the essence of his individual existence. Yet, it preserves the character of its origin. Through breath, a loan more than a possession, man and "anima-ls" partake in the divine principle that permeates the universe. In inhaling and exhaling, the individual, being monadic in its nature, remains, nevertheless, connected as a part with the whole of the world.

The usual Hebrew words for breath (*Neshimah*), breathing (*Nasham*), and soul (*Neshamah*) are in full agreement with the anthropology given in Genesis 2:7. The Biblical interpretation of life and breath has its exact counterpart in other cultures and in other language families. In Sanskrit, *Atman*—which we may spell with a capital "A"—is the all-pervading divine power, the soul of the cosmos, while *atman* signifies breath as the life-giving principle and therefore, also, as the individual soul. In modern German, *atman* persists almost unchanged—with *Atem* as the noun and *atmen* as the verb—corresponding to breath and breathing. The concept of *Atman*, to be sure, barely escaped extinction; it exists only in a few archaic and obsolete tropes. In contemporary English, the original relationship is more hidden than obvious, but the procedure of uncovering does not require much philological information. In Latin and Greek, the analogy with Hebrew and Sanskrit is clear and striking —as in the Latin pair of words *spirare* (to breathe, the root of "respiration") and *spiritus* and the Greek pairs *psychein* and *psyche*, *pneuein* and *pneuma*, with corresponding connotations. The *Sanctus Spiritus* of the Vulgate is in meaning and phrasing the literal translation of the New Testament Greek expression *Hagion Pneuma*.

One sees how the same idea returns, a true archetype, in various shapes. As these linguistic statistics gain in validity with every new item added to the etymological series, it is worth mentioning that a familiar Latin word for breath and soul, *anima*, is a namesake of *anemos*, the Greek word for wind. Like parallel lines converging in perspective drawing to the vanishing point, the linguistic parallels converge to the point of their common origin in immediate sensory experience. The complete agreement between terms so different in their ancestral lines of culture and language demonstrate that this common interpretation is but one step removed from the original experience.

The relation of *Neshima* and *Neshama*, of *Atman* and *atman*, of *pneo* and *pneuma*, and of *spiro* and *spiritus* are intuitive interpretations of breathing, half-way between image and concept. Purists, therefore, may condemn them as anthropomorphic. They certainly are anthropomorphic, but they do not deserve rejection, for human experience can only be anthropomorphic. Here, we are interested in how the world appears to a human being and not how, supposedly, it is in itself, that is, how it is conceived in relation to an incorporeal, mathematical intellect. One must not overlook the fact that through observation and communication, science rests on those anthropomorphic qualities of experience that positivistic scientists want to eradicate. Thus, accepting the counsel offered by language, we conclude that the primary experience of breathing is that of participation and exchange, of receiving and expelling, of doing and suffering, of acting and being compelled. In breathing, we experience our vital existence in its dependence and in its uniqueness, in its never-ending contact and exchange with the world.

Breathing as a medium of contact does not remain a silent function. Breath carries the voice. It can be transformed into an "utterance." The first breath of the newborn turns into a cry. In crying out, a sound proceeds from my mouth, but it returns to me; I hear myself. In crying out, I experience myself within the world as a part of it; the traditional dichotomy of inner–outer makes no sense. In crying out, I am acting, producing; but the product, which becomes a part of the surroundings, remains, nevertheless, my voice. In crying out, I surpass the confinement of the body scheme; I reach out; I call for attention. In crying out, I find myself accepted or rejected; I meet response or indifference, support or resistance. The sound, articulate or inarticulate, appears as if it were the original model of all property, for it is detachable, movable, and transferable; yet, it remains mine in all these transactions. In crying out, we experience our power or our infirmity.

Breath which, in exhaling, carries our voice brings in, in inhaling, smells and scents. The voice announces to the world our moods and wishes; smell orients us in the world. The oldest among the senses is assigned as scout and sentry to the indispensable and continuous function of breathing. A foul smell takes away our breath, while a pleasant smell induces a deep, wide breathing. Smell and breath are in reciprocal relation. Smell is the "warden and warner" of breathing; breath is the activator of smelling. While circulation—the driving of the blood through the closed "inland system" of vessels—is exempted from voluntary and anticipatory modulation, respiration, which establishes direct and incessant communication with the world, permits voluntary interference to a limited degree. Indeed, speech and smell both demand such interference. Accentuation, to single out just one factor of articulation, depends on accurate timing: retardation and acceleration, increase and diminution of breath. Likewise, orienting smelling requires voluntary but less precise regulation of breathing. Although upright posture, which contributed to the active control of breath, has reduced the importance of smell as a human sense of orientation and searching, still a bad odor chases us away, and a sweet fragrance invites us to stay and to absorb. Whether active or passive, smelling reveals the original character of sensory experience: to be dominated by attraction and repulsion. There is a motor element in sensory experience. The psychological content of attraction is that of "not yet being united." This "not yet being united" is not a statement about two phases, one of unification and the other preceding it; psychologically, it belongs to the first phase itself. Recent research in neurophysiology has cast some doubt on the strict topical separation of sensory and motor functions in the brain cortex. However this may be, sensory experience is not an accumulation of neutral sensory data; it is the attitude of a movable being, capable of unification and separation.

To sum up, the experience of breathing has three facets: first, participation and exchange; second, power and infirmity; and, third, attraction and repulsion. In this context—the psychology of breathing—the sigh—enigmatic to the physiology of respiration—becomes understandable.

Our thesis is that the sigh is a variation of breathing insofar as breathing is experienced as a relation to the world. A sigh occurs when the equilibrium between the individual and the world is disturbed, when pressure and resistance are increased. The focus of this disturbance is irrelevant. The sigh appears to be a futile effort to throw off the burden, and, yet, it is not an action which finally ends in frustration nor an action at all—for action leads from a start to a goal, and it brings about a change. At the end of action, the initial situation is abandoned. Sighing, however, does not lead from a start to a goal; failure is immanent from the beginning. Beginning and end, so to speak, are one. Sighing expresses an intolerable situation that it does not intend to change.

At this point, we may do well to expand our considerations. Thus far, we have identified the sigh with the sigh of grief, but there is also the sigh of relief, and there are other forms.

According to Webster, the sigh is "a deep and prolonged audible inspiration or respiration of air, especially when involuntary and expressing some emotion or feeling, as grief, yearning, weariness, relief" (1948). Webster does not say what differences, if any, there are between the sighs of grief, of yearning, and of relief. Obviously, the assumption is that we are able to distinguish between them, that we are not to take the sigh of relief for an expression of grief. Even so, sighing could always follow the same pattern; environmental conditions alone would permit a distinction, but this is not the case. Distinction does not depend on a commentary given by the actual situation. Expressive motions speak for themselves.

The sigh of relief resembles the sigh of grief in the first phase—that of inhaling. At the turning point, however, a sudden change occurs. The air is not forced out through a narrowed passage as if it were against the resistance of the world. At the turning point, the mouth is vigorously opened and the air flows out easily and rapidly, meeting no obstruction. The shoulders do not sink back in fatigue, in resignation; they are lowered as if freed from all burden. The chest is thrown out, the arms slightly stretched into the surrounding space.

The sigh of relief—just like the sigh of grief—is a variation of breathing, insofar as breathing is experienced as a relation to the world. It occurs when emotional pressure is lifted, when resistance has faded, and when the equilibrium between the individual and the world has been restored. The sigh of relief—like the sigh of grief—*expresses* a situation; it does not intend to produce any change. It does not release tension but expresses relaxation; the sigh of relief makes its appearance when—after an unexpected message, for instance—the tenseness of a situation has been decreased.

If only the sigh could be explained as a means of communication! The statement, however, that all expressive motions serve communication is a postulate—a dogmatic construction invented to overcome theoretical difficulties. It certainly would facilitate the theoretical issue if the proposition were correct. Expressive motions could be grouped with a class of familiar functions; we could avoid the difficulty of explaining why motions not aiming at communication could serve communication so well. Unfortunately, the postulate is not, as the sigh shows, in agreement with the facts. The sigh demands no witness; it has no social function, although it may secondarily affect interpersonal relations and may be arbitrarily produced for that purpose. Interpersonal relations, even if they are paramount in and decisive for most human behavior, are not omnipresent. There are elemental relations of the individual to the world—and, therefore, disturbances of such relations—which are not derived from interpersonal relations. Our thesis explains this point well. As breathing establishes a relation between the solitary individual and the world, sighing—a variation of the experience of breathing—shares in the solitude of breathing.

The sigh, it seems, does not fit into any familiar scheme. First we could not discover a physiological condition; now we are unable to find a psychological purpose. The sigh is an activity but not an action. It is communicative but not intended for communication. Its meaning is manifest, but the relation of the sign to the signified—sighing to grief or sighing to relief—is obscure. The sigh is understandable as a whole, but little known in its details. Its spontaneous production evokes immediate response, but neither performer nor observer can account for his behavior. The sigh does not have the character of a reflex, but it is not intentional either. Obviously, the traditional frames of reference prove insufficient. This is an alarming situation, a signal for a revision of the basic categories of psychology. Our thesis points to the direction which we should follow.

We turned our interest to the sigh with the expectation that an analysis of one of the many of the phenomena of expression would lead to an insight that could be generalized. The possibility of applying our thesis to other expressions than those for which it was originally designed[2] makes it probable that our explanation was not altogether wrong. We may, therefore, assume that the paradoxical situation just described is not limited to the sigh but inherent in expression in general. If this is so, our next move should be an attempt to generalize our thesis and to see whether this generalization will help us to a better understanding of expressions. Success or failure will decide whether the guiding assumptions have been correct.

Applied to expressions in general, our thesis may be formulated this way: Expressive motions are variations of fundamental functions in the performance of which the individual (man or animal) experiences his existence, his being-in-the-world, in a mode peculiar to him. One could also say that expressive motions are the variations of fundamental functions in the experience of which the individual performs his being-in-the-world. By "fundamental functions," I mean such forms of behavior as breathing, keeping upright, walking, seeing, or mating. Fundamental functions, varying from species to species, determine in their specificity for each member of the species the basic dimensions (possibilities and limitations) of his being-in-the-world.

If expressions are immediate variations of fundamental functions, every form of behavior needs to be expressive—the calm breath as well

---

[2] Sneering, snarling, and sniggering may be added here, all of which belong, as expressive variations of breathing, in the same group with sighing. They and many similar words share—for good reason—the initial onomatopoetic letters *sn* with sneezing, sniffling, and snorting. They are related by a common denominator: a brisk, short discharge of air. However, the vehement reflex action of sneezing serves the purpose of clearing the nasal airways. Sneering and snarling have no such physiological purpose; they do not produce any change. They express disdain through the accentuated but effortless elimination, the puffing out, of so much superfluous air.

as the sigh, the friendly or indifferent look as well as the paranoid one, the nonchalant walk or the gay step as well as the depressed gait. Because the extremes are frequently more easily accessible, we are inclined to give a special label to the extraordinary, which most catches our attention. We forget that the middle between the extremes belongs to the same order. We call smiling an expression, but not smiling is also expressive; under certain conditions it is a very strong expression, threatening and frightening. The concentration of research on a limited group of expressive motions, ignoring the ubiquity of expression, can but misguide us and prevent our understanding of the phenomena.

In formulating and elaborating our thesis, we have found ourselves faced with a peculiar difficulty: Thesis and commentary will not reveal their full meaning until a revision of the basic categories has been accomplished. Still I cannot avoid referring to something which does not yet exist in print.[3] The remarks in which I will try to explain my thesis should leave no doubt that this revision will gravitate around the phenomenon and the concept of experience—its nature, its content, and its subject.

Experiencing beings are directed toward the world in which they, nevertheless, keep themselves apart, maintaining their identity and integrity as individuals. Experiencing is synonymous with experiencing-the-world and with experiencing-oneself-in-the-world. It is directed to the Other; but one experiences the Other only in relation to oneself and vice versa. Experience is of the I–world relation. This relation, which is not a compound of two parts—I and the world—but exists only as a whole, cannot be translated into or replaced by the sequence "stimulus and response." Experiencing beings do not merely occur. In sleep—or to be more correct, in coma—they resemble inanimate things, which are simply present or at hand. Experiencing beings, while awake, always find themselves in a situation. One may as well say, "to find oneself in a situation"—this is exactly what experiencing signifies. Therefore, a motor element must be inherent in experience: directions to or fro, attraction or repulsion, attack or retreat. The fundamental functions delineate the possible situations. Men and animals experience and perform their existence as sensing, mobile beings in deporting[4] themselves toward the world—in opposing and yielding, searching and fleeing, ac-

---

[3] A beginning has been made in my book, *The Primary World of Senses* (1963). See also Binswanger (1942), Goldstein (1939), Merleau-Ponty (1945), and Buytendijk (1949).

[4] I have selected the word "deporting" because the original meaning of behaving has become obsolete, thanks to behaviorism, which turned the original connotation into its very opposite.

cepting and rejecting. They experience in their corporeality; experiencing is related, therefore, to gravity, air, light, space, distance, to incorporating, meeting, and avoiding. In every single one of the fundamental functions, the being-directed-to-the-world is realized in a particular form. In getting up, for instance, and in keeping upright, a man distances himself from the ground on which he finds his support. Thus, in opposing gravity, he experiences, in his exertion, his own strength and, at the same time, the counterforces which he resists; he experiences his being capable or failing.

Expressive motions, we have said, are variations of fundamental functions in which a person performs his being-in-the-world in a mode peculiar to him. Take, for example, a depressed person; his posture (a variation of keeping upright), his weary gait (a variation of walking), and his avoluminous voice (a variation of breathing and uttering) make manifest his being overcome by the counterforces, his succumbing. Or, to give another example, let us consider the expression of astonishment, of "breathtaking" amazement—the wide-open eyes, the gaze fixed on the object, the jaw dropping, the breath arrested at the height of inhaling. There, again, we have variations—homologous variations—of fundamental functions, this time of seeing, of incorporating, and of breathing. These and many other expressive motions are universal and uniform because they are variations of fundamental functions and, therefore, variations of basic human attitudes. We understand these and other expressions without preceding instruction because we meet the other one not as a body but as an individual who, in resisting and yielding, in searching and fleeing, is related to the world and to us, cor-responding to our own approach.

Expressions are not secondary, not additions subsequent to sensory data. The facts to prove this are plentiful and unambiguous. In their early months, babies answer in true meaningful responses the expressive behavior in their environment. The children's world of toys and fairy tales is understandable and appeals to them because it is full of physiognomies. That stones and trees, sun and wind, and wolf and rabbit all can talk is not surprising in a world where expressions reign. The existence of the inanimate, of mere things, is a late discovery. The magic world of primitive people is not an outgrowth of archaic functions but of a naïve interpretation where physiognomic characters are accepted as manifestations of essential qualities. The elimination of physiognomic characters is a slow process; it is never complete. They are always present; they regain their full power not only in dreams, in inebriety, and in psychoses but in all those situations where we still live in the landscape. The facts tell us that all this is so. The right concept of experience will explain that it cannot be otherwise.

Experience is the only authentic theme of psychology. Psychology deals or should deal with experiencing beings, not with a mind or an intellect nor with a nervous system or an apparatus, not with a consciousness and data of consciousness nor with stimuli and motor responses. Psychology can be defined as a branch of knowledge dedicated to the study of experiencing beings insofar as they are experiencing beings. This definition preserves the continuity with prescientific thinking and acting that has been interrupted ever since the attempt was made to establish psychology as a science. In everyday life, experience is taken for granted. It is never debated that experience alone makes possible interpersonal relations and communication. Everyone realizes that, through observation, demonstration, and communication, science itself owes its existence to experience. In short, no one ever doubts that experiencing beings as such are in a unique relation to their world. Experience, not as an abstract entity, but as a capacity of man and animal, is appraised as an incomparable endowment; it is respected as a formidable reality. Modern psychology, however, is proud of having risen far above this level of nonscientific, "medieval" belief. Even when the phenomenon is acknowledged, its reality is denied. Experience has become a mere phantom.

In 1900, Freud wrote in his *Interpretation of Dreams*, "What role is now left, in our representation of things, to the phenomenon of consciousness, once so all-powerful and over-shadowing all else? None other than *that of a sense-organ for the perception of psychic qualities*" (1938, p. 544).

A few years later, Watson made the final, extreme step; he denied the very existence of consciousness, for which he could not find any proof.[5] Before Watson started the movement known as behaviorism, Pavlov had already formulated his ideas of objective psychology, where a nervous system acted upon by stimuli takes the place of the experiencing being in his relation to the world. In a short time, objective psychology gained wide popularity and—with some modifications—has for a long time retained it despite its radical and patent deficiencies.[6]

[5] Watson's statement is a classical example of a *contradictio in adjectu*, for a proposition and the statements proving in logical sequence the correctness of its meaning are not physical things. There is no place for proofs in the realm of physical things. They are neither true nor false; they simply are. Whoever speaks about proofs speaks at the same time, by implication, about experiencing and thinking beings.

[6] The deficiencies are radical because they are the unavoidable consequences of the principle of the theory. They become patent whenever the rules of the game set by the theory are strictly observed and the phenomena fully explored and respected. Com-

Powerful motives must be at work to make such a destructive transformation of the familiar aspects of the world acceptable. The history of Western philosophy tells us what they are and where they are rooted. Passionate metaphysical partisanship is willing to pay the highest price, to tolerate inconsistencies, to ignore deficiencies, and to coerce the phenomena into the Procrustean bed of the theory.

Objective psychology and many other schools of contemporary psychology are late stages of a long development which began centuries ago. Since Descartes's metaphysics, man, the concrete living individual, has ceased to be—in theory—the subject of experience. A thinking substance, the *res cogitans*, took his place. It was this incorporeal substance —detached from space and motion—which underwent the mutation to "consciousness." In the course of time, it gradually lost its substantiality and degenerated into an epiphenomenon, a lofty "no-thing." To the unreality of this consciousness—the end product of a long chain of metaphysical metamorphoses—to this consciousness, "once so all-powerful and over-shadowing all else," Freud opposed the assumed reality of the unconscious and of the energy-charged id. Freud's idea of the unconscious was the exact counterpart of the mummified concept of consciousness, this derivative of Descartes's metaphysics. In substituting an apparatus for the experiencing being and, thereby, consciousness for experience, Freud followed the tradition that in all its turns is dominated by the Cartesian dichotomy of mind and body.

The truth, however, is that experience is still as "all-powerful and over-shadowing all else" as it has always been; it will remain so as long as men and animals exist as individual organisms. To reach an understanding of expressive motions, one has to be careful not to confuse experience with consciousness and to see to it that a mind, a nervous system, or an id does not take the place of the living, experiencing being. To regain the genuine theme of experience, we will have to remove the historical debris under which it is buried at present. When this will

---

munication is an example, one of many. Two experiencing beings can meet each other, converse together, and observe together the same thing. Two nervous systems cannot do anything like it. Two brains cannot communicate, neither by direct nor by indirect methods. While we, my neighbor and I, watch together the same events, my brain and his brain—or, to be more correct, Brain A and Brain B—are activated by different stimuli. Physical agents are turned into sensory stimuli the moment that they bring receptors into activity. Physical agents turned into stimuli act on the individual nervous system, which, in its function, remains separate and isolated from any other. We cannot share stimuli. It is loose talk to call light, sound, and heat stimuli, still more to use this word for visible and audible things. But this confusion is absolutely necessary to hide the weakness of a theory that substitutes nervous systems for experiencing beings. Objective psychology which uses observation, demonstration, and communication cannot account for its own existence.

have been done, the solution of the theoretical problems of expression will be relatively easy, the paradoxes will disappear, and principles for a systematic order of expressions will offer themselves, as I will show in another paper.

References

Alexander, F., & French, T. M. *Studies in psychosomatic medicine.* New York: Ronald Press, 1948.

Allport, G. W., & Vernon, P. *Studies of expressive movement.* New York: Macmillan, 1933.

Baker, D. M. Sighing respiration as a symptom. *Lancet*, 1934, 1, 174-177.

Bell, C. *Anatomy and philosophy of expression as connected with the fine arts.* (5th ed.) London: Bolin, 1865.

Binswanger, L. *Grundformen und Erkenntnis menschlichen Daseins.* Zurich: Max Niehaus, 1942.

Bohr, N. On the notions of causality and complementarity. *Dialectica*, 1948, 2, 312–319.

Buytendijk, F. J. J., & Plessner, H. Die Deutung des mimischen Ausdrucks. *Phil. Anz.*, 1925–1926, 1, 72–126.

Buytendijk, F. J. J. *Allgemene Theorie der Menselijke Houding en Beweging.* Utrecht: Heb Spectrum, 1949.

Cabot, R. C., & Adams, F. D. *Physical diagnoses.* (13th ed.) Baltimore: Williams & Wilkins, 1942.

Darwin, C. *Expression of the emotions in man and animals* (1872). New York: Appleton, 1904.

Duchenne, G. *Mécanisme de la physionomie humaine.* Paris: Baillière, 1876.

Engel, J. J. *Ideen zu einer Mimik.* Berlin: Mylins, 1786.

Freud, S. *The basic writings of* . . . New York: Random House, 1938.

Goldstein, K. *The organism, a holistic approach to biology derived from pathological data in man.* New York: American Book, 1939.

Gratiolet, F. *De la physionomie et des mouvements d'expression.* Paris: Hetzel, 1865.

Klages, L. *Ausdrucksbewegung und Gestaltungskraft.* (4th ed.) Leipzig: Barth, 1923.

Lavater, J. C. *Essays on physiognomy.* Boston: Spotswood & West, 1794.

Lessing, G. E. *Collected works of* . . . Vols. 5 & 6. Stuttgart: Göschen, 1874.

Merleau-Ponty, M. *Phénoménologie de la perception.* Paris: Librairie Gallimard, 1945.

Pagel, W. William Harvey and the purposes of circulation. *ISIS*, 1951, 42 (172), 22–37.

Piderit, T. *Wissenschaftliches System der Mimik und Physiognomik.* Detmold, 1867.

Straus, E. W. *The primary world of senses.* New York: The Free Press, 1963.

Webster's New International Dictionary. (2nd ed.) Springfield: Merriam, 1959.

White, P. D., & R. G. Hahn. Symptoms of sighing in cardiovascular diagnosis with spirographic observations. *Amer. J. med. Sci.*, 1929, 177, 179–188.

Wundt, W. *Völkerpsychologie.* (2nd ed.) Vol. 1. Leipzig: Engelmann, 1912.

PART III

Clinical Studies

CHAPTER FOURTEEN

Norm and Pathology
of I-World Relations

Heidegger's *Being and Time* (1962) made its entrance into the world of letters in an austere academic environment. The first edition was not a book in its own right. It was published in 1927 as an essay in Husserl's *Yearbook of Phenomenology*, a philosophical journal written by professionals for professionals. Yet, this newborn stood out from the other "brain children" because of its style, its scope, its themes, its depth, and its approach. The starting point was a consideration of man in everyday life, the goal was to reach an understanding of the meaning of Being, and the road leading from that start to this goal was the "analytic of *Dasein*." It is therefore not surprising that the author, the title, and even the book itself were in a short time enthusiastically accepted by many and rejected with no less passion by others.

Like so many readers, psychiatrists were fascinated by the "analytic of *Dasein*," revealing the basic structure of "existence" as being-in-the-world and being-with, dealing with such topics as authenticity and inauthenticity, throwness and project, dread and care, call of conscience and resolve, finiteness and temporality.

The Swiss psychiatrist Ludwig Binswanger (1958, 1960) became convinced that, with *Being and Time*, the philosophical foundation of psychiatry had finally been established. He tried to apply Heidegger's philosophy of existence to psychiatry, to translate the "analytic of *Dasein*" into *Daseinsanalysen* (existential analyses). Yet, on his way back and down from the ontological level to the ontic sphere he had appalling obstacles to overcome. Care, throwness, and project in Heidegger's work, just as bad faith, freedom, and choice in Sartre's philosophy, are ontological concepts. How can these existentials be applied to the lives of individuals—to their actions and motions? The crucial point is the exalted position which Heidegger assigns to man. "Concerned about his Being and behaving toward his Being as toward his own possibilities" (Heidegger, 1960, p. 42), man appears to him different from all other beings—not only from inanimate things and man-made machines but also radically different from all other living creatures. For this reason, Heidegger rejects the traditional definition of man as a rational animal. He acknowledges, of course, our kinship with the animals, yet he emphasizes that man in his existence is separated from them by a very abyss (Heidegger, 1962, p. 12). One cannot ask, according to Heidegger, What man is; still less can one answer this question. One can only ask for the Who and the How. There is no unchangeable order of natural qualities characteristic for the species, no essence in the traditional meaning of the term, which ultimately characterizes man. Therefore, Binswanger (1947) adds, one cannot make man the object of research. We understand the other only as a partner in an I–thou relation.

These theorems lead to serious consequences when applied to psychiatry. If it makes no sense to ask what man is, we no longer see him as a living creature in health and disease. Heidegger was familiar with these and other facts of life; the problem is whether and how he or his followers can incorporate such themes as physical existence, sexuality, animal nature, or disease into his ontological system. Actually, Binswanger leaves no doubt that his *Daseinanalyse* is by no means a specifically psychiatric method. That he used it primarily for the interpretation of schizophrenic cases is a kind of professional accident. Binswanger's existential analyses of Ellen West, Lola Voss, etc. move between the poles of authenticity and inauthenticity, of floundered and accomplished forms of existence—but not between normal and abnormal, healthy and sick. "Existential analysis," Binswanger wrote in 1945, "is not a psychopathology, nor is it clinical research nor any kind of objectifying research. Its results have first to be recast by psychopathology into forms that are peculiar to it, such as that of a psychic organism, or even of a psychic apparatus, in order to be projected onto the physical organism" (1947, p. 216).

However this may be, I shall make clinical experience my point of departure. In turning my attention to a typical case, I do not regard him as an apparatus but as an experiencing creature. Here, I believe I am entitled to claim Heidegger, if not as my master, at least as an ally, for two reasons: First, we encounter the mental patient as a stranger in our everyday-life world (*Lebenswelt*, in Husserl's terminology). Whatever theories we may offer to explain psychotic behavior—whether we accept the thesis that mental diseases are brain diseases or search for a conflict between ego and id, ego and reality, and ego and superego—the frame of reference from which we start and to which we return is the structure of the everyday-life world. When Freud speaks about a break with reality, he refers to the reality familiar and common to all of us—the reality of so-called naïve realism. This is the same for the learned and the illiterate, for the rich and the poor, for Lumumba and Hammerskjold. Its characteristics are not taught in school. We live it, enact it, and respond to it, but we do not know it. Indeed, the failure of the mental patient to conform may cause us to stop and think about the *Lebenswelt*. Psychoses are, so to speak, basic experiments arranged by nature; the clinical wards are the natural laboratories where we begin to wonder about the structure of the *Lebenswelt*. We realize that, in order to account for its breakdown, we have to study its norm first. We suddenly notice that we are beginners in a field where we deemed ourselves masters.

Another obstacle exists. The discovery or rediscovery of the *Lebenswelt* has been blocked by a scientific tradition reaching back into antiquity. The *Lebenswelt* was held in contempt and despised as illusory. Modern science has been even more radical in its censure and its demands. The world as it appears to us in its macroscopic structure and with its sensory qualities must be reduced to atomic events. This reduction supposedly leads from a mere appearance, in the sense of an apparition, to the real core of things. The scientific credo professes as an article of common faith, Lashley said, that "all phenomena of behavior and of mind are ultimately describable in the concepts of the mathematical and physical sciences" (1952, p. 112). The paradoxical consequence is that the science of physics must be understood as groups of physical events. Most psychologists, therefore, refuse to waste time in contemplating physics as a human accomplishment which originates in the *Lebenswelt*. They take the possibility of observing for granted. Satisfied with measurement, they do not inquire into the psychological conditions of measuring. The tables are turned; the physicist himself, or man—in all his activities—is considered as an object of physics, a body among other bodies. Human experience and conduct must forcibly be adapted to the ruling system of physicalistic concepts. But this theoretical bias obscures the very sight of the phenomena. Inadvertently and unintentionally, they are assimilated to the "underlying neural mechanisms." The dogma has it that sensations, perceptions, thoughts, and memories occur *within* a particular organism, accompanying excitations of the nervous system. They are side effects, like sparks flashing with the turn of synaptic switches which transmit afferent impulses to the motorium. Experience, and sensory experience, is supposed to be merely "subjective."

Since the days of Galileo, subjectivity has been interpreted in spatial terms. Sensory qualities do not reside—to use Galileo's terminology—in things themselves; they reside in our minds. Today, we let them reside in our brains. From their supposedly original position, percepts are carried outward—through reality testing, projection, or some other voodoo procedure—and finally located in an external world to which none of us has any direct access. Scientific theory, based on Galileo's, Descartes', and Hobbes' metaphysics, teaches a radical sejunction of subject and object. The experiencing creature is cut off from the world.

In the practice of life, however, we do not place others in an outside world; we meet them on common ground. Obviously, the reduction cannot be unilateral. One cannot reduce qualities to cortical stimulation and then talk about our brain. If the sensory qualities are relative to man, man is relative to them. The reduction does not actually change the appearance of things; it is performed in thoughts and words. The physicist never leaves the shores of the *Lebenswelt*. In fact, the reduction of the *Lebenswelt* silently presupposes its validity. We are *in* the world, not outside. There, we are in contact with all things in sight and in reach. The senses do not provide us with mere sensory data. In seeing, we are confronted with the objects themselves, not with their pictorial representations. The act of seeing demands our presence; it commits us to a definite position in relation to our environment. In sensory experience, we are aware of things *and* ourselves; not one before the other, not one without the other. This is the second point where I am at least in partial agreement with Heidegger, who, in the "analytic of *Dasein*," refutes the traditional subject–object dichotomy. I have avoided his telling term "being-in-the-world," because in *Being and Time* it is understood as an ontological concept. It signifies that mode of being which makes the ontic structure of human life possible and understandable. For this reason, the existential being-in-the-world is limited to *Dasein* and cannot be applied to sensory experience in general, i.e., not to animal experience. But medical anthropology cannot omit life and the animal nature of man, although man can and usually does detach himself from the primary modes of contact which he has in common with the animals.

All scientific observation begins on the level of sensory experience, but not all sensory experience ends on that level. Those who run for safety in a hurricane do not measure its velocity. Science demands a detached observer who projects events on an impersonal frame of reference that can always be identified and reconstructed. In science, observers are exchangeable; they all sit in the audience and watch the events on the stage. In primary sensory experience, however, there is no division of space into stage and auditorium; everyone is in the arena. In sensory experience, we are not neutral observers watching the outcome of remote events through a one-way mirror; we are affected, caught, seized, in an egocentric position. The light, the wind, heat and cold, and sounds and scents are obtrusive; we "realize" their impact. Things appear attractive or repulsive. We respond to their physiognomies rather than to their logical order. That we are beset is decisive; the How and What is secondary. The That of being engaged and seized precedes the What. The scientific observer explores and judges the reality of events. To him, the predicate "real" signifies that something has occurred in accordance with the established laws of nature. In sensory experience, however, "reality" has quite a different meaning; it means that something happens to me. Reality of sensory experience concerns me in my unique, vital existence. It is prior to reflection and doubt, as is so clearly demonstrated by the apodictic powers of hallucinations.

In some of my writings, I have tried to re-open the case of sensory experience, to reclaim a territory lost for a long time. In using the term aesthesiology, I have even made an attempt to reinstitute the forgotten meaning of "aisthesis." In this, I may appear quixotic because I am compelled to challenge such generally accepted doctrines of neurophysiology as "Mind can only be regarded, for scientific purposes, as the activity of the brain" (Hebb, 1949, p. xiv). To this statement Hebb adds, "Modern psychology takes completely for granted that behavior and neural functions are perfectly correlated, that one is completely caused by the other" (1949, p. xiii). In line with this postulate, perceptions must be considered as perfectly correlated with and caused by afferent conduction and cortical excitation. Indeed, the physiological problem of thought, Hebb explains, "is that of the transmission of excitation from sensory to motor cortex" (1949, p. xvi). If this is so, sensory experience cannot add anything essential to the function of the body machine. But these speculations of a tough-minded empiricist leave us completely at a loss as to how he could account for his knowledge of the activities of the brain. For, in every neurophysiological experiment, two brains are involved: the brain observed and the observer's brain. When someone studies the brain of a man or an animal, his own brain is excited by optical stimuli reflected from the surface of some remote object. The stimuli, on their arrival on the retina, will not tell whence they came. The so-called observations must be considered as activities which are located exclusively within the observer's brain and skull, a mere transmission of excitation from sensory to motor cortex. Not even the magic of projection could transform such intracerebral excitations into an object of observation.

Through sensory experience, a new dimension is opened to the experiencing organism. This is the basic fact on which all science rests, even the denial of the fact itself. In sensory experience, we are related to objects *qua* objects, to an environment in which we can orient ourselves and act. The intentional relation to the other enables us to finally comprehend the order and relation of one object to another in the physical world. The relation of a nervous system to stimuli is not commensurate with that of an experiencing being to objects. The work of neurophysiology and psychology is contaminated by the promiscuous usage of the terms "stimulus" and "object," a confusion unpardonably confounded.

The next step is to apply aesthesiology to pathological manifestations. I select a well-defined organic disturbance: a mild but characteristic failure in spatial orientation. I have in mind those patients who prove unable to draw the floor plan of a room or a house, with which they are familiar and in which they still move around at ease. As Henry Head noted (1926), aphasic patients, otherwise inconspicuous in their spatial orientation, are frequently incapable of performing this apparently simple task. Such disturbances are counted among neurological symptoms; they are considered as an impairment of a more or less isolated function, related to a focal derangement of the brain, a deficiency remote from the center of *Dasein*. However, I intend to show that accomplishment and failure in such cases is much more involved than assumed.

The observation of failures makes us wonder about the normal performance. The situation is typical; it illustrates the psychiatrist's embarrassment mentioned earlier. In everyday life, we take it for granted that a normal person will be able to draw, after a fashion, the floor plan of a familiar room. Psychiatric experience puts an end to such naïve confidence. We discover a problem where we had seen none before. Obviously, an explanation of this disturbance has to wait for an adequate understanding of the norm.

In the procedure characteristic of experiments, we watch a transformation produced under controlled conditions. A change occurs; the initial situation vanishes with the progress of the experiment. At the end, let us say, of a chemotherapeutic study, we pause and ask ourselves whether the patients might not have recovered spontaneously, without any medication. Yet, we cannot reverse the experiment; we cannot return to its beginning. The experimental code, therefore, requires controls. In order to provide for controls, we pair, in unwarranted optimism, treated and untreated patients. In our present investigation, we need no controls. We can directly match final and initial situations; both can be viewed simultaneously. The finished product will tell us more about its producer and his production than any introspective or objective methods of observation could reveal.

A floor plan of this auditorium somehow depicts this hall, although it would be difficult to discover any resemblance between the two. No likeness connects the representation with the original. The plan is not a portrait, not a facsimile; neither is it a sign or symbol; it represents but does not reproduce. In fact, comparing the representation with its prototype, one is struck by the obvious disparities, the enormous reduction of volume, size, and substance. In contrast to the fullness of the original view, the outline drawn in a floor plan appears pitifully meager. In spite of its obvious inferiority, the plan must in some way be superior to the original. Graphic representation, like any other set of symbols, cannot be a mere substitute for reality. The deficiencies are obvious. It will take more effort to uncover the virtues. Perhaps we must change our point of view and search for the shortcomings encountered in the actual situation. Is there nothing wanting? At this moment, we enjoy a spacious room. But let us lower the ceiling and bring the walls close together; soon we reach a point where we will feel shut in. Walls look grim to a prisoner in solitary confinement; they block his sight and action. A house in flame no longer shelters; it threatens to engulf its occupants. These are extreme situations, but they make us see, as though through a magnifying glass, traits which, albeit inherent in every sensory experience, pass unnoticed most of the time. All walls are enclosures. Every visible thing is an object in the literal sense of the word; an objectum— i.e., something thrown against—in German, a Gegenstand—something which stands against, resists and limits our view, like the tall man in the theater who always sits in front of us. Reality holds us in the confines of the here and now. In every concrete situation, the walls form barriers which our sight cannot penetrate. The floor plan, however, presents their outline as figures on a ground, as a demarcation in a space extended beyond the physical boundaries.

An architect's design shows spatial relations of rooms such as no mortal eye has ever seen. The rooms have lost their solidity. In reality, walls separate one room from the next; they hold us back in sight and motion. On a plan, all the neighboring rooms are open to simultaneous inspection. We recognize the walls, but we see them as partitions; we see them, so to speak, from both sides at once. The architectural design presents the single room as part of a whole which, as such, is out of reach. Under natural conditions, we can pass only from one part to another; we must leave one room to enter the next. On a floor plan, we transcend without effort the natural barriers of sight, location, and distance.

Blueprints and road maps are elaborate designs. But the discrepancy between the original and its representation is no less acute in the modest assignment given to our patients. The floor plan of a single room presents all four walls at once and shows inner and outer space simultaneously, a view unparalleled in reality. In the actual situation, we have to turn around, replacing in temporal sequence the sight of the front with that of the rear. Yet, the plan presents the whole and presents it at rest. True, it simplifies reality, but it also adds to it; it shows more than the actually visible. If abstraction means nothing but omission of details, the floor plan cannot be the result of abstraction. On a ground plan, the ceiling, of course, is omitted. One may even doubt whether the white space circumscribed by the pencil lines actually represents the floor, for we can indicate the position of windows or other structures which either do not reach to the floor or rise above it. In any case, the plan represents the floor of a room; it does not simply imitate the track of lines where walls and floor meet. The plan does not give a mutilated torso of reality; height has not been amputated. Three-dimensional extension is represented on a two-dimensional plane. The actual situation is drastically changed; it is radically transformed. Whoever draws a floor plan must be able to emancipate himself from the impact of reality. A change in his I–world relation is required.

The plan presents the original as it never will be seen. The spatial configuration of the room is represented not as seen from inside but as it happens to exist per se, visualized from nowhere and detached from the personal presence of any spectator. While paintings—at least from Giotto to Monet—pictured the world as seen by man from a concrete "point of view," the floor plan excludes its own maker. It does not show a perspective organization of space converging to a center. Reflecting on myself, I can mark my position on the plan, inserting myself like another object into the detached order of things. On the plan, I am no longer at the center of my environment. Space is not organized around me in zones of closeness and distance; space has no depth. The direction backward is eliminated and replaced by the dimension side by side. A plan does not present an abstraction from concrete sight; it translates visible space into the abstract, homogeneous, isometric, impersonal order of geometry. The categorical attitude required in the construction of a floor plan calls for a reflexive dislocation of one's own self.

On a floor plan, natural size is discarded. I can draw this room on a small sheet of paper; its natural size is of no consequence. The proportion (in Latin, *ratio*; in Greek, *logos*) of lengths and angles alone is important. Together with natural size, weight, location, and orientation are abandoned. The plan is weightless but not because the paper is light; the flimsiest sheet of paper will do because the design is insubstantial. It could be drawn on any other material. The material used does not "matter." In fact, it must be negligible, because a representation is not that which it materially is. It points to something else which it is not. The wall represented on a floor plan consists of bricks, mortar, and paint; but a plan does not consist of paper and ink. A painting, though *on* the surface, is not seen *as* the surface of the canvas on which it is painted; it has no physical depth. Like a painting, the plan is a weightless, immaterial representation of something which it is not. Although we cannot dispense with some material, the representation as such is im-material. Were it not so, it could not function as a representation. Therefore, also, its own orientation in space is irrelevant. We can place it in any position, lift it from a horizontal to a vertical plane, or turn it from north to south. All such variations do not count, because the plan does not belong to the continuum of physical space; neither has it a unique position in public time. We can draw the plan of a building in direct sight, preserve the plan of a demolished structure, or devise a plan for a building to be erected in the future. A plan serves planning. The representation, the ground plan, just as other symbols, permits a freedom of action and comprehension which excels our direct contact with the original.

Even though the final result, the plan, runs counter to sensory experience, the initial situation must allow and even provide for this metamorphosis. Indeed, our comparison of the original and its representation contains in itself the solution to the problem that it poses.

To lay it bare, we will have to part with the cherished idea that a sequence of stimuli is accompanied by a corresponding series of percepts and that this multitude of single perceptions, although originally separated from one another, like individual frames in a motion picture film, could, nevertheless, be somehow joined together.

It may be argued that there is no problem. We can draw a room as a whole, because, in turning around, we add the view of the rear to the preceding one of the front. It is as simple as that. Only a fool could miss this straightforward answer to our query. As plausible as such an explanation may sound, it is a classic example of a *petitio principii:* it presupposes what it tries to explain.

Every motion which has the character of "turning around" is, from the start, related to a firmly established whole as its frame of reference. Of course, if in a particular case we want to learn the conditions of a whole room, we would move and turn around. But those who offer the motion of turning around as a causal-genetic explanation for the apprehension of the whole as such make quite different claims. They believe that this movement produces a kind of fusion between two discrete bits of excitation. Notwithstanding their disseverance, they fit together in the same way that two photos, reproducing opposite segments of a room, might be joined together. The motion of turning around supposedly permits two cortical configurations, although produced by disparate groups of stimuli, to form one figure. If allowed to meet, the fragments cling to one another like two magnetic semicircles growing together into one iron ring. In this process of optical fusion, the motion of turning the body is only instrumental. It simply furnishes the occasion; the marriage broker does not share the nuptial bed. Nevertheless, because experience, as we have been told, is perfectly correlated with neural functions, our comprehension of a room as a whole is caused by the amalgamation of the two optical excitations and indirectly by the motion which allows their junction. The genetic theory, therefore, demands psychophysical harmony and strict correspondence.

We may test this hypothesis by means of a fictitious experiment. We place a human subject on a small, rapidly rotating turntable in the center of a room. A light is turned off with every revolution of the table. The subject is brought into a position in which his optical receivers are hit

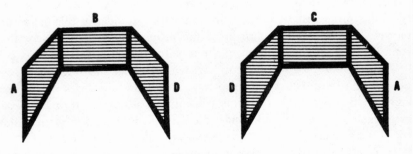

Figure 14-3

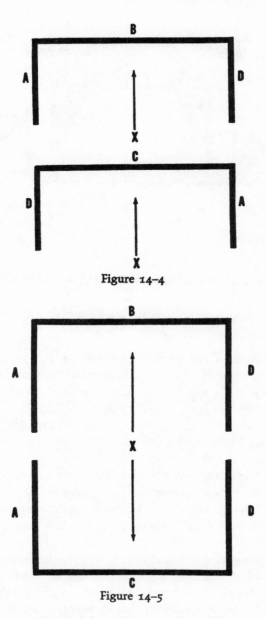

Figure 14-4

Figure 14-5

by stimuli reflected from one part of the room (Figure 14–1). After a turn of 180° his retinae will receive stimuli from the opposite sector of the room (Figure 14–2). In the subject's optical system, two volleys of stimuli will succeed each other (figures 14–3, 14–4). However, the two excitations, although following each other in objective time, can-

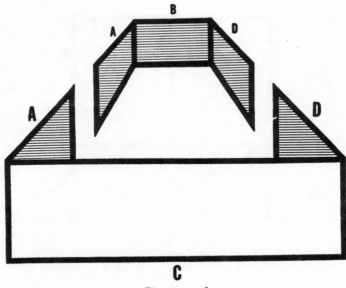

Figure 14–6

not realize their sequence. They remain isolated. But, even if they could somehow be associated, the optical system cannot provide for the supposed junction of the two halves because it is unidirectional. The polar articulation *forward–backward* (figures 14–5, 14–6) is alien to it. Throughout our lives, light enters our eyes in the single direction of pupil to retina; likewise, the direction of the afferent impulses and the spatial orientation of the cortical areas never change. In relation to optical stimuli, the polarity *rostral–caudal* does not apply. While we must rotate to expose our optical receivers to the light traveling in opposite directions, such change is not recorded by the optical system itself. In our subject's initial position (Figure 14–1), the wall B (figures 14–3, 14–4) was vis-à-vis his eyes. With a turn (Figure 14–2), the opposite wall C (figures 14–3, 14–4) is brought into obverse position to his eyes while the lateral walls A and D, to the right and left, exchange places (figures 14–7, 14–8). The two optical projections correlated with the positions of our subject do not complete each other as complementary halves. Instead of psychophysical harmony between the experienced order of the room and the corresponding physiological configuration, there are amazing discrepancies: the spatial ones just discussed and the temporal one mentioned earlier. While we actually see one segment after the other, we conceive the halves as belonging to each other simultaneously. Our recognition of a room as one whole structure at rest is apparently at variance with physiological facts, not in accordance with them. So, we are once again faced with the original question.

The answer has not to wait for the discovery of something radically new. But it does demand the courage to return to the oldest wisdom and to acknowledge, with all its consequences, a truth known to everyone but rejected by science. Stated in its simplest form, the truth is this: In seeing, we see something visible. This statement, I am afraid, comes as an anticlimax. Your reaction might well be expressed through the words of Horace: "Mountains labor and bring forth a ridiculous mouse." To make things worse, the statement sounds like a dubious application of Husserl's concept of intentionality. Yet, this apparent truism makes a bold claim. It describes seeing as an activity through which we attain an object without changing it—an action without a corresponding reaction. The statement implies that the relation connecting subject and object in sensory experience cannot be interpreted as the interaction of two bodies. Our everyday conviction that, in seeing, we apprehend things but nevertheless leave them as they are is not shattered through scientific criticism. It is the basis of all striving for objectivity.

Our maxim describes seeing as an activity. At the same time, it refers to something visible—that is to say, things appear to us; they manifest themselves as they are. Now, we are the recipients. The object dominates the scene. It affects us. We can see it; we must see it. We are convinced that an object visible to one must, under comparable conditions, be visible to all. What I can see and hear, my neighbor is expected to see and hear—neither less nor more. Dissenting is received with skepticism. Surfeit is an indication of a deception of the senses. The dissenter is judged as nearsighted, agnostic, even hysterical. And is it not our criterion for hallucinations that someone sees things, hears voices, or feels currents which others cannot see, hear, or feel?

Psychiatric practice is a segment of everyday life ruled by an axiom which is never challenged but, therefore, also never explicitly formulated—that we meet the Other as a partner in a world that we have in common. Observers are exchangeable. One goes and the other comes and occupies his position over against something visible. The grocer and his customer who exchange goods for money are convinced that the same dollar bill visible to both of them changes hands. The grocer and his customer do not share stimuli; they do not exchange muscle contractions; their brains do not communicate with each other. The visible thing must be a third party in relation to the two observers.

So, we have finally reached the point where we can announce the fundamental characteristic of sensory experience: In sensory experience, a living organism is related to the Other as the Other. The term "the Other" must be understood in the widest sense. It refers to the other one—our fellow-men just as well as to other things: the environment and finally the world. To avoid confusion, it might be better to use the special term "the Allon," derived from the Greek word signifying "the Other."

The relation to the Allon, self-evident in sensory experience, thwarts discernment—for good reason. In lieu of a full account, I will post ten theses and add some comments.

1. We meet the Allon in direct encounter, not as a ghost who sneaks into our chamber of consciousness from an outside world. The relation to the Allon is reciprocal. We move on the same level of reality.

In our macroscopic world, things are our partners that respond in their own manner, resisting or supporting our intentions. We put our feet on the ground and find it solid and safe or swampy and treacherous. Many are inclined to believe that such anthropomorphic interpretations are secondary, grafted on an initially realistic appraisal. But, even today, Western man gives proper names to rivers, winds, and mountains. The Alpinist who climbs the Matterhorn does not waste his energies on a heap of granite crystals; he wants to conquer that mountain rising before him in its individual grandeur. Even scientists tell us that sense organs receive information, that nerve fibers convey messages, that effectors respond to stimuli. The discovery of a world of faceless objects is late and never complete, and it is extremely painful when it occurs as an unreflected experience, as it does in cases of depersonalization. There, the original partnership with the Allon is cut asunder. Stimuli have not changed, but the I–world relation has. The patient continues to hear and see things, but he and the visible world no longer belong together. The individual knows the world as if it were seen on a floor plan, without any perspective in space or time. Seen by a depersonalized patient, space is deprived of depth. Much effort has been expended to detect the cues which determine the apprehension of the third dimension. But depth is not a purely optical phenomenon. It is relative to a mobile creature who can reach out to points "over there" from its egocentric position. Loss of depth, thus, refers to a loss of potentialities for action.

2. The Allon is accessible to us; nevertheless, it remains at a distance. It reaches us, but it must not be absorbed like stimuli nor digested like food. The moment we make it completely our own or surrender completely to it—as in sleep, renouncing our position opposite to it—it

ceases to be the Other. Stimuli do not exist apart from the receiver's organism which they excite, but the objects of sensory experience do. The relation to the Allon implies and demands a degree of mutual independence. Sensory experience is intrinsically linked with mobility. It can only occur in a creature capable of rising up from the ground and opposing the whole to which it belongs.

The Allon, in the dialectics of revealing and hiding, remains enigmatic. Disease estranges us even from our own bodies; falling sick, we discover the power of the Allon in ourselves. Distance, in spite of the most intimate contacts, is a general characteristic of sensory experience. The Allon, although manifest on its surface, is unfathomable in its depth. On their surface, things are well defined, clearly shaped, and precisely located, but their core eludes comprehension, description, and demarcation. It keeps its secret like the Other who—should he express himself with unrestrained candor, should he "be closer than breathing, nearer than hands and feet" (Tennyson)—will remain at a distance. Desdemona's oaths could not convince Othello. Jealousy has its roots in the unresolved ambiguity of the Allon. In schizophrenic experience, the balance between the open façade and the hidden core is disturbed; its presence is felt in its overwhelming power.

3. The Allon is apprehended in its suchness (in traditional terminology, in its secondary and primary qualities). We see the Empire State Building in its substantiality; we do not incorporate it materially. But this unilateral relationship to its suchness is mediated by physical agents. The stimulus does not cause perceiving. Its function can be compared to that of a catalyst that initiates the actuality of sensory experience. The stimulus delimits what will be seen and determines that it will be seen. From this point of view, intentionality of vision and causality of seeing are fully reconcilable.

Physiology and objective psychology acknowledge only the causal relation. They do not recognize a principal difference between suntan and sight. Just as the skin reacts to light with the production of pigments, so, supposedly, does the nervous system react with a motor response to photic stimulation. Perception, it seems, is but a dispensable byproduct; it is not the genuine correlate to retinal excitation. Behavior is determined by the relation of input and output; it is not understood as the relation of an experiencing being to his world.

Perhaps the following considerations will serve as a warning signal and start a critical re-evaluation. Whenever an observer studies a human subject or an animal, then the man as well as the rat, the material used as stimulus, and the motor responses must all be considered as stimuli acting on the *observer's* nervous system. According to behaviorist theory, they must be followed by the observer's motor responses. Of course, such motor effects do not know anything about the afferent impulses which released them. The output simply follows the input in time. The observer, however, actually relates the re-sponse backward to the stimuli, against the arrow of time. Unfortunately, stimuli cannot be observed, because, by definition, they are physical agents without visible or any other "secondary" qualities. Nor can they be manipulated; for the physical agent, when turned into a stimulus, no longer exists apart from the receiving organism. Those stimuli which provoke responses in the experimental animal never reach the eyes or ears of the observer. Stimuli cannot be shared by two organisms. Stimuli and objects are not synonymous terms; stimuli are constructs, never immediate objects of experience.

4. The relation to the Allon, although one of mutuality, is not one of equality. The Allon is the encompassing whole. It presents itself in fragments only. The actual situation is but a segment of a larger one, a part that, with open frontiers, borders on the next one. The whole is not a composite of originally solitary elements, like sensory data, impressions, or bits of information.

5. The relation I–Allon unfolds in a temporal continuum. The fragments of the Allon do not follow one another like slides projected on a screen, where one has to be removed to make room for the next. The present moment is but a focal point within the horizon of time, expanding into the future and the past.

Time is not experienced as a sequence of now-points. The actual moment is a phase in my state of becoming. In a sentence, words follow one another. The phonemes recorded on a tape follow one after the other; each one is strictly separated from the other. But, in listening to a speech, we understand the words as parts of a whole deployed in time. The first word opens the sentence pointing forward to those still to come. The grammatical subject will be defined by the predicate that follows, the end referring back to the beginning. Yet, this temporal sequence of words is apprehended as a whole presenting one definite meaning.

6. The present is prepossessed by that which is not yet. The future is imminent, but we do not know what the prospects are. We respond to this precarious condition by searching, exploring, and questioning. Dread is coeval with the actual situation, which is emotionally charged and threatened by the unknown, the unfamiliar, and the impending. Endless efforts are made to explore and to forecast, to conquer, or to pacify the Allon. In general, guided tours are preferred to the hazards of an ad-

venturous trip. In spite of all exertion, the dreadful remains omnipresent. Witness the agoraphobic who succumbs to its presence whenever he leaves the sheltering walls of his home and finds himself exposed to the incomprehensible immensity of the Allon. The tendency to consolidate and to tighten the defensive walls has its counterpart in the propensity to transcend the border and to enjoy the wider views—the penchant toward self-preservation has its counterpart in the striving for self-realization.

7. Every part, incomplete in itself, is capable of and in need of completion. The actual situation points to something else which is not, no longer, or not yet present; it points beyond its borders to the other parts and to the whole to which it belongs. The actual situation is not closed in by iron boundaries separating the given from the void.

Here, I believe, we can return to our initial problem. We wondered how one could represent a room on a floor plan as a whole, although in apparent contrast to direct experience. Now, it seems, the problem has been dissolved rather than solved. The simple reason is that we experience the part as part, as capable of and in need of completion. Experience alone can teach how the unseen sectors of a room will look in particular. That the actual situation is but a fragment makes experience possible.

Many questions still remain unsettled; for instance, how the physiological error, the reversal of sides, and the temporal parallaxis could be corrected.

8. As happens so frequently in our field, the first and probably the most difficult task is to discover the problems hidden by familiarity and by the facility of practice. No one pauses to marvel that we recognize a room as the same whether we turn to the right or to the left. The sequences a, b, c, d and a, d, c, b lead to the same result. We take it for granted that the walls seen one after the other co-exist. We are not surprised that one passing a street in the morning recognizes it as the same street at night. Not only does he recognize it as the same but he also recognizes that the street is seen in different perspectives—that the same What appears in different aspects of suchness. Finally, he is aware that his own position in relation to the street is turned in the opposite direction. In everyday life, we are not surprised, but the scientist has good reason to wonder, for there is no correspondence in the organization of stimuli and engrams to this experience. Yet, the classical theory of sensory experience is committed to the postulate that experience is strictly correlated with physiological events.

The traditional interpretation of sensory experience does not acknowledge the I—Allon relation. It never even considers the relation of an experiencing being to things experienced. It eliminates its real topic before it starts its discussion. Instead, traditional theory interprets sensory experience as the result of the interaction of two bodies. The sender produces in the recipient a phantom-like perception. Such sensory data do not belong to the outside world of objects; they represent them—it remains unclear how and to whom. In any case, while they represent an object, they are cut off from the outside world; they are said to be subjective; they belong to the subject. Since perceptions represent the outside world but belong to the subject, they cannot be an object of action. Every one, supposedly, carries in his consciousness a private gallery of such shadow images. The collector himself is not a part of his collection. He owns it; he has it; he does not belong to it. Sensory experience in classical theory does not include the experiencing being. The content of sensory experience is reduced to the appearance of a more or less distorted replica, a counterfeit of the outside world. Seeing is acknowledged as a physiological process, but not as the relation of seeing beings to things seen. The relation I–Allon is slashed. The Allon alone is left, but in a profoundly mutilated form. Perceptions are many; they follow one another in the order of objective time. They do not belong together in a meaningful context; they stick together through synaptic welding. Positivism from Hume to Skinner preaches the gospel that sense is repeated nonsense. The order and connection of perceptions is determined by the order and connection of afferent impulses and their traces. For this reason, classical theory cannot tolerate any discrepancies between the order of sensory data and physiological events.

Traditional interpretation claims that the world is presented subjectively in my consciousness. The relation I–Allon implies that, in our encounter with the world, we see things themselves; they are our partners, and we are theirs. My sensory experience includes myself as the one who sees visible things, who is directed to them but also opposite to them.

In sensory experience, we are aware of a dual order: the order of our own acts of seeing and the order of things seen. The two orders come into contact. They *do not coincide.*

In the sequence of our always limited views, we come to understand how the fragments of things seen belong together. In this process of assembling the fragments, significance provides the leitmotiv. Passing from one phase to the next in a state of becoming, we apprehend the permanent order of things in their own right. We are able to detach the order of the Allon from the order of its appearance to us. In fact, our understanding of our own position is dominated by our understanding of the whole to which we relate ourselves. With the question "What time is it now?" I order my personal now into the order of public time.

The capacity of discriminating the two orders in their mutual relation develops slowly during the years from early childhood to maturity. Not before the age of five or six will a child learn that games can be played according to rules and that things require being treated in a consistent manner. The Allon, lasting and resisting, demands our respect.

The relation I—Allon places each one of us in an egocentric position. From this central point, space opens before us as a stage for future action. Things seen over there at this moment now, nevertheless, present themselves as possible goals.

The dual order enables us to repeat, to see things again. It makes communication possible, because the Allon opens before us as the one all-encompassing world. Limited to his store of sensory data, every one would live in a private world.

9. In our physical existence, we are confined to fragments; we can exchange only one part for another, move from place to place, from day to day. The whole as such is inaccessible. We get hold of it through the mediation of language or other means of symbolic representation. Words are not substitutes for absent things or relations accessible to us before (the so-called) verbalization occurs. Symbolic representation enables us to break through the barriers that are set by our corporeal existence. The word "room" signifies a room as a whole. A map of the United States presents to us the country as a whole in its extension between the two oceans. Discarding natural size, the map delivers into our hands the spatial order of the whole in a scale adapted to our natural limits. A map of New York that equaled the city in size would be of no use. The natural relations are inverted. Symbolic representation gives us power over that whole of which we are but a tiny part. Yet, in using a map, we submit to the order of the whole and let our actions be ordered by it.

10. In our orientation in time and space, we descend from the whole to the here and now. We determine this moment as the eleventh hour of this day, this month, and this year. We determine the actual present through its relation to a whole that is never actually given. The word "today" signifies this day in its extension of twenty-four hours; the dial of a clock represents all the possibilities, the hands in motion mark the actual situation. Confined to one single point of the periphery, we use the word "today," signifying a day in its full circle. While we constantly change our position between morning and night, we mean this same whole of twenty-four hours: today. Only the one who can relate the actual moment, beyond its boundaries, to the not-present whole is

able to understand and therefore to remember, let us say, noontime, the luncheon hour, and the lunch.

We have made it our task to apply aesthesiology to pathology. In our efforts to account for a minor deficiency, we were forced to extend our runways farther and farther. Can we now jump higher? What are the results? The first one is, I believe, identical with the lengthy preparations themselves that demonstrate that ease of performance is not an indicator of psychological simplicity. In fact, I have tried to show that psychopathology has to be built on a psychology which is not the psychology of an apparatus—not a physiological but a psychological psychology—if I may say so, one which studies man as an experiencing being in his I–world relation.

"Behavior and the nervous system" has been a general theme of many conferences held during the last decade. Behavior was always treated as the dependent variable. While the exploration of the nervous system was highly sophisticated, the account given of the complex human behavior which made such sophistication possible was scanty and naïve. Seeing, observing, describing, remembering, measuring, and predicting were all taken for granted. To predict behavior is one thing; to understand predicting is the true psychological problem. All attempts to define consciousness or mind failed, to the satisfaction of most participants. Of course, one cannot define consciousness or mind as abstract entities; however, one can well define an experiencing being as an organism capable of apprehending the Other as the Other, and one can define the experiencing human being as one capable of comprehending the whole of which he is a part.

If the I–world relation is first acknowledged, it should not be too difficult to survey its disturbances. I have already pointed, in passing, to depersonalization, agoraphobia, the dysmnesic, the asymbolic, and the schizophrenic. Let me add a few remarks about the organic psychoses. The account given of the dual order leads directly into the psychopathology of symptomatic psychoses, with clouding of consciousness as the cardinal sign. It might not be inappropriate to revive the obsolete term "mental confusion" and to consider it as a manifestation of disturbances of the I–Allon relation, varying in degree from the mild stages of subacute delirium and perplexity to the wild excitement of psychomotor fugues and the severe mental disorganization in senile psychoses. One could place disturbances of the I–Allon relation side by side with the familiar symptomatology of organic psychoses and coordinate them like two columns in a bilingual dictionary. In one column, then, we would read about disorientation, fleeting attention, incoherence of thinking,

Figure 14–1   Figure 14–2

Figure 14–7

Figure 14–8

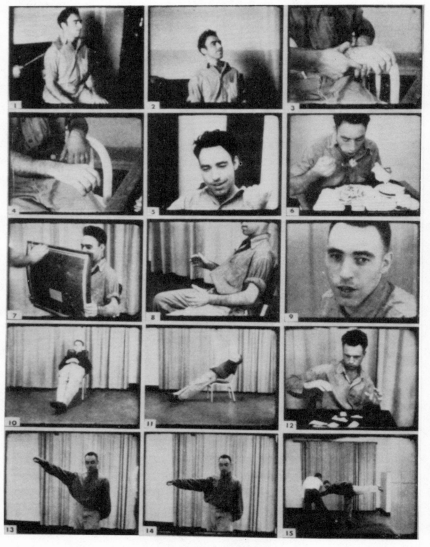

Figures 18–1 to 18–15

Figures 18–16 to 18–22

and purposeless action and in the other about disarray and fusion of the two orders, radical fragmentation, atomatization of the temporal continuum, the shrinking of the horizon of time, and the vanishing of the whole. The APA nomenclature enumerates impairments of orientation, memory, judgment, intellectual functions, and affect as characteristic of organic brain disorder. The I–Allon relation enables us to understand the inner unity of this aggregate. Here, picking the ripe berries from the I–Allon bush, we may go one step further and extend our interpretation to the optical hallucinations as they occur in acute delirium.

Under normal conditions, as long as the I–Allon relation is kept intact, we see things in relation to us but as their own order requires. When, however, this relation is not preserved in its integrity, the physiological error, the inversion of sides, and the temporal parallaxis can no longer be corrected. Under these conditions, the sequences a, b, c, d and a, d, c, b cannot be identified. Impressions succeeding one another in time do not coalesce into a meaningful whole. They contradict and counteract each other. Things seen, as the eyes see them, must look derisive, mocking, threatening, or bewitched. Every attempt to create order increases disorder. Stability breaks down in a whirling hypermetamorphosis. The panic-driven behavior in acute delirium and in psychomotor attacks is a dramatic manifestation of the breakdown of the I–Allon relation. In sharp contrast to schizophrenic voices, delirious hallucinations manifest directly a primary dissolution of those functions of the brain which normally sustain the I–Allon relation.

One may wonder if the conditions that empiricists consider fundamental are in fact reached only in the extreme pathological stages. In any case, the normal functions of the brain must be compatible with the sustenance of the I–Allon relation, and the principles of neurophysiology should be revised accordingly; for the existential categories of relation to potentialities, of meaningful correlation, of the historical order of time, in short, of the I–world relation, characterize all sensory experience.

References

Binswanger, L. *Ausgewählte Vorträge und Aufsätze.* Vol. 1. Bern: A. Francke, 1947.

Binswanger, L. *The case of Ellen West.* In R. May, E. Angel, & H. Ellenberger (Eds.), *Existence: a new dimension in psychiatry.* New York: Basic Books, 1958.

Binswanger, L. Existential analysis, psychiatry, schizophrenia. *J. exist. Psychiat.,* 1960, **1** (2), 157–175.

Head, H. *Aphasia and kindred disorders of speech.* Cambridge, Eng.: Cambridge University Press, 1926. 2 vols.
Hebb, D. O. *The organization of behavior.* New York: John Wiley, 1949.
Heidegger, M. *Being and time.* New York: Harper, 1962.
Heidegger, M. *Brief über den Humanismus.* Bern: A. Francke, 1947.
Lashley, K. S. *Cerebral mechanisms and behavior.* New York: John Wiley, 1952.

CHAPTER FIFTEEN

Phenomenology of Hallucinations

The obsolete expressions "alienist" and "alien asylum" still remind us that strangeness is the mark which leads to the prescientific discovery of psychotic behavior and directs its clinical observation and scientific explanation. Psychotic manifestations point, at least by implication, to a standard from which the patient deviates. Thanks to their strangeness, hallucinations are easily recognized as disturbances of sensory experience. Since the *actual* interpretation of the norm, however fragmentary, vague, and prejudiced it may be, predetermines any *possible* conception of pathological phenomena, a reappraisal of the norm of sensory experience has become mandatory; for in everyday life, we practice the norm— here familiarity prevents insight—and, in science, it is "more honor'd in the breach than in the observance." Psychological and psychopathological interpretations deal with a semblance rather than with the original.

Behavioral science, fascinated by the success of physics, labors to apply the methods of the natural sciences to the study of man and his world. In its effort to emulate physics, psychology reduces the experiencing human being to an organism, a nervous system, an apparatus, a field. It records stimuli and responses and measures input and output— completely oblivious to the fundamental differences between objects and stimuli. While man can be made an object of observation and measurement, he remains the subject who observes and measures. Physics is a part of the human world. The one who measures input and output in terms of space and time must reach beyond the actual here and now. The physicist may take the human possibilities of seeing, observing, and communicating, for granted, but the psychologist's very topic is the seeing of physical things, the observation of observable events. The validity of scientific findings is grounded in the validity of everyday-life experience.

To experiencing beings—man and animal—the world is opened; adjacent space is transformed and widened into an environment. In their corporeal existence, experiencing beings are in relation to the Other *as* the Other—a relation unknown to and inexplicable within the strict side-by-side physical order of spatiotemporal events. In sensory experience, we reach beyond the boundaries of our physical existence. Here and now are related to visible things over there as to our potential goals. Sensory experience is relative to a motile being.

A child may believe in Santa Claus, but a grownup knows that Santa's mask hides the real performer. A scientific child may accept the everyday-life world at its face value, but the man of science knows that colors and sounds are nothing but secondary qualities, purely subjective, that sensory experience is deceptive and illusory, and that the everyday world is nothing but a phantasm. The scientist, therefore, makes it his task to remove the overlay and to lay bare the neural mechanisms underlying behavior. True, in an uncritical attitude, we may say and believe that we look at visible things, cast an eye on them, and see them at a distance. But the physicist knows that, in reality, light has been traveling from a reflecting surface over there until it reached a distance receptor. The physiologist, following the physicist, locates the optical functions in the retina and in the cerebral cortex. And, finally, the psychologist, following the two others, does not hesitate to locate the accompanying sensations just there where the functions have their seat. "All sensa," says H. H. Price, "are identical with parts of the brain and not with the surface of the external physical objects" (1950).

There is no time today for a critique of this tradition, which reaches back to Descartes and Galileo. However, in order to justify the phenomenological approach, a method obviously at variance with accredited scientific procedures, I will have to give some reasons. From among many, I may mention the following points:

1. All statements about the illusory character of sensory qualities and the reality of neural mechanisms are metaphysical propositions to be evaluated as parts of the whole metaphysical system to which they belong.

2. The devaluation of sensory experience actually affirms what it denies, for the scientist remains in all his work a citizen of our every-

day world, with its macroscopic dimensions, its visible and touchable things, and its open horizons of time and space.

3. In spite of all efforts to dissipate it, the illusion never disappears.

4. The psychological observer uses a double standard; while he reduces the behavior of his subjects to neural mechanisms, he grants himself a privileged status; he continues to see and observe both the behavior and the brain in a macroscopic world.

5. And, finally, in every neuro-anatomic observation and neurophysiological experiment, two brains are involved: the brain observed and the observing brain. The same rules of explanation must apply to both. The observer's own behavior must be understood as a function of the underlying neural mechanisms, as responses to stimuli. But such logically required observance of the rules established for research would altogether eliminate its possibility. Strict adherence to the professed principles is tantamount to their *reductio ad absurdum*.

We may wonder, therefore, whether naïveté is the stigma of the phenomenologist. Actually, in phenomenology, naïveté may be taken as an asset because it indicates that we have successfully emanicipated ourselves from the bias of traditional theories and prejudices.

Now, I may return to my initial statement: In sensory experience, the world is opened to us. As experiencing beings we are related to the Other as the Other. The term "the Other" is used in the broadest sense signifying earth and sky, inanimate and living things, man and animal; to avoid ambiguity, I will replace the term "the Other" with the Greek word *allon*.

Whenever I consider an object, I find myself confronted with something else—the Allon—that exists apart from me. I may leave it to itself and return to it, see it again. Nevertheless, this something, characterized as being-not-me, presents itself to me; it is an object for me. The Allon is accessible to us; yet, it would lose its independent existence as an object were it completely accessible—could it be digested like food or absorbed in an organism like a stimulus. A stimulus has no existence apart from the organism which it excites, but an object of sensory experience has. That something is at the same time mine and not mine, so that I can establish a relationship with the Allon and yet leave it as it is—this is the logically offensive aspect of sensory experience. The striving for objectivity reveals the paradox of a situation dominated by two contradictory tendencies: letting things be what they are in themselves, independent of any observer—to eliminate the observer—and at the same time to submit the object completely to the observer's insight.

As a part of the Allon, any object is partly revealed and partly concealed. It always remains enigmatic. But the riddle is not given through a complex structure, which we can hope to disentangle in the future; there is a power which eludes our grasp. The Sphinx may well be taken as a symbol for the encounter of man and world on the primary level of sensory experience. In interpersonal relations, such "distance in contact" is more obvious. Although another person may reveal himself in friendship or surrender herself in love, even though the relation I–he or I–she may be transformed into an I–you and finally into a *we*, the other one keeps his secret. Jealousy has its roots in the unfathomable ambiguity of the Allon and the other one. Distance in contact, while better comprehended in interpersonal relations, is an all-pervasive characteristic of sensory experience—and necessarily so.

To the ambiguity of the situation corresponds the ambivalence of our attitudes. Partly revealed and partly concealed, the Allon forces our interest; it arouses our desire to know—not the intellectual curiosity to determine what a thing is but to ascertain how it behaves—for, in its independent existence, the Allon is threatening through its mere presence. To know, therefore, means here to master. In this sense, the word is still used in the idiom of carnal knowledge; as the Bible says, "Adam knew his wife."

That the Allon is partly revealed and partly concealed does not mean that the manifest and the veiled are clearly separated and located in different regions. The familiar and the strange interpenetrate each other. Suddenly, the hidden powers may pierce through, as in an earthquake when the solid ground proves treacherous. Even without any outward change, occult potentialities may manifest themselves. Some days when we open our eyes familiar things may look strange to us—a *jamais vu*. At the seashore in twilight, when the aesthetic charm begins to fail, we may suddenly discover the immense vastness of the ocean and, with it, the forlornness of our own existence. In some forms of depersonalization the insurmountable strangeness of the Allon, always present although not always obvious, manifests itself.

As long as we are in good health, we trust our body; it is our own, so much so that we live at ease in its functions and actions without any need for a conceptual or pictorial body image. Sickness estranges us from our body; then the body is turned into an object, a thing no longer to be trusted. Stricken by dis-ease, we discover the power of the Allon in ourselves. Just as the agoraphobic collapses when face to face with the boundlessness of open space, the hypochondriac reacts to this presence of the Allon in himself. That even without any mental disturbance something which is my very own can be experienced as belonging to the Allon is of great importance for an understanding of hallucinations.

Since the relation to the Allon is universal, encompassing all single experiences in their temporal sequence, we would expect variations of the I–world relation as a whole to occur under pathological conditions. We therefore may venture to say that, in the situation described as schizophrenic world catastrophe, the patient is overwhelmed by the Allon in its uncanny strangeness. The façade of things still stands, but, blank and meaningless, it no longer conceals the weird powers which seem to pervade the universe. The patient still recognizes things in their familiar shape, but there is something incomprehensible and unspeakable which strikes him with panic and horror.

The wondrous relation to the Allon—shared on equal footing by dog and master, by fools and wise men—appears to the reflecting mind absurd and repulsive, a blasphemy of the scientific spirit.

Borrowing from Husserl, I call the relation of the Allon a relation of intentionality. It is clear that intentionality, opening an environment to an experiencing being, differs from causality, connecting stimulus and nervous system. Sensory experience, while resting on a causal relation, transcends it. How the two can be reconciled remains a problem of first rank. It will never be solved if intentionality—basic to all experience—is not acknowledged and respected in its own right. Certainly, whoever tries to account for behavior in terms of neural mechanisms has first of all to take a complete inventory of that which he is going to explain.

In everyday experience, the relation of intentionality, the I–world relation, is characterized by coexistence and mutuality. Things over there —the Allon—and I move and meet on the same ground. Three centuries ago, the Cartesian dichotomy cut this relation to the Allon into two radically separate halves. The interpretation of sensory experience has never fully recovered from this drastic operation. A few words of comment are indispensable.

Descartes lifted the sensory qualities, so to speak, off the object. He assigned the objects, as far as they can be treated mathematically, to the extended substance, the physical world. He moved colors, sounds, and so on, as subjective sensory qualities, over to the other half, to the thinking substance—residing nowhere. Consciousness is exiled from the physical world; it is extramundane. The thinking substance, the *cogito*, alone with its cogitations which comprise also the sensations, reaches the world only in a round-about way by some methods of ratiocination, as, e.g., in Freud's reality testing. Although, according to Descartes, we may convince ourselves and firmly believe that there is an outside world, we can never gain any direct contact with it. In the Cartesian interpretation, self-awareness necessarily precedes the apprehension of the world. As we look at the world from outside, we must be aware of our thoughts before and even without recognizing the existence of an external world. When we speak today about an outside world, we still speak and think in terms of Descartes's metaphysics, a position taken by quite a few, surprisingly enough, for the proper point of departure in empirical research.

Current definitions of hallucinations, such as "perceptions without an object" (Lhermitte, 1951), prove the unbroken power of Descartes's philosophy. Here, perception is not understood as the relation of a perceiving creature to an object perceived. The experience of perceiving is reduced in its totality to a perception occurring in consciousness, a kind of picture made from mental colors. Intentionality is deleted. Although there is no external object inherent in a perception, we know, so one says, that certain sensations occur whenever a physically determined, a real body excites another one which happens to be an organism equipped with receptors. "Perception without an object" claims that, under normal conditions, objects in the outside world and perceptions in the mind are correlated; under abnormal conditions, perhaps through a kind of short circuit in the feeder system, a perception slide slips in and presents itself on the screen of consciousness without a typical stimulation. Hinsie and Schatzky's definition of hallucinations as a "sense perception to which there is no external stimulus" (1945) obviously indicates that, whether or not such stimulation actually occurs, this alternative does not affect a perception in its own structure. An hallucination *qua* perception, it seems, does not differ from a normal perception; it is characterized only in a negative sense, by the absence of an object or a stimulus, a deficiency unnoticed by the patient. In fact, contrary to all clinical experience, no reference is made to a patient and his psychosis. Yet, we all know that hallucinations manifest a pathological style of life, a deviant mode of "being-in-the-world."

In order to understand hallucinations in their proper context, we have to discard Descartes's dichotomy. If we do not sacrifice observable phenomena to a theory, if we allow ourselves to be truly empirical, then we gain a position for a new attack on the problem of hallucinations.

In everyday life, contrary to the traditional dogma of an "outside world" reached by inference, we find ourselves within the world. We do not survey from a grandstand a parade of objects filing by; we are in the game, face to face with other things, together with the Allon and related to it. The driver of a car does not look from Erewhon to the street and other cars; his body is not directed by his mind as by a kind of extra-mundane backseat driver. The driver finds himself in the midst of traffic, engaged and committed. In touching something, I feel touched; in seeing, I experience my own relation to visible things. Light illuminates the environment, but it may also strike my eyes and blind me. Sensory experience is the experience of an I–world relation. Self-awareness does not precede apprehension of the world: one is not before the other; one is not without the other. The world is the counterpart of my activities, and I am affected by its power.

Descartes's term "thinking substance" *(res cogitans)* indicates that the dispassionate attitude of a scientist was the pattern that served him as a model for the relation of consciousness to all its possible contents. However, in sensory experience, the Allon is not an indifferent object inviting peaceful contemplation by a neutral observer. From the start, sensory experience has an emotional component. The Allon is threatening or comforting, appealing or repelling, and we respond to its physiognomies with fear or confidence, trust or distrust. Sensory experience is egocentric. It serves the individual creature in its corporeal existence between life and death. In my sensory experience, I am not exchangeable, although under certain conditions I, as a human being, may succeed in establishing the attitude of a detached observer who no longer sees things in relation to himself. In short, in sensory experience, I am seized, caught up; my own case is called up.

In sensory experience, we move in a prelogical sphere where reality has the character of actuality. The real is that and only that which acts and seizes on an experiencing creature. That something is real means that something happens to me. It does not necessarily mean that something happened in accordance with the established laws of nature. The unreal, the merely possible or probable, has no place. *That* we are seized is the decisive factor. *What* it was may be found out later, if at all. Beyond the verdict of immediate experience, no appeal to a higher authority is either necessary or even possible. In fact, in sensory experience there is no judge who, after an impartial evaluation of the merits of the case, gives his judgment about it. In sensory experience, the situation is much more serious: the judge himself is attacked.

It is in this region, this prelogical sphere, that hallucinations and delusions occur. Hallucinations, therefore, do not yield to arguments. The immediateness of experience permits no doubt. Hallucinations are not in competition with the rest of a patient's perceptions. In fact, the reality of voices eclipses the reality of all other data and thwarts the effects of any rational analysis of circumstances.

There are, however, hallucinations and hallucinations. It is a familiar fact that visual hallucinations prevail in alcoholic delirium, while the schizophrenic is plagued by auditory and tactile hallucinations. Does recourse to phenomenology help us to understand better such clinical differences? I believe it does. The problem itself points the way to its solution.

Thus far, I have confined myself to a characterization of sensory experience in general, disregarding for the moment the modalities of seeing, hearing, and so on. Yet, every child, and first of all the proverbial burnt child, could tell us that there is a difference between seeing and touching a hot iron. And every boy could add something about the difference between looking at a pretty girl from a distance and approaching the same girl in a kiss and embrace. The craving for contact in delight has its counterpart in the revulsion from contact in disgust.

Once again, we find a striking contrast between everyday experience and the theories which try to elucidate it. The schema of an agreement between stimulus or, as Adrian (1947) says, between impulse discharge and sensation is much too narrow. The assumption of sensory data arranged in a temporal order fails to explain the very apprehension of time; it omits the relation to an object; it excludes any variations of contact; it cannot account for the full content of experience, not even in the most ordinary situations of everyday life.

Let us take a simple example. Whoever steps, jumps, or falls into the cold water of a swimming pool discovers, although not conceptually, (1) that he is involved; (2) that there is a dramatic change of involvement with transition from the first phase (seeing) to the second phase (feeling); (3) that he experiences himself *and* the water, experiences himself—his own body—in relation to the water; (4) that the modes of contact change from distance to closeness; (5) that, in relation to visible things, distance is extended in two directions—while things are remote from us, we also stand clear of them (depth perception is polar); (6) that an object is accessible in more than one modality; (7) that, in spite of the variance of the sensory data, one and the same object can be apprehended in seeing, touching, and so on.

In short, each one of the modalities shows the world in a particular aspect, each one relates us to the world in a specific contact, and each one determines our existence in a particular mode. The genus sense is unfolded in a spectrum where the modalities vary in regard to space, time, direction, distance, obtrusiveness, mineness, motion, measurability, and objectivity (see Table 15-1).

Under normal conditions, sound is perceived as an utterance. Sound

TABLE 15–1. Phenomenological Comparisons of Color and Sound

Colors	Sounds
1. Attribute	**Utterance**
Mode of being, expressed by an adjective	Activity, expressed by a verb
Adheres to things	Detachable from sounding body
	May develop into pure sound (music)
2. Identification	**Actuality**
The same thing visible again	The same sound never returns
Stabilization	Mobilization
Skeleton of things	Pulse of things
3. Articulates space	**Articulates time**
Simultaneity, yet no synchrony of sight and the visible goal over there	Originates, lasts, perishes—synchrony of hearing and the audible
4. Localization	**Localization (of sound)**
Over there, in definite directions	Fills and homogenizes space
Determines definite places	Abolishes local differences
Separates and divides (contour)	Binds together and unites (the cord)
5. Horizon	**Horizon**
Appear within spatial horizon	Appear within temporal horizon
Side by side, to be distinguished	One after the other, to be linked together
Beginning and end simultaneous	Beginning and end not simultaneous
Multiplicity	Frequency
Analytical	Synthetical
6. Motion	**Motion**
Identical thing changing places	Diverse tones following each other in time
Space in rest	The moment does not stay
7. Pathic	**Pathic**
Active—we cast an eye	Receptive—we lend an ear
Distance preserved	Distance abolished, I am caught
Space of attack and flight	Irrevocable, overpowering (Orpheus)
Sight and insight	Hearing and obedience
Beckoning	Calling

and sounding body do not share the same locality. Detached from the sounding body, sound moves toward us; it permeates, fills, and homogenizes space; it captures our ear. In music, sound is transformed into pure sound—at least in approximation, although the ideal case is never fully realized. We listen to the symphony, but we are still able to hear the orchestra. Detached sounds point back toward the sounding body, with its definite localization and, thereby, limited range of interference.

Such topographic limitations are no longer valid for the schizophrenic. In the auditory hallucinations of the schizophrenic, the normal pattern of the acoustical modality is deformed. The severance of the sound from the sounding body is brought to a pathological extreme. Voice and speaker are radically disjoined.

The schizophrenic hears voices, not persons. Occasionally, it is but one voice, but more often it is some, many, or "they" voices emanating from an anonymous group: the Communists, the Masons, the Jews, or the Catholics. Even if recognized as the voice of one individual, the *voice* continues to talk; the individual does not take over. Voice and speaker remain separate. Reference to fantastic machines, supposedly used for transmission, confirms that voices alone are immediately present.

Voices have no determinable position. They are ubiquitous. They call from the side, from above, from the rear; it seems as if the sector of frontal attack alone is spared. Voices do not fall upon the patient in a straightforward assault. Occasionally, a patient reports that voices penetrate his head, his ears, or his heart. There, he feels them rather than sees them. This experience confirms once again the pseudo-acoustical character of auditory hallucinations.

Lack of localization is not a simple deficiency. Indeed, voices do not lack—they mock—spatial determination. Eluding all limits and boundaries and not hindered by walls or distances, voices are overwhelming and irresistible in their power. The patient is helpless! There is no escape from the attacking voices.

Sound detached from the sounding body is something; yet, it is not a thing one can manipulate like the piano which produces the sound; it is not a thing, but neither is it no-thing. Sound is somewhere between thing and no-thing. It does not belong to the category of objects which we can handle. In hearing, we have already heard. We cannot escape from a sound in the manner by which we escape from visible things. Sound is obtrusive; it reaches us. We cast an eye on visible things at their distant place; we lend our ear to the words which come toward us and claim us. A voice calls and orders. No wonder, therefore, that, in many languages—in Greek and Latin, Hebrew, French and German, and Russian—the words "hearing" and "obeying" are derived from the same root. English makes no exception; for the verb "to obey" stems from the Latin *obaudire* (literally, to listen from below), a relation more clearly preserved in the noun "obedience."

Struck by the irresistible power of voices, the schizophrenic feels no need to test the reality of his experience. He is not shocked by physical absurdities; he is not surprised that he alone hears the voices; he does not wonder that the voices aim at him. But perhaps we might wonder whether the patient is singled out from among many others, honored, so to speak, by the persecution, or whether he is alone in immediate confrontation with a world of horror.

The schizophrenic is not a hermit who, frightened and disappointed, withdraws in seclusion from which he could return any day. The disturbance goes deeper; voices are atmospheric. They behave like the elements—the wind, the rain, the fire—and yet they speak, deride, and threaten. This metamorphosis indicates that the patient has lost his place in the human world, that its framework has collapsed. In alcoholic hallucinosis, the patient also hears voices, but he still relates them to people talking nearby, behind a wall, or below a window. The speakers are out of sight but not out of reach. They are held to a definite place somewhere in the neighborhood. The schizophrenic never tries to find out where the voices originate; the alcoholic not infrequently searches for the people who speak around him, not to him. He still lives in a human environment, forced to overhear a conversation which expresses moral criticism and threatens severe punishment. He is still concerned with physical reality. In a discussion about his hallucinations, he will not always be found recalcitrant.

The ubiquity of schizophrenic voices indicates that the general order of things—assigning definite places with limited zones of reach and influence—disintegrates in the catatonic mode of being caught. The physiognomy of horror effaces all differences. The world as a whole is turned into one realm of hostile powers that threaten the patient from all sides. He is alone and defenseless. He is paralyzed in his action, for human action is related to an "anisotropic space" or, to put it in less abstract words, voluntary motion is limited to an environment in which the goods of life are unevenly distributed, in which zones of danger alternate with zones of safety. Voluntary motion, aiming at some goal, is always directed toward a place of preference. But, in the schizophrenic world, homogeneous in its physiognomy of the uncanny, the patient has nowhere to turn. Akinesis, mutism, and auditory hallucinations that occur together in a catatonic stupor are all manifestations of the same alteration: the schizophrenic mode of being-in-the-world.

Tactile hallucinations, next in frequency to the hearing of voices, reveal a similar pattern. The tactile aggressions resemble the voices in their fluidity and fitfulness. A hostile power touches the patient and yet remains beyond reach. The reciprocity of normal tactile experience is annulled. Touching is performed from a distance; the victim is blown at, sprayed at, electrified, or hypnotized. The aggressors penetrate the innermost life of the patient. They clutch at his heart, they assault him sexually, and yet they remain at a distance. The incubus that takes possession of a woman is not at the same time embraced by her (Straus, 1958).

That optical hallucinations are rare in schizophrenia is not surprising. Seeing is the sense of identification, stabilization, and delineation. In seeing, we experience ourselves as active; we set our eyes on something. This extroverted direction of gaze is inverted in optical hallucinations of the schizophrenic: the patient is blinded, beams of light are turned against him, pictures are thrown upon him.

Such metamorphosis of existence cannot be limited to sensory experience. Indeed, the patient's experience, that his mind is read, that thoughts are put into his mind—all the so-called automatisms of thought denote that the barriers of his intimate life have been leveled, that he is denied a free survey of the world. To the automatisms of thinking there correspond the well-known motor automatisms—e.g., induced movements, automatic obedience, flexibilitas cerea. Echolalia and echopraxia are analogues of the echo of thoughts. Obviously, the patient is no longer the master of his body. The border that separates mineness from otherness has vanished.

To summarize this necessarily incomplete presentation, hallucinations are not a mere addition, a kind of foreign body in a normal modality. They originate in distorted modalities. As caricatures of normal structures, the distortions signify pathological modes of being-in-the-world. Here, phenomenology is the method of choice. Instead of explaining behavior by means of physiological hypotheses, reducing the I–world relation to events within an isolated organism, phenomenology tries to understand the mentally sick by understanding first the norm of man as an experiencing being.

It seems that Esquirol (1833) anticipated this situation when, one hundred fifty years before Lhermitte (1951), he gave a definition not of the hallucination but of the hallucinary. "A man," Esquirol said, "who has the inner conviction of a sensation actually perceived while no object fitting for its excitation is at the threshold of his senses, such a man is in a condition of hallucinating" (1833).

References

Adrian, E. D.: *The physical background of perception.* Oxford: Clarendon Press, 1947.

Esquirol, J. E. D. *Observations on the illusions of the insane.* London: Renshaw & Rush, 1833.

Hinsie, L. E., Shatzky, J. *Psychiatric dictionary.* New York: Oxford Univer. Press, 1945.

Lhermitte, J. *Les hallucinations.* Paris: Doin, 1951.

Price, H. H. *Perception.* London: Methuen, 1950.

Straus, E. Aesthesiology and hallucinations. In R. May, E. Angel, & H. Ellenberger (Eds.) *Existence: a new dimension in psychiatry.* New York: Basic Books, 1958.

CHAPTER SIXTEEN

Disorders of Personal Time in Depressive States

Depressive patients sometimes tell us about peculiar changes in their experience of space, time, and motion. The change is not that of one detail or another. The basic structure of space and time, of the world in its spatial and temporal aspects, is altered. Familiar surroundings become estranged, everything shows a new, bewildering physiognomy. The relations of the patient to the world are changed.

The patients, aware of the change, try to resist it, to force back former conditions, but their fight is in vain. They can remember the past; they cannot revive it. Their attempts to throw off the spell only increase their pain. Whereas many depressive patients do not reveal their sufferings easily, patients undergoing these experiences report them spontaneously. Distortions of time are not seldom the chief complaint.

These symptoms, if noted once, will then be seen frequently. In a survey of a large number of cases, one finds a striking similarity. The following quotations, arranged systematically, illustrate how statements made by one patient are almost literally repeated by another one.

In regard to the present, a patient said, "Time doesn't seem to move at all." Another said, "I can't explain. All is timeless, unchanging, hopeless." A third said, "I had no feeling of time at all. Time is nothing to me." A fourth said, "Absolute rigidity surrounds me."

In regard to the past, complaints were: "Everything seems ages ago." "Getting up this morning, I feel I have forgotten it," or "I can't remember the last morning; yesterday is as remote as events years ago." "Everything I have done seems like a long time ago; when the evening comes, and I think back over the day, it seems years away."

About the future, a patient said, "The future to me is remote. I feel hopeless. Before I could look for the future, but I can't now. There's something that won't let me." Or "I want to get something back to my mind that seems to have gone, to let me see the present and the future rather than to keep me looking toward the past. There is in me a kind of routine which does not permit me to envisage the future."

With these changes, the flow of time becomes homogeneous. Time loses its articulation: "There is no break in time. I am passing through time; there is no day and no night. There is nothing divided between my getting up and coming here and going back. It's all joined into one." "There is no beginning and no end to things."[1] In some cases, the alteration of the experience of time is strong enough as to produce hallucination-like distortions of the tools for measuring time. A clock appears strangely changed in its shape, or the hands seem to move backward.

Observations like these present us with the following problems: (1) to understand the phenomena; (2) to clarify their role in depressive states, and (3) to see whether there is an intrinsic temporal structure in depressive symptoms which do not have time as their manifest theme.

Our understanding of the psychopathology of time depends on our understanding of its norm. In this field, much remains to be done. As psychiatrists, we test our patients for their orientation in time. There our curiosity ends; that is, it ends just at the point where it should begin. We record temporal disorientation as a pathological symptom, but we have little or no interest in the condition of the normal accomplishment. We take it for granted that experiences follow one another in time. However, sequences of experiences do not explain the experience of sequence. Psychologists have studied perception of time. Yet, chronology and chronometry are but two, and certainly not the most important, aspects of time experience. With all interests centered on the perception of time, the scope of the problem is narrowed; with the naïve assumption of a plurality of experiences, the phenomenon is obscured. Indeed, if impression would follow impression, one to the exclusion of the other, we would not be able to experience time at all. The juncture of experiences cannot be mere sequence. Even so, perception of time and statements about time remain casual.

Yet, time is an intrinsic factor in all experiences, for each experience is either familiar or strange, transitory or lasting, finite or infinite, unique or repeatable, initial or recurring, rehearsal or performance.

---

[1] These quotations are compiled from personal observations and from papers by Lewis (1932), Mayer-Gross (1935), and Minkowski (1933).

In other words, we live and we experience in a state of becoming. External events may succeed one another like the cars of a train that crosses in front of us. Things we experience might be ordered in the temporal frame of sequence into the scheme of one-after-the-other. But our experiencing does not have the same temporal structure. In the unity of experiencing, every moment is a phase only of a larger whole, a transition from the "not yet" to the "no longer." Every moment in itself is incomplete and, therefore, capable of and in need of completion. Because of its incompletion, it is related to the adjacent ones in the past and the future and, even beyond the actual horizon, to the whole of our vital, social, historical existence. Every experience receives its specific significance, its specific value, from its temporal position. Even in its content, each moment is determined by its place in our life history. We all know that we will have to die. Fortunately, we do not know when. But let death come close—the night preceding a battle—or let it be imminent—the last dawn of a man sentenced to die—with such transitions from indefiniteness to finality, everything changes its physiognomy. Within the developing whole of our life history, we experience our existence in each moment as growing or shrinking, advancing or standing still. The experience of growth and decline depends on the environment; it depends no less on our personal conditions, our actions, moods, and capacities. Youth, élan, and health open the world; they diminish distances for our anticipation. Old age, fatigue, and weakness expand them. A bright day annoys the depressive. He, who has no abundance in himself, cannot see the beauty surrounding him. In our emotions, we experience the varying tensions between the actuality of the moment and the potentialities of our existence. Dynamics, mentioned frequently today in psychology and psychopathology, belong to a being whose temporal order is that of a state of becoming.

About all actual experience we say that it happens "now!"—a word understood by everybody and yet enigmatic in its meaning. The Now is a moment of my personal becoming. It is always my, his, or your Now. In relation to the speaker, it is a precise expression. Detached from the presence of the speaker or his listeners, it loses all definite meaning. But I can relate this, my personal Now, the actuality of my becoming, to an objective, common, general order of time. I ask, "What time is it now?" With this question, I relate my personal existence to an embracing order of time, determined by the calendar and the clock—that is, by universal history and cosmic events. The types of chronology and chronometry varied through the ages. The Greeks, the Romans, the Jews, and the Christians each invented a calendar of its own. But, wherever they fixed the beginning of their era, to the creation of the world or to the foundation of the city; however they divided days, months, and years; and whatever instruments they used for measurement, they agreed in principle. The idea was that of a cosmic order of time that is one and the same for everybody and, thereby, indifferent to the fate of the single individual. It is the time which flows uniformly; in it, one day is as long as the other, and it is quantifiable, determined by measure and number. Personal time, however, is not homogeneous; in it, a year is not as long as another one, and it is not determined by measure and number but articulated by values, by the importance or unimportance of events. There is a deep contrast between the cosmic objective order of time and the individual time of our personal becoming.

This contrast is experienced as accordance or discordance of these two orders. In our experience, time passes fast or slowly. With both terms, we express a relation—namely, a discordance—between the uniform time of the clock and the variable order of our historical becoming. On a boring day, time passes slowly, but, in retrospect, the day appears to be short. On an eventful day, time passes quickly, but the distance between morning and night appears to be long.

In depressive psychoses, this discordance reaches a maximum. "All is timeless." "Everything seems ages ago." "Something does not permit me to envisage the future." These were the complaints of our patients; the present, the past, and the future are changed. Present, past, and future are all phenomena in the temporal order of our personal becoming. In chronometric time, there is a relation of earlier and later but not of today, yesterday, and tomorrow. The actual moment of our experience divides past and future. The relation earlier–later of two events does not change; the relation yesterday–tomorrow does change. In this moment, the morning belongs to the past and the evening to the future. But soon will it be evening; another day will come. Then, both the last morning and this evening belong to the past. In relation to my experience, events change their temporal qualities, while their objective positions remain the same. The patients who speak about the future—which they are unable to envisage—or the past—which is far remote—refer to disorders of personal time. Thereby, they call our attention to the pathology of becoming.

With a standstill of becoming, future is rendered inaccessible. We do not proceed anymore toward the future. The Now loses its position between "not yet" and "no longer." The present is no longer the continuation of the past; the morning does not grow into the noon and the evening. The context and continuity of time crumbles. The patients cannot experience the present as a completion of the past: "Everything seems ages ago." Even the recent past is moved off and separated from the actual moment by an empty distance. "I cannot remember the last morning" implies, "It no longer belongs to my life." With the disturbance of becoming and the consequent change in experiencing personal time, the objective order of time also is altered. We relate our Now to the common time of clock and calendar, but we have also to reintegrate this world time into our personal becoming. In the pathological discordance of personal and objective time, as it occurs in depressions, this reintegration fails. Patients may experience this as a vanishing of time. They do not move on while the hands of the clock move over the dial, adding minute to minute. Their own existence does not grow any longer in the irresistible stream of time. Other patients do not complain so much about the vanishing of time as about its unreality. Reality—whatever its scientific definition may be—in concrete experience, is not sensed as an impersonal, objective, logical order of events but as coexistence of the world and myself. With the standstill of personal becoming, world time is transformed into a mere sequence of events that, finally, being meaningless, loses even the character of temporality.

Although the cases to which I refer are not extreme rarities, they certainly are a minority among the whole group of depressions. The question, therefore, arises whether the disturbances in the state of becoming, sometimes experienced as disorders in time, may find other expressions in symptoms more familiar to the observer of manic-depressive psychoses. Indeed, in any experience, normal as well as pathological, an intrinsic temporal structure can be revealed. This time element, although concealed to superficial observation, is a determining factor in the genesis of our experiences.

At this meeting, clock time forces me to confine myself to the analysis of a single symptom. The depressive delusion may serve for a demonstration of intrinsic time elements hidden in seemingly different experiences. In his delusion of guilt, the depressive patient is overwhelmed by the impact of the past. Under normal conditions, we liquidate the past, we let the past be past, by advancing toward the future; there is never a task completely finished. Using grammatical terms, I could say our *modus vivendi* is in the "imperfect." We turn to new problems before the old ones have found a "perfect" solution; an unsettled entry is carried over. Thereby, the past is extended into the present, but our history is also constantly re-interpreted in the light of new experiences. Our views of the past vary with the changes in our state of becoming. Looking backward on a good day, we see the past as a territory which we left behind us or as a solid ground which supports us; on a bad day, however, we experience the past as a burden which crushes us. Yet, there remain permanent characters of both the past and the future. The past is defined, determined, fixed; it is the area of success or failure, pride or guilt. Guilt ties us to the past; confidence frees us from its fetter. The future is open, undetermined; it is the area of possibilities, goals, desires, hope, or despair.

The past is always a limitation of our potentialities. Every decision means resignation. With every action, we have to give up other possibilities. In choosing medicine for my profession, I have to renounce a career as a businessman, a lawyer, or a diplomat. How can I know whether my choice was the right one? In our curriculum vitae, we mention what we have accomplished. Yet, our past is inevitably a record also of missed opportunities. We are always debtors to the past. Confronted with the past, we are at the bar of justice, and there is nobody who can plead not guilty.

The blocking of the future throws the depressive patient back to the past. Thence, he hears a terrible judgment pronounced, a judgment that knows no appeal. For his guilt, the depressive faces ultimate reprobation, eternal punishment. In depressive delusion, history is experienced in its absolute irrevocability, the past as unpardonable guilt, the future as inevitable catastrophe, and the present as irreparable ruin. Disaster may still have to come but that it will come is sure; its approach is predetermined by the past. Nothing can stop the fateful course of events. In guilt and retribution, there is an intrinsic temporal element, not of the clock time but the time of personal history.

The depressive delusion, that is, the mode in which the depressive patient is forced to read his history, points to a change in his state of becoming. Depressive experience originates in an essentially changed mode of vital existence. If this interpretation is correct, psychopathological analysis opens an approach into the research of the pathogenesis of psychotic processes, beyond the familiar zone of conflicts between desires and conventions.

References

Lewis, A. The experience of time in mental disorder. *Proc. royal Soc. Med.*, 1931–1932, **25**, 611–622.

Mayer-Gross, W. On depersonalisation. *Brit. J. med. Psychiat.*, 1935, **15**, 103–126.

Minkowski, E. *Le temps vécu*. Paris: Collection de l'Evolution Psychiatrique, 1933.

Straus, E. Das Zeiterlebnis in de endogenen Depression und in der psychopathischen Verstimmung. *Mschr. Psychiat. Neur.*, 1928, **68**, 640–656.

CHAPTER SEVENTEEN

The Pathology of Compulsion

The young and the old do not learn in the same way. No matter how hard and how systematically an adult applies himself to the learning of a foreign language, it will never become as much a part of him as his mother tongue, which he acquired without effort. We are all extremely skillful in *that* language whose rules we do not know or, more precisely, whose rules we follow without explicitly recognizing them as such. But isn't almost everything that falls within the province of psychology at once both hidden from and familiar to us? It is not surprising, then, that such divergent standards are placed on the natural sciences and psychology! While we appear to be getting closer and closer to the reality of animate and inanimate nature through scientific knowledge, it seems as if scientific knowledge has removed us more and more from psychic reality.

The postulates and formulas in which modern physics expresses its various kinds of knowledge are, to be sure, completely understandable to only a limited number of persons—to this, there is no objection. The structure of nature appears so complex that just such formulas are commensurate with it. Yet, striving for psychological insight, we will always meet with the persistent complaint that it is we who have actually complicated things and relationships which are simple by themselves, that it is we who have obscured the obvious—in short, that we plague ourselves with difficulties of our own creation.

Of course, as psychiatrists, we are at first sight in a favorable situation with regard to such misinterpretation. Practical needs force us to take up theoretical problems, but, when we do so, we come to feel that the very ease with which we can reach a consensus serves to hinder rather than help our understanding of psychic life. Nothing that we immediately experience is known immediately. As soon as we begin to speak of psychic life, we are already shackled by the tradition of a particular language, and we are already in the grip of a scientific terminology peculiar to a particular historical age. Both circumstances tend to work against psychology as a systematic discipline.

Language serves both for communication among people and for understanding subject matter. As a medium of communication, it serves everyone; as a means for understanding, it serves only a few. Thus, it is more suited to the former task than to the latter. The wisdom of language, too, is a concealed wisdom that must be continually rediscovered.

Furthermore, since the start of the modern era, the formation of scientific concepts has been decisively shaped by the natural sciences. Ever since Descartes, psychological categories have been assimilated to those of physics. In the course of time, the conceptual structure of physics, suitably modified, accommodated, and distorted, has become common property. Today, it has even entered the speech and thinking of the ordinary man, so that everyday psychological judgments are rife with theoretical prejudgments.

As long as we are only concerned with trying to secure an understanding with those in our own milieu, all seems to be in order. But, as soon as we try to pass from communication to insight, everything is changed. Even in trying to make an exact translation from one contemporary language into another, we meet with difficulties. These difficulties are compounded when we attempt translation of writings from another culture or age, and they are almost insurmountable when we try to translate the language of the sick person into the language of those who are well.

Because of this, we cannot simply begin our investigation of a special psychopathological problem like compulsion at the usual level of conceptual specification. Rather, we must turn backward, away from special pathological problems to the general problems of normal psychic life. In doing so, pathological manifestations may be useful in leading us to concealed questions. Later, when we have secured fresh possibilities of understanding through the solution of such problems, we can return to special problems. In this connection, we may refer to the history of psychoanalysis which, starting with an investigation of hysterical reactions, was forced farther and farther away from its original goal, until it was eventually compelled to attempt a universal interpretation of man's psychic life.

Therefore, we are not free to proceed directly toward our goal. Like a mountain climber, we must pursue a zigzag course. We must be ready to make wide detours, even to reach a base from which an ascent can be made. In attempting a deeper understanding of compulsion phenomena, we should not shy away from detours, even though it might seem at times that we have turned our backs on the goal, that we are going away from it, or that we have utterly lost sight of it. I will not discuss here how compulsion should be classified clinically (see Binder, 1936). Perhaps I can show most easily what cases and phenomena I have in mind by offering a compulsive patient's brief account of her lifelong suffering.

This patient, forty years old and married to a store clerk, writes:[1]

At a birthday party in November, 1918, a bouquet of flowers was placed on the bed. My cousin, who had a darling three-year-old boy, took the bouquet from the bed, saying flowers should not be laid on the bed. Three weeks later the child was ————. From then on, I was very careful that no more flowers were laid on the bed. I like beautiful flowers very much, but can't pick them up any more or stand to have them in the house. That happened only after I had had a child myself, when it was already more than a year and a half old. I kept dreading that the child could be taken away from me.

In January 1931, a very dear, good, old acquaintance, who had become a member of the family ————. His wife, who didn't have friends here any more, visited us every Sunday just after having visited the ————. That didn't bother me at first. After about four to six months, her gloves made me uneasy, then her coat, her shoes, etc. I was careful that these things didn't get too close to ours. That went on until the lady noticed it and stopped visiting us, because she thought I felt disgusted with her. Since we live near the ————, I am disturbed by all the people who go there, and that is quite a few, whenever the summer is very dry. It is a real mass migration. If one of them brushed against me, I had to wash the particular piece of clothing with detergent or gasoline. Or someone would come into our house who had been there, then I am no longer able to move around right. I feel as though the rooms had all shrunk, and that I keep on brushing things with my dress. I have to go through the door sideways. To get some peace, I wash everything with soapy water, and, afterwards, I have to wash the dress, too, I was just wearing. Then everything becomes wide and open again, and I have room. If I go shopping and someone is in the shop, I can't go in, because the particular man or woman could run into me, or I might receive bills and coins paid by them. So I am restless all day long, and have to keep moving back and forth. First, I have to wipe away something here, then there, or start in washing. If I sit down for a while, I get tired and go to sleep sitting or standing up. There is no peace anywhere. When I take the streetcar, I always worry that someone in ———— could get on. If that happened and the lady or gentleman would sit near me, I would have to leave. Pictures in newspapers, too, and magazines that show such things upset me. If I happen to touch them with my hand, the washing with detergent begins again. I am simply unable to write down everything that is bothering me. My insides are continually stirred up, and this beautiful saying fits me exactly: "Where you go, peace is no."

—*Margarethe Sch., Spandau*

[1] The blanks in the text match those in the original. The missing words should prove easy to fill in.

Although it is short, this letter contains much that is characteristic. The empty spaces allude to the recurrent theme in many if not all severe cases of so-called primary compulsion neurosis—the theme of death, corpse, and decay. Simultaneously, the patient tells us of her interminable anxiety-laden defense against it. What she fears and what she tries to protect herself against is omnipresent; it shows up everywhere and at every moment. In whatever direction she turns, it encompasses her; nowhere is she safe from it.

What the patient says about the shrinking of space is also characteristic. She is a simple woman of limited education. When she writes that the rooms contract and that the doorways narrow so that she can hardly pass through them, she is not just repeating something she has read or something she imagines she feels. Rather, what we can glean from her words is that the space we live in is experienced very differently from the way in which we conceive mathematical forms of space. This lived space has a dynamics of its own that confines or liberates, according to the vital reach of the sick or healthy person.

We know that many compulsives are eventually compelled to pass their lives in a single room or even in one corner of a room. In our case, we see how the patient is becoming enclosed at the onset of her illness. She has neither place nor time to rest—she has lost her stance—having lapsed from lived space and lived time. She is always in a state of activity but without anything to show for it. One hour is like another and each day like the one before. Winter or summer, work day or holiday, nothing affects this way of life. The patient's existence no longer has the rhythm of beginning and ending; it has lost historical articulation so that its historicality has been reduced to a dead level.[2] Important and characteristic in this self-report is, finally, the omission of the crucial words referring to her particular theme. The sick woman reports the torture she suffers from merely reading such words in the newspaper. And, when inadvertently she touches such a word in print with her hand, the sequence of defense and purification as a whole is activated.

Her report does not exhaust the symptomatology of compulsion sickness. But what it does mention—the theme, the so endless warding off, magical communication, contraction of space, breakdown of history— these are all strikingly common symptoms in many severe cases. I could have used other case histories, and it would not have made any appreciable differences. Yet, the sick persons whose stories are so surprisingly

---

[2] While the compulsive patient suffers a fall from historical existence, the case of the phobic is otherwise. This difference is a fundamental one that makes it impossible to consider compulsion and phobia as linked or related forms of disturbance.

similar are from widely different social strata, in terms of family background, education, and occupation. This by itself tends to weaken the assumption that compulsion sickness is a neurosis. Such doubt is sustained by findings from genetic studies, observations of the course of illness, and the limited effects of psychotherapy.

Thus, we are but following conventional usage when we term the compulsion sickness "compulsion neurosis," just as, until recently, paralysis agitans and chorea minor were still classed under the heading of motor neuroses even though their organic bases were already determined or considered probable. I tend to the view that the phenomena of compulsion do not originate in the circumstances of the sick person's life history. At the same time, I believe that it is only an existential analysis that will enable us to penetrate more deeply into its pathology.

The case that was reported here is to serve as a paradigm for the subsequent investigation. But is such a procedure legitimate?

We call a case paradigmatic whenever the various symptoms usually distributed through a number of case histories are most fully present and distinct in that single case. But, in psychological analysis, a case may be paradigmatic in another sense—namely, when it permits us, by virtue of its structure, to move from the manifest symptoms to the hidden origins of the phenomena, when it enables us to advance from the idiographic to the essential. Only the fruitfulness of an investigation can determine the legitimacy of taking a case as paradigmatic in this sense.

As an objection to the use of the case of M. Sch. as a paradigm for compulsion sickness, it might be interposed that nothing has been mentioned about the genesis of her illness. I would like to make clear here that I don't consider that a shortcoming. Under certain circumstances, of course, the careful elucidation of a life history may permit us to understand how just this person has become sick in just this way.

The converse view, that an analysis of the life history should not only allow us to explain the fact of becoming ill but the actual content of the disturbance as well, is entirely untenable. This view would be justifiable only if the phenomena were already, in some specific sense, understood as spurious or sham. Then their hidden meaning could be divined with the help of a psychoanalytic or some other kind of key. Here, however, we are inquiring into the anthropological possibility of such disturbances, i.e., we are looking at the symptoms as expressions and not as masks of human Being.

Anyone trying to peer behind a mask prefers a position to one side, above, or below, from where he can apprehend the other with a quick look. Such gazing at phenomena from one side has come to be the habitual stance of "unmasking" psychology. But anyone who, on the contrary, is interested in establishing the anthropological possibility of phenomena must observe them *en face* in order to penetrate them. Because, in this procedure, we do not "reduce" one symptom to another, we can do without the life history data, which can be added easily enough later.

For now, I shall limit my observations to what I earlier called the theme of compulsion and the interminable warding off so intimately conjoined with it. Thus, I am choosing only one feature from the full symptomatology of compulsion sickness, not just any feature but a feature that is indispensable and extremely characteristic. Of course, we can approach a complex problem only by viewing one facet at a time, just as we can climb a mountain from one side only. But, once we have discovered the path that leads to the top, we are admitted to a panoramic view of the whole.

The compulsive's warding off has diverse shadings—shadings of terror, dread, repulsion, and disgust. From all these shadings of parrying I shall take only one—disgust. But I shall not be able to adhere to this limitation too strictly, since disgust is modified in the individual instance by dread, terror, and repulsion.

We have now reached the point mentioned in the beginning, where we will briefly turn away from our explicit goal in order to reapproach it by a wide detour.

Disgust and its counterpart, craving, are psychic phenomena of far-reaching consequence in our relationships to nature, to the animals and people influencing our manners, customs, fashions, eating, drinking, and clothing, as well as the construction of our houses and cities. The influence of disgust extends from the lowest to highest dimensions of human existence. Considering its scope and its significance, one might expect that psychology would have devoted due attention to this phenomenon. But a psychology textbook has more to say about the conditions under which color may be perceived monocularly in the peripheral visual field than about disgust. To be sure, psychoanalysis often mentions the barriers of disgust and shame, and Freud attributes great significance to their being erected for the course of the life history; he takes note of the phenomenon but without analyzing it as such more precisely.

All that remains, then, apart from several studies, are a number of widely scattered case histories. To proceed inductively, we could first attempt to collect the complete case materials and then see whether and how this diversity can be ordered. But that would be love's labors lost, for the objects of disgust vary with the historical period, nationality, social class, sex, and age. We don't even need to travel or to wait for social change to occur; for one and the same person, the object of disgust can change from hour to hour. Hunger lowers the barriers of disgust, and satiation raises them up again.

Examination of the case materials, then, must be inconclusive, since we are unable to agree on any particular object indispensable for disgust. But we cannot stop at this negative finding, because this doesn't alter the fact that, however various the objects of disgust, the disgust reaction to all these different objects remains the same. So there must be something that all these various objects have in common. Perhaps we have only looked wrongly, looking for characteristics identical in all the objects of disgust, having in mind a thing x with the properties yz.

And here is another point where everyday speech confuses us. We talk about the characteristics, features, and signs of things, using these expressions very loosely as if they were interchangeable. Even in scientific observation. we often do not realize that, in this way, we fail to discriminate differences sharply enough. A few illustrative examples will elucidate. Books are usually printed in editions of which each copy is exactly like another. Occasionally, however, there is reason to distinguish single copies so that they may always be individually identified. Then they are numbered. The number is the present sign of the single copy. We say that the book *has* such or such a number. Here, there is no inherent connection between the sign and the signified. Now to the second case: There are only a few copies in a limited edition. To distinguish them, their bindings are in different colors—blue, red, and green. Here, we usually do not say that the book *has* a red color but that it *is* red, green, etc. What was just now a sign now seems to have become a characteristic. This shift, from being a mark to being an intrinsic characteristic, is only possible because both number and color are members of a particular class denominated "accidental," in the classical sense of the Aristotelian *symbebekos* (Metaphysics, V).

There are other characteristics, too, that we must be careful to distinguish from these accidental ones. Tennis balls are discarded when they are old and worn out from use. Doesn't age affect the very being of the object in a much more immediate way than the application of color? We prefer the patina of age and weathering to a fresh coat of paint because then the actual being of a thing can be seen, while it is only hidden by the paint. Yet we don't make the distinction in our speech; we use the same particle, "is," in both cases. We say this house *is* red, just as we say this house *is* old.[3] Still, the applied color is a contingent, accidental property while age is essential.[4]

Contingent characteristics are mostly manifest ones; essential characteristics, on the other hand, are hidden. Age is a hidden characteristic, and necessarily so. As a particular mode of an object's being, it shows itself in certain signs and physiognomic characters. Actually, the expression of hidden essential characteristics can be so full and so rich that we believe we see age itself in these features. But this is an illusion. When a collector of bronzes, for example, strikes the surfaces of his little statuettes, the smoothness of the bronze skin is taken as a sign of age and authenticity and not as age itself. Here, the case of Dossena comes to mind. Dossena was extremely skillful in endowing art works of his own manufacture with the physiognomy and signs of antiquity. His creations were accepted by many as "real" products of the ancient world. Such deception is always possible because age is a hidden characteristic, however it may express itself.

With the foregoing distinctions—accidental–essential and manifest–hidden—we have not finished our drawing of distinctions, for it is easy to ascertain that manifest and hidden characteristics have very different relationships to space. When psychological aptitude tests made their first appearance, they were constructed so as to determine testees' skills in specialized and limited kinds of task. To be sure, it is quite possible that in some instances it may be justified to select out persons who performed highest on the task of adjusting two movable dials to the same setting, but no one would allow his choice of a true friend to be turned over to psychological tests.[5] Whatever may lead us to place our trust in a fellow man, whether we find him to be kind, serious, or reliable, each

[3] Both Spanish and Portuguese have two different words for "being." Here, the logical distinction between characteristics has had a lasting effect on linguistic forms. The Spaniard uses the verb *ser* for necessary characteristics and the verb *estar* for accidental ones.

[4] The antithesis between accidental and necessary does not coincide with that between contingent and essential, insofar as we include under necessary properties only those which are lasting, intrinsic, and generic, and insofar as we include under essential ones—as I mean to do here—moments of individual existence and becoming.

[5] Of course, even for such purposes, procedures showing some resemblance to scientific experiments have been proposed. But that ought not to lead anyone to the mistaken assumption that they are as dependable and exact as physiological diagnoses. What makes these tests useful, namely, their enabling us to evaluate single factors within a complex happening, is also what makes their value as personality tests so questionable. They especially cannot be used to measure any isolated performance, since, in personality testing, the individual needs to be appraised in an over-all manner. But, for that task, the laboratory is rarely appropriate.

one of these characteristics reveals him in his entirety. Each of the hidden characteristics is true of the object in its entirety, yet no single one is true to the exclusion of another. The hidden characteristics are without any particular locus or spatial demarcation and do not, in their multiplicity, form any kind of aggregate. For this reason, they are inaccessible in the laboratory and through the experiment. Manifest characteristics, on the other hand, do form an aggregate with certain spatial limits and relationships within which the individual parts are interchangeable.

Now, there are some peculiar correspondences between manifest and hidden characteristics. Cleanliness and purity form one such pair of characteristics which, because correlated, show the opposition even more clearly. Cleanliness is a manifest characteristic while purity is hidden. Cleanliness has its place and its boundaries while purity does not. Someone may have clean hands, but it might prove embarrassing were he to show his feet. Although purity may manifest itself in cleanliness, it need not. Yes, it even seems as if an excessive need for cleanliness is an effort to replace lost purity. Lady Macbeth could wash her hands of the blood of her victim, but she could not purify herself of her deed. Yet, the language of her dream images embodies, in her futile efforts to clean her hands of the blood stains, her longing to be purified of the murder. In her pangs of conscience, Lady Macbeth cries out, "All the perfumes of Arabia will not sweeten this little hand."

There is one more example I would like to give of the opposition and correspondence between manifest and hidden characteristics, in which, also, magic takes shape. Human beauty can be an altogether external beauty, of the mask, so to speak. But beauty can also be expressive, of essential, hidden characteristics, and it is then sure to cast a spell over us. In the classical "Walpurgis Night" of Goethe, Chiron lectures Faust, who has just asked, "Who is the most beautiful woman?"

> What! . . . when woman's beauty means
> All too often a frozen image,
> My praise to her and her alone
> Who brims with joy, sparkles with life.
> Beauty is enraptured by herself;
> But charm is irresistible,
> As Helena whom once I bore.[6]

Hidden characteristics can emerge in many different ways. They can emerge loudly and clearly or softly, in a barely audible fashion. How they are apprehended in the particular instance depends on the one who

---

[6] Translated by E. E.

expresses himself and the other who listens. King Lear was deaf to Cordelia's tender love; he trusted the specious glibness of Goneril and Regan. An expression defies measurement. I can exactly ascertain the presence of and perceive those characteristics that are manifest and incidental; I can measure them. But characteristics that are hidden and essential elude such determination and measurement. Thus it is that the former are used to describe a particular "Man Wanted," even though the "Man Wanted" description never tells us what is essential to the man. The specifications of the "Man Wanted" poster are exact but without life; poets don't write such paragraphs. The figures of poetry live because poetry discloses the hidden; it produces the shape of what is essential in things and not a copy of everyday reality.

In the perspective of natural science, the antithesis between manifest and hidden characteristics disappears. Mathematical natural science aspires to comprehend everything in terms of manifest or exactly "manifestable" relations. We could even say that it is the dream of mathematical natural science to construct a "Man Wanted" characterization of the world. Psychological understanding cannot follow in the footsteps of natural science. The very object of psychology resists it, since our relationships to nature and men are not those of the "Man Wanted" poster. As living, experiencing beings, we belong to the physiognomic world.

To be sure, an additional qualification is in order; we belong not only to the world as physiognomic landscape but also to the physical world, although in a different communicative mode. That we belong to both worlds and, consequently, to neither one of them completely will soon become important to our understanding of compulsion.

But what does this digression on signs and characteristics contribute to our understanding of disgust? As long as we sought for things with manifest and invariant signs among all the case studies of disgust, we found nothing. But what if we look for the hidden characteristics and the physiognomic characters in which they express themselves?

For the sake of brevity, let us begin with this: Disgust is the defense against invasion by decay. In using this definition, it must be kept in mind that I am referring to decay as a hidden characteristic and, thus, one that can express itself in many different ways.

In a study of disgust published some years ago, Gustav Kafka (1929) asserted that disgust is directed toward all outgrowths of the organic. This interpretation of the phenomenon comes so close to being correct that it is doubly misleading. First of all, it is factually incorrect. We aren't disgusted by ivory tusks, antlers, bits of coral, pearls, or snail shells—all organic products—nor, probably, by mummies, dried sea horses, and skeletons. The dried starfish, like deer's antlers, are beyond the process of decay; both have assumed fixed forms. They are petrified, dead, but not decaying. Kafka's view is also incorrect in a still deeper sense, for he is looking for manifest characteristics instead of hidden ones with their manifold changing expressions. Of course, organic outgrowths often have the character of decay but not necessarily so. A purely physiognomic dissolution of organic form is at times sufficient to evoke disgust in us for sheer life and not merely for its outgrowths. Even a "swarm," which obscures organic form or in which it seems to dissolve, can produce a feeling of disgust that we are spared when seeing a single individual of the same species. On the other hand, inanimate nature, taken in a strictly scientific sense, can exhibit the physiognomic characters of generation and decay. The "winking lake," the wide-open ocean, and the carefree stream all invite us in—quite different from the stagnating pond, even when, objectively speaking, we must grant that it is "clean." In the first instance, we plunge in, becoming one with the lightness, joy, wide openness, and play of the waves; in the second instance, we are repelled by its murkiness and lifelessness. In other words, while eager longing and the defense against disgust are both entirely sensual, the expressive characters exciting the longing and the aversion are neither rigidly determinate nor simply given by nature. The expressive characters are also partly shaped by tradition, in ecstasy and longing no less than in disgust and defense. Some centuries are enamored of fleshiness while others look for slenderness; there are ages that award the palm to the mature, and others in which the juvenile takes the prize. The individual bows to the mode, style, and taste of his time, even in those of his tendencies apparently the most individual. Thus it is that prohibitions originating in one sphere are able to make what is in another sphere forbidden and disgusting. One need only consider food prohibitions and their effect. We have a horror of touching a murderer, no matter how clean he may have washed. The world of human senses takes its final form in part from our intellectual existence; but the reverse is also true—and important for understanding compulsion. Our *behavior* in the first situation is affected by our *condition* in the second.[7]

---

[7] Thus, there is a revulsion near to disgust in experiencing renewed contact with what might be called "outgrowths of intellect," such as one's own letters, diaries, and old notes. "How disgusting my descriptions are when I read them again; only your advice, your urging, your demand, can make me do it!" begin the "Letters from Switzerland," which, according to the fiction of Goethe, were found among Werther's

I am very far from asserting that the decaying things that disgust us are actually conceived as decay. Quite the contrary! In the sensual realm, we are not acting as observers or conceivers but as seekers and avoiders. Man, and only man, has two different basic ways of communicating with his world: one is thinking, viewing, and knowing and the other is sensual arousal, desire, or aversion. Our perceptions, to be sure, are mediated by our senses; yet, as observers, we are in a mode of communication with the world that is quite different from that of sensing. How different are the modes of communication in the gentle fondling of another's body and in medical palpation! This divergence of communicative modes enables us as observers, say physicians or anatomists, to contact things we would strictly avoid in immediate sensual communication. In making the transition, we are not always immediately successful, since the world of the senses does not easily give us up. And, once it is accomplished, a return to the world of the senses may not be easy. How quickly a word from the world of thought can disrupt our idyllic hours.[8]

In this way, all sensory communication differs fundamentally from intellectual communication. Among the senses, however, each particular sense once again has its own characteristic mode. The individual senses do not convey materials to be intellectually worked up, differing only as media while remaining otherwise the same. No, our contact with the world is altogether different if through the eye rather than through the ear or touch. Things that it would disgust us to touch can be looked at without exertion, because whatever we see is always experienced at a distance greater than what is touched. But what we see can also arouse disgust; this shows two things: First, that unification does not begin with bodily introception but rather, in communicating through the senses, we live alternatively, systolically and diastolically uniting and separating.[9] But it also proves that the events we are here discussing

---

papers. When the feeling in which such notes first took form has evaporated, then there is a curious mustiness about them. Often, we are at ease reading even our more exact contributions only when the process of separation has ended, when our own productions have taken on for us an existence of their own.

[8] I believe we can order disgust, aversion, dread, and horror in the following hierarchy: As valuing persons, we react with aversion to the contemptible; as living persons, we react with disgust to the decaying; as mortal persons, we react with awe to the overpowering; as existing persons, we react with horror to nothingness. Since we do not, as living persons, ever cease being valuing persons, mortal persons, and existing persons, we rarely meet with "pure" impulses of aversion, disgust, dread, or horror. Is this in any way different from the laws that apply to freely falling bodies?

[9] Things are either far off or near in sensory communication, but the frame of reference for farness and nearness is not that of metric space. Nearness and remoteness emerge as different levels of out-reaching openness in a creature constituted by the possibility of being able to move itself.

cannot be understood as reflex events; rather, they have to be understood as behavior toward the world. Reflexes are hyletic events *in* an organism set off by an invariant, physically definable stimulus. But, in disgust and in actually all sensory reactions, we respond to a complex variety of different and changing expressive characters.

In his psychology, Aristotle taught that we, in sensing, receive the *eidos* without the *hylé. (De Anima,* 424a 17ff.) In modern psychology, which begins with Descartes, precisely the opposite is asserted. (*The Passions of the Soul,* I, 23; *Dioptric,* fourth discourse.) Sensation is considered as a hyletic material event. Impressions are transmitted to the soul by means of material events, always equal impressions through equal events.

Yet, we would be unable to react in the same way to such a changing variety of stimuli, as well as to stimuli of different senses, if these reactions were reflexes. And it would be even less understandable that we are able to react differently to the same impressions.

Expressive characters are many and various; in addition, things themselves change their expressive character from one situation to another. Something that is disgusting in one situation may lose that character in another. The athlete's profusion of sweat may be sensed as expressive of vital strength and activity. Then it provokes a very different feeling than does the fever perspiration of a patient or the odor of a sweating throng. Taken as a thing, a hair is still a hair whether on another's curly head, on a coat collar, in a soup, or used as material, such as horsehair. I need not descend to details to show how the same thing—hair—changes its expressive character entirely with these changes of situation. Combed-out hair disgusts us, but, in some historical periods, a true cult of snipped locks has existed. Cut hair is every bit as much an outgrowth of the organic as combed-out hair or horsehair. One last example: Faust demands that Mephistopheles bring him a cloth from Gretchen's breast as a love-token. Used clothing, our own as well as others', disgusts us, but, for Faust, the cloth is not a piece of underclothing; for him, it is part of the beloved, saturated with her scent and essence. A cloth from Gretchen's linen chest would not have served equally well. The antithesis between clean and used does not coincide with that of pure and impure. The expressive character that something reveals does not depend only on its qualities as a thing and on the particular situation; it is just as much a matter of whose eyes alight on it.

Here, I must point out a circumstance that is important for the understanding of our theme as a whole. One could ask whether decay is anything but an excrement or corpse? If that were so, then decaying would of course be limited to particular things with particular manifest characteristics. We could get rid of them by burial and burning; we could segregate the area of decay from the rest of the life space. Actually, however, decay is in the midst of life, inextricably involved with life. We cannot escape it; it is everywhere life is. To these nether regions, the lines of Goethe are figuratively appropriate.

> Of earth is left to us
> A painful scrap to bear,
> And were it of asbestos,
> It isn't very fair.[10]

The skin, even while it rejuvenates and renews itself, exudes wastes. It is the same with all the other organs. So it is that rapture and disgust occur so closely together, for what was just now expressive of a fullness of vital abundance turns into excretion and secretion. Because the organism lives only as long as it renews itself, as long as it produces its dross and keeps casting its skins, everything about the living body is equivocal; here, something can be taken as expressive of the abounding, of the living, or the presence of the decaying is already sensible. Just how it will appear depends on the vitality or poverty of the person who approaches it.

The Flemish painters—Rubens, Jordaens, and others—saw the world with eyes different from the Nazarenes or Pre-Raphaelites who came later. Rubens is indefatigable in portraying the live world in all its luxuriant fullness. If the milk spurts from a woman's breast in the midst of drunken festive processions or a curly-locked urchin gives free play to his inner prompting,[11] then all of this can only aid the painter to represent the brimming, and brimming over, abundance of life.

This particular sense of life has undergone a pervasive change since the days of the Dutch painters. The world is no longer experienced in terms of its wide openness, largesse, and abundance but, rather, in its narrowness, meagerness, and deficiencies. One need but compare the still lifes of Snyders and other Dutch painters with the melancholy apples

[10] Translated by E. E.
[11] For the child and in the child, many things are still free from the often very considerable disgust felt when met in grown, especially aged, persons. Disgust remains a stranger to the child as long as he is unacquainted with death and decay. In the child, we can still accept much that will later provoke disgust because it is an integral feature of his burgeoning life. The "Mannekin-Pis" in Brussels has survived decades without challenge. Of course, another circumstance also plays a part. His display is no offense to human dignity because the child has not yet gained dignity; in him, nature is without odium. Indignation does not pave the way for disgust. The innocent eye allows us to discover the fullness of life in the goings-on of the Brussels "Manneken," too.

of Cézanne. This change from abundance to scarcity, from wide openness to constriction, is the word of the day in every sphere of human life. It is perhaps most evident in clothing, fashions, and men's hair styling. Wherever one looks, the same change of style is observable: number of children in a family, eating and drinking, research, language, or architecture. Neither intention, coercion, nor commands are able to do anything against such style-forming influences.

Around the turn of the century, people became more sensitive to sickness and death. Where life abounds, death is easier to take. But, nowadays, hospitals are our most imposing secular buildings. Within their walls, everything is done to dispel thoughts of sickness and death. In these halls, corridors, and rooms, one could almost imagine oneself in a place meant for merrymaking. *Memento mori* seems to have been erased from the hospital as far as it is humanly possible.

Rubens' paintings of fauns and nymphs are a perfect example of how, even in its details, the physiognomy of the world always depends on the observer and how quickly what is appealing can become disgusting without any actual change in the thing itself. Some persons are irritated rather than delighted by a painting of Rubens. Its lushness they see only as corpulence; its abundance, only as bulkiness; its burgeoning, only as swollenness. For them, the living metamorphoses into the decaying.

One must be up to such abundance. The richly set table attracts only the healthy person and frightens away the sickly. Hunger is the best cook, but only the healthy have this hunger that itself expands the boundaries of what is appetizing. The depressive patient suffers from lack of sleep, appetite, and sexual desire. Begetting and banqueting spring from an abundance of vitality; appetite is evoked by plenty and actually enters into it. Thus, it is inadvisable to give a sick person a full plate, lest it drive away his appetite. Children often put too much on their plates. As we say, their eyes are bigger than their stomachs, i.e., they have not yet learned to adjust plenty and quantity in relation to each other.

In this sphere, the norm cannot be exactly determined, and yet it is clear when the limits, in either direction, have been violated. A person who claims that Rubens overdoes things, that he errs by his excess, is not so easily controverted. But there is just as surely a falling short of the norm. We may think of the "Décadence" of Baudelaire and the appeal of the feeble, weary, crumbling, and sickly—the enjoyment of *haut goût*. At this level, the appeal is still one of a delight in beauty, even if the beauty is that of transience and autumn. One step lower, one meets with delight in the vulgar for its own sake, the hateful for itself. To discover just how universal Thersites, is, one need only open any newspaper. The need for the horrifying seems almost insatiable. Even as abundance sensitizes one for plenty, so need sensitizes one for scarcity. True, it is a lack *in* the other we are talking about here. The other person is mean, the other person is cowardly, the other person is false. One's own being is still obscured.

I do not intend to descend any farther on this slope. These allusions should be enough to show that there is such a thing as a pathology of sympathetic relationships, and to show that the phenomena of compulsion fall within it.

From these comments, one might conclude that I would trace all decadence to degeneration, all intellectual and spiritual decline to biological failure. But that is not at all my view. In periods more or less correctly termed decadent, there are at least leading figures who show no signs of biological pathology in their personal existence or way of life. Just as in Aristotle's view *(De Anima* 424a 2–10), sensation is intermediate between the extremes of what can be sensed (white and black, for example) but must contain both potentially without actually being either, so the healthy person is also potentially between the two value extremes; he can turn in this direction or in that. The sick person, however, has been displaced toward one pole. His center has shifted to such an extent that he finds himself completely surrounded by decay. Thus, he is no longer able to discriminate; he is without insight.

For the compulsive patient, the world is filled with the decaying. Wherever he looks, he sees only decay; wherever he goes, he meets only with decay. All his activity is expended in warding off the decayable that presses in on him from every side and at every instant; and so these patients are never finished washing and scrubbing their own body.

The following case history will illustrate this more clearly.

A twenty-five-year-old woman, Mrs. F. L., who had suffered from compulsions for several years, reported that her illness had appeared suddenly at the time of her first pregnancy, when she was twenty-one. She still recalled the day and the particular circumstances. Her mother had asked her to come along to the cemetery to visit her father's grave. She had cried and hadn't wanted to go (although in previous years she had frequently visited the cemetery); she had become frightened: there was such a smell there; there were vapors from what the buried persons there had died of. She hadn't wanted to give the reason for her refusal; finally, she had overcome her distaste and gone along. On the way, however, she was terribly frightened, and, at the cemetery, she had to be "on guard" continually, lest she breathe normally and inhale some of the vapors.

Her examination was made more difficult by the fact that the patient made strong warding-off movements almost continually; struck herself in the face; wiped her cheeks and neck; screamed; made clicking, gurgling noises; and threw herself around in bed, first pulling her pajama tops and then the covers over her head. She only quieted down when the conversation was directed toward rather impersonal topics. Whenever the theme of her compulsion came up, her outbursts started again. The patient termed these uncontrolled movements "showing off" and added that she was no longer able to suppress them. Her back and shoulders were sore all over from rubbing. After the first interview, the patient had to vomit because "everything had been called by its plain name."

Since that visit to the cemetery, the patient continued, it had been one thing after another. At first she had been unable to say or listen to anything about *dead people* or *coffins*. She felt disgusted at everything old and grayheaded. Earlier she wouldn't have sent any beggar away, but now she couldn't even look at an old man's hand. When she did so, she had to scream and run away. She felt frightened, but there was something else, something inside her she couldn't describe. She had tried to control herself, but the more she tried the less she was able to. It was as if a strange power directed her, like in hypnosis. She had "lost her grip"; that was how she had gotten sick. The only one who understood her was her husband. Having "lost her grip," she didn't know where "to stay." It simply took hold of her. It was as if she had no life of her own, as if someone were squeezing her together. For the past three years, she had also been having frequent bad dreams. When she awoke, she had told them to her husband, and this had been a big "show off." Afterwards, she demanded that her husband take deep breaths so that she could be sure that someone else could stand to hear such thoughts, and that made her strong again. She was living like a *parasite*, from others' strength. She had demanded that her husband sleep in the same bed with her[12] so she could cling to him and be protected.[13]

For the past three years, everything had revolved around dust. Her child lived in the next room with her mother, so she had "strange dust." Because of this, she had to reject the child. Her own mother and child were not allowed to enter her room. She suffered greatly because of this; she loved her child and wanted to kiss her, but then it would bring germs into her room.

The patient is no longer able to do her own housework. She stays almost all the time in one room of her two-room house, constantly fighting the dust. It is almost impossible for her to go out, for coffins are sold on one street, someone once killed himself on another street, she once met a cripple on another, and the fourth street runs by the cemetery, etc., etc.

Compulsive thoughts keep coming like ants, like a car going faster and faster without being able to stop. Then she has to fight off her thoughts and doesn't know where "to stay." She screams for something to hold on to, hides in a corner, crawls into the closet or in bed, hides underneath her husband's

---

[12] In Germany it is customary for married couples to sleep in twin beds. (E. E.)
[13] This morbid clinging is easily differentiated from the "grip" a phobic patient secures from another's presence. More sharply formulated, one could say that the phobic person cannot exist on his own in the world, while the compulsive person lives in isolation.

coat, or tries to call up something beautiful in her imagination; then she has something to hold on to.

During her stay in a sanitarium, she once saw a coffin standing in front of the house and had to run away. She ran all the way home from the suburb to her husband because she had "lost her grip." When her doctor later stood on the spot where the coffin had been and breathed deeply to show her that he was able to bear the thought of the coffin, she was also able to.

The illness, whose numerous symptoms I have only sketched here, ran its course with some ups and downs while becoming progressively worse.

What is unusual about this case is the pervasiveness with which the patient experiences the disturbance of her sympathetic relationships. Remarkable, too, are the simultaneous defensive measures: the rudimentary warding-off movements, the magical participation in her husband's and her doctor's vitality, and the technique of cleansing.

In the psychopathology of compulsion, it has been customary to distinguish compulsive thoughts, compulsive fears, and compulsive impulsions, and this patient, too, employs such terms. Nevertheless, such distinctions do not hit the mark. The patient does not suffer from isolated thoughts, imaginings, impressions, and impulsions. She suffers from having to live in a world filled with evil demons. In the dust with which the patient constantly struggles, the demonic can still be detected. The dust, like a demon, is both ubiquitous and elusive. The struggle against dust is an effort to endow the demonic with the rational form of a thing, rendering it susceptible to being warded off; but the effort is futile.

In the hope of understanding compulsion better, attempts have been made to spot experiences of healthy persons comparable to the symptoms of compulsion—e.g., the inability to get rid of a tune that keeps running through one's head. Actually, as the preceding case history shows, there is no analogy at all between such disturbances and compulsion phenomena.

Finally, there has been a controversy about whether the experience of compulsion is a disturbance of thinking or feeling. But the compulsive patient does not experience a disturbance of a psychological function; rather, with such a disturbance as basic, he lives in a world whose structure is altered from that of the normal world. His world and his being in the world has undergone a fundamental change. Only by taking account of this transformed style of life is it possible to make the compulsive syndrome intelligible. Such a radical disturbance of sympathetic relationships alters the over-all physiognomy of the world, even in the mere reception of it. This is something to which psychoanalysis has not given sufficient attention. The Freudian doctrine construes the compulsive phenomena as action that fails in a conflict situation. It always looks as if the patient were engaged in action and could always decide otherwise or approach things differently; the aim of psychoanalytic therapy is to enable the patient to behave differently. Psychoanalysis will give him power over the id. Actually, however, psychosis transforms man in his being as creature; the psychosis leaves him without any possibility of behaving otherwise or making a different decision.

Through this analysis of disgust, I have tried to obtain some insight into the structure of the compulsive patient's world. I started from one symptom frequently met with in compulsion sickness. Now it is time to judge whether our attempt has succeeded. If it has, then it ought to be possible also to better understand other typical symptoms not yet discussed—e.g., doubt, pedantry, magical behavior, and miserliness. (See Binswanger, 1933.)

All these symptoms are met with at times even in healthy persons, so they seem to differ from normal behavior in degree only. However, I wish to maintain that the mode of being of the compulsive is essentially different from that of the healthy person. Since the compulsive's symptoms are not merely phenomena incidental to his illness, it must also be possible to demonstrate their essentially compulsive character. This, in turn, requires that the world of the normal person be contrasted with that of the obsessive in an even more radical manner. Such a confrontation promises a reciprocal clarification of the normal and the pathological.

To the norm as integral are opposed the multiple forms of pathology. So it is not enough to simply indicate that there is deviation from the norm; the specific deviation must be shown. The truly characteristic feature of the norm, in its opposition to compulsion, is, it seems to me, ease (Gelassenheit).[14]

This we know, that even the most conscientious work will draw critical fire. Unexpected events upset the most beautiful plans of the politician or businessman; the accidents reported in the newspapers day after day show that all the measures taken to prevent them are still inadequate. From this standpoint, compulsive patients, in the last analysis, would be justified in their endless doubting, controlling, and searching

[14] There are many related words in German suggesting the importance of ease or "looseness" in normal behavior, e.g., lässig, nachlässig, zuverlässig, sich verlassen auf.

for reasons. They are actually right insofar as it is possible to improve precautions by taking new measures or insofar as all reasons can be supplanted by better ones. Yet, we call obsession morbid and consider it a vital disturbance. And justifiably so! If we had to wait for an absolutely reasonable basis, for absolute certainty in our actions, then everything would come to a stop. We live "for the time being," and we know—more or less clearly—that we live in the *provisional*. However much we strive for conscientiousness, we still put an end to our deliberations. In all action, we give up certainty and entrust ourselves to the future, relying on ourselves, on the circumstances, and on others. Closing a deal in everyday life is always pragmatic.

But we are only able to live while "letting things be" because we feel ourselves joined by a sympathetic tie with other parts of the world and borne along by them. But anyone who—like the compulsive—cannot live in the provisional, as a single part in a sympathetic tie with other parts, is *opposed* by the world in its totality. And both the methods and aims of life together undergo a radical change.[15]

This inability shows itself even under normal circumstances. Anyone who aims at the whole has more required of him; at the same time, he is more exposed socially than the man who is content to repeat the habitual, guaranteed performances of everyday life. Because of this, we use a different scale for judging the former. We demand that he have a better basis for his conclusions, a broader outlook in his planning. We expect the language of the statesman to be different from that of the man in the street. But even the statesman could never end his deliberations if he did not eventually take a chance. To take a chance, however, means to trust oneself and to entrust oneself to one's fellow men and circumstances—to depend on one's luck.

In the figure of Julius Caesar, history has given us the great example of a man who, aiming at the whole and trusting to the moment in ever new and ingenious improvisations, surmounted all difficulties. He seemed to be in league with the very elements. Historians have eulogized his *clementia*. His mildness and his easy poise made him stand out among his enemies and also brought about his downfall. Wouldn't he have benefited from a bit more foresight? Wouldn't Caesar have done better to have paid attention to the warnings and the augurs? Of course. Yet, the same *clementia* that brought Caesar to his downfall had originally raised him to his greatness and fame. Without it, he would not

---

[15] From the incapacity of the melancholic to establish the past as past, we can derive the relation of compulsion to manic-depression, and, from the disturbance of the sympathetic relations, its connection with schizophrenia.

have fallen because without it he would not have risen so high. His fate teaches us the painful truth that we are only able to reach toward totality from the provisional and that, however near totality, we must nevertheless continue on in the provisional.

Anyone who insists on determining his actions solely in relation to the perfect will never reach the point of *acting*, for all action is directed and, as such, is necessarily one-sided and particular. Since the compulsive patient is unable to live in the provisional or the particular, he is also unable to act.

We know how compulsive patients seek to avoid the necessity of personal responsibility, how they—sworn enemies of improvisation—would even like to regulate everyday life according to a plan elaborated to the last detail. One of my patients was rarely able to fall asleep before daybreak because she passed night after night making schedules in which she tried to include everything that she would have to do as a housewife the following day, down to the tiniest detail. Travel was a nightmare for her. The change from everyday routine, the unpredictable, the little bit of adventure that even tourist bureaus have not been able to eliminate, all interfered with her making plans and spoiled any pleasure she might have had in the trip from the very beginning. As soon as she would try to make a travel decision, the trouble began, for, in such a decision, deliberate choice, curiosity, and mode became relevant—all unmeasurable factors.

Because all action is directed and, therefore, of necessity directed in a one-sided way, the patient is plagued by a wish to undo what has been done. If it were only wicked thoughts that the patient wished undone, then one could consider this tendency as a kind of repentance. But the undoing is to be understood literally. An effort is made to reverse the personal history, to return to the starting point, to literally retrace a path. Time loses its quality as historical time. When a healthy person, on the way home from work, takes the same streets he used in going to work, he has no intention of annulling his earlier way thence. But this is precisely the meaning of the compulsive's urge to retrace a present or past path in the opposite direction.

This compulsion to undo was particularly marked in the following case.

A biologist, Dr. B., had received from his university a stipend for several years of study abroad. He went first to Berlin. After some time, without any warning, he began to suffer from compulsive disturbances. At first, "images" came to him while he was working with the microscope, images he had great difficulty warding off. He never said anything about the theme of these images.

With painful effort, he was able to continue his researches for a time. But he experienced increasing interference not only from his struggle against the images but also from his compulsion to count and recheck his preparations many times. Hoping for improvement from a change of surroundings, he discontinued his studies in Germany and went to England. But he was unable to stay there for more than a few months because the professors used words that he could not bear to hear. Later, he was not even able to repeat these words. One could only gather from his remarks that they must have been words like death, dying, and corpse.

His next stop was France. But, there, the sight of so many men dressed in black frightened him. He quickly realized that their clothes had nothing to do with mourning; nevertheless, the sight of black so disturbed him that he returned to Germany.

When he returned to Berlin, it seemed to him that the porter who carried his trunk had a skin disease, so he had the trunk put in storage. During the subsequent ten months, he was unable to decide whether to claim the trunk, although it contained scientific records and important official documents along with his clothing and underwear. It was impossible for him to resume his studies during his second stay in Berlin. If a "bad thought" came to him on awakening, his entire day was ruined. He was unable to use many of his books because they had been printed in places which were taboo for him. He could no longer visit the library and laboratory because of particular impressions that interfered. As before, these were men in mourning, persons with badges indicating blindness, and mortuaries. On one occasion, he had sat opposite a blind man on the streetcar. Subsequently, he was unable to use this particular line any more, and, soon after that, he was unable to take any streetcar at all. Disturbing impressions came to color anything that stood in even the slightest relation to it.

But, when Dr. B., after a long struggle, finally resolved to go for a walk, he was then gripped by a compulsion to undo. This compulsion was particularly strong on bridges and railroad overpasses. Sometimes he was successful in going on in his original direction after a single return trip over the bridge. This compulsion to undo was not a façade of anxiety in the presence of rejected impressions; Dr. B., rather, sought for definite objectives so that he could retrace a particular path he had taken some time previously. He was particularly bothered by recurrent thoughts about a place he had once passed more than three years before. Several attempts at undoing had failed because new building made a reversal in exact detail impossible. Now, to the need to undo was added the need to restore the way to its original condition. This, more than anything else, was what kept him in Germany. When his money finally ran out and his visa had expired, he was still unable to make the decision to leave. At the same time, he was unable to do what was necessary to extend his stay. His situation became desperate. The day I decided to bring his case to the attention of his consul, he suddenly disappeared. He had been careful to see that all his responsibilities would be attended to. I have never learned what became of him.

The tendency to undo is the distinctive feature of this case; its theme, its defense, its anxiety at the spoken word and its life-space structure are the same as in the earlier cases. The power of the compulsion over the patient is also clear.

Many psychotherapists do not seem very impressed by compulsion. Stekel, for example, says of his treatment method: "I try to make the patient's attitude understandable to him, I explain the central ideas of his illness to him, his leitmotivs, life directions, and life goals, I teach him how to take charge of his daydreams, at the same time requiring him to give up his system without any further ado" (1930a, p. 235).

To Owen Glendower's boasting of his knowledge of magic, science, and arts—"I can call spirits from the vasty deep"—Percy gives the answer, "Why, so can I, or so can any man, / But will they come, when you do call for them?" (*King Henry IV*, Part I, Act III, sc. 1).

So may one call on compulsive patients to give up their system from one day to the next. Only I fear they will not do so, for even the possibility of death will not bring many of them to renounce their ritual. A patient I knew for a long time literally washed herself to death. During her compulsion sickness, her tuberculosis flared up and spread from her lungs to her larynx. Despite serious warnings from her doctor, she continued her hour-long daily ablutions, finally making it necessary to discharge her from the tuberculosis sanitarium. Quite aware of the imminent danger, she kept up with her purification ritual as long as she had the strength to move.

What good can it do in such cases to try to prove to the patient that "he is playing with reality?" Of what use is "breaking up his system" to him? Of what use is the insight that he is "abusing logic?" Most patients know these things anyway, before treatment. The symptoms of compulsion actually stem from the incapacity, following the breakdown of sympathetic relationships, to live in that nonlogically grounded tentativeness and particularity on which man's capacity for action depends.

In every action, we must impose an *order* on things. This means that a tension must necessarily arise between the private individual order and the general order. Such opposition is especially clear when the rights, duties, and power of the acting person are particularly broad. Within the narrow bounds of everyday bourgeois existence, this tension remains hidden, even though it is never completely absent from it. The compulsive patient would like to act according to a constituted general order; he would like to act in accordance with the categorical imperative. But the categorical imperative is a general formula. When we try to apply it to the concrete instance, we are once more thrown back upon ourselves.

The pedant gives up a personally serviceable order even in his private life; he goes so far as to subordinate himself utterly and slavishly to an impersonal and general order accepted as an end in itself.

A philologist is unable to finish his studies because he is compelled to read every book word for word. He cannot skim a book, cannot read it by paging back and forth, arranging passages from his own viewpoint; rather, he must crawl from word to word so that everything he reads forms an endless chain he can never articulate as a whole.

Another patient had sorted out the individual items of wash in his linen closet according to their importance and age. Among them were two dozen brand new shirts. But he continued to wear only his old and worn ones because the two dozen had to be kept unbroken.

To someone no longer able to guide his daily affairs according to need, wish, mood, and possibility of success, numbers seem to offer certitude. Numbers, of course, are well-defined, exactly determinable individuals, many even, through their particular position in the number series or through their preferred use, are downright individualities. But even this security doesn't last. For the certitude afforded by the full meaning of the single number is soon placed in doubt by the multitude of numbers. When I have resolved not to leave the house before brushing my coat twenty times from top to bottom and twenty times from bottom to top, why should it be just twenty times? Why not thirty or fifty times? Why not two or three times twenty times? And did I do it exactly twenty times? Did I make a mistake? Must I not start over again from the beginning? The guarantee of numbers breaks down, too; the requirements must be raised repeatedly.

The principles of order to which obsessives subordinate themselves consequently become increasingly odd and bizarre. In this connection, I suspect that the following factor is also involved: What is sought as a solution for specific personal difficulties is an impersonal general schema. But none is forthcoming because what is being demanded, in a sphere ruled by mere opinion (doxa), is certitude itself (episteme). The place of the suprapersonal principle actually intended is now assumed by that which lies at the farthest remove from everything familiar, personal, and intimate: The odd offers itself as a substitute for the impersonal, the extraneous. The end result is that what should lead away from all arbitrariness reveals itself as the very extreme of the arbitrary and unreasonable.

The avarice of the compulsive patient also reveals his effort to maintain a rigid grip on the status quo. This stinginess tries to prevent every form of use and is not specifically tied up with money. Because of the lack of fruition in their own lives, the patients are merely aware of use and disappearance while they remain blind to budding, growth, and regeneration. In a case reported by Störring (1933), avarice took unusually strange forms, together with a bizarre demand for strictly determined order. The patient flew into a rage whenever anything was used from his hoard of supplies during the severe war and postwar periods. At times, his fright about consuming anything reached such a point that he swallowed his own sperm. Such actions suggest a schizophrenic illness. But its clinical classification is not crucial here.

Whatever we may attempt to do, we can act only when we place our trust in the world and rely on ourselves. The compulsive patient, however, distrusts himself no less than he distrusts the world. As healthy persons, we live in sympathetic contact with our surroundings, yet every bit as much with our own past and our own future. The presence of compulsive frights and compulsive drives indicates that these sympathetic ties are disturbed. Did he remember to stamp the letter? Did he actually turn off the gas? Maybe he wrote a self-compromising comment in the folder? Will he not put poison in the baby's milk? Because the sympathetic ties with his own past and future self are deranged, because he is not integral with the doer whose deeds after all belong to the past or the future, such thoughts are interminable.

A patient who consulted me described his trouble in a way very relevant here. This forty-two-year-old man said that he had suffered from compulsive apprehensions of criminality for the past nine years. Therapeutic efforts of every kind to reduce his worry that he could mistreat children, murder, or steal had been of no avail. To meet these dangers, the patient has devised a series of precautions. But, at one point in his ritual, he is still completely unsure whether his devices are for preventing a future action or for assuring him that he has not already committed one of the crimes mentioned. The following is a typical example: The patient has stored his rarely used bicycle in a shed, but he keeps the bicycle lamp in his house. When he sees any unfamiliar bicycle parked along the street, the patient is overcome with anxiety lest the lamp he has at home is the one he is going to steal. As a precaution, the patient crosses to the other side of the street long before he comes to the bicycle; but, if there should happen to be bicycles on both sides, all he can do is walk down the center of the dangerous street. "I will certainly get run over some day doing this," the patient said, being quite able to give an account of his temporal confusion without being able to interpret it. Here, we see a compulsive apprehension and a compulsive drive that are indistinguishable with any degree of reliability. The loss of sympathetic contact with his own development removes the patient from a temporal perspective. Future and past then lose their characteristic difference and appear interchangeable. In other words, the compulsive drive is not a genuine drive at all; the compulsive apprehension is not a genuine apprehension. The patient realizes evil in his own nature but as if it were in another. Evil is experienced as possibility through the interruption of contact with one's own development; evil is experienced as nontemporal, potential Being never actualized as deed but which also never abjures its power by ultimately repudiating the deed.

Now, we must say a word about doubt as it takes the form of theoretical doubt in compulsion sickness. All questions lead to ultimate questions. Accordingly, answers to every conceivable sort of question can be final only when they are based on the final questions and principles. As healthy persons, we seek, in the principles, to attain a grasp of the totality. But neither are the principles themselves fixed. The healthy person discovers peace in religious devotion to the totality; or he seeks it within a tradition where the historical and changing seems final and unchanging; or he accepts makeshift answers and lives for the day, alternating between satisfaction and resignation. All these paths are closed to the compulsive patient. His doubts never leave him, and they develop into an impotent interrogation of the final meaning of everything. Thus, there is definitely a relationship between religion and compulsion neurosis, but it is just the reverse of the connection assumed by Freud.

The history of human thought bears witness to man's incessant struggle to secure a grasp on the whole, to rise above particularity and tentativeness. But the very same history teaches us that, as long as we are healthy, we remain inexorably confined to both.

A man's actual relation to totality determines his historical status. The possible relation to totality divides the sexes; here there are barriers that are insurmountable. In the zone of human life lying between *wholeness* and *particularity*, our life takes on aspects of tragedy and comedy. To be sure, both satirist and humorist are concerned with the same thing: the perpetuation of particularity in our every effort to achieve the totality—in all our claims to status that, in their hierarchical subordination to highest authority, still derive from the relationship to totality. The satirist, however, measures the imperfect in terms of its distance from the perfect and makes himself its judge; the humorist gives to the imperfect as such its place and its due and makes himself its advocate.

If this is so and if it is also true that the compulsive patient is unable to live with the imperfect because of the destruction of his sympathetic relationships, then we could infer that he must be lacking in humor. Experience seems to confirm this. Among my compulsive patients, I have met some who were malicious and deceitful and some who took a wicked delight in spotting others' weak points, but I have never yet met a single one with a sense of humor. The situation of compulsive patients in their acosmic world renders them incapable of seeing men and things in a relaxed and reasonable manner. Just as they lack humor, so they lack the capacity for enjoyment. Has anyone ever seen a compulsive who enjoyed nature, hiking, and camping or who had a good time just eating and drinking? Hardly a single one of my patients has ever been intoxicated. To enjoy—what else does it mean but, while fully aware of the tension between the perfect and the imperfect, to accept the imperfect and to bide in it for the time being? If the compulsively sick person occasionally seems to have an insight into the absurdity of his actions, he does not go so far as to smile at himself or to become angry with himself. Therefore, we may assume that the compulsive's insight differs from that of the healthy person in this respect, that his ec-centric viewpoint, the transformation of his world, nevertheless persists, even for those with "insight."

As particular beings we live in *perspective*. (See Litt, 1926.) Human existence has a perspectival character. Perspective is not only an optical phenomenon. Our existence itself is perspectival—i.e., from our center, our today, and our home, we articulate times and spaces in terms of closeness and remoteness. From our perspective, we are able to assign places to things, even to those of a generic character; from our perspective, we are able to separate the sacred from the profane and germination from decay. The healthy person is, consequently, able to rid himself—in the real sense of the word—of the disgusting. He assigns it to the cloaca as its appropriate place. He rises above disgust without any apparent psychic effort. The compulsive patient, on the other hand, must call on technology, both natural and magical, to help him.

Technology has labored with growing success for the past several centuries to disrupt the perspectival attachments of human existence. In Napoleon's day, a trip from England to America lasted many weeks, and news from the "Far" East took many months to reach us. At that time, the Alps still divided northern and southern Europe; most of the Alpine passes were closed in winter. What was near and what was far was determined by the natural reach of man and animal. In that respect, everything was still as it had been from the earliest times. In such things, the contemporaries of Goethe were scarcely ahead of Dante, Virgil, or even Homer; they were closer to them than to us citizens of the twentieth century. In hardly a hundred years, the basic forms of human life have been fundamentally transformed. Modern man no longer lives at a natural center from which he reaches outward in thought to comprehend the totality. Technology has conquered particularity without affording us the totality. It has replaced the particularity with a multitude of details. To the extent that the proportion between particularity and totality has been disturbed, one may well term the spirit of the intellect the "adversary of the soul." (See Klages, 1960 [E. E.].) But not insofar as this spirit obliges us to give up particularity and impels us to prehend the whole from our perspective. By observing the woes and delights of modern man, one may begin to realize what loss of perspective means. When we say that human existence is perspectival, we are not using a metaphor.

The disturbance of sympathetic relationships affects the compulsive patient in his relations with the world as a totality, so that he is no longer able to dwell in the tentative, the particular, and the perspectival. His avarice, his pedantry, his temporizing, and his lack of humor can be interpreted in terms of their contrast to the norms of everyday life. We could now conclude, since we seem to have achieved our initial aim. But a more thoughtful treatment of the symptoms of compulsion cannot afford to by-pass the problem of the "magical." In taking it up here, I hope to be able to tie the beginning and end of this study more closely together.

I would like to return to the distinction between manifest and hidden characteristics. Like the dream, the world view of magic and magical techniques are situated in that intermediate realm of correspondences between hidden and manifest characteristics—the realm of their analogical confusions and exchanges. In the magical world, the topical indeterminacy of hidden characteristics becomes ubiquity, while the lack of spatial boundaries results in a transcendence of all distances.

Because the hidden qualities of a thing apply to it as a whole, it seems that what happens to a part must also happen to the whole. One can have a share in the hidden characteristics, in a sense, because they are not spatially demarcated nor specifically located; we can participate in strictness, gentleness, and earnestness. But this sharing can neither be forced nor prevented. In other words, there is no such thing as a technique of participation. Nevertheless, everything in the magical world tends strongly in the direction of a magical technique of participation.

Arme Heinrich was to be healed through the sacrifice of a virgin.[16]

[16] "Der Arme Heinrich" is the central figure of the medieval German verse epic by Hartmann von der Aue. (E. E.)

His cure was considered a purification through magical participation in the purity of a maiden. But the magic healer requires a magic means for his rite; he needs the live heart of a maiden. In the poem, Arme Heinrich himself prevents the awful operation at the last moment; he submits to his fate and chooses to bear his illness. Yet, after his return from Salerno, it is manifest that he has been cleansed. The power of love has saved him, and he no longer needs magic; a miracle has occurred. Arme Heinrich has outgrown the world of enchantment.

Although enchantment is technique, it is still magical technique. Technique, in the full sense of the word, requires that each event and intervention be linked to a particular place and particular time, linked to the application of particular means in a particular sequence, and to a particular range of effectiveness. The magician, too, makes use of particular magical agents and formulas; if it is to work, the spell must be cast at a particular time and on a particular spot. Thus far, magic appears to be in agreement with technique, but the very means used and the effects expected both reveal that interchange of the manifest and the hidden qualities that is so characteristic of the magical world.

"The Pangwe girls use lush flowers and fruits as beauty magic, because they make them just as lush. . . . If one aims a sharp point at an enemy from near or far, he will waste away and die" (Jaide, 1937).[17] It is not the point itself that is effective but pointedness, as its inner nature, that results in the effectiveness of the point. The pointedness enters into direct spatial action with the thrust of the spear, but it can be just as effective at a distance. Despite such general efficacy one can make special use of the pointedness by aiming the point in a particular direction. Originally, then, the point acquires its potency from being filled with the "mana" of pointedness; thereby, its effect is no longer confined to any particular place or spatial area. But then the same pointedness participates also in the local and directional determination of the point. The sorcerer can make the pointedness serve him by setting up a sharp object at a certain time, in a certain spot, and pointing in a certain direction. In this way, the strength of the magic, despite its ties to place, hour, and means, is nevertheless able to overcome all spatial distance and limitations. Thus, although both magic and genuine technique have the determination of time and place of action in common, the motives for magical determinations differ from those of technique.

Magic is a technique in the realm of the physiognomic. Just because

[17] Jaide's is a comprehensive collection of material systematically arranged. I agree in most points with Jaide's interpretation of primitive magic.

we are trying to do greater justice to the uniqueness of this realm, every instance of magic appears bogus to us.

The world of magic is dominated by the physiognomic character of things and events; even we modern men live in a physiognomic world. The decisive difference between ourselves and the "primitive" is that the latter interprets all the physiognomic characters at once as real and effective. The primitive's way of construing the world distinguishes his world from our own; but, once completed, this construction in turn affects the appearance of things themselves. In a world construed a particular way, we can see things only in a particular way. The world construed as magical, prior to all specific experiences and observations, interferes with the clear differentiation of appearance and appearing, expression and expressed, manifest and hidden. For this reason, it is possible to treat the hidden as if it were manifest.

We call the magical world "primitive." Such an evaluation is not a prejudice of intellectual pride but is solidly founded, for the primitive remains at the center of his world, surrounded by apparitions to which he reacts individually and inconsistently. His reactions remain isolated ones, joined together only by the unity of their style. They do not fit into one single order that embraces the multiplicity of the whole.

The so-called primitive interpretation of the world is a first step toward any kind of world interpretation. We encounter it on a primary level in the history of human thought; it is not a protoform in the biological genesis of thinking. Just because magic corresponds to the primitive's interpretation of the world, it comes always to the fore when men, as individuals or as members of a group, are surrounded and overcome by the physiognomic. This is exactly the situation in which the compulsive finds himself. The physiognomy of his world has been altered in its very depth. It is not only the new and increased power of the physiognomic that distinguishes his world from that of the healthy; it is the dominating physiognomy of decay—the radical absence of wholesome forces—that marks this world.

It is perfectly correct to speak here of the physiognomy of the decaying; still, we ought not to overlook that, by contrast to the world of the primitive, this is a decaying more sensed than seen. Moreover, the world of the compulsive is fraught with decay in a monotonous manner; it does not have the physiognomic spectrum and articulation of the primitive world. Because the decaying is more "scented" than seen, the compulsive suffers a violent shock whenever the decaying assumes a definite form. He is no less frightened at the sight of a sick person, a cripple, a corpse, a coffin, or mourning wear than he is at the written, printed, or spoken words referring to these things.

A healthy person also knows such anxieties. Convention dictates that we pass over many things in silence or that we employ a euphemism or circumlocution. The names of things enable us to take hold of them; the unnamed and anonymous does not yet seem to exist for us. The name establishes a new communication—not only naming but also evoking and convoking things; it gives us power over them at the same time that it puts us in their power. The name lifts things from undefined possibility into definite reality. The pathic moment is complemented by the gnostic. What was said goes into the record, is put down in chronicles, becoming valid and real thereby. The spoken word also lifts the decaying from a vague indefiniteness to unassailable certainty.

While the spoken word is general and repeatable, the object seen appears to be confined to one particular spot. The sick person ought to feel good when, with the sight of a cripple, the decaying is brought from vague ubiquity to a precise location and thereby limited. But an opposite force immediately takes control of what was just defined; decay, omnipresent decay, once more casts its spell. One day, the patient has to leave a streetcar because someone in mourning has gotten on; the next day, he is no longer able to ride on that line, and the day following, all streetcars have become "taboo." The initial delimitation and condensation are forthwith followed by a process of dissolution and diffusion. Thereby, the intensity of the decaying is only enhanced. After such an encounter, the world of the compulsively sick person is even more frightening than it was before.

Against these omnipresent frights, the sick person develops his particular ritual. The details of the ritual may be understood from the life history; incidental features, such as the requirement to knock three times, may be traced back to associative linkages. But the design of the patient's "magic" ritual corresponds, in the first place, to the magic character of the world in which he lives.

The literature contains many references to compulsives' beliefs in the omnipotence of their thoughts. It has been thought that this belief could mask a hidden neurotic pride. This interpretation does not seem to be accurate. The compulsive lives within a continuum of evil in which everything continues to affect everything else without limit.

Isn't it only wicked thoughts that have such power? A compulsive woman, childless and unmarried and whose sister had to be hospitalized, is seized by the idea that if her sister should die, she would get her child to raise. A few days later, this sister actually dies; from then on, the patient was unable to get free of a self-indictment that her own wish could have brought about her sister's death.

Most of us at one time or another have played with such thoughts, but we reject them; we know we are playing a dubious *game,* and we attribute no more power to such thoughts than to their opposites. For the compulsive, on the contrary, whether he looks at the world or at himself, evil alone appears real to him. The compulsive's feeling of guilt is more a sense of horror about his being evil than about any particular evil deed. He is crushed by his universal feeling of guilt before he has ever begun to act.

Consequently, compulsive patients combat an enemy who is at once overpowering, omnipresent, and intangible; with inadequate weapons, they join a hopeless battle. Their fate is that of Sisyphus and the Danaïdes. The particular experience of compulsion is rooted in his self-contradictory situation.

In every action into which we have been coerced, assent and refusal, our yes and our no, are joined in a peculiar way. In resolutely opposing an alien power, we reject its demand and affirm our own conduct. If we yield to it, then we acknowledge the extraneous demand and are once more in agreement with our correspondingly altered behavior. If we are coerced by force, our no continues; we are unable to oppose ourselves in such a case since we have suspended action. But the person who has been coerced to act can still make a decision. His opposition, to be sure, reverts to submission; even he who acts under coercion must, in acting, affirm his own doing as well as the other's demand. The conflict, however, remains; he rejects his own conduct and repudiates the other's demand. Avoiding final commitment, he submits to the power of a demand whose right he contests.

Now, in compulsion sickness the conflict is not, of course, with the power and right of an alien demand.

As long as the strength of the compulsive's opposition continues, he straightforwardly resists the power of decay. Only with collapse does his experience become ambivalent. Only when overtaxed does he begin to reflect. But in reflection, the invisibly decaying cannot be comprehended. The standpoint of the compulsive patient is definitely not so "far out" that he would not interpret the world in accord with general opinion. The compulsive still shares with the healthy person the reflected gnostic evaluation of the world. But he understands the modifications of the pathic no better than the healthy person. Consequently, in reflection, his own doing is incomprehensible; it seems absurd to him, as if it were happening under coercion. His own warding off is interpreted as an inner compulsion. So it is that we are wont to say that the compulsive has "insight" into his absurd behavior. Yet, if his insight were perfect, he would long since have given us an interpretation of compulsion and would have spared us the trouble of attempting one.

I have made but passing reference to the literature on compulsion. But I do not consider polemics indispensable for a scientific paper. Instead of a polemic, however, I would like to emphasize the following points as essential:

1. This entire investigation keeps strictly within the boundaries of psychological or, if you prefer, anthropological understanding. At no point have I sought refuge in physiological hypotheses. The physiological hypotheses given to explain psychic occurrences are usually freely and—since a kind of family resemblance between psychic phenomena and physiological processes is often supposed to exist—badly invented at the same time. It should be sufficient to realize that physiological processes take place in objective time and that they are conceived as impersonal processes, while the symptoms of compulsion belong to historical time and are expressive of a disturbance in personal becoming. The two systems are conceptually incommensurable. It is not that the process of thinking is interminable but that the thinker, in his world, is unable to terminate. Reference to "psychosomatic unity" does not help, since this term, in the absence of clear concepts, is simply a verbal artifact. Anyone using the phrase "psychosomatic unity" still means a union of the diverse and not a unitariness. We can specify the terms in the union of the diverse; the unit, on the contrary, we have thus far been incapable of grasping, even though it is a matter of everyday experience. Just when it may be justifiable to view thought disturbances as disturbances "of thinking" cannot be discussed here.

2. An attempt has been made to comprehend the manifold variety of symptoms as congeneric changes in the life style under the condition of illness.

3. This has made it necessary to ascertain the structure of healthy life more precisely. The norm, however, which must guide psychopathology in such problems is not the sum total of the performances of discrete psychic and physical functions. The norm is man as a questioning, erring being.

References

Aristotle. *De anima.*
Aristotle. *Metaphysics.*
Binder. H. *Zur Psychologie der Zwangsvorgänge.* Berlin: Karger, 1936.

Binswanger, L. *Über Ideenflucht.* Zurich: Orell Füssli, 1933.

Descartes, R. *Philosophical Works.* New York: Dover, 1931. 2 vols.

Jaide, W. *Das Wesen des Zaubers in den primitiven Kulturen und in der Is-landssaga.* Leipzig: Borna, 1937.

Kafka, G. Zur Psychologie des Ekels. Z. *angew. Psychol.,* 1929, 34.

Klages, L. *Der Geist als Widersacher der Seele* (4th ed.). Bonn: Bouvier, 1960.

Litt, T. *Individuum und Gemeinschaft.* (3rd ed.) Leipzig und Berlin: Teubner, 1926.

Stekel, W. Die Psychologie der Zwangskrankheiten. *V. Kongressber. Psychother.,* 1930. Cp. Z. *ges. Neurol. Psychiat.,* 1930, 57.

Störring, G. E. Ein Beitrag zum Problem der Zwangspsychopathie. Z. *ges. Neurol. Psychiat.,* 1933, 139.

CHAPTER EIGHTEEN

Pseudoreversibility of Catatonic Stupor

Catatonia was presented by Kahlbaum in 1874 as a nosological entity, a brain disease of a specific kind. Kahlbaum, therefore, did not confine himself to a mere description of those symptoms which we still enumerate under the heading of a catatonic type of schizophrenic reaction; he went further and tried to give an explanation of the catatonic disturbances. His theory is embodied in the title of his book, *Katatonie oder das Spannungs-Irresein*. While *Katatonie* has been accepted as a psychiatric term, the second part of the title is not easily translated. The word *Spannungs-Irresein* may be best represented—preserving the style of the period—through "tension-" or "tone-vesania." As these terms reflect the psychiatric tendencies prevailing in Kahlbaum's epoch, a few words about the historical background are appropriate.

We must not forget that the struggle between somatogenic and psychogenic theories of psychoses extends far into the past. It is intimately related to the special topic of psychiatry. While medicine in general is concerned with man as a living organism and the disturbances of its biological functions, the basic theme of psychiatry is man as a citizen or, more accurately, man failing as a citizen—man with whom no further communication is possible, who has become irresponsible and incompetent, whose civic rights may be suspended, who may be forced if not into treatment at least into custody by judge and jury. The loss of outer freedom appears to be necessitated by a preceding loss of inner freedom. It is, therefore, small wonder that one group of physicians

This chapter was co-authored by Richard M. Griffith.
Figures 18–1 to 18–22 follow page 274.

should ascribe this loss of freedom to the soul and its passions and the other, to the body and its disturbances. Today, old arguments, of course with characteristic variations, are repeated in the discussion between the dynamic and the biological schools of psychiatry. Toward the middle of the last century, the protracted fight appeared to be decided in favor of the somaticists. Griesinger (1845), in line with Rush (1812), and others, gave the terse formulation: *Mental diseases are brain diseases.* This thesis, far ahead of the knowledge of details, presented in a nutshell a program with no small demands on future research. It asked for a system of clinical syndromes or entities, related to the still unborn physiology of the brain, combined with the not yet existing pathology of the nervous system, and sustained by some kind of anticipated physiological psychology. With Broca's observations (Broca, 1861), Hitzig's experiments (Hitzig, 1874), and Fechner's psychophysics (Fechner, 1860), decisive steps had been made, first in the field of basic sciences, to substantiate Griesinger's ideas. Kahlbaum and his pupil Hecker (1871), who gave the first description of hebephrenia, tried to enact on their part the clinical section of that extensive plan. In their attempt to single out specific nosological entities, they used general paresis as their model, just as Kraepelin (1883) did later on. General paresis was impressive to psychiatrists a hundred years ago because in it there was found—at least once in the field of psychiatry—a disease with a specific etiology,[1] symptomatology, course, and pathology. The fascination must have been very strong indeed, for Kahlbaum adhered very closely to the pattern established for the interpretation of general paresis.

When Bayle (1822), Delaye (1824), and Calmeil (1826) described the symptomatology and macroscopic pathology of general paresis, they shared the common psychiatric view that all psychoses followed the same course, running through four or five stages of vesania: mania, melancholia, delirium, dementia. The term "general paralysis" was used not to designate an impairment of mental faculties but to indicate a paresis of all motor functions in cases of mental disease. Delaye (1824) entitled his paper "Considerations about a Kind of Paralysis Which Affects Especially the Insane" *(Considérations sur une espèce de paralysie qui affecte particulièrement les aliénés)*. In other words, they assumed a combination of two syndromes, a psychosis combined with a general paralysis.

---

[1] The French authors who gave the first description of general paresis had not come to consider syphilis as a possible cause of paresis. Years went by until, in 1857, Esmarch and Jessen pointed out this relationship. In a short time, their hypothesis gained wide although not universal approval.

Kahlbaum used the same scheme. He declared:

Catatonia is a brain disease, running in cycles, in which the mental symptoms present in sequence the picture of melancholia, mania, stupor, confusion, and finally dementia; besides these mental symptoms—one or another of these five stages could be missing—there are found as essential symptoms disorders in the motor part of the nervous system with the general character of spasms (1874) [translation ours].

He described incomplete contractions and epileptiform and choreiform spasms; he compared verbigeration—a term coined by Kahlbaum—with clonic spasms and mutism with tonic spasms. To him, speech disorders appeared to be a result of coordinated spasms of the speech pathways. In short, Kahlbaum described catatonic behavior as presenting a motor disturbance; akinetic and hyperkinetic movements, catalepsy and waxy flexibility, stupor and excitement, mannerisms and stereotypies are neurological symptoms.

Kahlbaum's tenets were soon accepted in their descriptive parts; his theoretical attitude, however, did not go long unchallenged. Bleuler (1911), to mention only one outstanding authority, insisted that rigidity, catalepsy, and stupor are of psychic origin. Dynamic psychiatry was inclined to follow Bleuler. Yet, the observations made later on in the study of epidemic encephalitis and of the extrapyramidal motor system gave new impetus to a physiological theory of catatonia. Kleist (1908) tried to give an exact topology of catatonia. DeJong (1945) believed, with some vacillation, that he could reproduce catatonia with bulbocapnine. Strecker and Ebaugh (1945) mentioned that an extract of the pineal glands produced a similar effect. Others claimed to have found anomalies of tone or action potentials; some assumed a tone fixation of muscle without action current; the similarity to shortening and lengthening reactions in decerebration was pointed out. Ranson (1934) and later Gellhorn (1953) related catatonic manifestations to corticohypothalamic disturbances. Hill (1952) reported anomalies of EEG in catatonia.

While DeJong (1945) and Baruk (1933) used drugs to produce catatonic-like disturbances in normal animals, many of us have used sodium amytal or carbon dioxide to reduce the catatonic stupor. Both observations—the pharmacological production of catatonic stupor and its reduction—seem to confirm Kahlbaum's idea that catatonic symptoms are directly related to disturbances of certain motor elements or segments of the nervous system. Nielson and Thompson, for instance, think it most likely that "this salt [sodium amytal] alters the cell permeability of neurons. . . . Nerve cell membranes become more permeable," and, because of this, "in catatonic schizophrenia the stuporous patient usually awakens after the injection of about 5 grains of the drug" (1947, p. 238). This sounds plain and simple; but perhaps matters are somewhat more complex. Although the common clinical experience of sudden, unpredictable, transitory changes from stupor to action need not contradict this or similar assumptions, it warns us not to accept them in haste. That sodium amytal should awaken a stuporous patient is certainly in sharp contrast with its usual narcotic effect. We may well wonder, therefore, whether the stuporous patient is actually in a sleep-like condition from which he could awake.

Whenever one tries to give an explanation, he must make sure of the facts he intends to explain. Catatonic behavior is obtrusive; it promptly fulfills our requirements for reliable diagnostic symptoms. Furthermore, catatonic patients, because of their excitement or stupor, are usually seen under the limiting conditions of a disturbed ward. Contented for such reasons with the global aspect of catatonia, we are prone to overlook many important details. We realized this when we began to study catatonic expression in our photographic laboratory.

Not satisfied with casual observations in the ward, we tested the responsiveness of catatonic patients to varying situations more systematically, only to discover a surprising regularity instead of capricious reaction. Our experiments, we believe, confirm with conclusive evidence the opinion that the catatonic symptoms are manifestations of a disturbance of action and not due to a direct impairment of the motorium.

From our film library, we have assembled some selections to illustrate the points under discussion. Photographic recording, superior in many but not in all respects to direct observation, offers the opportunity of preserving evanescent behavior for repeated and communal inspection.

The first patient, Tim, is seen the day after his admission to the hospital.[2] He is waiting just outside the admission staff room. This anteroom, somewhat remote from the general hospital traffic, is an environment less artificial than the ward. As we wanted a record under the most natural conditions possible, we let things go as they would.

On occasions like this, we are quick to use the labels "stupor" and "withdrawal" and thereby may be blinded by our own words. This man, notwithstanding his frozen attitude and muteness, is not shut off from his environment; he segregates himself as a nonparticipant. If withdrawal means separation and severance from all connecting avenues, he is not withdrawn, in spite of his stupor, but vigilant. Catatonic stupor should not be interpreted as a sleep-like condition; this patient, although

[2] The following section of the paper was written to be accompanied by a motion-picture film. Single frames from the film have been enlarged for figures 18–1 to 18–22.

stuporous, is really alert. He keeps his eyes on the scene of events. While he permits a fly to crawl over his face without so much as twitching a muscle (Figure 18–1), he responds with a suppressed smile to some remark of a passerby. At one point, he throws himself back into position, as if he had just caught himself relaxing (Figure 18–2). His rigid gaze finally yields to excessive blinking.

In the following section, the same patient is seen at lunch time in the doctor's office. Seated behind a table, he retains his rigid posture, ignoring the food. Waxy flexibility is easily demonstrated; his right cataleptic arm remains in position (figures 18–3, 18–4) as the sodium amytal injection is started. The needle still in the vein, the patient begins to smack his lips, to grin, and to talk. "Keep it coming, Doc" were his first words (Figure 18–5). A few grains of the drug sufficed to turn him from one who refused food into a voracious eater (Figure 18–6). There certainly had been no lack of hunger, no metabolic disturbance, and no condition resembling hibernation but plainly a rejection of food. Obviously, the patient is overcome by the typical soporific effect of sodium amytal; in his drowsinesss, his guard down, he succumbs to the temptation of food. Now hunger asserts itself.

The third section shows the patient a few hours later in our photo laboratory. The effect of the sodium amytal has abated, and the patient has relapsed into stupor (figures 18–7, 18–8). Once again, we are able to turn immobility into lively and cooperative action. This time, no sodium amytal, carbon dioxide, or any other drug was needed. A device as simple as ball-playing proved sufficient (figures 18–16, 18–17). Without hesitation, the patient participates in the game; he no longer appears stiff, and his motions are fluent, expansive, and well coordinated. Apparently he enjoys the situation.

We could easily duplicate—and triplicate—this observation. We have in our film archives many other samples of catatonic behavior, in complete agreement with this one. In fact, we have films where the sudden transition from stupor to fluent motions is still more striking, as will be seen in the following "shorts."

There is method in this madness. The change from stupor to action is not accidental but follows certain rules. Some situations are without effect, whereas others produce a change with great regularity. Among the situations tried in our experiments, the first in order is ball-playing, where the patients—not always and not all but most of them and most of the time—become responsive and cooperative. Some react freely, some in a clownish manner, and some with inappropriate vigor and occasionally with aggressiveness (figures 18–20, 18–21). But, again, in the great majority, action is well coordinated with all the typical and familiar synergies and with a total surrender to the play. The start is often slow (Figure 18-18). It may take several attempts before a patient catches on and several more to make him enter the game with some enthusiasm (Figure 18-19). The initiative always has to be with the examiner. A ball placed near the patient or even directly in his hand has no effect whatsoever.

In some cases, at the end of a provocative situation, the patients immediately or after a very short while return to their stupor (Figure 18-10 to 12). Examining our films carefully, we found that even during the short intervals between throwing a ball and catching it some patients show conation toward a relapse into stupor (Figure 18-22). Sometimes, the relaxation lasts for a considerable time once the spell has been broken, but always the patient sinks back into stupor. The power of ball-playing need not be exhausted with one responsive reaction; during the same laboratory session, the patient may participate in the play for a second time and relapse for a second time.

With a regularity corresponding somewhat to the breaking of stupor, we were also able to produce it (figures 18-7, 18-8). The procedure and results resembled those in testing waxy flexibility. Obviously, catalepsy is not a mere motor manifestation but is related to the total experience of the patient—how he attacks objects and how he dwells in his own body. Waxy flexibility would appear to be arrested action rather than arrested motion. Catatonic behavior, as a motor expression, corresponds to the schizophrenic experience of the world. It expresses no less the patient's estrangement from his own corporeal existence.

Our rheoscopic studies permit us to do away with the assumption that due to a change of tone stuporous patients can and do remain in frozen attitudes without visible signs of effort and exhaustion. The last part of the film shows Tim, our first patient, two months later, more catatonic than ever. He sits down in the laboratory, staring at the camera. The eyes are motionless, but the gaze is attentive (Figure 18-9). A smile softening the mute lips betrays the patient's comprehension and grasp of the situation when a harmless trick is played on him. We ask the patient to get up; we lift his right arm to the horizontal; it remains in position (Figure 18-13). In the photographic record, one can observe how the patient, after a short while, glides into a more comfortable position, putting his left foot forward and bending his trunk to the left side to counterbalance the weight of the lifted right arm. The abducted arm begins to shake; then, gradually, it is lowered, the hand sinks down, and the elbow and wrist are bent (Figure 18-14).

Perhaps the least flexible of catatonic attitudes is the well-known stance kept seemingly unchanged for hours. But, even here, our films reveal signs of adaptation. We do well to remember that nonpsychotic persons also learn to stand upright nearly motionless for a long time. In Hitler's Germany, sentinels had to stand immobile, resembling a stone monument more than a human being. Cataleptic positions must not be interpreted as abnormal duration of innervation but as persevera- tion of attitude, perhaps as an incapacity to initiate any change.

If there is an increase of tone in the stuporous patient, the "stupor" is certainly distributed quite unevenly; it is never complete, and the dis- tribution does not follow any neurological pattern. An attempt to en- gage our patient in hand-wrestling resulted in a bizarre combination of passivity with resistance. The patient surrenders to the action of the ex- aminer. He surrenders—but only partially. He does not start any counter- movement by himself; at the same time, he resists; he is not completely passive. He allows himself to be pulled over into an extreme position, yet he does not yield. He skillfully frustrates the efforts of his opponent. Finally, using the other's hand as a kind of support, he balances on his right toes, his trunk bent forward and his left leg extended in the axis of the trunk, approaching the horizontal (Figure 18–15), suggesting a somewhat unorthodox Degas. Whatever the artistic deficiencies, the dancing act makes it clear that there is no lack of action currents in this kind of "attitudinizing."

These pictures taken together leave no doubt that the motor system in the proper sense is not disturbed in the catatonic. These patients are not immobilized in the panzer of their musculature but hold themselves immobile. There is no irreducible increase of tone, as in patients with paralysis agitans or in a pallidum syndrome. If this were so, the patient could not change his attitude from one moment to the next, from a stu- porous, negativistic posture to well-coordinated movements and back to frozen attitudes with mannerisms.

Neurological examinations in the cases presented here were negative, as were the EEG's which showed but occasional insignificant deviations —the same as found in many noncatatonic cases.

Our experiments, while they help to decide the controversy about the nature of catatonic motor disturbances, are a beginning rather than an end of research in this line. They present many new problems. First of all, we would like to know why the catatonic patient responds to ball- playing, why this situation produces a change of attitude comparable, within limits, to the effect of sodium amytal or carbon dioxide. "Regres- sion?" Neither H. Jackson's concept of dissolution of functions (1884) nor Freud's idea of a return to earlier stages of libidinal development (1963) is applicable. Perhaps the answer may be found in the observation itself. We prompted the catatonic patient to participate in playing, in playing ball. Both factors count. Ball-playing is communication but communication at a distance, and, as play without rules and aims, it is a communication and partnership without obligations and consequences. There is something more to be said. In playing, the catatonic patient responds to a specific situation, but this situation gains its meaning primarily in relation to and in contrast with the permanent situation of catatonia. We cannot expect to explain the transitory reversal fully without understanding catatonia itself.

The proposition that catatonic symptoms are manifestations of a disturbance of action rather than an impairment of motility makes sense only if there is an essential difference between motion and action, between the means of transportation and the travel, or—if you will—between the physiological and psychological aspects of motion.

Those who interpret catatonic behavior as a manifestation of a motor disturbance have chosen the more comfortable route; they do not have to explain how the many varieties of catatonic symptoms are related to each other. They may try to give such an explanation, but they need not; they could be satisfied with the assumption that the same, still unknown agent affects a number of suborgans of the brain, be it the cortex, the pallidum, the putamen, the caudate, the hypothalamus, or any other locus. However, if one assumes a basic disturbance of activity, he must go further and give an account of the inner relations of all catatonic symptoms. Therefore, we shall have to answer this question: How are the manifold catatonic motor symptoms related to one another and how to the rest of the catatonic syndrome? This presents a still wider problem: How are the catatonic symptoms related to schizophrenic manifestations in general?

The answer to these questions may be facilitated if we consider the possibility that the schizophrenic patient does not live in a space or a world in common with us and that, therefore, his behavior should not be understood as an eccentric mode of action still related to the structure of space familiar to us but as corresponding to the structure of the peculiar world in which he lives. The next question to be answered is: What is the structure of the world in which the catatonic patient exists? Formulated differently, the question is: What is the schizophrenic's mode of being-in-the-world?

Closely related to these questions is the following: Does the schizophrenic experience his own body like a normal person, or is his experience of his own body changed in catatonia—and if so, in what way?

All this leads to the last two questions: Can we describe a (or the) fundamental disorder of schizophrenic experience? Can we relate it to one biological disturbance?

We have found rheoscopic studies supplementing clinical experience and general theoretical considerations a promising tool for answering this array of questions. The method permits, within limits, an experimental approach to problems in psychopathology, providing evidence of facts and thereby helping to decide debatable opinions.

The experimental demonstration of the reversibility of catatonic stupor establishes a fact not unknown to the clinical psychiatrist; it reminds us that, even in severe cases, the modes of schizophrenic responses need not be coarctated to one. Even the severe schizophrenic may still have a variety of reactions at his disposal—but, with all of them, he remains schizophrenic. The pseudoreversibility warns us not to overrate prognostically minor changes in the behavior of catatonic patients.

Evidence that the disturbance is psychomotor rather than motor, an impairment of action rather than of motion, does not necessarily imply a psychogenic origin of catatonia. In fact, seen in its full context, catatonic behavior leads to the opposite conclusion—not revealing defenses originating from unconscious or conscious biographical experience in a world common to all of us but pointing, in its radical estrangement, to biological changes which transform the mode of being-in-the-world beyond the reach of normal or abnormal purpose and motivation.

References

Baruk, H. La catatonie expérimentale par la bulbocaprine et les autres catatonies expérimentales toxiques. *Encéphale*, 1933, **28**, 645–662.

Bayle, A. L. J. Recherches sur l'arachnite chronique (1822). In *Centenaire de la thèse de Bayle*. Paris: Masson, 1922.

Bleuler, E. Dementia Praecox oder die Gruppe der Schizophrenieen. In *Aschaffenburgs Handbuch der Psychiatrie*. Leipzig-Wien: Deuticke, 1911.

Bleuler, E. The physiogenic and psychogenic in schizophrenia. *Amer. J. Psychiat.*, 1930, **10**, 203–211.

Broca, P. Remarque sur le siège de la faculté du langage articulé. *Bull. Soc. Anthrop.*, 1861, **6**, 330–357.

Calmeil, L. F. *De la paralysie considerée chez les aliénés*. Paris: Baillière, 1826.

DeJong, H. *Experimental catatonia*. Baltimore: Williams & Wilkins, 1945.

Delaye, J. B. Considérations sur une espèce de paralysie qui affecte particulièrement les aliénés. Inaugural dissertation, Paris, 1824.

Esmarch, P., & R. Jessen. Syphilis und Geistessörungen. *Allg. Z. Psychiat.*, 1857, **14**.

Fechner, G. T. *Elemente der Psychophysik*, 1860.

Friedreich, J. B. *Handbuch der allgemeinen Pathologie der Psychischen*. Krankheiten, Erlangen, 1839.

Freud, S. *Three essays on the theory of sexuality*. New York: Basic Books, 1963.

Gellhorn, E. *Physiological foundations of neurology and psychiatry*. Minneapolis: University of Minnesota Press, 1953.

Griesinger, W. *Pathologie und Therapie der psychischen Krankheiten*. Stuttgart: 1845.

Hecker, H. Die Hebephrenie. *Virch. Arch.*, 1871, 52.

Hill, D. EEG in episodic psychotic and psychopathic behavior. *EEG Clin. Neuro-physiol.*, 1952, 4, 419–442.

Hitzig, J. E. (Ed.) Untersuchungen über das Gehirn. Berlin: Hirschwald, 1874.

Homburger, A. Motorik der Schizophrenieen. In *Handbuch der Psychiatrie* Vol. IX. Berlin: Springer, 1932.

Jackson, H. Croonian lectures on the evolution and dissolution of the nervous system. *Lancet*, 1884.

Kahlbaum, K. *Die Katatonie oder das Spannungs-Irresein*. Berlin: Hirschwald, 1874.

Kleist, K. *Untersuchungen zur Kenntnis der Psychomotorischen Bewegungsstoerungen bei Geisteskranken*. Leipzig: Klinkhardt, 1908.

Kraepelin, E. *Lehrbuch der Psychiatrie*. (8th ed.) Leipzig: Barth, 1955.

Nielsen, J. M., & G. N. Thompson. *The engrams of psychiatry*. Springfield, Ill.: Charles C Thomas, 1947.

Ranson, S. W. *Trans. Coll. Physic.*, 1934, 2 (4), 222.

Rush, B. *Medical inquiries and observations upon the diseases of the mind*. Philadelphia: 1812.

Strecker, E. A., & F. G. Ebaugh. *Practical clinical psychiatry*. Philadelphia: Blakiston, 1945.

Acknowledgments

Acknowledgment is due the following publishing houses and journals for permission to reprint Professor Straus's essays:

1. Translated from the original German paper, "Die Formen des Räumlichen." *Der Nervenarzt*, Vol. 3 (1930), 633–656.
2. Translated from the original French paper, "Le Mouvement vécu." *Recherches Philosophiques*, Vol. 5 (1935–1936), 112–138.
3. *Acta Psychotherapeutica et Psychosomatica*, Vol. 8 (1960), No. 5, 334–350. Paper presented at the International Congress of Psychotherapy, Barcelona, 1958.
4. *Tijdschrift voor Philosophie*, Vol. 24 (1962), No. 1, 2–32. Translated from the German, "Über Gedächtnisspuren," *Der Nervenarzt*, Vol. 31 (1960), 1–12, by R. Krambach, M.D., D.P.M., London.
5. *Tijdschrift voor Philosophie*, Vol. 18 (1956), No. 3, 1–20.
6. Jahrbuch für *Psychologie und Psychotherapie* (Karl Alber Verlag), Vol. 6 (1958), 65–78.
7. *The Psychiatric Quarterly*, Vol. 26 (1952), 529–561.
8. *Tijdschrift voor Philosophie*, Vol. 14 (1952), No. 4, 1–22.
9. Reprinted from *Congrès Descartes: Actualités scientifiques et industrielles*. Vol. 3. Paris: Hermann, 1937. Pp. 52–59. Paper read at the Ninth International Congress of Philosophy, Paris, 1937.
10. *Confinia Psychiatrica* (S. Karger, Basel/New York), Vol. 2 (1959), Nos. 3–4, 148–171.
11. *Schweizer Archiv für Neurologie und Psychiatrie* (Orell Füssli, Zürich), Vol. 31 (1933), No. 2.
12. *The American Journal of Psychiatry*, Vol. 108 (1951), No. 6, 439–443.
13. *Tijdschrift voor Philosophie*, Vol. 17 (1955), No. 1, 3–29.
14. *Diseases of the Nervous System*, Monograph Supplement, Vol. 22 (1961), No. 4, 57–68.
15. *Hallucinations*, Louis J. West (Ed.). New York: Grune & Stratton, 1962. Pp. 220–232.
16. *Southern Medical Journal*, Vol. 40 (1947), No. 3, 254–259.
17. *Monatsschrift für Psychiatrie und Neurologie* (S. Karger, Basel/New York), Vol. 98 (1938), No. 1, 61–101.
18. *The American Journal of Psychiatry*, Vol. 111 (1955), No. 9, 680–685.

Index